D0065475

REJOICE IN THE LORD

A Hymn Companion to the Scriptures

Edited by

Erik Routley

GRAND RAPIDS, MICHIGAN

WM. B. EERDMANS PUBLISHING COMPANY

Copyright © 1985 by Wm. B. Eerdmans Publishing Co.
255 Jefferson Ave. SE, Grand Rapids, Mich. 49503

Reprinted, October 1989

The publisher gratefully acknowledges permission to reprint texts, tunes, and
arrangements granted by the publishers, organizations, and individuals listed on
pp. 636–640.

Prepared by a Committee
of the Reformed Church in America
Music set by Moonye Korea Publications, Seoul, Korea
Design and layout by Joel Beversluis
Text type: Goudy Old Style
Printed and bound by Eerdmans Printing Company, Grand Rapids, Michigan

Library of Congress Cataloging in Publication Data

Main entry under title:

Rejoice in the Lord.

Includes indexes.

1. Reformed Church in America — Hymns.   I. Routley, Erik.
M2124. R26R44   1985   85-751586

ISBN 0-8028-9009-1

TABLE OF CONTENTS

PART III: SPIRIT OF TRUTH, SPIRIT OF POWER   371-497

PART IV: THE HOPE OF GLORY   498-624

PREFACE

The General Synod of the Reformed Church in America at its meeting in 1979 appointed a committee to explore the possibility of producing a new hymnal. Acting upon the committee's positive recommendation, the Synod of 1980 appointed a committee composed of the undersigned to prepare a new hymnal for the Reformed Church in America. In 1983 the Synod gave its approval to the committee's work.

One of the first actions of the committee was to secure the services of Erik Routley as its editor. Through a happy providence, he was able to complete his work before he was suddenly called home. The committee wishes to express its thanks to Ann MacKenzie, whose painstaking editorial work made possible the completion of the book on schedule. Thanks also to Mildred Schuppert, who compiled the Topical Index and index of Hymns with Descants.

Rejoice in the Lord is now offered as an instrument for the praise of the people of God. While it has been designed with the needs of the Reformed Church in America in mind, we believe that it can be of wide use for all churches of the Reformed and Presbyterian tradition. We have sought to create a hymnal that is biblical in its basic design, Reformed in its theological orientation, and catholic in its scope. We have tried to avoid any exclusive use of one musical style or one theological period, attempting rather to provide as wide a range of hymnological material as is possible within the confines of a single book.

The plan of the book is very simple: the canonical order of the Bible has provided the outline for the selection and arrangement of hymns. The hymns begin where the Bible begins—with God's act of creation—and they conclude where the Bible concludes—with the great vision of God's eternal city. In between are hymns that celebrate God's care for and salvation of Israel; the promise of the Messiah; the life, death, resurrection, and ascension of our Lord Jesus Christ; the encouragement, comfort, and direction of the Holy Spirit; the worship, witness, and fellowship of the Church; the gift of Scripture and Sacraments; and the abiding promise of the sure and total triumph of God in Christ over evil.

Deeply mindful that it is our duty and delight to glorify God and enjoy him forever, we offer *Rejoice in the Lord*, a hymn companion to the Scriptures, for the use of the churches. The preparation of this book has been a joy to all of us and we trust that the same joy may be the experience of all who use it.

THE HYMNBOOK COMMITTEE

Howard G. Hageman, *Chairman*

Robert J. DeYoung   Roger J. Rietberg
Norman J. Kansfield   Merwin Van Doornik
Gloria L. Norton   Lawrence Van Wyk

EDITOR'S INTRODUCTION

In introducing our hymnal, we cannot do better than quote a short passage from the preface that John Wesley wrote for his 1780 hymnbook. The following passage was laid before this editorial committee at the outset of their deliberations, and it was agreed to be as good a general guide to what we were attempting as we could find. This is what Wesley wrote:

> What we want is a Collection not too large, that it may be cheap and portable; nor too small, that it may contain a sufficient variety for all ordinary occasions. Such a hymnbook you now have before you. It is not so large as to be either cumbersome, or expensive: and it is large enough to contain such a variety of hymns as will not soon be worn threadbare. It is large enough to contain all the important truths of our most holy religion, whether speculative or practical; yea, to illustrate them all, and to prove them both by scripture and reason: and this is done in a regular order. The hymns are not carelessly jumbled together, but carefully arranged under proper heads, according to the experience of real Christians. So that this book is, in effect, a little body of experimental and practical divinity.

We started there. Wesley's hymnal contained 525 hymns: ours has about 20 percent more. Wesley's hymnal was the first in the English language to present the hymns arranged under sections. While our arrangement is not his, we present our hymns according to a pattern determined by Christian experience as we follow it through the Bible, beginning with God the Creator, and ending with the final and profoundest mysteries of the faith. Wesley called his hymnal a "little body of experimental [that is, "experiential"] and practical divinity," and we are convinced that a believer, or a seeker, who reads through this book from one end to the other, using it as a companion to the Scriptures, will find that it is just that: theology for people who are not theological specialists, poetry for those who claim not to be literary, and a lyric illumination of the Christian way.

THE POETRY

In our choice of texts we have sought to offer examples of all the best styles in hymnody, as all editors do. What will be especially apparent, however, is that often we have presented texts in a more complete form than current hymnals do, restoring stanzas that have recently been dropped. Our principle has been that, by presenting all the stanzas of a text, we allow the user to abridge a hymn, when necessary, by selecting from them. Had we omitted certain stanzas, they would naturally be unavailable, and the user's choice would be to that extent limited. In long hymns, therefore, we "star" certain stanzas which can be omitted where brevity is needed. We do so without (normally) making any judgment about the quality of those stanzas; the star indicates only that a stanza may be omitted without doing too much violence to the text as a whole. Ideally it is best to sing the whole of a hymn, but hasty and ill-considered abridgments have in practice been found to produce bizarre results, which is why we offer this guidance.

We have done our best to stay close to each author's original text, and the occasional archaism has not deterred us from doing that. But two considerations have quite often made alterations necessary. We considered first those cases in which a fine poem would be placed beyond the reach of ordinary singers because its author uses a word in a sense it does not now carry. The disappearance of the language of the King James Version of the Bible from our religious vocabulary makes a phrase like "If thou but suffer God to guide thee" needlessly difficult to apprehend, and now and again we have, as gently as possible, attempted to release the author's true meaning.

The other much more compelling need today is a sensitivity for "inclusive language" in hymns and liturgical speech. Here we will say at once that in the very large majority of cases where "man" is used meaning "humanity," and "brother" for "other people," we have made such changes as seem to us to meet the need, and not to damage the original too much. In just a few cases such an amendment has proved impossible, and still we thought the hymn must be included. There are probably not more than four or five of these, and we have occasionally used the "dagger" to alert sensitive singers that a verse contains an undesirable expression.

But we have not attempted, except in a few twentieth-century hymns, to rephrase in the plural hymns written in the singular; and we have not often embarked on the extremely hazardous and difficult task of adjusting all language so that it gives no offense to those who regard it as wrong to use the male pronoun for God the Father or God the Holy Spirit. What is appropriate to precise theological discourse is, we believe, not necessarily appropriate to religious lyric. Ours is an era of sensitivity to this issue but it is also a time which has not yet developed a genderless pronoun. In this context, the selection or adjustment of texts to accommodate this awareness would commit us either to omit a very large number of established classics, or so to alter their diction and style as to make them unrecognizable to singers (and probably to make them a travesty of what their authors intended). For better or for worse, we have gone as far in this matter as our times and good sense would allow. We leave this struggle to those who will edit the hymnbooks of succeeding decades.

THE MUSIC

Our principles of musical choice were basically the same. We looked for tunes that are accessible to people who enjoy singing (which is almost everybody) and that are satisfying to people of musical achievement (who are fewer). A good hymn tune is one that can be sung by ear after two or three hearings; it is one in which, without too much musical sophistication, the singer can hear the next note coming. Compared with some hymnals, our offerings will probably appear conservative, but we wanted to help close the gap between the highly musical and the rest of us which in recent years has been widening. In a letter on this subject in 1946, C. S. Lewis wrote: "The door is low, and we must stoop to enter it." As with some texts, so with some tunes, it is wise to remember that.

The present collection is, however, distinguished by the inclusion of more than twenty-five tunes from the Genevan Psalters of 1551 and 1562. It is the special distinction of the Reformed Church to have preserved the old Psalter tunes of Calvin's church in regular use, and, though they are sometimes long and demanding, they are always satisfying to sing when they are mastered.

9

In three classic cases we have included medieval plainsong tunes, but we urge that in most instances these should be sung by a soloist or a group, with refrain-verses sung by the congregation. Psalm tunes of the English and Scottish type, always so simple, often so magnificent, appear in greater quantity because our collection demands more Common Meter tunes than any contemporary American book; sometimes we give them in their primitive rhythms, which are always easy to sing (especially for those who sing by ear) and are often far more eloquent in that form.

German chorales appear as often as they are suitable for singing in English; some of the simpler of J. S. Bach's arrangements, whose singular beauty has made them widely loved, are given here and there. The extraordinary "con-gregational sense" displayed in the French diocesan tunes of the period 1680 to 1780 has encouraged us to make wider use of them than former hymnals in this tradition have done; and their English contemporaries, in the school of Purcell and Handel, have proved their worth elsewhere, and have been gladly added to our repertory.

It is when we come to the nineteenth century that we have, perhaps, made the most conspicuous changes, and it is here that the American traditions come into their own. For our present purposes, we draw on two distinct American traditions: that of the "north" (as it then was), including such venerable names as Billings, Holden, and Lowell Mason; and that of the "south," the source of that American "folk hymnody" which has, during the past generation, become so greatly loved outside the region of its origin. It is undeniable that both in America and in England there was a serious "inflation of the currency" that left us with a very large number of mediocre tunes. But the real quality of the best stands out when some of the mediocre underbrush has been cleared, and we entirely agree with those who say that the wholesale condemnation of nineteenth-century hymnody which was fashionable a generation ago was grossly misconceived. Mason in America and Dykes in England had, at their best, a sense of what people could sing which ought to be the envy of many later composers.

As for the twentieth century, it has of course been the age of adventure and experiment and has—as we can now see during its last years—produced as much disposable music as did the century before. Cutting a path, as best we could, through this new jungle, we have tried to keep our basic aim steadily in view, which is to select twentieth-century tunes, including those not before published, for their essential singability more than for their aggressive original-ity. Regarding the most recent contemporary compositions we have, as editors always must, had to make what we might call prayerful guesses about what will last and what will not. But all through the music of this book we hope that the singer will recognize a continuous tradition of truly congregational song. If there are a few tunes which the "average congregation" might be expected to find difficult, we have usually provided easier alternatives either by direct display or by reference. But even the unfamiliar tunes, we judge, are in fact less difficult in practice than they might appear on paper.

Now and again we have decorated a tune with a descant. It should be understood that all such descants are entirely optional and should be used only for the stanzas suggested. In almost all cases the tune is well known, and in every case the descant goes with the harmonies used for the tune. More complex descants and varied harmonies abound in easily obtained publications, which most organists are familiar with.

Some tunes are composed in "unison" texture. On the whole we have done all we could to present tunes (even when they usually appear as unison tunes) in SATB; but there are some which cannot be so adapted. They are always strong tunes and almost always vigorous; but a choir director may well use some imagination, in the longer hymns set to such tunes, in allocating stanzas for antiphonal singing, by women and men, or from side to side of the congregation. Varied textures of accompaniment, and indeed varied harmonies, are specially helpful here.

THE NEW AND THE OLD

Inevitably, a singer will find that something he or she is looking for is not in this book. The exclusion of some familiar pieces to make room for our response to modern needs is always the most painful part of the editors' work. A few hymns still receive great respect but are in fact (as we discovered) hardly ever sung. Some can be replaced easily by new hymns which say better what the others said. A few, we must admit, are still widely used, but we ventured to judge them inappropriate for today's worship, or theologically dubious. And we decided altogether to exclude songs of special national reference which, being not hymns but patriotic songs, are well known and easily accessible.

Many individual hymns and categories of hymns—old and new, those used before in Reformed churches and those not, the widely known and the worthy but little known—must inevitably be excluded from a collection even as broad as this one is. We have reasoned, however, that just as very few congregations will sing all the hymns in a collection, but will make their own selection within it, so, nowadays, few congregations limit themselves rigidly to the choices offered by their hymnal. It will, then, not be difficult for those who miss certain "old favorites" to provide their own supplies—always observing the law of copyright where it is relevant.

But in replacing the "old with the new" we are not in fact merely replacing the ancient with the modern. Not infrequently we are recovering the ancient and inviting the less distinguished modern to make way for it. Our own prayerful guess has been that today, after a generation of rejection of the old, we are ready for exactly such a rediscovery. For the provision of a healthy hymnody, in which the best of all ages is honored, is our best defense against addiction to this or that style, which breeds a barbarous intolerance in singing congregations. All we hope for in our singers is that they manifest toward hymnody that flexibility and alertness which in today's church life is constantly called for, and by most congregations unquestioningly accepted.

Wherever this hymnbook is hospitably accepted, by congregations of the Reformed Church and of the whole Church of Jesus Christ, it is our hope that this singing companion to the Christian faith may enable the people of God, with heart and voice and mind, and with pleasure and delight, to *Rejoice in the Lord.*

September 1982

—ERIK ROUTLEY,
MUSICAL EDITOR

Our God, Our Help in Ages Past

ST. ANNE

Our God, Our Help in Ages Past

Isaac Watts, 1719 (alt'd)

ST. ANNE, CM

Later form of tune attributed
to William Croft, 1678–1727

1. Our God, our help in a - ges past, our hope for years to come,
2. un - der the shad - ow of thy throne thy saints have dwelt se - cure;
3. Be - fore the hills in or - der stood, or earth re - ceived her frame,
4. A thou-sand a - ges in thy sight are like an eve - ning gone,

1. our shel - ter from the storm - y blast, and our e - ter - nal home:
2. suf - fi - cient is thine arm a - lone, and our de - fense is sure.
3. from ev - er - last - ing thou art God, to end - less years the same.
4. short as the watch that ends the night, be - fore the ris - ing sun.

Alternative tune: OLD 107th, 165

*5. Time, like an ever - rolling stream,
bears all our years away;
they fly forgotten, as a dream
dies at the opening day.

6. Our God, our help in ages past,
our hope for years to come,
be thou our guard while troubles last,
and our eternal home.

Ps. 90:1–5

CREATOR OF HEAVEN AND EARTH

2

O Worship the King

Sir Robert Grant, 1833

HANOVER, 5.5.5.5.6.5.6.5

Supplement to the New Version (1708)

Descant, st. 6, by John Wilson

5. Frail children of dust, and feeble as frail,
in thee do we trust, nor find thee to fail;
thy mercies how tender, how firm to the end!
Our maker, defender, redeemer, and friend.

6. O measureless Might, ineffable love!
While angels delight to hymn thee above,
thy humbler creation, though feeble their lays,
with true adoration shall sing to thy praise.

Alternative tune:
LYONS, 598

CREATOR OF HEAVEN AND EARTH

Ps. 104

Praise the Lord! Ye Heavens, Adore Him

3

Foundling Hospital Collection, Anon., c. 1798

AUSTRIA, 8.7.8.7 D

F. J. Haydn, 1796

1. Praise the Lord! ye heavens, a - dore him; praise him, an - gels in the height;
2. Praise the Lord! for he is glo - rious; nev - er shall his prom - ise fail;

1. sun and moon, bow down be - fore him; praise him, all ye stars of light.
2. God hath made his saints vic - to - rious: sin and death shall not pre - vail.

1. Praise the Lord! for he hath spo - ken; worlds his might - y voice o - beyed:
2. Praise the God of our sal - va - tion; hosts on high, his power pro - claim;

1. laws which nev - er shall be bro - ken for their guid - ance he hath made.
2. heav'n and earth, and all cre - a - tion, laud and mag - ni - fy his name!

Alternative tunes: ABBOT'S LEIGH, 393, RUSTINGTON, 348

Ps. 148

CREATOR OF HEAVEN AND EARTH

4

All Creatures of Our God and King

St. Francis of Assisi, c. 1225; tr. W. H. Draper, 1855–1933

Melody in *Auserlèsene . . . Geistliche Gesänge*
(Cologne, 1623); in this form from 1635;
harmonized by R. Vaughan Williams, 1906

LASST UNS ERFREUEN, LM with additions

1. All crea-tures of our God and King, lift up your voice and with us
2. Thou rush-ing wind that art so strong, ye clouds that sail in heav'n a -
3. Thou flow-ing wa - ter, pure and clear, make mu-sic for thy Lord to
*4. Dear moth-er earth, who day by day un - fold - est bless-ings on our

1. sing, Al-le - lu - ia! Al-le - lu - ia! Thou burn - ing
2. long, O praise him, Al-le - lu - ia! Thou ris - ing
3. hear, Al-le - lu - ia! Al-le - lu - ia! Thou fire so
4. way, O praise him, Al-le - lu - ia! The flowers and

1. sun with gold - en beam, thou sil - ver moon with soft - er
2. morn, in praise re - joice; ye lights of eve-ning, find a
3. mas - ter - ful and bright, that giv - est us both warmth and
4. fruits that in thee grow, let them his glo - ry al - so

1. gleam, O praise him, O praise him!
2. voice! O praise him, O praise him!
3. light, O praise him, O praise him!
4. show! O praise him, O praise him!

Unison

1. Al - le - lu - ia! Al - le - lu - ia! Al - le - lu - ia!
2. Al - le - lu - ia! Al - le - lu - ia! Al - le - lu - ia!
3. Al - le - lu - ia! Al - le - lu - ia! Al - le - lu - ia!
4. Al - le - lu - ia! Al - le - lu - ia! Al - le - lu - ia!

*5. All ye who are of tender heart,
     forgiving others, take your part.
          Sing his praises, Alleluia!
     Ye who long pain and sorrow bear,
     praise God and on him cast your care!
          O praise him, O praise him, Alleluia!
     Alleluia! Alleluia!

*6. And thou, most kind and gentle death,
     waiting to hush our latest breath,
          O praise him, Alleluia!
     Thou leadest home the child of God,
     and Christ our Lord the way hath trod:
          O praise him, O praise him, Alleluia!
     Alleluia! Alleluia!

7. Let all things their Creator bless
     and worship him in humbleness!
          O praise him, Alleluia!
     Praise, praise the Father, praise the Son,
     and praise the Spirit, Three in One:
          O praise him, O praise him, Alleluia!
     Alleluia! Alleluia!

CREATOR OF HEAVEN AND EARTH

5

For the Beauty of the Earth

Adapted from a hymn by F. S. Pierpoint, 1867

Adapted 1861 from a chorale
by C. Kocher, 1838

DIX, 7.7.7.7.77

Descant, st. 5, by S. H. Nicholson

5. For thy Church that ev-er-more lift-eth ho-ly hands a-bove,

1. For the beau-ty of the earth, for the beau-ty of the skies,
2. For the won-der of each hour of the day and of the night,
3. For the joy of ear and eye, for the heart's and mind's de-light,
4. For the joy of hu-man love, broth-er, sis-ter, par-ent, child,
5. For thy Church that ev-er-more lift-eth ho-ly hands a-bove,

5. of-f'ring up on ev-'ry shore her pure sac-ri-fice of love,

1. for the love which from our birth o-ver and a-round us lies,
2. hill and vale and tree and flower, sun and moon and stars of light,
3. for the mys-tic har-mo-ny link-ing sense to sound and sight,
4. friends on earth and friends a-bove; for all gen-tle thoughts and mild,
5. of-f'ring up on ev-'ry shore her pure sac-ri-fice of love,

5. Lord of all, to thee we raise this, our hymn of grate-ful praise.

Refrain

Lord of all, to thee we raise this, our hymn of grate-ful praise.

This tune in a higher key: 228

CREATOR OF HEAVEN AND EARTH

Praise to the Living God! 6

Yigdal: Jewish hymn of praise, tr. M. Landsberg and N. Mann, 1914

Thomas Olivers and Meyer Lyon, 1770;
based on a Jewish melody

LEONI, 6.6.8.4 D

1. Praise to the liv-ing God! All prais-ed be his name,
2. Form - less, all love-ly forms de - clare his love-li - ness:
3. His spir-it flow-eth free, high surg-ing where it will:
4. E - ter-nal life hath he im-plant-ed in the soul;

1. who was, and is, and is to be, for aye the same.
2. ho - ly, no ho-li - ness of earth can his ex - press.
3. in proph-et's word he spoke of old; he speak-eth still.
4. his love shall be our strength and stay while a - ges roll.

1. The one e - ter-nal God, ere aught that now ap - pears:
2. Lo, he is Lord of all; cre - a - tion speaks his praise,
3. Es - tab-lished is his law, and change-less it shall stand,
4. Praise to the liv-ing God! All prais-ed be his name,

1. the first, the last, be - yond all thought his time - less years.
2. and ev - 'ry-where, a - bove, be - low, his will o - beys.
3. deep writ-ten on the hu-man heart, on sea, on land.
4. who was, and is, and is to be, for aye the same.

Alternative tune: SEVENTH TUNE, 271

CREATOR OF HEAVEN AND EARTH

Immortal, Invisible, God Only Wise

Walter Chalmers Smith, 1867

ST. DENIO (JOANNA), 11 11.11 11 anapaestic

Welsh melody, *Canaiadau y Cyssegr* (1839)

1. Im - mor - tal, in - vis - i - ble, God on - ly wise,
2. Un - rest - ing, un - hast - ing, and si - lent as light,
3. To all life thou giv - est, to both great and small;
4. Great Fa - ther of glo - ry, pure Fa - ther of light,

1. in light in - ac - ces - si - ble hid from our eyes,
2. nor want - ing, nor wast - ing, thou rul - est in might;
3. in all life thou liv - est, the true life of all;
4. thine an - gels a - dore thee, all veil - ing their sight;

1. most bless - ed, most glo - rious, the An - cient of Days,
2. thy jus - tice like moun - tains high soar - ing a - bove,
3. we blos - som and flour - ish as leaves on the tree,
4. all laud we would ren - der, O help us to see

1. al - might - y, vic - to - rious, thy great name we praise.
2. thy clouds which are foun - tains of good - ness and love.
3. and with - er and per - ish, but nought chang - eth thee.
4. 'tis on - ly the splen - dor of light hid - eth thee.

Alternative tune: ST. BASIL, 344

CREATOR OF HEAVEN AND EARTH

Dan. 7:9; Ps. 36:6; Isa. 6:2–3

Let All the World Rejoice

Variant (1965) from a hymn by John Hunt, 1853

CHRIST CHURCH, 6.6.6.6.88

Charles Steggall, 1865

1. Let all the world re-joice, the Lord al-might-y reigns;
2. Glad was the an-gel throng to see his might pre-vail;
3. The heav'ns and earth he made by his pre-vail-ing might;
4. But this fair world shall die, the crea-ture of a day,

1. the thun-ders are his voice, our life his will or-dains: un-e-qualled,
2. they sang their joy-ful song the u-ni-verse to hail; while yet in
3. his eye all things sur-veyed, he scat-tered an-cient night, and heav'n and
4. in cool-ing ash-es lie, its glo-ry passed a-way; the pride and

1. sov-'reign and a-lone in maj-es-ty he fills his throne.
2. ra-diant youth it stood, th'e-ter-nal Word pro-nounced it good.
3. earth and sky and sea pro-claimed his glo-rious maj-es-ty.
4. glo-ry of the earth shall be as ere they had their birth.

*5. Yet ever fixed the throne
  of the eternal One
shall stand when earth is gone,
  and time its race has run.
New worlds his power can make at will,
new creatures can his praise fulfill.

6. The outskirts of his ways
  appear to mortal sight;
the fullness of his praise
  exceeds an angel's flight;
but here is truth all truth above:
mortals may bless immortal love.

Gen. 1:12; Job 26:14

CREATOR OF HEAVEN AND EARTH

9

All Beautiful the March of Days

Frances Whitmarsh Wile, 1912 (alt'd)

FOREST GREEN, CMD

English folk song, arranged by
R. Vaughan Williams, 1906

1. All beau-ti-ful the march of days, as sea-sons come and go;
2. O'er white ex-pans-es spar-kling pure the ra-diant morns un-fold;
3. O thou from whose un-fath-omed law the year in beau-ty flows,

1. the hand that shaped the rose hath wrought the crys-tal of the snow,
2. the sol-emn splen-dors of the night burn bright-er through the cold;
3. thy-self the vi-sion pass-ing by in crys-tal and in rose,

1. hath sent the hoar-y frost of heaven, the flow-ing wa-ters sealed,
2. life mounts in ev-ery throb-bing vein, love deepens round the hearth,
3. day un to day doth ut-ter speech, and night to night pro-claim,

1. and laid a si-lent love-li-ness on hill and wood and field.
2. and clear-er sounds the an-gel hymn, "Good will to all on earth."
3. in ev-er-chang-ing words of light, the won-der of thy name.

Alternative tunes: HALIFAX, 481, SHEPHERD'S PIPES, 253

This tune in a lower key: 193

CREATOR OF HEAVEN AND EARTH

Ps. 19:2

I Sing th'Almighty Power of God

Isaac Watts, 1715

ELLACOMBE, CMD

Later form (1868) of melody
in *Württemberger Gesangbuch* (1784)

1. I sing th'al-might-y power of God that made the moun-tains rise,
2. I sing the good-ness of the Lord that filled the earth with food;
3. Crea-tures, as num'rous as they be, are sub-ject to thy care;

1. that spread the flow-ing seas a-broad, and built the loft-y skies.
2. he form'd the crea-tures with his word, and then pro-nounced them good.
3. there's not a place where we can flee, but God is pres-ent there.

1. I sing the wis-dom that or-dained the sun to rule by day;
2. Lord, how thy won-ders are dis-played wher-e'er I turn my eye,
3. His hand is my per-pet-ual guard, he keeps me with his eye;

1. the moon shines full at his com-mand, and all the stars o-bey.
2. if I sur-vey the ground I tread, or gaze up-on the sky!
3. why should I then for-get the Lord, who is for-ev-er nigh?

Gen. 1:12

CREATOR OF HEAVEN AND EARTH

11

Let All the World

George Herbert, 1593–1633

AUGUSTINE, 10 4.66.66.10 4   Erik Routley, 1964

CREATOR OF HEAVEN AND EARTH

2. The Church with psalms must shout; no door can keep them out;

2. The Church with psalms must shout; no door can keep them out; (but)

2. but a - bove all, the heart must bear the long - est part.

2. but a - bove all, the heart must bear the long - est part.

(Org.)

Unison

2. Let all the world in ev - 'ry cor - ner sing, my God and King!

CREATOR OF HEAVEN AND EARTH

Let the Whole Creation Cry

Stopford A. Brooke, 1881

Melody by Jakob Hintze, 1678,
harmonized by J. S. Bach

SALZBURG, 77.77 D

1. Let the whole cre - a - tion cry, "Glo - ry to the Lord on high."
2. War - riors fight - ing for the Lord, proph - ets burn - ing with his word,
3. Men and wom - en, young and old, raise the an - them man - i - fold;

1. Heav'n and earth, a - wake and sing, "God is good and there - fore King."
2. those to whom the arts be - long, add their voic - es to the song.
3. and let chil - dren's hap - py hearts in this wor - ship bear their parts;

1. Praise him, all ye hosts a - bove, ev - er bright and fair in love;
2. Kings of knowl - edge and of law, to the glo - rious cir - cle draw;
3. from the north to southern pole, let the might - y cho - rus roll:

1. sun and moon, up - lift your voice, night and stars, in God re - joice!
2. all who work and all who wait, sing, "The Lord is good and great!"
3. "Ho - ly, ho - ly, ho - ly One, glo - ry be to God a - lone!"

CREATOR OF HEAVEN AND EARTH

Now All the Woods Are Sleeping

Nun ruhen alle Walder, by Paul Gerhardt, 1653; paraphrased in the
Lutheran Book of Worship (1978); st. 3 mostly by Robert Bridges, 1899

H. Isaak, c. 1450–1517,
adapted by J. S. Bach, 1729

INNSBRUCK, 77.6.7 7.8

13

1. Now all the woods are sleep - ing, through fields the
2. The ra - diant sun has van - ished, its gold - en
3. Now all the heav'n - ly splen - dor breaks forth in
4. Though long our an - cient blind - ness has missed God's

1. shad - ows creep - ing, and cit - ies sink to rest:
2. rays are ban - ished from dark - 'ning skies of night;
3. star - light ten - der from myr - iad worlds un - known;
4. lov - ing - kind - ness and plunged us in - to strife,

1. let us as night is fall - ing, on God our Mak - er
2. but Christ the Sun of glad - ness, dis - pell - ing all our
3. and we, this mar - vel see - ing, for - get our self - ish
4. one day when life is o - ver shall death's fair night un -

1. call - ing, give thanks to him, who loves us best.
2. sad - ness, shines down on us in warm - est light.
3. be - ing for joy of beau - ty not our own.
4. cov - er the fields of ev - er - last - ing life.

CREATOR OF HEAVEN AND EARTH

This Is My Father's World

Maltbie D. Babcock, 1901

English traditional melody
adapted by Franklin L. Sheppard, 1915;
harmonized by David Hugh Jones, 1953

TERRA BEATA, SMD

1. This is my Fa-ther's world, and to my lis-tening ears
2. This is my Fa-ther's world: the birds their car-ols raise,
3. This is my Fa-ther's world: oh, let me ne'er for-get

1. all na-ture sings, and round me rings the mu-sic of the spheres.
2. the morn-ing light, the lil-y white, de-clare their Mak-er's praise.
3. that though the wrong seems oft so strong, God is the Rul-er yet.

1. This is my Fa-ther's world: I rest me in the thought
2. This is my Fa-ther's world: he shines in all that's fair;
3. This is my Fa-ther's world: the bat-tle is not done;

1. of rocks and trees, of skies and seas; his hand the won-ders wrought.
2. in the rus-tling grass I hear him pass, he speaks to me ev-ery-where.
3. Je-sus who died shall be sat-is-fied, and earth and heaven be one.

CREATOR OF HEAVEN AND EARTH

Gen. 1

Cecil Frances Alexander, 1848 (alt'd)

17th-century English melody;
arranged by Martin Shaw, 1915

ROYAL OAK, 7.6.7.6.7.6.7.6
Stanza 1 to be sung as refrain after stanzas 2 to 5

1. All things bright and beau-ti-ful, all crea-tures great and small,

1. all things wise and won-der-ful: the Lord God made them all.

2. Each lit-tle flower that o-pens, each lit-tle bird that sings:
3. The rock-y moun-tain splen-dor, the haunt-ing cur-lew's call,
4. the cold wind in the win-ter, the pleas-ant sum-mer sun,
5. He gave us eyes to see them, and lips that we might tell

2. he made their glow-ing col-ors, he made their ti-ny wings.
3. the great lakes and the prai-ries, the for-ests in the fall:
4. the ripe fruits in the gar-den: he made them ev-ery one.
5. how great is God Al-might-y, who has made all things well.

Gen. 1:31   CREATOR OF HEAVEN AND EARTH

Father, We Thank You

Caryl Micklem, 1975

ALL KINDS OF LIGHT, 5.8.85.5

Caryl Micklem, 1975

1. Fa - ther, we thank you for the light that shines all the
2. Fa - ther, we thank you for the lamps that light - en our
3. Fa - ther, we thank you for the friends that bright - en our
4. Fa - ther, we thank you for your love in Je - sus to -

1. day: for the bright sky you have giv - en,
2. way: for hu - man skill's ex - plo - ra - tion
3. play: for your com - mand to call oth - ers
4. day, giv - ing us hope for to - mor - row

1. most like your heav - en, Fa - ther, we thank you.
2. of your cre - a - tion, Fa - ther, we thank you.
3. sis - ters and broth - ers, Fa - ther, we thank you.
4. through joy or sor - row, Fa - ther, we thank you.

CREATOR OF HEAVEN AND EARTH

Gen. 1:9-19

We Plow the Fields and Scatter

Wir pflugen, M. Claudius, 1782; tr. Jane Montgomery-Campbell, 1861

J. A. P. Schulz, 1800;
harmonized by J. B. Dykes, 1861

WIR PFLUGEN, 7.6.7.6.7.6.7.6 with refrain

1. We plow the fields and scat-ter the good seed on the land, but it is
2. He on-ly is the Mak-er of all things near and far; he paints the
3. We thank Thee, then, O Fa-ther, for all things bright and good, the seed-time

1. fed and wa-tered by God's al-might-y hand; he sends the snow in
2. way-side flow-er, he lights the eve-ning star; the winds and waves o-
3. and the har-vest, our life, our health, our food; ac-cept the gifts we

1. win-ter, the warmth to swell the grain, the breez-es and the sun-shine, and
2. bey him, by him the birds are fed; much more to us, his chil-dren, he
3. of-fer, for all thy love im-parts, and what thou most de-sir-est, our

Refrain

1. soft re-fresh-ing rain.
2. gives our dai-ly bread. } All good gifts a-round us are sent from heaven a-
3. hum-ble, thank-ful hearts.

bove; then thank the Lord, O thank the Lord for all his love.

Ps. 145:16

THE EARTH IS THE LORD'S

18   Come, Ye Thankful People, Come

Based on hymns by H. Alford, 1810–1871, and Anna L. Barbauld, 1743–1825

ST. GEORGE'S WINDSOR, 77.77 D   G. J. Elvey, 1858

1. Come, ye thank-ful peo-ple, come, raise the song of har-vest home;
2. All the bless-ings of the field, all the stores the gar-dens yield,
3. We our-selves are God's own field fruit un-to his praise to yield,

1. all is safe-ly gath-ered in ere the win-ter storms be-gin;
2. all the fruits in full sup-ply, rip-en'd 'neath the sum-mer sky,
3. wheat and tares to-geth-er sown, un-to joy or sor-row grown:

1. God, our Mak-er, doth pro-vide for our wants to be sup-plied;
2. all that spring with boun-teous hand scat-ters o'er the smil-ing land,
3. first the blade and then the ear, then the full corn shall ap-pear;

1. come to God's own tem-ple, come, raise the song of har-vest home!
2. all that lib-'ral au-tumn pours comes from God's o'er-flow-ing stores.
3. grant, O har-vest Lord, that we whole-some grain and pure may be.

This tune in a higher key: 601

THE EARTH IS THE LORD'S   Mt. 13:24ff

Sing to the Lord of Harvest

J. S. B. Monsell, 1863

STEURLEIN, 7.6.7.6 D

Melody by J. Steurlein, 1575

1. Sing to the Lord of harvest, sing songs of love and praise;
2. By him the clouds drop fatness, the deserts bloom and spring,
3. Heap on his sacred altar the gifts his goodness gave,

1. with joyful hearts and voices your alleluias raise.
2. the hills leap up in gladness, the valleys laugh and sing.
3. the golden sheaves of harvest, the souls he died to save.

1. He filleth with his fullness all things with large increase;
2. By him the rolling seasons in fruitful order move;
3. Your hearts lay down before him when at his feet you fall,

1. he crowns the year with goodness, with plenty and with peace.
2. sing to the Lord of harvest a song of happy love.
3. and with your lives adore him, who gave his life for all.

THE EARTH IS THE LORD'S

Praise and Thanksgiving

Albert F. Bayly, 1970

BUNESSAN, 5.5.5.4 D

Hebridean folk melody

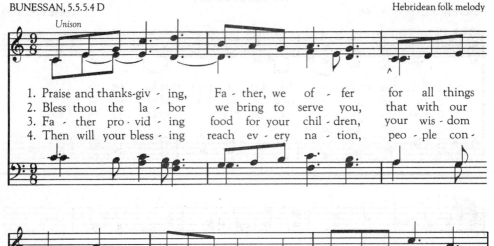

1. Praise and thanks-giv - ing, Fa - ther, we of - fer for all things
2. Bless thou the la - bor we bring to serve you, that with our
3. Fa - ther pro - vid - ing food for your chil - dren, your wis - dom
4. Then will your bless - ing reach ev - ery na - tion, peo - ple con -

1. liv - ing you have made good: har - vest of sown fields,
2. neigh - bor we may be fed. Sow - ing or till - ing,
3. guid - ing bids us to share one with an - oth - er,
4. fess - ing your gra-cious hand. Where your will reigns, no

1. fruits of the or - chard, hay from the mown fields, blos-som, and wood.
2. we would work with you, har - vest-ing, mill - ing for dai - ly bread.
3. so that re - joic - ing, sis - ter and broth - er may know your care.
4. mor - tal will hun - ger; your love sus -tains, so fruit-ful the land!

Alternative harmonization (SATB): 215

THE EARTH IS THE LORD'S

Ps. 104:13f

For the Fruits of His Creation

Fred Pratt Green, 1970

EAST ACKLAM, 8.4.8.4.888.4

Francis Jackson, 1969

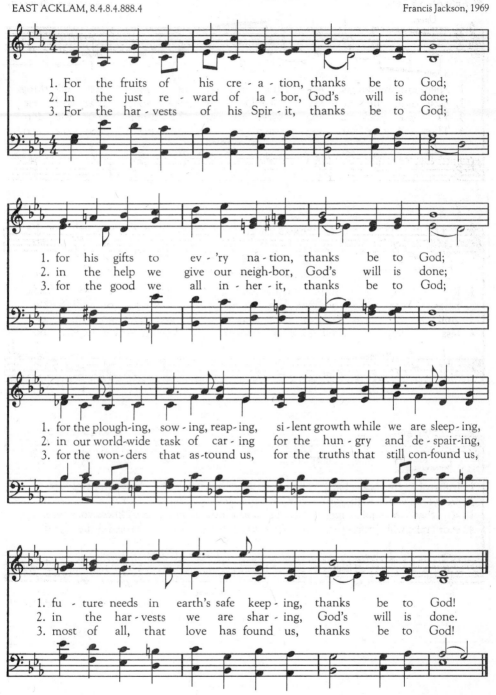

1. For the fruits of his cre - a - tion, thanks be to God;
2. In the just re - ward of la - bor, God's will is done;
3. For the har - vests of his Spir - it, thanks be to God;

1. for his gifts to ev - 'ry na - tion, thanks be to God;
2. in the help we give our neigh-bor, God's will is done;
3. for the good we all in - her - it, thanks be to God;

1. for the plough-ing, sow - ing, reap - ing, si - lent growth while we are sleep-ing,
2. in our world-wide task of car - ing for the hun - gry and de - spair-ing,
3. for the won - ders that as-tound us, for the truths that still con-found us,

1. fu - ture needs in earth's safe keep - ing, thanks be to God!
2. in the har - vests we are shar - ing, God's will is done.
3. most of all, that love has found us, thanks be to God!

Lk. 15:31–32

THE EARTH IS THE LORD'S

22   Thank You, God, for Water, Soil, and Air

Brian Wren, 1973

LONSDALE, 9.10.10.9

Erik Routley, 1979

1. Thank you, God, for wa - ter, soil, and air,
2. Thank you, God, for min - er - als and ores—
3. Thank you, God, for price - less en - er - gy,
4. Thank you, God, for weav - ing na - ture's life

1. large gifts sup-port - ing ev - 'ry-thing that
2. the ba - sis of all build - ing, wealth, and
3. stored in each at - om, gath - ered from the
4. in - to a seam - less robe, a frag - ile

1. lives. For - give our spoil-ing and a - buse of them.
2. speed. For - give our reck-less plun-der - ing and waste.
3. sun. For - give our greed and care-less - ness of power.
4. whole. For - give our haste, that tam-pers un - a-wares.

1. Help us
2. Help us
3. Help us   re - new the face of the earth.
4. Help us

5. Thank you, God, for making planet earth,
   a home for us and ages yet unborn.
  Help us to share, consider, save, and store.
   Come and renew the face of the earth.

THE EARTH IS THE LORD'S

Gen. 1:28–29

God in His Love for Us Lent Us This Planet

Fred Pratt Green, 1971

ECOLOGY, 11.10.11.10 dactylic

Austin C. Lovelace, 1974

1. God in his love for us — lent us this plan - et, gave it a
2. Thanks be to God — for its bount - y and beau - ty, life that sus-
3. Long have our hu-man wars — ruined its — har - vest: long has Earth
4. Earth is the Lord's! it is ours to en - joy it, ours as his

1. pur - pose in time — and in space; small as a spark — from the
2. tains — us in bod - y and mind: plen - ty for all, — if we
3. bowed to the ter - ror of force; long have we wast - ed what
4. stew - ards, to farm — and de - fend. From its pol - lu - tion, mis-

1. fire of cre - a - tion, cra - dle of life — and the home — of our race.
2. learn how to share — it, rich - es un-dreamed of to fath - om and find.
3. oth - ers have need — of, poi-soned the foun - tain of life — at its source.
4. use and de-struc-tion, good Lord, de-liv-er us, — world — with-out end!

Ps. 115:16

THE EARTH IS THE LORD'S

24

Lord, Bring the Day to Pass

Ian Fraser, 1964

CAMANO, 6.6.6.6.88

Richard Proulx, 1977

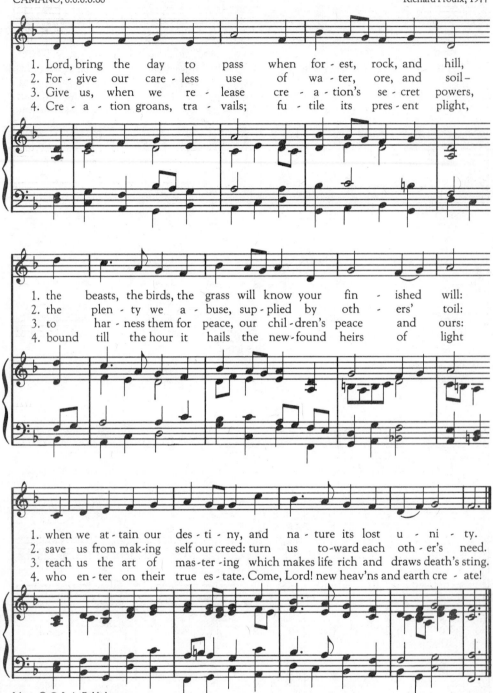

1. Lord, bring the day to pass when for-est, rock, and hill,
2. For-give our care-less use of wa-ter, ore, and soil—
3. Give us, when we re-lease cre-a-tion's se-cret powers,
4. Cre-a-tion groans, tra-vails; fu-tile its pres-ent plight,

1. the beasts, the birds, the grass will know your fin-ished will:
2. the plen-ty we a-buse, sup-plied by oth-ers' toil:
3. to har-ness them for peace, our chil-dren's peace and ours:
4. bound till the hour it hails the new-found heirs of light

1. when we at-tain our des-ti-ny, and na-ture its lost u-ni-ty.
2. save us from mak-ing self our creed: turn us to-ward each oth-er's need.
3. teach us the art of mas-ter-ing which makes life rich and draws death's sting.
4. who en-ter on their true es-tate. Come, Lord! new heav'ns and earth cre-ate!

THE EARTH IS THE LORD'S

Rom. 8:19–22

God Folds the Mountains out of Rock 25

ROUTLEY, LM
Thomas H. Troeger, 1985
Carol Doran, 1985

1. God folds the mountains out of rock and fuses elemental powers in
2. From veins of stone we lift up fire and too impressed with our own skill we
3. Our instruments can probe and sound the folded mountain's potent core, but
4. Yet wisdom is the greater need, and wisdom is the greater source, for
5. Lord, grant us what we cannot mine, what science cannot plumb or chart: your
6. Then we like mountains richly veined will be a source of light and flame whose

1. ores and atoms we unlock to claim as if their wealth were ours.
2. use the flame that we acquire not thinking of the Maker's will.
3. wisdom's ways are never found among the lodes of buried ore.
4. lacking wisdom we proceed to waste God's other gifts on force.
5. wisdom and your truth divine enfolded in a faithful heart.
6. energies have been ordained to glorify the Maker's name.

Job 28

God, You Have Given Us Power to Sound 26

WALSALL, CM
G. W. Briggs, 1945
Psalm Tunes, W. Anchors, c. 1721

1. God, you have giv'n us power to sound depths hitherto unknown;
2. Great are your gifts; yet greater far this gift, O God, bestow,
3. Let wisdom's godly fear dispel all fears that hate imparts;
4. So for your glory and our good may we your gifts employ,

1. to probe earth's hidden mysteries and make their might our own.
2. that as to knowledge we attain, we may in wisdom grow.
3. give understanding to the mind, and with new mind, new heart.
4. lest, maddened by the lust of power, we shall ourselves destroy.

Alternative tunes: BANGOR, 288, and ST. FLAVIAN, 28   THE EARTH IS THE LORD'S

27 **Can We by Searching Find Out God?**

Elizabeth Cosnett, 1980

METROPOLITAN, CM

Melville Cooke

1. Can we by search-ing find out God, or for-mu-late his ways?
2. Al - though his be - ing is too bright for hu-man eyes to scan,
3. Our boast-ful - ness is turned to shame, our prof - it counts as loss,
4. We there may rec - og - nize his light, may kin -dle in its rays,
5. There God breaks in up - on our search, makes birth and death his own,

1. Can num-bers meas - ure what he is, or words con-tain his praise?
2. his mean-ing lights our shad-owed world through Christ, the Son of Man.
3. when earth-ly val - ues stand be - side the man - ger and the cross.
4. find there the source of pen - i - tence, the start - ing point for praise.
5. he speaks to us in hu - man terms, to make his glo - ry known.

This tune in a higher key: 385

Job 11:7

28 **From Thee All Skill and Science Flow**

Charles Kingsley, 1871

Richard Redhead, 1853; based on the first
half of the OLD 132nd, *English Psalter* (1562)

ST. FLAVIAN, CM

1. From thee all skill and sci - ence flow, all pi - ty, care, and love,
2. Im - part them, Lord, to each and all, as each and all shall need,
3. And has - ten, Lord, that per - fect day when pain and death shall cease,
4. When ev - er blue the sky shall gleam, and ev - er green the sod,

1. all calm and cour - age, faith and hope; O pour them from a - bove!
2. to rise like in - cense, each to thee in no - ble thought and deed.
3. and thy just rule shall fill the earth with health and light and peace.
4. and our rude work de - face no more the par - a - dise of God.

THE EARTH IS THE LORD'S

Alternative tune: WALSALL, 26

God Who Stretched the Spangled Heavens

Catherine Cameron, 1967

HOLY MANNA, 8.7.8.7 D

American folk hymn tune

1. God who stretched the span-gled heav-ens in - fi - nite in time and space,
2. Proud-ly rise our mod-ern cit - ies, state-ly build-ings, row on row:
3. We have con-quered worlds un-dreamed of since the child-hood of our race;
4. As thy new ho - ri - zons beck - on, Fa - ther, give us strength to be

1. flung the suns in burn - ing ra-diance through the si - lent fields of space,
2. yet their win-dows, blank, un - feel - ing stare on can-yoned streets be-low,
3. known the ec - sta - sy of wing-ing through un-chart - ed realms of space,
4. chil - dren of cre - a - tive pur-pose, think - ing thy thoughts af - ter thee,

1. we thy chil-dren, in thy like-ness, share in-ven-tive powers with thee:
2. where the lone-ly drift un - no-ticed in the cit - y's ebb and flow,
3. probed the se-crets of the at - om, yield-ing un - im - ag - ined power,
4. till our dreams are rich with mean-ing, each en-deav-or, thy de - sign;

1. great Cre - a - tor, still cre - at - ing, teach us what we yet may be.
2. lost to pur - pose and to mean - ing, scarce-ly car - ing where they go.
3. fac - ing us with life's de - struc-tion, or our most tri - um-phant hour.
4. great Cre - a - tor, lead us on - ward till our work is one with thine.

This tune in a lower key: 381

THE EARTH IS THE LORD'S

Beyond the Mist and Doubt

Donald Hughes, 1911–1967 (1969)

MAIDEN WAY, 6.6.88.6

Erik Routley, 1969

1. Be - yond the mist and doubt of our un - cer - tain
2. Our rest - less in - tel - lect has all things in its
3. Still in hu - mil - i - ty we know thee by thy

1. day, I trust in thine e - ter - nal name, be -
2. shade, but still to thee my spir - it clings, se -
3. grace; for sci - ence - 's re - mot - est probe feels

1. yond all chang - es still the same, and in that
2. rene be - yond all shak - en things, and I am
3. but the fring - es of thy robe: love looks up —

st. 1,2 *st. 3*

1. name I pray.
2. not a - fraid.
3. on thy face.

THE EARTH IS THE LORD'S

Job 26:14

O Lord of Every Shining Constellation

Albert F. Bayly, 1950

VICAR, 11.10.11.10

V. Earle Copes, 1964

Unison

1. O Lord of ev - 'ry shin - ing con - stel - la - tion
2. You, Lord, have made the at - om's hid - den forc - es,
3. You, Lord, have stamped your im - age on your crea - tures,

1. that wheels in splen - dor through the mid - night sky,
2. your laws its might - y en - er - gies ful - fill;
3. and though they mar that im - age, love them still;

1. grant us your Spir - it's true il - lu - mi - na - tion
2. teach us, to whom you give such rich re - sourc - es,
3. lift up our eyes to Christ, that in his fea - tures

1. to read the se - crets of your work on high.
2. in all we use, to serve your ho - ly will.
3. we may dis - cern the beau - ty of your will.

Job 38:31-33

THE EARTH IS THE LORD'S

32

O God of Space and Time

Herbert Ritsema, 1982

WILHELMUS, 12 12.12 12

16th-century Dutch melody;
harmony mostly by John Wilson

1. O God of space and time, e-ter-nal is your name.
2. O God of love and grace re-vealed in Christ your Son,
3. O God of truth and light, so bright-en ev-'ry heart,
4. Keep now our spir-its pure, our minds on things a-bove;

1. In you no here nor there, from age to age the same;
2. who died that we might live, in whom your will was done:
3. that we re-flect your beau-ty through cre-a-tive art.
4. help us to walk with - in the free-dom of your love.

1. re-ceive our heart - felt praise for show-ing us your love,
2. grant us the zeal to love be-yond mere hu-man ways,
3. In sci - ence we ob-serve the or-der of your ways;
4. Grant us a vi - sion clear, your wis-dom to re-veal,

or

1. as through the years you gave pro-tec-tion from a-bove.
2. that sweet and self - less toil may mark our earth-ly days.
3. in speech and mu - sic joined, we of-fer you our praise.
4. that we may per - se-vere, to love and teach and heal.

THE EARTH IS THE LORD'S

Earth and All Stars

Herbert Brokering, 1964

David Johnson, 1968

33

DEXTER, 4.5.7 D with refrain

1. Earth and all stars, loud rush-ing plan - ets sing to the
2. Hail, wind and rain, loud blow-ing snow - storm sing to the
3. Trum-pet and pipes, loud clash-ing cym - bals sing to the
*4. Ma - chines and steel, loud pound-ing ham - mers sing to the
5. Knowl-edge and truth, loud sound-ing wis - dom sing to the

1. Lord___ a new song! O vic-to - ry, loud shout-ing ar - my
2. Lord___ a new song! Flow-ers and trees, loud rus-tling dry leaves
3. Lord___ a new song! Harp, lute and lyre, loud hum-ming cel - los
4. Lord___ a new song! Lime-stone and beams, loud build-ing work - men
5. Lord___ a new song! Daugh-ter and son, loud pray-ing mem - bers

sing to the Lord___ a new song! He hath done

mar - vel-ous things. I, too, will praise him with a new___ song!

Ps. 98:1ff

THE EARTH IS THE LORD'S

34 God Is Love: Let Heaven Adore Him

Timothy Rees, 1922

RODLAND, 8.7.8.7 D

Gene Traas, 1977

1. God is love: let heav'n a-dore him; God is love: let earth re-joice;
2. God is love, and he en-fold-eth all the world in one em-brace;
3. God is love, and though with blind-ness sin af-flicts these hu-man hearts,

1. let cre-a-tion sing be-fore him and ex-alt him with one voice.
2. with un-fail-ing grasp he hold-eth ev-'ry child of ev-'ry race.
3. God's e-ter-nal lov-ing-kind-ness nev-er from his world de-parts.

1. He who laid the earth's foun-da-tions, he who spread the heav'ns a-bove,
2. And when hu-man hearts are break-ing un-der sor-row's i-ron rod,
3. Sin and death and hell shall nev-er o'er us fi-nal tri-umph gain;

1. he who breathes through all cre-a-tion, he is Love, e-ter-nal Love.
2. then they find that self-same ach-ing deep with-in the heart of God.
3. God is love, so love for-ev-er o'er the u-ni-verse must reign.

Alternative tune: BLAENWERN, 115

Great God of Wonders!

Samuel Davies, 1723–1761 (alt'd)

Melody in Schumann's *Geistliche Lieder* (1539);
most of the harmony from J. S. Bach (Cantata 102)

VATER UNSER, 8.8.8.8.88

1. Great God of won-ders! all thy ways are match-less, god-like
2. Such dire of-fens-es to for-give, such guil-ty, dar-ing
3. O may this strange, this match-less grace, this god-like mir-a-

1. and di-vine; but the fair glo-ries of thy grace more
2. souls to spare: this is thy grand pre-rog-a-tive, and
3. cle of love fill the wide earth with grate-ful praise, and

1. god-like and un-ri-valed shine. Who is a par-doning
2. none shall in the hon-or share! Who is a par-doning
3. all th' an-gel-ic hosts a-bove. Who is a par-doning

God like thee? And who has grace so rich and free?

♮ last time only

Dan. 9:9

WHO PARDONS ALL YOUR INIQUITIES

36 God Moves in a Mysterious Way

William Cowper, 1774

LONDON NEW, CM

Playford's Psalms (1671)

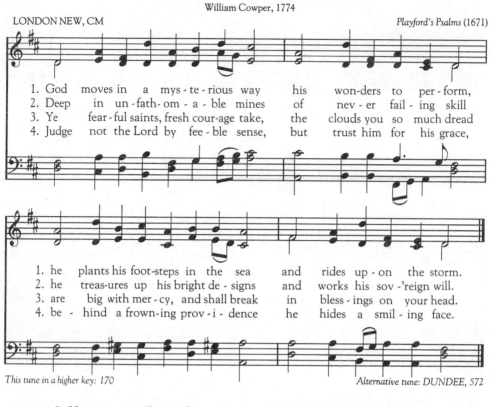

1. God moves in a mys-te-rious way his won-ders to per-form,
2. Deep in un-fath-om-a-ble mines of nev-er fail-ing skill
3. Ye fear-ful saints, fresh cour-age take, the clouds you so much dread
4. Judge not the Lord by fee-ble sense, but trust him for his grace,

1. he plants his foot-steps in the sea and rides up-on the storm.
2. he treas-ures up his bright de-signs and works his sov-'reign will.
3. are big with mer-cy, and shall break in bless-ings on your head.
4. be-hind a frown-ing prov-i-dence he hides a smil-ing face.

This tune in a higher key: 170

Alternative tune: DUNDEE, 572

5. His purposes will ripen fast,
   unfolding ev'ry hour;
   the bud may have a bitter taste,
   but sweet will be the flower.

6. Blind unbelief is sure to err
   and scan his work in vain;
   God is his own interpreter,
   and he will make it plain.

Ps. 77:19

37 Come, Let Us to the Lord Our God

John Morison, in *Scottish Paraphrases* (1781)

KILMARNOCK, CM

Neil Dougall, 1831

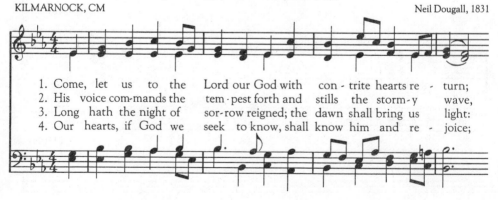

1. Come, let us to the Lord our God with con-trite hearts re-turn;
2. His voice com-mands the tem-pest forth and stills the storm-y wave,
3. Long hath the night of sor-row reigned; the dawn shall bring us light:
4. Our hearts, if God we seek to know, shall know him and re-joice;

WHO PARDONS ALL YOUR INIQUITIES

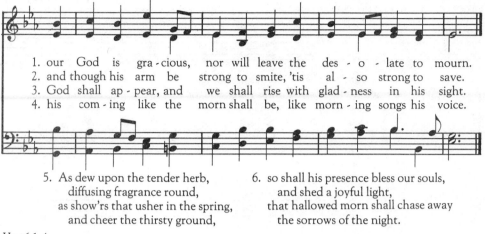

1. our God is gra-cious, nor will leave the des-o-late to mourn.
2. and though his arm be strong to smite, 'tis al-so strong to save.
3. God shall ap-pear, and we shall rise with glad-ness in his sight.
4. his com-ing like the morn shall be, like morn-ing songs his voice.

5. As dew upon the tender herb,
   diffusing fragrance round,
   as show'rs that usher in the spring,
   and cheer the thirsty ground,

6. so shall his presence bless our souls,
   and shed a joyful light,
   that hallowed morn shall chase away
   the sorrows of the night.

Hos. 6:1–4

O God of Truth, Whose Living Word 38

Thomas Hughes, 1857

MARTYRS, CM

Scottish Psalter (1635)

Descant, st. 5, by Erik Routley

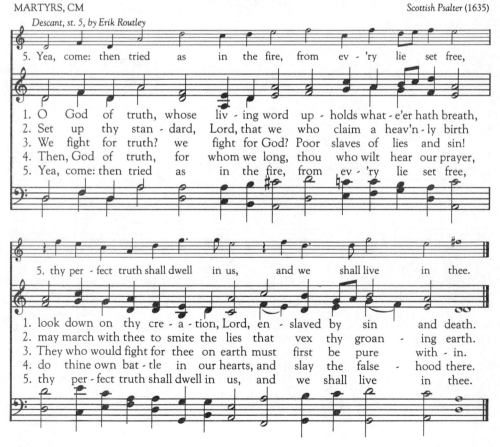

5. Yea, come: then tried as in the fire, from ev-'ry lie set free,

1. O God of truth, whose liv-ing word up-holds what-e'er hath breath,
2. Set up thy stan-dard, Lord, that we who claim a heav'n-ly birth
3. We fight for truth? we fight for God? Poor slaves of lies and sin!
4. Then, God of truth, for whom we long, thou who wilt hear our prayer,
5. Yea, come: then tried as in the fire, from ev-'ry lie set free,

5. thy per-fect truth shall dwell in us, and we shall live in thee.

1. look down on thy cre-a-tion, Lord, en-slaved by sin and death.
2. may march with thee to smite the lies that vex thy groan-ing earth.
3. They who would fight for thee on earth must first be pure with-in.
4. do thine own bat-tle in our hearts, and slay the false-hood there.
5. thy per-fect truth shall dwell in us, and we shall live in thee.

39 God of Compassion, in Mercy Befriend Us

John J. Moment, c. 1933

O QUANTA QUALIA, 11.11.11.11 dactylic

Later form of melody in
Paris Antiphoner (1681)

1. God of com-pas-sion, in mer-cy be-friend us;
2. Wan-d'ring and lost, thou hast sought us and found us,
3. How shall we stray, with thy hand to di-rect us,

1. giv-er of grace for our needs all a-vail-ing,
2. stilled our rude hearts with thy word of con-sol-ing;
3. thou, who the stars in their cours-es are guid-ing?

1. wis-dom and strength for each day do thou send us,
2. wrap now thy peace, like a man-tle, a-round us,
3. What shall we fear, with thy pow'r to pro-tect us,

1. pa-tience un-tir-ing and cour-age un-fail-ing.
2. guard-ing our thoughts and our pas-sions con-trol-ling.
3. we who walk forth in thy great-ness con-fid-ing?

This tune in a lower key: 583

Alternative (later) version of
this measure

WHO PARDONS ALL YOUR INIQUITIES

Isa. 55:9

Searcher and Savior of My Soul

John Henry Livingston, 1814

Henry K. Oliver, 1832
harmonized by Carol Doran, 1985

FEDERAL STREET, LM

1. Search - er and Sav - ior of my soul, my Sun, my
2. Oft to thy Word my soul re - pairs; thence I my
3. Sus - tain me then with prom - ised grace, re - vive my
4. Su - preme - ly wise and good and great; O! search my

1. Shield, my sov - ereign Judge; all things are na - ked
2. high - est com - forts draw; though foes may fight and
3. heart, in - crease my faith: seal to my soul thy
4. heart and try my ways. Thy word I love, thy

1. to thy view — my heart, my thoughts, my words, my ways.
2. dev - ils rage, if God be for me, all is well.
3. pard' - ning love, let strength be e - qual to my day.
4. judg - ments fear, and trem - ble while I pray and praise.

40

Ps. 119:153–160

WHO PARDONS ALL YOUR INIQUITIES

41   Eternal Light! Eternal Light!

Thomas Binney, 1829

CHALFONT PARK, 8.6.88.6   Erik Routley, 1942

1. E - ter - nal light! E - ter - nal light! How pure the soul must be,
2. The spir - its that sur - round thy throne may bear the burn - ing bliss;
3. O how shall I, whose na - tive sphere is dark, whose mind is dim,
4. There is a way for us to rise to that sub - lime a - bode,
5. These, these pre - pare us for the sight of ho - li - ness a - bove;

1. when, placed with - in thy search - ing sight, it shrinks not,
2. but that is sure - ly theirs a - lone, since they have
3. be - fore th'in - ef - fa - ble ap - pear, and on my
4. an of - f'ring and a sac - ri - fice, a Ho - ly
5. the heirs of ig - no - rance and night may dwell in

1. but with calm de - light can live and look on thee.
2. nev - er, nev - er known a fall - en world like this.
3. na - ked spir - it bear the un - cre - at - ed beam?
4. Spir - it's en - er - gies, an Ad - vo - cate with God.
5. the e - ter - nal light, through the e - ter - nal love!

WHO PARDONS ALL YOUR INIQUITIES   *Ex. 33:20*

God of Love

Timothy Rees, 1916

CAROLYN, 8.5.8.5.888.5

Herbert Murrill, 1951

1. God of love and truth and beau-ty, hal-lowed be thy name;
2. Lord, re-move our guil-ty blind-ness, hal-lowed be thy name;
3. In our wor-ship, Lord most ho-ly, hal-lowed be thy name;

1. fount of or-der, law, and du-ty, hal-lowed be thy name.
2. show thy heart of lov-ing kind-ness, hal-lowed be thy name.
3. in our work, how-ev-er low-ly, hal-lowed be thy name.

1. As in heav'n thy hosts a-dore thee, and their fa-ces veil be-fore thee,
2. By our heart's deep-felt con-tri-tion, by our mind's en-light-ened vi-sion,
3. In each heart's im-ag-i-na-tion, in the Chur-ch's a-do-ra-tion,

1. so on earth, Lord, we im-plore thee, hal-lowed be thy name.
2. by our will's com-plete sub-mis-sion, hal-lowed be thy name.
3. in the con-science of the na-tion, hal-lowed be thy name.

Mt. 6:9

WHO PARDONS ALL YOUR INIQUITIES

43   Creator of the Earth and Skies

Donald W. Hughes, 1964

PLAISTOW, LM

Melody from *Magdalen Hymns* (c. 1760)

1. Cre - a - tor of the earth and skies, to whom the words
2. We have not known you: to the skies our mon - u - ments
3. We have not loved you: far and wide the wreck - age of
4. For this, our fool - ish con - fi - dence, our pride of knowl -
5. Teach us to know and love thee, Lord, and hum - bly fol -

1. of life be - long, grant us your truth to
2. of fol - ly soar, and all our self - wrought
3. our ha - tred spreads, and e - vils wrought by
4. edge and our sin, we come to you in
5. low in your way. Speak to our souls the

1. make us wise, grant us your pow'r to make us strong.
2. mis - er - ies have made us trust our - selves the more.
3. hu - man pride re - coil on un - re - pen - tant heads.
4. pen - i - tence; in us the work of grace be - gin.
5. quick - 'ning word, and turn our dark - ness in - to day.

WHO PARDONS ALL YOUR INIQUITIES

Gen. 11; Phil. 1:6

Faith, While Trees Are Still in Blossom

44

Tron sig sträcker efter Frukten, by Anders Frostenson, 1960;
tr. Fred Kaan, 1972

MERTON, 8.7.8.7

W. H. Monk, 1861

1. Faith, while trees are still in blos-som, plans the pick-ing of the fruit;
2. Long be-fore the dawn is break-ing, faith an-tic-i-pates the sun.
3. Long be-fore the rains were com-ing, No-ah went and built an ark.
4. Faith, up-lift-ed, tamed the wa-ter of the un-di-vid-ed sea,
5. Faith be-lieves that God is faith-ful— "He will be what He will be."

1. faith can feel the thrill of har-vest when the buds be-gin to sprout.
2. Faith is ea-ger for the day-light, for the work that must be done.
3. A-bra-ham, the lone-ly mi-grant, saw the light be-yond the dark.
4. and the peo-ple of the He-brews found the path that made them free.
5. Faith ac-cepts his call, re-spond-ing, "I am will-ing, Lord: send me."

Gen. 6; Ex. 3:3; Ex. 14:26; Isa. 6:8

O God of Bethel

45

Text from the *Scottish Paraphrases* (1781);
based on Philip Doddridge, 1740 (alt'd)

DUNDEE, CM

Scottish Psalter (1615);
harmony from *Ravenscroft's Psalter* (1621)

1. O God of Beth-el, by whose hand thy peo-ple still are fed,
2. our vows, our prayers, we now pre-sent be-fore thy throne of grace;
3. Thro' each per-plex-ing path of life our wan-d'ring foot-steps guide;
4. O spread thy cov-'ring wings a-round, till all our wan-d'rings cease,

...[NO PAUSE]

1. who through this wea-ry pil-grim-age hast all thy ser-vants led,
2. God of past a-ges, be the God of each suc-ceed-ing race.
3. give us each day our dai-ly bread, and rai-ment fit pro-vide.
4. and at our Fa-ther's loved a-bode our souls ar-rive in peace.

Later version of this tune: 572
Alternative tune: LONDON NEW, 36
Gen. 28: 10–22

GOD OF ABRAHAM, ISAAC, AND JACOB

46 Come, O Thou Traveler Unknown

Charles Wesley, 1739
First Tune

WOODBURY, 8.8.8.8.88

Erik Routley, 1969

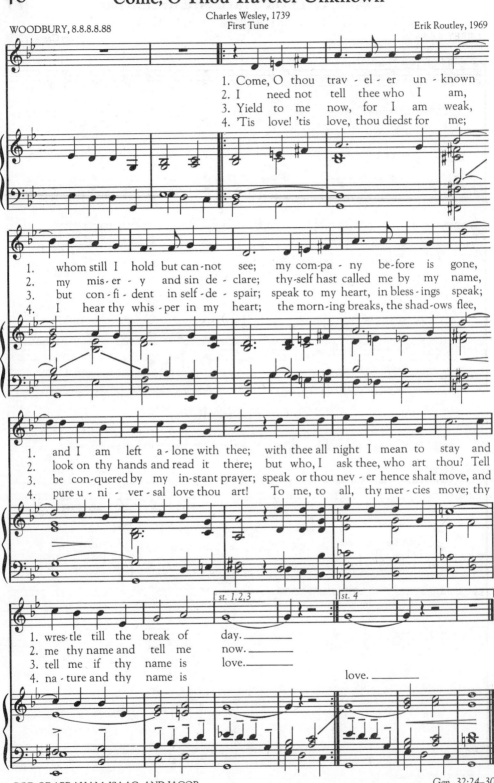

1. Come, O thou trav-el-er un-known
2. I need not tell thee who I am,
3. Yield to me now, for I am weak,
4. 'Tis love! 'tis love, thou diedst for me;

1. whom still I hold but can-not see; my com-pa-ny be-fore is gone,
2. my mis-er-y and sin de-clare; thy-self hast called me by my name,
3. but con-fi-dent in self-de-spair; speak to my heart, in bless-ings speak;
4. I hear thy whis-per in my heart; the morn-ing breaks, the shad-ows flee,

1. and I am left a-lone with thee; with thee all night I mean to stay and
2. look on thy hands and read it there; but who, I ask thee, who art thou? Tell
3. be con-quered by my in-stant prayer; speak or thou nev-er hence shalt move, and
4. pure u-ni-ver-sal love thou art! To me, to all, thy mer-cies move; thy

st. 1,2,3   st. 4

1. wres-tle till the break of day.
2. me thy name and tell me now.
3. tell me if thy name is love.
4. na-ture and thy name is love.

GOD OF ABRAHAM, ISAAC, AND JACOB

Gen. 32:24–30

Come, O Thou Traveler Unknown

Second Tune

SURREY, 8.8.8.8.88

Henry Carey, 1723

1. Come, O thou trav-el - er un-known whom still I hold but can-not see;
2. I need not tell thee who I am, my mis-er-y and sin de-clare;
3. Yield to me now, for I am weak, but con-fi-dent in self-de-spair;
4. 'Tis love! 'tis love, thou diedst for me; I hear thy whis-per in my heart;

1. my com-pa-ny be - fore is gone, and I am left a-lone with thee;
2. thy-self hast called me by my name, look on thy hands and read it there;
3. speak to my heart, in bless-ings speak; be con-quered by my in-stant prayer;
4. the morn-ing breaks, the shad-ows flee, pure u - ni - ver - sal love thou art!

1. with thee all night I mean to stay and wres-tle till the break of day.
2. but who, I ask thee, who art thou? Tell me thy name and tell me now.
3. speak or thou nev - er hence shalt move, and tell me if thy name is love.
4. To me, to all, thy mer - cies move; thy na-ture and thy name is love.

GOD OF ABRAHAM, ISAAC, AND JACOB

Our Voice in Song We Gladly Raise

John B. Geyer, 1980

Charles Hutcheson, 1832;
harmonized by Eric H. Thiman

STRACATHRO, CM

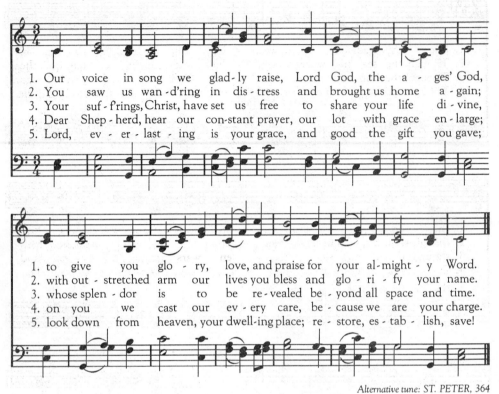

1. Our voice in song we glad-ly raise, Lord God, the a - ges' God,
2. You saw us wan-d'ring in dis-tress and brought us home a - gain;
3. Your suf-f'rings, Christ, have set us free to share your life di - vine,
4. Dear Shep-herd, hear our con-stant prayer, our lot with grace en - large;
5. Lord, ev - er - last - ing is your grace, and good the gift you gave;

1. to give you glo - ry, love, and praise for your al-might - y Word.
2. with out - stretched arm our lives you bless and glo - ri - fy your name.
3. whose splen - dor is to be re - vealed be - yond all space and time.
4. on you we cast our ev - ery care, be - cause we are your charge.
5. look down from heaven, your dwell-ing place; re - store, es - tab - lish, save!

Alternative tune: ST. PETER, 364

GOD OF ABRAHAM, ISAAC, AND JACOB

Deut. 26:5

Lift Thy Head, O Zion, Weeping

49

Karoly Jeszensky, c. 1674; tr. William Toth, 1940

MAGYAR, 8.7.8.7.77.88

Hymn of the Hungarian Galley Slaves, c. 1674

1. Lift thy head, O Zi-on, weep-ing, still the Lord thy Fa-ther is;
2. Though the sea his waves as-sem-ble and in fu-ry fall on thee,
3. Though the hills and vales be riv-en God cre-at-ed with his hand,
4. Though in chains thou now art griev-ing, though a tor-tured slave thou die,

1. thou art dai-ly in his keep-ing, and thine ev-'ry care is his.
2. though thou cry, with heart a-trem-ble, "O my Sav-ior, help thou me!"
3. though the mov-ing signs of heav-en wars pre-sage in ev-'ry land,
4. Zi-on, if thou die be-liev-ing, heav-en's path shall o-pen lie.

1. Rise and be of glad-some heart, and with cour-age play the part;
2. Though un-trou-bled still he sleep who thy hope is on the deep,
3. yet, O Zi-on, have no fear: ev-er is thy help-er near;
4. Up-ward gaze and hap-py be, God hath not for-sak-en thee;

1. soon a-gain his arms will fold thee to his lov-ing heart and hold thee.
2. Zi-on, calm the breast that quak-eth; nev-er God his own for-sak-eth.
3. he hath sought thee, he hath found thee; lo! his wings are walls a-round thee.
4. thou his peo-ple art, and sure-ly he will fold his own se-cure-ly.

Ps. 137:1; Ps. 46:2

GOD OF ABRAHAM, ISAAC, AND JACOB

50

Guide Me, O Thou Great Jehovah

Arglwydd arwain trwy'r anialwch, William Williams,
1745; st. 1 tr. Peter Williams, 1771;
st. 2-3 tr. William Williams, 1772

CWM RHONDDA, 8.7.8.7.8.7.7

John Hughes, 1907

1. Guide me, O thou great Je - ho - vah, pil - grim through this
2. O - pen now the crys - tal foun - tain, whence the heal - ing
3. When I tread the verge of Jor - dan, bid my anx - ious

1. bar - ren land; I am weak, but thou art might - y; hold me with thy
2. stream doth flow; let the fire and cloud - y pil - lar lead me all my
3. fears sub - side; death of death, and hell's de - struc - tion, land me safe on

1. power - ful hand; bread of heav - en, bread of heav - en,
2. jour - ney through; strong de - liv - erer, strong de - liv - erer,
3. Ca - naan's side; songs of prais - es, songs of prais - es

1. feed me till I want no more, feed me till I want no more.
2. be thou still my strength and shield, be thou still my strength and shield.
3. I will ev - er give to thee, I will ev - er give to thee.

GOD OF ABRAHAM, ISAAC, AND JACOB

Ex. 16:4; Ex. 17:6; Ex. 40:38

Captain of Israel's Host

St. 1–2, Charles Wesley, 1762, based on Matthew Henry, c. 1700;
st. 3, Charles Wesley, 1747

COLERAINE, 8.8.8.8.88

La Scala Santa (Ireland, 1681)

1. Cap-tain of Is-rael's host and guide of all who seek the land a-bove,
2. By thine un-err-ing Spir-it led, we shall not in the des-ert stray;
*3. We've no a-bid-ing cit-y here, but seek a cit-y out of sight;

1. be-neath thy shad-ow we a-bide, the cloud of thy pro-tect-ing love;
2. we shall not full di-rec-tion need, nor miss our prov-i-den-tial way;
3. thith-er our stead-y course we steer, as-pir-ing to the plains of light:

1. our strength, thy grace; our rule, thy word; our end, the glo-ry of the Lord.
2. as far from dan-ger as from fear while love, al-might-y love, is near.
3. Je-ru-sa-lem the saints' a-bode, whose found-er is the liv-ing God.

Ex. 13:21; Heb. 13:14; Deut. 29:29   GOD OF ABRAHAM, ISAAC, AND JACOB

52   Arm of the Lord, Awake, Awake!

Charles Wesley, 1739

DEUS TUORUM MILITUM, LM   Melody in Grenoble *Antiphoner* (1753)

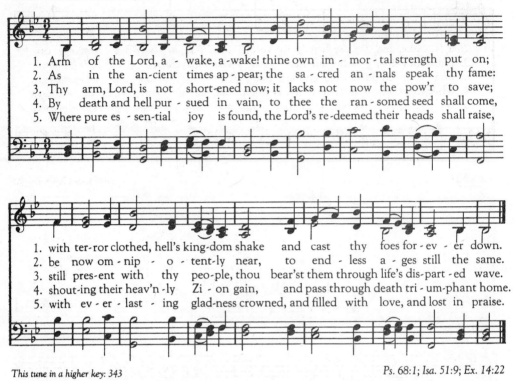

1. Arm of the Lord, a - wake, a - wake! thine own im - mor - tal strength put on;
2. As in the an - cient times ap - pear; the sa - cred an - nals speak thy fame:
3. Thy arm, Lord, is not short - ened now; it lacks not now the pow'r to save;
4. By death and hell pur - sued in vain, to thee the ran - somed seed shall come,
5. Where pure es - sen - tial joy is found, the Lord's re - deemed their heads shall raise,

1. with ter - ror clothed, hell's king - dom shake and cast thy foes for - ev - er down.
2. be now om - nip - o - tent - ly near, to end - less a - ges still the same.
3. still pres - ent with thy peo - ple, thou bear'st them through life's dis - part - ed wave.
4. shout - ing their heav'n - ly Zi - on gain, and pass through death tri - um - phant home.
5. with ev - er - last - ing glad - ness crowned, and filled with love, and lost in praise.

This tune in a higher key: 343   Ps. 68:1; Isa. 51:9; Ex. 14:22

53   Awake, Our Souls, Away, Our Fears

Isaac Watts, 1707

CHURCH TRIUMPHANT, LM   Melody by J. W. Elliott, 1874

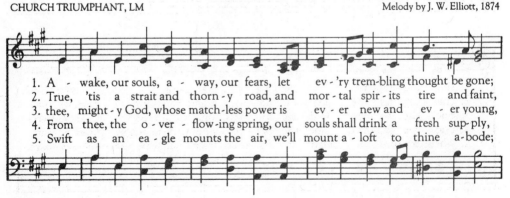

1. A - wake, our souls, a - way, our fears, let ev - 'ry trem - bling thought be gone;
2. True, 'tis a strait and thorn - y road, and mor - tal spir - its tire and faint,
3. thee, might - y God, whose match - less power is ev - er new and ev - er young,
4. From thee, the o - ver - flow - ing spring, our souls shall drink a fresh sup - ply,
5. Swift as an ea - gle mounts the air, we'll mount a - loft to thine a - bode;

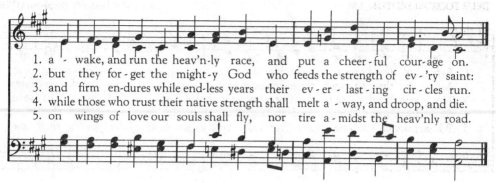

1. a - wake, and run the heav'n-ly race, and put a cheer-ful cour-age on.
2. but they for - get the might-y God who feeds the strength of ev-'ry saint:
3. and firm en-dures while end-less years their ev - er - last-ing cir - cles run.
4. while those who trust their native strength shall melt a - way, and droop, and die.
5. on wings of love our souls shall fly, nor tire a-midst the heav'nly road.

Isa. 40:31

This tune in a higher key: 70

Through the Night of Doubt and Sorrow 54

Igjennem nat og traengsel, by B. S. Ingemann, 1825;
tr. Sabine Baring-Gould, 1867

MARCHING, 8.7.8.7

Martin Shaw, 1915

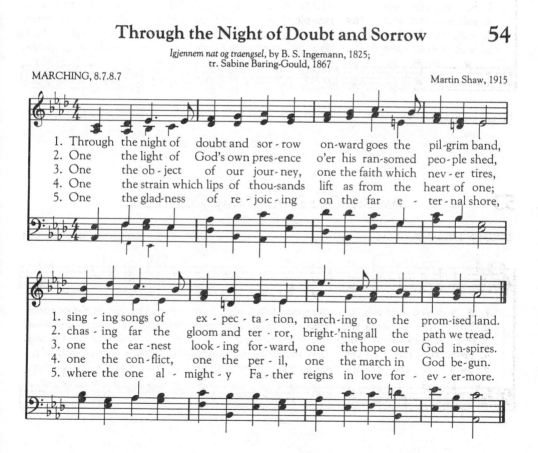

1. Through the night of doubt and sor - row on-ward goes the pil-grim band,
2. One the light of God's own pres-ence o'er his ran-somed peo-ple shed,
3. One the ob - ject of our jour-ney, one the faith which nev - er tires,
4. One the strain which lips of thou-sands lift as from the heart of one;
5. One the glad-ness of re - joic - ing on the far e - ter - nal shore,

1. sing - ing songs of ex - pec - ta - tion, march-ing to the prom-ised land.
2. chas - ing far the gloom and ter - ror, bright-'ning all the path we tread.
3. one the ear -nest look - ing for-ward, one the hope our God in-spires.
4. one the con-flict, one the per - il, one the march in God be-gun.
5. where the one al - might-y Fa-ther reigns in love for - ev - er-more.

Eph. 4:4–6

GOD OF ABRAHAM, ISAAC, AND JACOB

55   By Gracious Powers So Wonderfully Sheltered

Von guten Mächten, by Dietrich Bonhoeffer, 1944;
tr. Fred Pratt Green, 1972

INTERCESSOR, 11.10.11.10

C. H. H. Parry, 1904

1. By gracious powers so wonderfully sheltered,
2. Yet is this heart by its old foe tormented,
3. And when this cup you give is filled to brimming
4. Yet when again in this same world you give us

1. and confidently waiting, come what may,
2. still evil days bring burdens hard to bear;
3. with bitter sorrow, hard to understand,
4. the joy we had, the brightness of your sun,

1. we know that God is with us night and morning,
2. O give our frightened souls the sure salvation
3. we take it thankfully and without trembling,
4. we shall remember all the days we lived through,

1. and never fails to greet us each new day.
2. for which, O Lord, you taught us to prepare.
3. out of so good and so beloved a hand.
4. and our whole life shall then be yours alone.

♮ *last time only*

GOD OF ABRAHAM, ISAAC, AND JACOB

Ps. 116:13; Lam. 2:21; Mt. 14:36

God Is My Strength! I Bless His Name 56

Philip Doddridge, 1702–1751 (alt'd)

KENT, LM

J. F. Lampe, 1746

1. God is my strength! I bless his name; the same his pow'r, his grace the same;
2. I 'midst ten thou-sand dan-gers stand, sup-port-ed by his guard-ian hand,
3. Thus far his arm has led me on, thus far I make his mer-cy known,
4. My grate-ful soul on Jor-dan's shore shall raise one sa-cred pil-lar more,

1. the to-kens of his friend-ly care o-pen and close and crown the year.
2. and see, when I sur-vey my ways, ten thou-sand mon-u-ments of praise.
3. and while I tread this des-ert land, new mer-cies shall new songs de-mand.
4. then bear in his bright courts a-bove, in-scrip-tions of im-mor-tal love.

I Sam. 7:12

This tune in a higher key: 476

Great God, We Sing That Mighty Hand 57

Philip Doddridge, c. 1740

WAREHAM, LM

William Knapp, 1738

1. Great God, we sing that might-y hand by which sup-port-ed still we stand;
2. By day, by night, at home, a-broad, still are we guard-ed by our God,
3. With grate-ful hearts the past we own; the fu-ture, all to us un-known,
4. In scenes ex-alt-ed or de-pressed, thou art our joy and thou our rest;

1. the o-pening year thy mer-cy shows; thy mer-cy crowns it till it close.
2. by his in-ces-sant boun-ty fed, by his un-err-ing coun-sel led.
3. we to thy guard-ian care com-mit, and peace-ful leave be-fore thy feet.
4. thy good-ness all our hopes shall raise, a-dored through all our chang-ing days.

This tune in a higher key: 173

Acts 26:22ff

GOD OF ABRAHAM, ISAAC, AND JACOB

58

God of Our Life

Hugh T. Kerr, 1916
First Tune

ALBERTA, 10.4.10.4.10 10

W. H. Harris, 1931

Unison

1. God of our life, through all the cir-cling years, we trust in thee;
2. God of the past, our times are in thy hand; with us a-bide.
3. God of the com-ing years, through paths un-known we fol-low thee;

1. in all the past, through all our hopes and fears, thy hand we see.
2. Lead us by faith to hope's true prom-ised land; be thou our guide.
3. when we are strong, Lord, leave us not a-lone; our ref-uge be.

1. With each new day, when morn-ing lifts the veil,
2. With thee to bless, the dark-ness shines as light,
3. Be thou for us in life our dai-ly bread,

1. we own thy mer-cies, Lord, which nev-er fail.
2. and faith's fair vi-sion chang-es in-to sight.
3. our hearts' true home when all our years have sped.

Original key: D flat
GOD OF ABRAHAM, ISAAC, AND JACOB

Ps. 139:13; Heb. 13:8

God of Our Life

Second Tune

SANDON, 10.4.10.4.10 10

Charles H. Purday, 1860

1. God of our life, through all the cir-cling years, we trust in thee;
2. God of the past, our times are in thy hand; with us a-bide.
3. God of the com-ing years, through paths un-known we fol-low thee;

1. in all the past, through all our hopes and fears, thy hand we see.
2. Lead us by faith to hope's true prom-ised land; be thou our guide.
3. when we are strong, Lord, leave us not a-lone; our ref-uge be.

1. With each new day, when morn-ing lifts the veil,
2. With thee to bless, the dark-ness shines as light,
3. Be thou for us in life our dai-ly bread,

1. we own thy mer-cies, Lord, which nev-er fail.
2. and faith's fair vi-sion chang-es in-to sight.
3. our hearts' true home when all our years have sped.

GOD OF ABRAHAM, ISAAC, AND JACOB

60   Lead Us, O Father, in the Paths of Peace

William H. Burleigh, 1859

LONGWOOD, 10.10.10.10

Adapted from a melody by Joseph Barnby, 1874

1. Lead us, O Fa - ther, in the paths of peace;
2. Lead us, O Fa - ther, in the paths of truth;
3. Lead us, O Fa - ther, in the paths of right;
4. Lead us, O Fa - ther, to thy heav'n - ly rest,

1. with - out thy guid - ing hand we go a - stray,
2. un - helped by thee, in er - ror's maze we grope,
3. blind - ly we stum - ble when we walk a - lone,
4. how - ev - er rough and steep the path - way be,

1. and doubts ap - pall, and sor - rows still in - crease;
2. while pas - sion stains and fol - ly dims our youth,
3. in - volved in shad - ows of a dark - 'ning night;
4. through joy or sor - row, as thou deem - est best,

1. lead us through Christ, the true and liv - ing way.
2. and age comes on, un - cheered by faith or hope.
3. on - ly with thee we jour - ney safe - ly on.
4. un - til our lives are per - fect - ed in thee.

GOD OF ABRAHAM, ISAAC, AND JACOB

Jn. 14:6

Nun danket alle Gott, M. Rinckart, 1636;
tr. Catherine Winkworth, 1863

NUN DANKET, 6.7.6.7.6.6.6.6

Melody edited by J. Cruger, c. 1636;
harmony mostly by F. Mendelssohn-Bartholdy, 1840

1. Now thank we all our God with heart and hands and voic - es,
2. O may this boun-teous God through all our life be near us,
3. All praise and thanks to God the Fa - ther now be giv - en,

1. who won - drous things hath done, in whom this world re - joic - es;
2. with ev - er joy - ful hearts and bless - ed peace to cheer us;
3. the Son, and him who reigns with them in high - est heav - en,

1. who, from our moth -ers' arms hath bless'd us on our way
2. and keep us in his grace, and guide us when per - plexed,
3. the one e - ter - nal God, whom heav'n and earth a - dore;

1. with count-less gifts of love, and still is ours to - day.
2. and free us from all ills in this world and the next.
3. for thus it was, is now, and shall be ev - er - more.

Sirach 50:22

GOD OF ABRAHAM, ISAAC, AND JACOB

62   We Praise Thee, O God, Our Redeemer

Julia C. Cory, 1902 (alt'd)

Netherlands melody, in
A. Valerius's *Collection* (1626)

KREMSER, 12.11.12.11

1. We praise thee, O God, our Re - deem - er, Cre - a - tor;
2. We wor - ship thee, God of the a - ges, we bless thee;
3. With voic - es u - nit - ed, our prais - es we of - fer,

1. in grate - ful de - vo - tion our trib - ute we bring.
2. through life's storm and tem - pest our guide hast thou been.
3. and glad - ly our song of true wor - ship we raise;

1. We lay it be - fore thee, we kneel and a - dore thee,
2. When per - ils o'er - take us, es - cape thou wilt make us,
3. our sins now con - fess - ing, we pray for thy bless - ing;

1. we bless thy ho - ly name, glad prais - es we sing.
2. and with thy help, O Lord, life's bat - tles we win.
3. to thee, our great Re - deem - er, ev - er be praise.

This tune in a lower key: 574

GOD OF ABRAHAM, ISAAC, AND JACOB

We Gather Together to Ask the Lord's Blessing 63

Netherlands Folk Hymm
Tr. Theodore Baker

Tune KREMSER, facing page

1. We gather together to ask the Lord's blessing;
   he chastens and hastens his will to make known;
   the wicked oppressing now cease from distressing,
   sing praises to his name: he forgets not his own.

2. Beside us to guide us, our God with us joining,
   ordaining, maintaining his kingdom divine;
   so from the beginning the fight we were winning;
   thou, Lord, wast at our side; all glory be thine!

3. We all do extol thee, thou leader triumphant,
   and pray that thou still our defender wilt be.
   Let thy congregation escape tribulation;
   thy name be ever praised! O Lord, make us free!

The Lord in Mercy Bless Us Now 64

John B. Geyer

ST. ETHELDREDA, CM

W. T. Turton, 1860

1. The Lord in mer-cy bless us now and watch our course each day;
2. The Lord look kind-ly on us here and give us peace and joy;
3. Make known, most gra-cious God, your work to na-tions far and wide,

1. his face with bright-ness shine on us, his grace ap-point our way.
2. may praise and ser-vice all our days our lips and lives em-ploy.
3. that ev-'ry tongue may glad-ly praise the love that will a-bide.

Num. 6:24

GOD OF ABRAHAM, ISAAC, AND JACOB

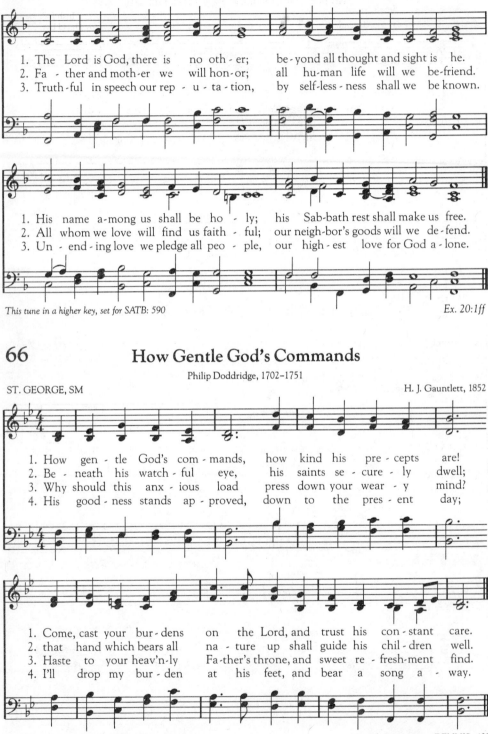

65

The Lord Is God, There Is No Other

The Ten Commandments, paraphrased by Daniel James Meeter, 1980

COMMANDMENTS, 9.8.9.8

Melody in *Genevan Psalter* (1551)

1. The Lord is God, there is no oth-er; be-yond all thought and sight is he.
2. Fa-ther and moth-er we will hon-or; all hu-man life will we be-friend.
3. Truth-ful in speech our rep-u-ta-tion, by self-less-ness shall we be known.

1. His name a-mong us shall be ho-ly; his Sab-bath rest shall make us free.
2. All whom we love will find us faith-ful; our neigh-bor's goods will we de-fend.
3. Un-end-ing love we pledge all peo-ple, our high-est love for God a-lone.

This tune in a higher key, set for SATB: 590

Ex. 20:1ff

66

How Gentle God's Commands

Philip Doddridge, 1702–1751

ST. GEORGE, SM

H. J. Gauntlett, 1852

1. How gen-tle God's com-mands, how kind his pre-cepts are!
2. Be-neath his watch-ful eye, his saints se-cure-ly dwell;
3. Why should this anx-ious load press down your wear-y mind?
4. His good-ness stands ap-proved, down to the pres-ent day;

1. Come, cast your bur-dens on the Lord, and trust his con-stant care.
2. that hand which bears all na-ture up shall guide his chil-dren well.
3. Haste to your heav'n-ly Fa-ther's throne, and sweet re-fresh-ment find.
4. I'll drop my bur-den at his feet, and bear a song a-way.

FULL OF GRACE AND TRUTH

Alternative tune: DENNIS, 408

Be Thou My Vision

Rob to mo bhoile, ancient Irish poem;
tr. Mary Byrne, 1905; versified by Eleanor Hull, 1912 (alt'd)

SLANE, 10 10.9 10 dactylic (irregular)

Irish folk melody
harmonized by David Evans, 1927

1. Be thou my vi - sion, O Lord of my heart;
2. Be thou my wis - dom, and thou my true word;
3. Rich - es I heed not, nor earth's emp - ty praise,
4. High King of heav - en, my vic - to - ry won,

1. nought be all else to me, save that thou art —
2. I ev - er with thee and thou with me, Lord;
3. thou mine in - her - i - tance, now and al - ways:
4. may I reach heav - en's joys, O bright heaven's Sun!

1. thou my best thought, by day or by night,
2. thou my great Fa - ther, thy child let me be;
3. thou and thou on - ly, first in my heart,
4. heart of my own heart, what - ev - er be - fall,

1. wak - ing or sleep - ing, thy pres - ence my light.
2. thou in me dwell - ing, and I one with thee.
3. high King of heav - en, my trea - sure thou art.
4. still be my vi - sion, O rul - er of all.

FULL OF GRACE AND TRUTH

68 Lord of Creation, to You Be All Praise!

Jack C. Winslow, 1964

Irish folk melody
harmonized by Erik Routley, 1951

SLANE, 10 11.11 11 dactylic

1. Lord of cre - a - tion, to you be all praise!
2. Lord of all pow - er, I give you my will,
3. Lord of all wis - dom, I give you my mind,
4. Lord of all boun - ty, I give you my heart;

1. Most might - y your work - ing, most won - drous your ways!
2. in joy - ful o - be - dience your tasks to ful - fill.
3. rich truth that sur - pass - es our knowl - edge to find.
4. I praise and a - dore you for all you im - part;

1. You reign in a glo - ry no tongue e'er can tell;
2. Your bond - age is free - dom; your ser - vice is song;
3. What eye has not seen and what ear nev - er heard
4. your love to in - flame me, your coun - sel to guide,

1. you deign in the heart of the hum - ble to dwell.
2. and, held in your keep - ing, my weak - ness is strong.
3. is taught by your Spir - it and shines from your Word.
4. your pres - ence to shield me what - e'er may be - tide.

5. Lord of all being, I give you my all;
if ever I disown you, I stumble and fall;
but sworn in glad service your word to obey,
I walk in your freedom to the end of the way.

FULL OF GRACE AND TRUTH

Isa. 57:15

O God, My Faithful God

O Gott du frommer Gott, by Johann Heermann, 1585–1647;
tr. the editors of the *Lutheran Book of Worship* (1978);
based on the version by Catherine Winkworth, 1863

DARMSTADT (WAS FRAG ICH NACH DER WELT),
6.7.6.7.6.6.6.6.

Ahasuerus Fritsch, 1679;
arranged by J. S. Bach, 1685–1750 (Cantata 45)

1. O God, my faith-ful God, true foun-tain ev-er flow-ing,
2. Give me the strength to do with read-y heart and will-ing,
3. Keep me from say-ing words that lat-er need re-call-ing;
4. When dan-gers gath-er round, oh, keep me calm and fear-less;

1. with-out whom noth-ing is, all per-fect gifts be-stow-ing:
2. what-ev-er you com-mand, my call-ing here ful-fill-ing—
3. guard me, lest i-dle speech may from my lips be fall-ing:
4. help me to bear the cross when life seems dark and cheer-less;

1. give me a health-y frame, and may I have with-in
2. to do it when I ought, with all my strength; and bless
3. but when, with-in my place, I must and ought to speak,
4. help me, as you have taught, to love both great and small,

1. a con-science free from blame, a soul un-stained by sin.
2. what-ev-er I have wrought, for you must give suc-cess.
3. then to my words give grace, lest I of-fend the weak.
4. and, by your Spir-it's might, to live at peace with all.

Ps. 141:3; Isa. 50:4

FULL OF GRACE AND TRUTH

70
The Lord Is King!

Josiah Conder, 1836

CHURCH TRIUMPHANT, LM

Melody by J. W. Elliott, 1874

1. The Lord is King! Lift up thy voice, O earth, and all ye heav'ns, re-joice!
2. The Lord is King! Who then shall dare re-sist his will, dis-trust his care?
3. The Lord is King! Child of the dust, the Judge of all the earth is just;
4. He reigns! Ye saints, ex-alt your strains. Your God is King, your Fa-ther reigns,
5. One Lord, one em-pire, all se-cures; he reigns, and heav'n and earth are yours;

1. From world to world the song shall ring, "The Lord om-nip-o-tent is King!"
2. Or mur-mur at his wise de-crees, or doubt his roy-al prom-is-es?
3. ho-ly and true are all his ways; let ev-'ry crea-ture speak his praise.
4. and Christ is at his Fa-ther's side, the Man of Love, the Cru-ci-fied.
5. through earth and heaven one song shall ring: "The Lord om-nip-o-tent is King!"

This tune in a lower key: 53

Ps. 98:1; Gen. 18:25b

71
Awake, My Soul, and with the Sun

Thomas Ken, 1695, 1711

HERONGATE, LM

English traditional melody

1. A-wake, my soul, and with the sun thy dai-ly stage of du-ty run;
2. By in-flu-ence of the light di-vine let thy own light in good works shine;
3. Lord, I my vows to thee re-new; scat-ter my sins as morn-ing dew;
4. Di-rect, con-trol, sug-gest this day all I de-sign or do or say,
5. Praise God from whom all bless-ings flow; praise him all crea-tures here be-low;

FULL OF GRACE AND TRUTH

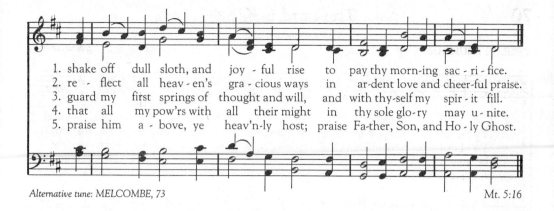

1. shake off dull sloth, and joy-ful rise to pay thy morn-ing sac-ri-fice.
2. re-flect all heav-en's gra-cious ways in ar-dent love and cheer-ful praise.
3. guard my first springs of thought and will, and with thy-self my spir-it fill.
4. that all my pow'rs with all their might in thy sole glo-ry may u-nite.
5. praise him a-bove, ye heav'n-ly host; praise Fa-ther, Son, and Ho-ly Ghost.

Alternative tune: MELCOMBE, 73

Mt. 5:16

Thou Hast Made Us for Thy Glory 72

Anna Marie Sywulka, 1961

MAHON, 8.7.8.7

C. Edgar Knowles, 1916

1. Thou hast made us for thy glo-ry;
2. As the bride is for her bride-groom,
3. Thou hast made us for thy-self, Lord;

1. thou hast planned in won-drous ways to re-deem us
2. as the stream-let for the sea, as the soft clay
3. ful-ly thine we now would be, for our souls are

1. for thy plea-sure, and per-fect us for thy praise.
2. for the pot-ter, we are made a-lone for thee.
3. ev-er rest-less till they find their rest in thee.

New Every Morning Is the Love

John Keble, 1827

MELCOMBE, LM

Melody by Samuel Webbe, 1782

1. New ev-'ry morn-ing is the love our wak-ing and up-ris-ing prove;
2. New mer-cies each re-turn-ing day hov-er a-round us while we pray;
3. If on our dai-ly course our mind be set to hal-low all we find,
4. The triv-ial round, the com-mon task will fur-nish all we need or ask:

1. through sleep and dark-ness safe-ly brought, re-stored to life, and pow'r, and thought.
2. new per-ils past, new sins for-giv'n, new thoughts of God, new hopes of heav'n.
3. new treas-ures still of count-less price God will pro-vide for sac-ri-fice.
4. room to de-ny our-selves, a road to bring us dai-ly near-er God.

This tune in a lower key: 519

Alternative tune:
HERONGATE, 71

*5. Seek we no more; content with these,
    let present rapture, comfort, ease
    as God shall bid them, come and go —
    the secret, this, of rest below.

*6. Only, O Lord, in thy dear love
    fit us for perfect rest above,
    and help us this and every day
    to live more nearly as we pray.

Lam. 3:23; Gen. 22:8

Lord, as I Wake I Turn to You

Brian Foley, 1971

Tune MELCOMBE, above

1. Lord, as I wake I turn to you,
    yourself the first thought of my day:
    my King, my God, whose help is sure,
    yourself the help for which I pray.

2. There is no blessing, Lord, from you
    for those who make self-will their way;
    no praise for those who will not praise,
    no peace for those who will not pray.

3. Your loving gifts of grace to me,
    those favors I could never earn,
    call for my thanks in praise and prayer,
    call me to love you in return.

4. Lord, make my life a life of love,
    keep me from sin in all I do;
    Lord, make your law my only law,
    your will my will for love of you.

Come, Labor On

Jane Laurie Borthwick, 1859, 1863

ORA LABORA, 4.10 10.10 4

T. Tertius Noble, 1918

Unison

1. Come, la - bor on. Who dares stand i - dle on the har - vest plain
2. Come, la - bor on. Claim the high call - ing an - gels can - not share —
3. Come, la - bor on. A - way with gloom - y doubts and faith - less fear!
4. Come, la - bor on. No time for rest, till glows the west - ern sky,

1. while all a - round us waves the gold - en grain? And to each ser - vant
2. to young and old the gos - pel glad - ness bear; re - deem the time; its
3. No arm so weak but may do ser - vice here: by fee - blest a - gents
4. till the long shad - ows o'er our path - way lie, and a glad sound comes

1. does the Mas - ter say, "Go work to - day."
2. hours too swift - ly fly. The night draws nigh.
3. may our God ful - fill his right - eous will.
4. with the set - ting sun, "Well done, well done!"

Jn. 4:35–37; Mt. 9:37–38; Eph. 5:16

FULL OF GRACE AND TRUTH

76 O Splendor of God's Glory Bright

Splendor paternae gloriae, by Ambrose of Milan, c. 340–397;
tr. composite

PUER NOBIS NASCITUR, LM

Melody adapted by M. Praetorius, 1609;
harmonized by G. R. Woodward, 1910

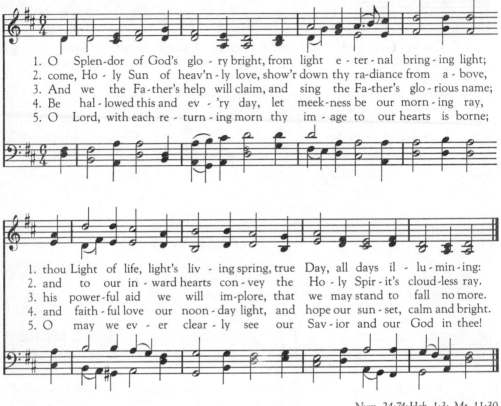

1. O Splen-dor of God's glo-ry bright, from light e-ter-nal bring-ing light;
2. come, Ho-ly Sun of heav'n-ly love, show'r down thy ra-diance from a-bove,
3. And we the Fa-ther's help will claim, and sing the Fa-ther's glo-rious name;
4. Be hal-lowed this and ev-'ry day, let meek-ness be our morn-ing ray,
5. O Lord, with each re-turn-ing morn thy im-age to our hearts is borne;

1. thou Light of life, light's liv-ing spring, true Day, all days il-lu-min-ing:
2. and to our in-ward hearts con-vey the Ho-ly Spir-it's cloud-less ray.
3. his power-ful aid we will im-plore, that we may stand to fall no more.
4. and faith-ful love our noon-day light, and hope our sun-set, calm and bright.
5. O may we ev-er clear-ly see our Sav-ior and our God in thee!

Num. 24:74; Heb. 1:3; Mt. 11:30

77 All Praise to Thee, My God, This Night

Thomas Ken, 1695, 1771

TALLIS' CANON, LM

Thomas Tallis, 1557

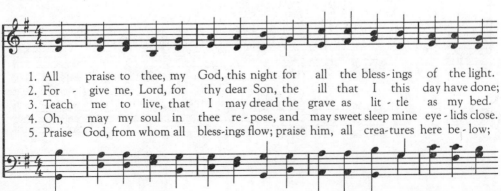

1. All praise to thee, my God, this night for all the bless-ings of the light.
2. For-give me, Lord, for thy dear Son, the ill that I this day have done;
3. Teach me to live, that I may dread the grave as lit-tle as my bed.
4. Oh, may my soul in thee re-pose, and may sweet sleep mine eye-lids close.
5. Praise God, from whom all bless-ings flow; praise him, all crea-tures here be-low;

FULL OF GRACE AND TRUTH

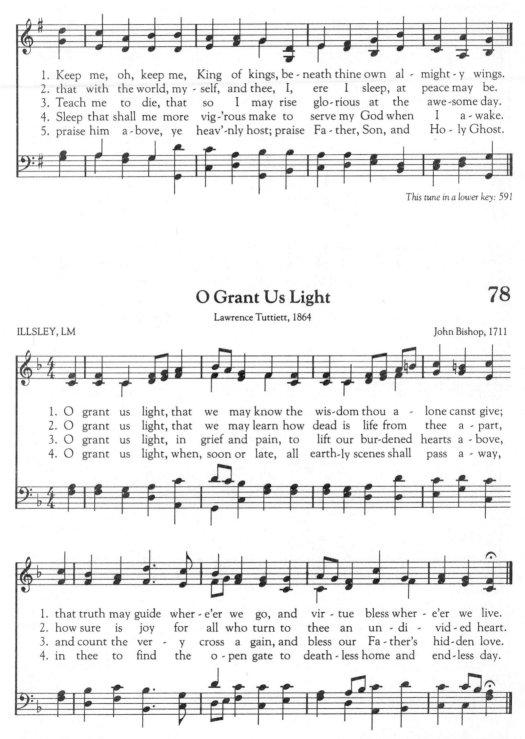

1. Keep me, oh, keep me, King of kings, be-neath thine own al - might-y wings.
2. that with the world, my - self, and thee, I, ere I sleep, at peace may be.
3. Teach me to die, that so I may rise glo-rious at the awe-some day.
4. Sleep that shall me more vig-'rous make to serve my God when I a-wake.
5. praise him a - bove, ye heav'-nly host; praise Fa - ther, Son, and Ho - ly Ghost.

This tune in a lower key: 591

O Grant Us Light

78

Lawrence Tuttiett, 1864

ILLSLEY, LM

John Bishop, 1711

1. O grant us light, that we may know the wis-dom thou a - lone canst give;
2. O grant us light, that we may learn how dead is life from thee a - part,
3. O grant us light, in grief and pain, to lift our bur-dened hearts a - bove,
4. O grant us light, when, soon or late, all earth-ly scenes shall pass a - way,

1. that truth may guide wher - e'er we go, and vir - tue bless wher - e'er we live.
2. how sure is joy for all who turn to thee an un - di - vid - ed heart.
3. and count the ver - y cross a - gain, and bless our Fa - ther's hid-den love.
4. in thee to find the o - pen gate to death-less home and end-less day.

Ps. 43:3   FULL OF GRACE AND TRUTH

79 Forth in Thy Name, O Lord, I Go

Charles Wesley, 1749

ANGELS' SONG, LM

Melody and bass by Orlando Gibbons, 1623

1. Forth in thy name, O Lord, I go, my dai-ly la-bor to pur-sue;
2. The task thy wis-dom hath as-signed O let me cheer-ful-ly ful-fill;
*3. Pre-serve me from my call-ing's snare, and hide my sim-ple heart a-bove.
4. Thee may I set at my right hand, whose eyes my in-most sub-stance see,

1. thee, on-ly thee, re-solv'd to know, in all I think or speak or do.
2. in all my works thy pres-ence find, and prove thy good and per-fect will.
3. A-bove the thorns of chok-ing care, the gild-ed baits of world-ly love.
4. and la-bor on at thy com-mand, and of-fer all my works to thee.

This tune in a lower key: 543

5. Give me to bear thy easy yoke,
   and ev'ry moment watch and pray,
   and still to things eternal look,
   and hasten to thy glorious day;

6. for thee delightfully employ
   whate'er thy bounteous grace hath giv'n.
   and run my course with even joy,
   and closely walk with thee to heav'n.

FULL OF GRACE AND TRUTH

Rom. 12:1–2

O God of Earth and Altar

G. K. Chesterton, 1906 (alt'd)

LLANGLOFFAN, 7.6.7.6 D

David Evans, in *Hymnau a Thonau* (1865)

1. O God of earth and altar, bow down and hear our cry;
2. From all that terror teaches, from lies of pen and tongue;
3. Tie in a living tether the prince and priest and thrall;

1. our earthly rulers falter, our people drift and die;
2. from all the easy speeches that satisfy the throng;
3. bind all our lives together, smite us and save us all;

1. the walls of gold entomb us, the swords of scorn divide;
2. from sale and profanation of honor and the sword;
3. in ire and exultation aflame with faith, and free,

1. take not thy thunder from us, but take away our pride.
2. from sleep and from damnation, deliver us, good Lord!
3. lift up a living nation, a single sword to thee.

This tune in a lower key: 587   *Alternative tunes: KING'S LYNN, 395, LANCASHIRE, 423*

Ex. 20:24   FULL OF GRACE AND TRUTH

81 How Blest Are They Who, Fearing God

Based on *The Psalter* (1912)

ST. MATTHIAS (Song 67), CM

Archbishop Prys's *Psalter* (1621);
bass by O. Gibbons, 1623

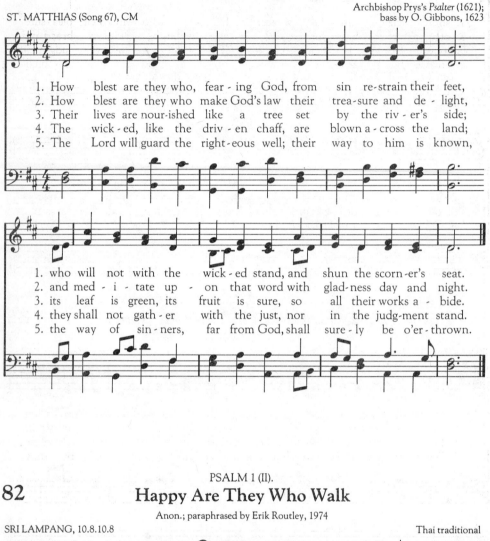

1. How   blest are they who, fear - ing God, from   sin re-strain their feet,
2. How   blest are they who make God's law their   trea-sure and de - light,
3. Their   lives are nour-ished like   a   tree set   by the riv - er's   side;
4. The   wick - ed, like the driv - en chaff, are   blown a - cross the land;
5. The   Lord will guard the right-eous well; their   way to him is known,

1. who will   not with the   wick - ed stand, and   shun the scorn-er's   seat.
2. and med - i - tate up - on that word with   glad-ness day and night.
3. its   leaf   is green, its   fruit   is sure, so   all their works a - bide.
4. they shall not gath - er   with the just, nor   in the judg-ment stand.
5. the   way of   sin - ners,   far from God, shall   sure - ly be o'er-thrown.

82 Happy Are They Who Walk

Anon.; paraphrased by Erik Routley, 1974

SRI LAMPANG, 10.8.10.8

Thai traditional

1. Hap - py are   they who walk in   God's wise   way;   hap - py who
2. Theirs   is the   life where du - ty   and de - light   nour - ish each
3. Fret - ful and   anx - ious are the   sin-ner's   days,   bar - ren and
4. Lord,   in your   mer - cy spare me,   keep me   still;   let   me not

1. shun the sin - ful choice; hap - py who find their plea - sure
2. oth - er bliss - ful - ly; as when be - side a broad and
3. lone - ly is their path; like wind on dust the judg-ment
4. choose the sin - ner's way; prom - ise and law you e - qual-

1. in God's law, hap - py who heed God's right - eous voice.
2. gen - 'rous stream proud - ly stands ev - er green the tree.
3. of the Lord scat - ters their pride in sud - den wrath.
4. ly, have giv'n: let them be my de - light to - day.

PSALM 8.

Lord, Our Lord, Thy Glorious Name 83

Based on *The Psalter*, 1912

SAVANNAH, 77.77   Melody in Herrnhut *Choralbuch* (Moravian, c. 1735)

1. Lord, our Lord, thy glo-rious name all thy won-drous works pro-claim;
2. In - fant lips thou dost or - dain wrath and ven-geance to re-strain;
3. Moon and stars in shin-ing height night - ly tell their Mak - er's might;
4. What are we that we should be loved and vis - it - ed by thee,

1. in the heav'ns with ra - diant signs ev - er - more thy glo - ry shines.
2. weak - est means ful - fill thy will, might - y en - e - mies to still.
3. hu - man strength can - not com - pare with the glo - ry pres - ent there.
4. raised to an ex - alt - ed height, crowned with hon - or in thy sight?

5. With dominion crowned we stand,   6. Lord, our Lord, thy glorious name,
   o'er the creatures of thy hand;   all thy wondrous works proclaim;
   all to us subjection yield   thine the name of matchless worth,
   in the sea and air and field.   excellent in all the earth.

PSALMS PRAISE HIM

84

Keep Me, O God of Grace

Nichol Grieve, 1951

ST. DUNSTAN'S, 6.5.6.5.666.5

C. Winfred Douglas, 1916

1. Keep me, O God of grace; from ill de-fend me; my trust in thee I place;
2. My good-ly her-i-tage thou, Lord, main-tain-est; from child-hood un-to age
3. By thee my soul is blest with joy o'er-flow-ing; in con-fi-dence I rest,

1. do thou be-friend me; thou art the Lord most high; save thee no
2. my lot main-tain-est; thy wis-dom doth im-part in-struc-tion
3. thy mer-cy know-ing; Lord, from the si-lent grave thou wilt thy

1. good have I; when sor-rows mul-ti-ply, thy peace at-tend me.
2. to my heart; thou who al-might-y art, to guide me deign-est.
3. ser-vant save, that life for which I crave at last be-stow-ing.

85

My Inheritance Is from the Lord

Adrienne Tindall, 1981

SOUTH CERNEY, 9.8.8.8.88

William H. Hadow, 1906

1. My in-her-i-tance is from the Lord: no world-ly wealth can win my praise.
2. I have set the Lord be-fore my face, and he has held me safe, se-cure.
3. God is show-ing me the path of life, my steps de-pend up-on his care.

PSALM 18.

O God, My Strength and Fortitude

86

Thomas Sternhold, 1549

MONTROSE, CM

Gilmour's *Psalm-Singer's Assistant* (Scotland, 1793)

87
Behold the Morning Sun

Isaac Watts, 1719

SANDYS, SM

English carol melody

1. Be - hold the morn-ing sun be - gins its glo - rious way;
2. How per - fect is thy word! and all thy judg-ments just!
3. I hear thy word with love, and I would fain o - bey:
4. O who can ev - er find the er - rors of their ways?
5. While with my heart and tongue I spread thy praise a - broad,

1. its beams through all the na - tions run, and life and light con - vey.
2. For - ev - er sure thy prom - ise, Lord, in which we sure - ly trust.
3. send thy good Spir - it from a - bove to guide me lest I stray.
4. Yet with a bold, pre - sump-tuous mind I would not dare trans - gress.
5. ac - cept the wor-ship and the song, my Sav - ior and my God!

This tune in a higher key: 514

88
All Ye That Fear God's Holy Name

The Psalter (1912)

CANNOCK, LM

Walter K. Stanton, 1951

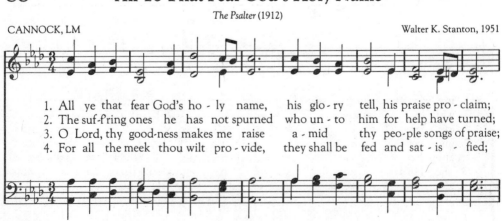

1. All ye that fear God's ho - ly name, his glo - ry tell, his praise pro - claim;
2. The suf-f'ring ones he has not spurned who un - to him for help have turned;
3. O Lord, thy good-ness makes me raise a - mid thy peo-ple songs of praise;
4. For all the meek thou wilt pro - vide, they shall be fed and sat - is - fied;

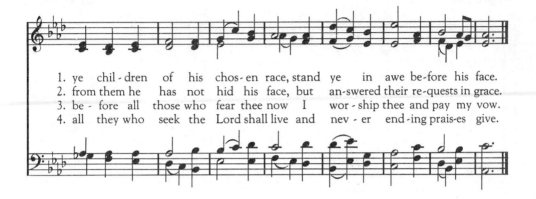

1. ye chil‑dren of his chos‑en race, stand ye in awe be‑fore his face.
2. from them he has not hid his face, but an‑swered their re‑quests in grace.
3. be‑fore all those who fear thee now I wor‑ship thee and pay my vow.
4. all they who seek the Lord shall live and nev‑er end‑ing prais‑es give.

PSALM 23 (I).

The Lord's My Shepherd

Scottish Psalter (1650) First Tune

89

CRIMOND, CM

Jessie Seymour Irvine, 1872;
harmonized by T. C. L. Pritchard, 1929

1. The Lord's my Shep‑herd, I'll not want; he makes me down to lie
2. My soul he doth re‑store a‑gain; and me to walk doth make
3. Yea, though I walk in death's dark vale, yet will I fear none ill;
4. My ta‑ble thou hast fur‑nish‑ed in pres‑ence of my foes;
5. Good‑ness and mer‑cy all my life shall sure‑ly fol‑low me;

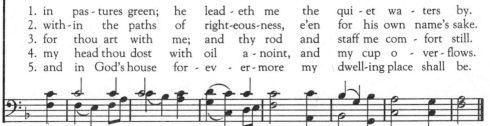

1. in pas‑tures green; he lead‑eth me the qui‑et wa‑ters by.
2. with‑in the paths of right‑eous‑ness, e'en for his own name's sake.
3. for thou art with me; and thy rod and staff me com‑fort still.
4. my head thou dost with oil a‑noint, and my cup o‑ver‑flows.
5. and in God's house for‑ev‑er‑more my dwell‑ing place shall be.

The Lord's My Shepherd

Second Tune

SEARCHING FOR LAMBS, CM

Scottish folk song arranged in
Church Hymnary III (1973)

90

1. The Lord's my Shep-herd, I'll not want; he makes me down to lie
2. My soul he doth re-store a-gain; and me to walk doth make
3. Yea, though I walk in death's dark vale, yet will I fear none ill;
4. My ta-ble thou hast fur-nish-ed in pres-ence of my foes;
5. Good-ness and mer-cy all my life shall sure-ly fol-low me;

1. in pas-tures green; he lead-eth me the qui-et wa-ters by.
2. with-in the paths of righ-teous-ness, e'en for his own name's sake.
3. for thou art with me; and thy rod and staff me com-fort still.
4. my head thou dost with oil a-noint, and my cup o-ver-flows.
5. and in God's house for-ev-er-more my dwell-ing place shall be.

NOTE: *When this tune is used, st. 1, and perhaps also st. 3, can be sung by solo voices.*

My Shepherd Is the Living Lord

91

First quatrain by Thomas Sternhold, 1549;
the rest by Isaac Watts, 1719

American folk hymn,
Southern Harmony (1835);
harmonized by Erik Routley, 1976

RESIGNATION, CMD

1. My Shep-herd is the liv-ing Lord, noth-ing there-fore I need;
2. When I walk through the shades of death, thy pres-ence is my stay;
3. The sure pro-vi-sions of my God at-tend me all my days;

1. in pas-tures fair, near pleas-ant streams he set-teth me to feed.
2. a word of thy sup-port-ing breath drives all my fears a-way.
3. O may thy house be mine a-bode, and all my work be praise.

1. He brings my wan-d'ring spir-it back when I for-sake his ways,
2. Thy hand, in sight of all my foes, doth still my ta-ble spread;
3. There would I find a set-tled rest, while oth-ers go and come —

1. and leads me for his mer-cy's sake in paths of truth and grace.
2. my cup with bless-ings o-ver-flows, thine oil a-noints my head.
3. no more a strang-er or a guest, but like a child at home.

92 Earth Is Eternally the Lord's

The Murrayfield Psalms (1954)

ST. MATTHEW, CMD

William Croft, 1708

1. Earth is e - ter - nal - ly the Lord's, its full - ness his a - lone;
2. Who may as - cend the mount where stands God's ho - ly dwell-ing place,
3. Such are they all who from the Lord a bless - ing rich shall win;

1. the world and all that dwell there - in he made to be his own.
2. or in his sanc - tu - ar - y may ap - pear be - fore his face?
3. God with his mer - cies crowns their life and shields their souls with - in.

1. For on the wide ex - panse of seas he found - ed it se - cure;
2. The clean of hands, the pure of heart, who ne'er their souls have lent
3. Such must their gen - er - a - tion be who to the heights as - pire,

1. he on the floods es - tab - lished it, and made it to en - dure.
2. to wrong - ful act, nor sworn an oath that masked a false in - tent.
3. who seek the face of Is - rael's God, and af - ter him in - quire.

Alternative tune: LADYWELL, 616

PSALMS PRAISE HIM

Ye Gates, Lift Up Your Heads

Scottish Psalter, 1650 (alt'd)

ST. ASAPH, CMD

Melody adapted from *Sacred Music*
(Edinburgh, 1825)

1. Ye gates, lift up your heads on high; ye doors that last for aye,
2. Ye gates, lift up your heads; ye doors, doors that do last for aye,

1. be lift-ed up, that so the King of glo-ry en-ter may.
2. be lift-ed up, that so the King of glo-ry en-ter may.

1. But who of glo-ry is the King? The might-y Lord is this;
2. But who is he that is the King of glo-ry? who is this?

1. e'en that same Lord that strong in might and great in glo-ry is.
2. The Lord is hosts, and none but he the King of glo-ry is.

94

Show Me Thy Ways, O Lord

Adapted from the *Murrayfield Psalms* (1954)

OLD 25th, SMD

Anglo-Genevan Psalter (1558)

1. Show me thy ways, O Lord, and teach thy paths to me;
2. Thy ten-der mer-cies, Lord, re - mem-ber thou, I pray;
3. The Lord is good in - deed, and faith-ful he a - bides;
4. All the Lord's ways are love; he faith-ful is and true

1. guide thou my foot-steps in thy truth, teach me to fol-low thee.
2. thy lov-ing-kind-ness-es re - call, for from of old are they;
3. he in the way of right-eous-ness re - pen-tant sin-ners guides.
4. to those who keep his cov-e-nant, his pre-cepts' path pur - sue.

1. For thou the ver - y God of my sal-va-tion art;
2. my youth-ful sins for - get, as mer-cy is with thee;
3. He teach-es hum-ble souls his jus-tice to dis - cern;
4. I wait for thee, O God; to thee, O Lord, I call;

1. a - new each day I look to thee, to make thine own my heart.
2. as thou art mer-ci-ful and good, O Lord, re-mem-ber me.
3. he lead-eth hum-ble souls that they his way of life may learn.
4. Re - deem-er be to Is - ra - el from their dis-tress-es all.

PSALM 27.

God Is My Strong Salvation

James Montgomery, 1817

CHRISTUS DER IST MEIN LEBEN, 7.6.7.6   Melody by M. Vulpius, 1609

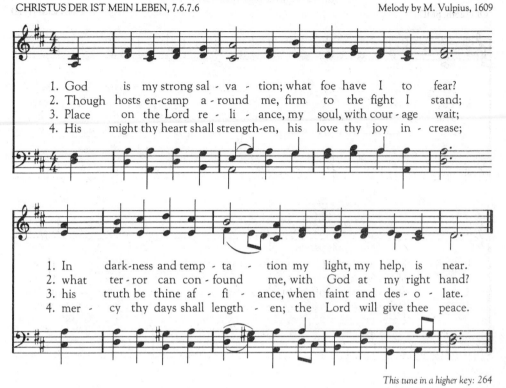

1. God   is my strong sal - va - tion; what foe have I   to   fear?
2. Though hosts en-camp a - round me, firm to the fight I   stand;
3. Place   on the Lord re - li - ance, my soul, with cour - age wait;
4. His   might thy heart shall strength-en, his love thy joy in - crease;

1. In   dark-ness and temp - ta - tion my light, my help, is   near.
2. what   ter - ror can con - found me, with God at my right hand?
3. his   truth be thine af - fi - ance, when faint and des - o - late.
4. mer - cy thy days shall length - en; the Lord will give thee peace.

This tune in a higher key: 264

PSALMS PRAISE HIM

96
O Lord by Thee Delivered

The Psalter, 1912 (alt'd 1953)

MEIRIONYDD, 7.6.7.6 D

William Lloyd, 1840

1. O Lord, by thee de - liv - ered, I thee with songs ex - tol;
2. His ho - ly name re - mem - ber; ye saints, give thanks and praise:
3. My grief is turned to glad - ness; to thee my thanks I raise,

1. my foes thou hast not suf - fered to glo - ry o'er my fall.
2. his an - ger lasts a mo - ment; his fa - vor, all our days;
3. who hast re - moved my sor - row and gird - ed me with praise;

1. O Lord, my God, I sought thee, and thou didst heal and save;
2. for sor - row, like a pil - grim, may tar - ry for a night,
3. and now, no long - er si - lent, my heart thy praise will sing;

1. thou, Lord, from death didst ran - som and keep me from the grave.
2. but joy the heart will glad - den when dawns the morn - ing light.
3. O Lord, my God, for - ev - er my thanks to thee I bring.

How Blest Are They Whose Trespass

The Psalter, 1912 (alt'd 1950)

Melody of Psalm 130, Genevan
Psalter (1542)

AU FORT DE MA DETRESSE, 7.6.7.6 D

1. How blest are they whose tres - pass hath free - ly been for - giv'n,
2. While I kept guil - ty si - lence, my strength was spent with grief,
3. So let the god - ly seek thee in times when thou art near;

1. whose sin is whol - ly cov - ered be - fore the sight of heav'n,
2. thy hand was heav - y on me, my soul found no re - lief;
3. no whelm-ing flood shall reach them, nor cause their hearts to fear;

1. to whom the Lord in mer - cy im - put-eth not their sin,
2. but when I owned my tres - pass, my sin hid not from thee;
3. in thee, O Lord, I hide me; thou sav - est me from ill,

1. who hath a guile-less spir - it, whose heart is true with - in.
2. when I con-fessed trans-gres-sion, then thou for - gav - est me.
3. and songs of thy sal - va - tion my heart with rap - ture thrill.

98 Through All the Changing Scenes of Life

Tate & Brady's Psalms, 1696 (alt'd)

WILTSHIRE, CM

George T. Smart, 1797

1. Through all the chang-ing scenes of life, in trou-ble and in joy,
2. Of his de-liv-'rance I will boast, till all that are dis-tressed
3. O mag-ni-fy the Lord with me, with me ex-alt his name;
4. The hosts of God en-camp a-round the dwell-ings of the just;

1. the prais-es of my God shall still my heart and tongue em-ploy.
2. from my ex-am-ple com-fort take, and soothe their griefs to rest.
3. when in dis-tress to him I called, he to my res-cue came.
4. de-liv-'rance he af-fords to all who in his prom-ise trust.

5. O make but trial of his love;
   experience will decide
   how blest are they, and only they,
   who on his truth confide.

6. Fear him, ye saints, and you will then
   have nothing else to fear;
   make you his service your delight,
   your wants shall be his care.

99 High in the Heavens, Eternal God

Isaac Watts, 1719

TRURO, LM

Psalmodia Evangelica (1789)

1. High in the heav'ns, e-ter-nal God, thy good-ness in full glo-ry shines:
2. For-ev-er firm thy jus-tice stands, as moun-tains their foun-da-tions keep;
3. From the pro-vi-sions of thy house we shall be fed with sweet re-past;
4. Life, like a foun-tain rich and free, springs from the pres-ence of the Lord;

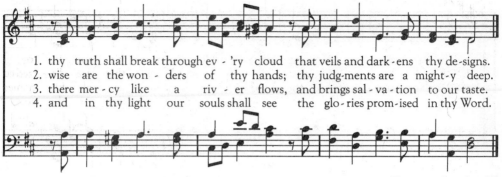

1. thy truth shall break through ev - 'ry cloud that veils and dark - ens thy de - signs.
2. wise are the won - ders of thy hands; thy judg-ments are a might - y deep.
3. there mer - cy like a riv - er flows, and brings sal - va - tion to our taste.
4. and in thy light our souls shall see the glo - ries prom - ised in thy Word.

This tune in a lower key: 185

PSALM 40.

I Waited for the Lord My God

100

The Psalter (1912)

ABRIDGE, CM

Isaac Smith, c. 1770

1. I wait - ed for the Lord my God, yea, pa - tient - ly drew near,
2. He took me from de - struc-tion's pit, from out the mi - ry clay;
3. A new and joy - ful song of praise my thank - ful heart he taught,
4. And man - y who be - hold how good the Lord has been to me

1. and he at length in - clined to me, my plead - ing cry to hear.
2. he set my feet up - on a rock, and stead - fast made my way.
3. a song of glo - ry to our God for all that he has wrought.
4. shall learn to fear, and in his name their trust hence - forth shall be.

101 Seeking Water, Seeking Shelter

Cantate Domino, tr. Erik Routley, 1974

Melody in the *Genevan Psalter* (1551)
(slightly adapted)

PSALM 42, 8.7.8.7.77.88

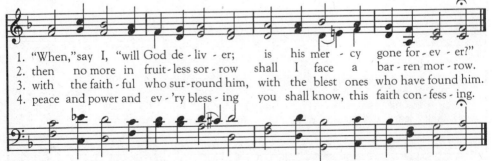

1. Seek-ing wa-ter, seek-ing shel-ter, gasps the thirst-y, wea-ry deer;
2. No! he is my soul's true for-tress; though I hear those voic-es wild—
3. Send your light and truth to lead me; then the path shall I dis-cern
4. So, my soul, why such dis-qui-et? why such mourn-ing, why such fear?

1. so my soul in days of trou-ble longs for God's re-fresh-ment here.
2. "Where's your God? why has he left you?" — he will not for-get his child.
3. to my fa-ther's house, where wel-come waits the prod-i-gal's re-turn.
4. Day al-read-y breaks on dark-ness, God has sought you, God is near.

1. In this stress-ful course of life, in its lone-li-ness and strife,
2. Come then, be my ad-vo-cate, come, your ser-vant vin-di-cate;
3. Then new songs shall fill my days, ev-'ry mo-ment full of praise,
4. Hope in God and you shall live; all de-light he waits to give;

1. "When," say I, "will God de-liv-er; is his mer-cy gone for-ev-er?"
2. then no more in fruit-less sor-row shall I face a bar-ren mor-row.
3. with the faith-ful who sur-round him, with the blest ones who have found him.
4. peace and power and ev-'ry bless-ing you shall know, this faith con-fess-ing.

PSALMS PRAISE HIM

God Is Our Refuge and Our Strength

The Psalter (1912)

YORK, CM
Descant, st. 5, adapted from S. Stubbs

Melody in *Scottish Psalter* (1615);
harmony by S. Stubbs and John Milton, 1621

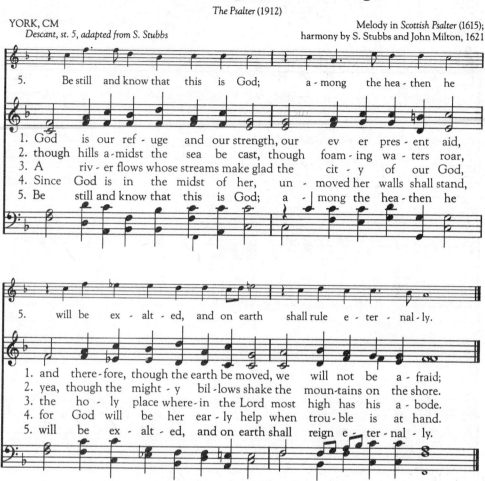

5. Be still and know that this is God; a - mong the hea - then he

1. God is our ref - uge and our strength, our ev er pres - ent aid,
2. though hills a - midst the sea be cast, though foam - ing wa - ters roar,
3. A riv - er flows whose streams make glad the cit - y of our God,
4. Since God is in the midst of her, un - moved her walls shall stand,
5. Be still and know that this is God; a - | mong the hea - then he

5. will be ex - alt - ed, and on earth shall rule e - ter - nal - ly.

1. and there - fore, though the earth be moved, we will not be a - fraid;
2. yea, though the might - y bil - lows shake the moun - tains on the shore.
3. the ho - ly place where - in the Lord most high has his a - bode.
4. for God will be her ear - ly help when trou - ble is at hand.
5. will be ex - alt - ed, and on earth shall reign e - ter - nal - ly.

103 People, Gather Round!

Marie J. Post, 1980

PSALM 47, 5.5.5.5.5.5.5 D

Melody from *Genevan Psalter* (1551)

1. Peo - ple, gath - er round! Shout! in tri-umph sing! Awe - some is the Lord
2. Shout! Our King as-cends with a trum-pet's call. Peo - ple, gath - er round!

1. o - ver ev - 'ry-thing. He sub - dues all lands, na - tions of the earth,
2. He is God of all. Shout loud songs of joy. Sing to God your Lord,

1. gives them to his seed — her - i - tage of love. From for - ev - er God
2. who sub - dues all lands with his might - y sword. Princ - es, praise his name,

1. chose us for his own. Peo - ple, gath - er round! Sing be-fore his throne!
2. make his glo - ries known. Kings of earth, give thanks now be-fore his throne.

God Be Merciful to Me

Adapted from *The Psalter* (1912)

ABERYSTWYTH, 77.77 D

Joseph Parry, 1879

1. God be mer - ci - ful to me; on thy grace I rest my plea.
2. Wash me, wash me pure with - in, cleanse, O cleanse me from my sin;
3. Gra - cious God, my heart re - new, make my spir - it right and true;

1. Plen - teous in com - pas - sion thou, blot out my trans - gres - sions now;
2. I con - fess thy judg - ments just; speech - less, I thy mer - cy trust.
3. from my sins O hide thy face, blot them out in bound - less grace.

1. my trans - gres - sions I con - fess; grief and guilt my soul op - press;
2. Thou a - lone my Sav - ior art, teach thy wis - dom to my heart;
3. Cast me not a - way from thee: let thy Spir - it dwell in me;

1. I have sinned a - gainst thy grace, and pro - voked thee to thy face.
2. make me pure, thy grace be - stow; make me thus thy mer - cy know.
3. thy sal - va - tion's joy im - part; stead - fast make my will - ing heart.

105 O God, Thou Art My God Alone

James Montgomery, 1822

WAINWRIGHT, LM

Richard Wainwright, 1822

1. O God, thou art my God a - lone; ear - ly to thee my soul shall cry,
2. Yet thro' this rough and thorn - y maze I fol - low hard on thee, my God;
3. Thee in the watch - es of the night when I re - mem - ber on my bed,
4. Bet - ter than life it - self thy love, dear - er than all be - side to me;
5. Praise with my heart, my mind, my voice, for all thy mer - cy I will give;

1. a pil - grim in a land un - known, a thirst - y land whose springs are dry.
2. thy hand un - seen up - holds my ways; I safe - ly tread where thou hast trod.
3. thy pres - ence makes the dark - ness light; thy guard - ian wings are round my head.
4. for whom have I in heav'n a - bove, or what on earth, com - pared with thee?
5. my soul shall still in God re - joice; my tongue shall bless thee while I live.

Praise Waits for Thee in Zion, Lord

St. 1 and 4, *Scottish Psalter* (1650);
st. 2-3, 5-6, *Murrayfield Psalms* (1954)

BALFOUR, CM

G. J. Knowles, 1749–1789

1. Praise waits for thee in Zi - on, Lord: to thee vows paid shall be.
2. To thee must all come pen - i - tent who would in thee find peace;
3. Bless'd are all those whom thou dost choose and call - est to thy side,
4. We sure - ly shall be sat - is - fied with thy a - bun - dant grace,

1. O thou that hear - er art of prayer, all flesh shall come to thee.
2. guilt weighs us down, but thou from sin dost con - trite hearts re - lease.
3. that they with - in thy courts may dwell, and close to thee a - bide.
4. and with the good - ness of thy house, e'en of thy ho - ly place.

Alternative tune: ARDEN, 128

5. O God of our salvation sure,
   thou answerest when we pray,
   and dost thy perfect righteousness
   in deeds of awe display.

6. In all the ends of earth, and far
   in islands of the sea,
   our fallen race has learned to place
   its confidence in thee.

107 Thy Might Sets Fast the Mountains

The Psalter (1912)

MORNING LIGHT, 7.6.7.6. D

G. J. Webb, 1837

1. Thy might sets fast the moun-tains; strength girds thee ev - er - more
2. To bless the earth thou send - est from thy a - bun - dant store
3. The year with good thou crown - est, the earth thy mer - cy fills,

1. to calm the rag - ing peo - ples and still the o - cean's roar.
2. the wa - ters of the spring - time, en - rich - ing it once more.
3. the wil - der - ness is fruit - ful, and joy - ful are the hills.

1. Thy maj - es - ty and great - ness are through all lands con - fessed,
2. The seed by thee pro - vid - ed is sown o'er hill and plain,
3. With corn the vales are cov - ered, the flocks in pas - tures graze;

1. and joy on earth thou send - est a - far, from east to west.
2. and thou with gen - tle show - ers dost bless the spring - ing grain.
3. all na - ture joins in sing - ing a joy - ful song of praise.

PSALMS PRAISE HIM

God of Mercy, God of Grace

H. F. Lyte, 1834

108

HEATHLANDS, 77.77.77

Henry Smart, 1867

1. God of mer - cy, God of grace, show the bright - ness of thy face;
2. Let the peo - ple praise thee, Lord; be by all that live a - dored;
3. Let the peo - ple praise thee, Lord; earth shall then her fruits af - ford;

1. shine up - on us, Sav - ior, shine; fill thy church with light di - vine;
2. let the na - tions shout and sing "Glo - ry!" to their Sav - ior King;
3. God to us his bless - ing give, we to God de - vot - ed live;

1. and thy sav - ing health ex - tend un - to earth's re - mot - est end.
2. at thy feet their trib - utes pay, and thy ho - ly will o - bey.
3. all be - low and all a - bove, one in joy and light and love.

109

Great God, Arise

Norman J. Kansfield, 1976, 1981

Melody of Psalms 36 and 68 in
Genevan Psalter (1551)

PSALM 68, 88.7.88.7 D

1. Great God, a - rise, and by your might de - feat all foes of truth and right;
2. But wid - ows and the fa - ther - less the Lord shall com - fort, heal, and bless;
3. To God we lift our fer - vent praise, who o - ver - whelms us all our days
4. Now come, all peo - ples of the earth: choose songs that apt - ly laud God's worth,

1. save us from e - vil's ter - ror. As smoke is driv - en by the storm,
2. he is their faith - ful Fa - ther. God gives the des - o - late a place
3. with good things be - yond mea - sure. God cares for us: our Lord is he,
4. his grace and gran - deur tell - ing. Praise him who reigns in glo - ry high,

1. as wax by fire is left no form, drive out all hu - man er - ror.
2. and pris - 'ners find re - lease and grace; the lost ones he will gath - er.
3. whose love is shown e - ter - nal - ly by gifts from his own trea - sure.
4. whose Word like thun - der splits the sky, all powers on earth com - pel - ling.

1. But let the righteous joyful be, exultant in your majesty
2. Exalt, exalt the name of God, proclaim his royal worth abroad
3. Struggle and pain cannot obscure the trust that makes us always sure
4. Yet he it is keeps us from harm, God cradles us within his arm,

1. with joyful jubilation. Let us arise, go forth, and sing
2. with fervent exultation; build up a highway smooth and wide,
3. that God is our salvation, who for us wills to use that power
4. and smiles on us with favor. This God of gods with us shall dwell,

1. in praise of heaven's gracious King, the Lord, our sure salvation.
2. that thro' the desert he may ride, the Lord of our salvation.
3. which gives us in our darkest hour escape from desolation.
4. till the whole world joins Israel to bless the Lord our Savior.

PSALMS PRAISE HIM

110 Lord of the Worlds Above

Isaac Watts, 1719 *(alt'd)*

DARWALL, 6.6.6.6.4.44.4   John Darwall, 1770

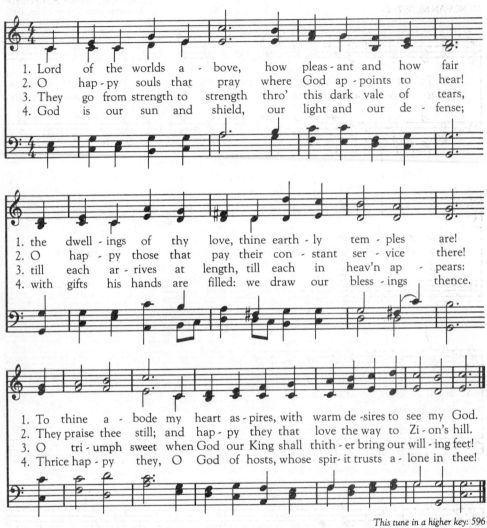

1. Lord of the worlds a - bove, how pleas - ant and how fair
2. O hap - py souls that pray where God ap - points to hear!
3. They go from strength to strength thro' this dark vale of tears,
4. God is our sun and shield, our light and our de - fense;

1. the dwell - ings of thy love, thine earth - ly tem - ples are!
2. O hap - py those that pay their con - stant ser - vice there!
3. till each ar - rives at length, till each in heav'n ap - pears:
4. with gifts his hands are filled: we draw our bless - ings thence.

1. To thine a - bode my heart as - pires, with warm de - sires to see my God.
2. They praise thee still; and hap - py they that love the way to Zi - on's hill.
3. O tri - umph sweet when God our King shall thith - er bring our will - ing feet!
4. Thrice hap - py they, O God of hosts, whose spir - it trusts a - lone in thee!

This tune in a higher key: 596

To My Humble Supplication

J. Bryan, c. 1620

Melody in the *Genevan Psalter* (1551);
harmony from Gustav Holst, 1906

GENEVAN 86, 88.77 D

1. To my hum-ble sup-pli-ca-tion, Lord, give ear and ac-cep-ta-tion;
2. to thee, rich in mer-cies' trea-sure and in good-ness with-out mea-sure,

1. save thy ser-vant that hath none help nor hope but thee a-lone.
2. nev-er fail-ing help to those who on thy sure help re-pose.

1. Send, O send re-liev-ing glad-ness to my soul op-prest with sad-ness,
2. Heav'n-ly Tu-tor, of thy kind-ness, teach my dull-ness, guide my blind-ness,

1. which from clog of earth set free, winged with zeal, flies up to thee;
2. that my steps thy paths may tread which to end-less bliss do lead.

112 Jerusalem, the City on the Mountain

Daniel Meeter, 1982

GENEVAN 87, 11.10.10.11

Genevan Psalter (1562)

1. Je - ru - sa - lem, the cit - y on the moun - tain,
2. O cit - y, glo - rious things of you are spo - ken,
3. God speaks his word to all the for - eign na - tions,
4. God reg - is - ters the name of ev - 'ry na - tion

1. the Lord our God has cho - sen for his own.
2. your walls pro - claimed in God's own proph - e - cy:
3. "Come back to me, come, kneel be - fore my throne."
4. up - on the roll of his Je - ru - sa - lem.

1. Far more than Ja - cob's towns and peace - ful fields
2. the walls be - tween the peo - ples of the earth
3. E - gypt the an - cient and great Bab - y - lon,
4. Their danc - ing princ - es lead a thou - sand tongues,

1. God loves each tow - 'ring gate and flow - ing foun - tain.
2. shall be for - ev - er by your wit - ness bro - ken.
3. come, make your home on Zi - on's firm foun - da - tions.
4. sing - ing to God e - ter - nal ad - o - ra - tion.

My Song Forever Shall Record

The Psalter (1912)

ST. PETERSBURG, 88.88.88

Adapted from a melody by
Dmitri Bortniansky, 1825

1. My song for-ev-er shall re-cord the ten-der mer-cies of the Lord;
2. Al-might-y God, thy loft-y throne has jus-tice for its cor-ner-stone,
3. The swell-ing sea o-beys thy will; its an-gry waves thy voice can still;
4. With bless-ing is that na-tion crowned whose peo-ple know the joy-ful sound;

1. thy faith-ful-ness will I pro-claim, and ev-'ry age shall know thy name.
2. and shin-ing bright be-fore thy face are truth and love and bound-less grace.
3. the heav'ns and earth by right di-vine, the world and all there-in is thine;
4. they in the light, O Lord, shall live— the light thy face and fa-vor give.

1. I sing of mer-cies that en-dure for-ev-er build-ed firm and sure.
2. The heav'ns shall join in glad ac-cord to praise thee for thy works, O Lord.
3. the whole cre-a-tion's won-drous frame pro-claims its Mak-er's glo-rious name.
4. Their fame and might to thee be-long, for in thy fa-vor they are strong.

PSALMS PRAISE HIM

114

Lord, Thou Hast Been Our Dwelling Place

The Psalter (1912)

GOTTLOB, 88.88.88

Collection of J. G. Wagner, 1742;
harmonized by J. S. Bach

1. Lord, thou hast been our dwell-ing place through all the a - ges of our race;
2. O teach thou us to count our days, and set our hearts on wis - dom's ways;
3. O send the day of joy and light, for long has been our sor - row's night;
4. So let there be on us be - stowed the beau - ty of the Lord our God;

1. be - fore the moun - tains had their birth, or ev - er thou hadst formed the earth,
2. turn, Lord, to us in our dis - tress, in pit - y now thy ser - vants bless;
3. af - flict - ed through the wea - ry years, we wait un - til thy help ap - pears;
4. the work ac - com - plished by our hand es - tab - lish thou, and make it stand;

1. from ev - er - last - ing thou art God, to ev - er - last - ing our a - bode.
2. let mer - cy's dawn dis - pel our night, and all our day with joy be bright.
3. from age to age with us a - bide; in us let God be glo - ri - fied.
4. yea, let our hope - ful la - bor be es - tab - lished ev - er - more by thee.

Alternative tune: ST. CATHERINE, 459

PSALMS PRAISE HIM

Call the Lord God Thy Salvation

115

James Montgomery, 1822 *(alt'd)*

BLAENWERN, 8.7.8.7 D

William Rowlands, 1915

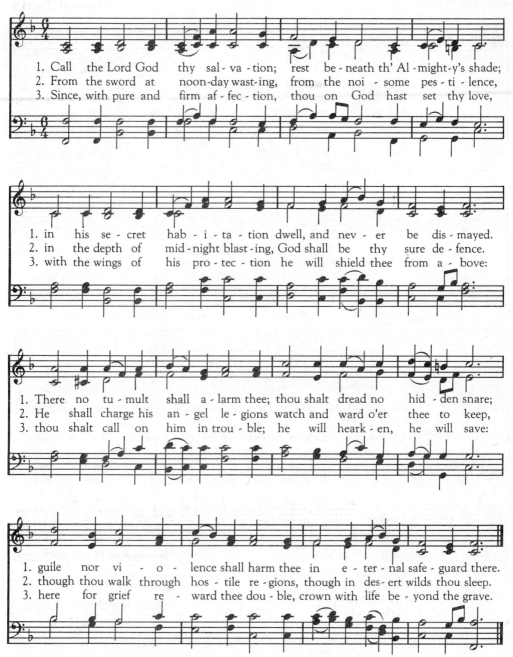

1. Call the Lord God thy sal-va-tion; rest be-neath th' Al-might-y's shade;
2. From the sword at noon-day wast-ing, from the noi-some pes-ti-lence,
3. Since, with pure and firm af-fec-tion, thou on God hast set thy love,

1. in his se-cret hab-i-ta-tion dwell, and nev-er be dis-mayed.
2. in the depth of mid-night blast-ing, God shall be thy sure de-fence.
3. with the wings of his pro-tec-tion he will shield thee from a-bove:

1. There no tu-mult shall a-larm thee; thou shalt dread no hid-den snare;
2. He shall charge his an-gel le-gions watch and ward o'er thee to keep,
3. thou shalt call on him in trou-ble; he will heark-en, he will save:

1. guile nor vi-o-lence shall harm thee in e-ter-nal safe-guard there.
2. though thou walk through hos-tile re-gions, though in des-ert wilds thou sleep.
3. here for grief re-ward thee dou-ble, crown with life be-yond the grave.

Alternative tunes: HYFRYDOL, 346, RODLAND, 34; may be sung in half-stanzas to STUTTGART, 183

PSALMS PRAISE HIM

116

To Thank the Lord Our God

Variant from *Scottish Psalter* (1650)

Attributed to R. Boyd in
Kentucky Harmony (1816)

SALVATION, CMD

1. To thank the Lord our God it is a good and come-ly thing,
2. How great, Lord, are thy works; each thought of thine, how deep it is!
3. Ho - san - na! Up - right is the Lord: he is a rock to me,

1. and to thy name, O thou Most High, due praise a - loud to sing;
2. A brut - ish mind this know - eth not: fools un - der - stand not this.
3. and he from all un - right - eous - ness is al - to - geth - er free.

1. thy lov - ing - kind - ness forth to show when first ap - pears the light,
2. No! through thy works, Lord, thou hast made our souls right glad to be;
3. Lord, let thy grace and glo - ry stand on us thy ser - vants thus;

1. and to de - clare thy faith - ful - ness with plea - sure ev - 'ry night.
2. and in thy works we will tri - umph, which have been wrought by thee.
3. con - form the works we take in hand; Lord, pros - per them and us.

God, the Lord, a King Remaineth

117

John Keble, 1839 (alt'd)

BRYN CALFARIA, 8.7.8.7.4.7

William Owen, *Y Perl Cerddorol* (1852)

Slowly

1. God, the Lord, a King re-main-eth, robed in his own glo-rious light;
2. In her ev-er-last-ing sta-tion earth is poised, to swerve no more;
3. With all tones of wa-ters blend-ing, glo-rious is the break-ing deep;
4. Lord, the words thy lips are tell-ing are the per-fect ver-i-ty;

1. God hath robed him-self and reign-eth; he hath girt him-self with might.
2. thou hast laid thy throne's foun-da-tion from all time where thought can soar.
3. glo-rious, beau-teous, with-out end-ing, God, who reigns on heaven's high steep.
4. of thine high e-ter-nal dwell-ing, ho-li-ness shall in-mate be:

1. Al-le-lu-ia! Al-le-lu-ia! Al-le-lu-ia!
2. Al-le-lu-ia! Al-le-lu-ia! Al-le-lu-ia!
3. Al-le-lu-ia! Al-le-lu-ia! Al-le-lu-ia!
4. Al-le-lu-ia! Al-le-lu-ia! Al-le-lu-ia!

1. God is King in depth and height! God is King in depth and height!
2. Lord, thou art for-ev-er-more! Lord, thou art for-ev-er-more!
3. Songs of o-cean nev-er sleep. Songs of o-cean nev-er sleep.
4. Pure is all that lives with thee. Pure is all that lives with thee.

118 O Come and Sing unto the Lord

The Psalter (1912)

IRISH, CM

Melody from *A Collection
of Psalm Tunes* (Dublin, 1749)

1. O come and sing un-to the Lord, to him our voic-es raise;
2. Be-fore his pres-ence let us come with praise and thank-ful voice;
3. The Lord our God is King of kings, a-bove all gods his throne;
4. To him the spa-cious sea be-longs, he made its waves and tides;
5. O come, and bow-ing down to him our wor-ship let us bring;

1. let us in our most joy-ful songs the Lord, our Sav-ior, praise.
2. let us sing psalms to him with grace, with grate-ful hearts re-joice.
3. the depths of earth are in his hand, the moun-tains are his own.
4. and by his hand the ris-ing land was formed, and still a-bides.
5. yea, let us kneel be-fore the Lord, our Mak-er and our King.

PSALMS PRAISE HIM

New Songs of Celebration Render

119

Erik Routley, 1972

Strasbourg Psalter (1545); revised in *Genevan Psalter*
(1551); harmonized by John Wilson, 1979

RENDEZ A DIEU, 9.8.9.8 D

1. New songs of cel - e - bra - tion ren - der to him who has great
2. Joy - ful - ly, heart - i - ly re - sound - ing, let ev - 'ry in - stru -
3. Riv - ers and seas and tor - rents roar - ing, hon - or the Lord with

1. won - ders done; love sits en - throned in age - less splen - dor; come
2. ment and voice peal out the praise of grace a - bound - ing, call -
3. wild ac - claim; moun - tains and stones, look up a - dor - ing, and

1. and a - dore the might - y One. He has made known his great sal - va -
2. ing the whole world to re - joice. Trum - pets and or - gans, set in mo -
3. find a voice to praise his name. Right - eous, com - mand - ing, ev - er glo -

1. tion which all his friends with joy con - fess. He has re -
2. tion such sounds as make the heav - ens ring; all things that
3. rious, prais - es be his that nev - er cease: just is our

1. vealed to ev - 'ry na - tion his ev - er - last - ing righ - teous - ness.
2. live in earth and o - cean make mu - sic for your might - y King.
3. God, whose truth vic - to - rious es - tab - lish - es the world in peace.

This tune in a lower key and with different harmony: 551

Words Copyright © 1974 by Hope Publishing Company, Carol Stream, IL 60188. International Copyright secured. All Rights
Reserved. Used by Permission.

PSALMS PRAISE HIM

120 All People That on Earth Do Dwell

Theodore Beza, 1551; tr. William Kethe, 1560, and *Scottish Psalter* (1565)

OLD HUNDREDTH, LM

English form of Psalm 134
in *Genevan Psalter* (1551)

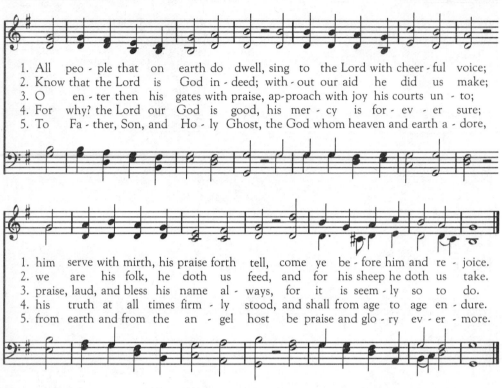

1. All peo-ple that on earth do dwell, sing to the Lord with cheer-ful voice;
2. Know that the Lord is God in-deed; with-out our aid he did us make;
3. O en-ter then his gates with praise, ap-proach with joy his courts un - to;
4. For why? the Lord our God is good, his mer-cy is for-ev-er sure;
5. To Fa-ther, Son, and Ho-ly Ghost, the God whom heaven and earth a-dore,

1. him serve with mirth, his praise forth tell, come ye be-fore him and re - joice.
2. we are his folk, he doth us feed, and for his sheep he doth us take.
3. praise, laud, and bless his name al - ways, for it is seem-ly so to do.
4. his truth at all times firm - ly stood, and shall from age to age en - dure.
5. from earth and from the an - gel host be praise and glo-ry ev-er-more.

121 Bless, O My Soul, the Living God

Isaac Watts, 1719

PARK STREET, LM

Adapted from a melody by
F. M. A. Venua, c. 1810

1. Bless, O my soul, the liv-ing God; call home thy thoughts that rove a - broad;
2. Bless, O my soul, the God of grace; his fa-vors claim thy high-est praise;
3. How slow-ly doth his wrath a - rise! On swift-er wings sal-va-tion flies.
4. 'Tis he, my soul, that sent his Son to die for crimes which thou hast done;
5. Our God, his love is ev-er sure to all his saints, and shall en-dure;

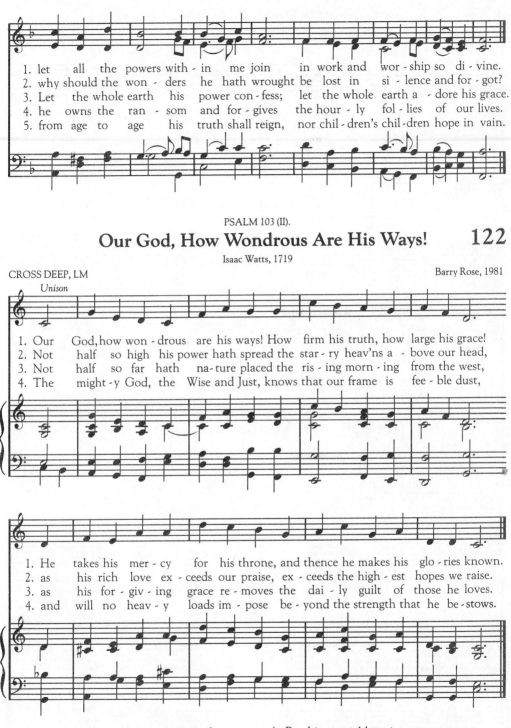

1. let all the powers with-in me join in work and wor-ship so di-vine.
2. why should the won-ders he hath wrought be lost in si-lence and for-got?
3. Let the whole earth his power con-fess; let the whole earth a-dore his grace.
4. he owns the ran-som and for-gives the hour-ly fol-lies of our lives.
5. from age to age his truth shall reign, nor chil-dren's chil-dren hope in vain.

PSALM 103 (II).

Our God, How Wondrous Are His Ways!　122

Isaac Watts, 1719

CROSS DEEP, LM

Barry Rose, 1981

Unison

1. Our God, how won-drous are his ways! How firm his truth, how large his grace!
2. Not half so high his power hath spread the star-ry heav'ns a-bove our head,
3. Not half so far hath na-ture placed the ris-ing morn-ing from the west,
4. The might-y God, the Wise and Just, knows that our frame is fee-ble dust,

1. He takes his mer-cy for his throne, and thence he makes his glo-ries known.
2. as his rich love ex-ceeds our praise, ex-ceeds the high-est hopes we raise.
3. as his for-giv-ing grace re-moves the dai-ly guilt of those he loves.
4. and will no heav-y loads im-pose be-yond the strength that he be-stows.

5. He knows how soon our nature dies,
   withered by ev'ry wind that flies;
   like grass we spring, and die as soon,
   or morning flowers that fade at noon.

6. But his eternal love is sure
   to all the saints, and shall endure;
   from age to age his truth shall reign,
   nor children's children hope in vain.

PSALMS PRAISE HIM

123 Praise the Lord!

Marjorie Jillson, 1970

LAUDATE PUERI, Irregular

Heinz Werner Zimmermann, 1970

1. Praise the Lord! Praise, you ser-vants of the Lord, praise the name of the Lord!
2. Praise the Lord! Thanks and prais-es sing to God, day by day to the Lord!
3. Praise the Lord! Praise and glo - ry give to God, who is like un -to him?
4. Praise the Lord! Praise, you ser-vants of the Lord, praise the love of the Lord!

1. Bless-ed be the name of the Lord! Bless-ed be the name of the Lord
2. High a - bove the na-tions is God, high a - bove the na-tions is God,
3. Rais-ing up the poor from the dust, rais - ing up the poor from the dust,
4. Giv - ing to the home-less a home, giv - ing to the home-less a home,

1. from this time forth and for - ev - er - more. Praise the Lord! Praise the Lord!
2. his glo - ry high o - ver earth and sky. Praise the Lord! Praise the Lord!
3. he makes them dwell in his heart and home. Praise the Lord! Praise the Lord!
4. he fills their hearts with new hope and joy. Praise the Lord! Praise the Lord!

Not to Us Be Glory Given

Timothy Dudley-Smith, 1974

HILLINGDON, 8.7.8.7 D

Walter S. Vale, 1936

1. Not to us be glo-ry giv-en, but to him who reigns a-bove:
2. Not what hu-man fin-gers fash-ion, gold and sil-ver, deaf and blind,
3. Not in them the hope of bless-ing: hope is in the liv-ing Lord!
4. Not the dead, but we the liv-ing praise the Lord with all our powers;

1. glo-ry to the God of heav-en for his faith-ful-ness and love!
2. dead to knowl-edge and com-pas-sion, hav-ing nei-ther heart nor mind—
3. High and low, his name con-fess-ing, find in him their shield and sword.
4. of his good-ness free-ly giv-ing, his is heav-en, earth is ours.

1. What tho' un-be-liev-ing voic-es hear no word and see no sign,
2. life-less gods some yet a-dore them, nerve-less hands and feet of clay;
3. Hope of all whose hearts re-vere him, God of Is-rael, still the same!
4. Not to us be glo-ry giv-en, but to him who reigns a-bove:

1. still in God my heart re-joic-es, work-ing out his will di-vine.
2. all be-come, who bow be-fore them, lost in-deed, and dead as they.
3. God of Aa-ron! Those who fear him he re-mem-bers all by name.
4. glo-ry to the God of heav-en for his faith-ful-ness and love!

PSALMS PRAISE HIM

125 O Thou, My Soul, Return in Peace

St. 1-2, *Murrayfield Psalms* (1950); st. 3-6, *The Psalter* (1912)

MARTYRDOM, CM

Hugh Wilson; arranged by
R. A. Smith, 1825

1. O thou, my soul, re - turn in peace to thine un - trou - bled rest,
2. He did in - deed re - deem my soul that else in death had slept;
3. What shall I ren - der to the Lord, what shall my of - f'ring be,
4. Sal - va - tion's cup my soul shall take while to the Lord I pray,

1. for thee the boun - ty of the Lord a - bun - dant - ly hath bless'd.
2. he hath mine eyes from tears set free, my feet from stum - bling kept.
3. for all the gra - cious ben - e - fits he hath be - stowed on thee?
4. and with his peo - ple I will meet my thank - ful vows to pay.

5. Not lightly does the Lord permit
   his chosen saints to die;
   from death thou hast delivered me;
   thy servant, Lord, am I.

6. Within his house, the house of prayer,
   my soul shall bless the Lord,
   and praises to his holy name
   let all his saints accord.

From All That Dwell Below the Skies

Isaac Watts, 1719

Melody in *Auserlèsene . . . Geistliche Gesänge*
(Cologne, 1623); in this form from 1635;
harmonized by R. Vaughan Williams, 1906

LASST UNS ERFREUEN, LM with additions

Unison

1. From all that dwell be-low the skies let the Cre-a-tor's praise a - rise:
2. E - ter-nal are thy mer-cies, Lord; e - ter-nal truth at-tends thy Word:

Harmony   *Unison*

1. O praise him, Al-le-lu - ia! Let the Re-deem-er's name be sung
2. O praise him, Al-le-lu - ia! Thy praise shall sound from shore to shore,

Harmony

1. through ev-'ry land, by ev-'ry tongue: O praise him, O praise him,
2. till suns shall rise and set no more: O praise him, O praise him,

Unison

1. Al-le-lu - ia, Al-le-lu - ia, Al-le-lu - ia!
2. Al-le-lu - ia, Al-le-lu - ia, Al-le-lu - ia!

127 O Give Ye Thanks unto the Lord

Murrayfield Psalms (1954); st. 6, Isaac Watts, 1719

STROUDWATER, CM

Melody in Matthew Wilkins's *Psalmody* (c. 1725)

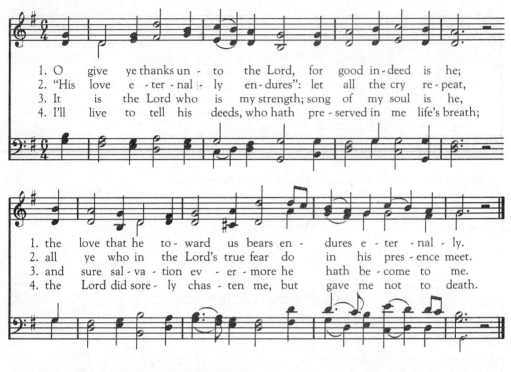

1. O give ye thanks un - to the Lord, for good in - deed is he;
2. "His love e - ter - nal - ly en - dures": let all the cry re - peat,
3. It is the Lord who is my strength; song of my soul is he,
4. I'll live to tell his deeds, who hath pre - served in me life's breath;

1. the love that he to - ward us bears en - dures e - ter - nal - ly.
2. all ye who in the Lord's true fear do in his pres - ence meet.
3. and sure sal - va - tion ev - er - more he hath be - come to me.
4. the Lord did sore - ly chas - ten me, but gave me not to death.

5. The stone the builders cast aside
   is now head cornerstone;
   we look and wonder at the work
   that is the Lord's alone.

6. This is the day the Lord hath made;
   he calls the hours his own;
   let heaven rejoice, let earth be glad,
   and praise surround the throne!

128 This Is the Day the Lord Hath Made

St. 1, *Murrayfield Psalms*; st. 2-5, Isaac Watts, 1719

ARDEN, CM

George T. Thalben-Ball, 1951

1. This is the day the Lord hath made, and un - to us did give;
2. To - day he rose and left the dead, and Sa - tan's em - pire fell;
3. Ho - san - na to th'a - noint - ed King, to Da - vid's ho - ly Son!
4. Blest be the Lord, who comes in power with mes - sag - es of grace,
5. Ho - san - na in the high - est strains the church on earth can raise:

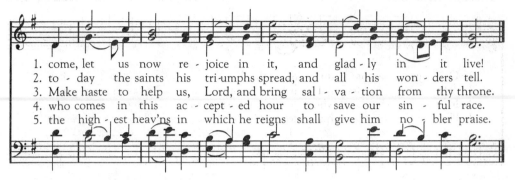

1. come, let us now re - joice in it, and glad - ly in it live!
2. to - day the saints his tri - umphs spread, and all his won - ders tell.
3. Make haste to help us, Lord, and bring sal - va - tion from thy throne.
4. who comes in this ac - cept - ed hour to save our sin - ful race.
5. the high - est heav'ns in which he reigns shall give him no - bler praise.

NOTE: *The whole of Psalm 118 can be sung by combining the texts of hymns 127 and 128.*
This tune in a lower key: 147   Alternative tunes: BALFOUR, 106, NUN DANKET ALL', 278

PSALM 119 (I).

Behold Thy Waiting Servant

129

Cento from Isaac Watts, 1719

WETHERBY, CM   S. S. Wesley, 1872

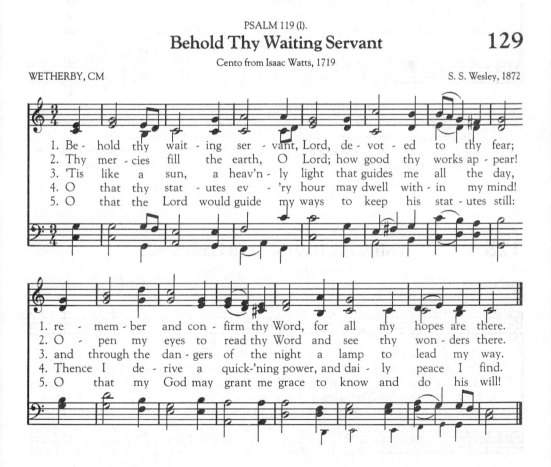

1. Be - hold thy wait - ing ser - vant, Lord, de - vot - ed to thy fear;
2. Thy mer - cies fill the earth, O Lord; how good thy works ap - pear!
3. 'Tis like a sun, a heav'n - ly light that guides me all the day,
4. O that thy stat - utes ev - 'ry hour may dwell with - in my mind!
5. O that the Lord would guide my ways to keep his stat - utes still:

1. re - mem - ber and con - firm thy Word, for all my hopes are there.
2. O - pen my eyes to read thy Word and see thy won - ders there.
3. and through the dan - gers of the night a lamp to lead my way.
4. Thence I de - rive a quick-'ning power, and dai - ly peace I find.
5. O that my God may grant me grace to know and do his will!

130
Lord, I Have Made Thy Word My Choice

Isaac Watts, 1719

BEULAH, CM

G. M. Garrett, 1889

1. Lord, I have made thy word my choice, my last-ing her-i-tage;
2. I read the his-tories of thy love and keep thy laws in sight,
3. 'Tis a broad land of wealth un-known, where springs of life a-rise,
4. My faith and love, and ev-'ry grace fall far be-low thy Word,

1. there shall my no-blest pow'rs re-joice, my warm-est thoughts en-gage.
2. while through thy prom-is-es I rove with ev-er fresh de-light.
3. seeds of im-mor-tal bliss are sown, and hid-den glo-ry lies.
4. for per-fect truth and right-eous-ness dwell on-ly with the Lord.

131
I to the Hills Will Lift My Eyes

The Psalter (1912)

DUNDEE, CM

Scottish Psalter (1615);
harmony from Ravenscroft, 1621

1. I to the hills will lift my eyes. O whence shall come my aid?
2. He will not let thy foot be moved; thy Guard-ian nev-er sleeps;
3. Thy faith-ful keep-er is the Lord, thy shel-ter and thy shade;
4. From e-vil he will keep thee safe; for thee he will pro-vide;

1. My help is from the Lord a-lone, who heav'n and earth has made.
2. with watch-ful and un-slum-b'ring care, his own he safe-ly keeps.
3. 'neath sun or moon, by day or night, thou shalt not be a-fraid.
4. thy go-ing out and com-ing in for-ev-er he will guide.

This tune in a higher key: 45
Alternative tune: LONDON NEW, 36

With Joy I Heard My Friends Exclaim

132

The Psalter (1912)

GONFALON ROYAL, LM

Percy C. Buck, 1918

1. With joy I heard my friends ex - claim, "Come, let us
2. How beau - ti - ful doth Zi - on stand, a cit - y
3. They come to learn the will of God, to pay their
4. For Zi - on's peace let prayer be made; may all that
5. For love of friends and kin - dred dear, my heart's de -

1. in God's tem - ple meet"; with - in thy gates, O Zi - on blest, shall
2. built com - pact and fair; the peo - ple of the Lord u - nite with
3. vows, his grace to own, for there is judg - ment's roy - al seat, Mes -
4. love thee pros - per well! With - in thy walls let peace a - bide, and
5. sire is Zi - on's peace, and for the house of God the Lord my

1. ev - er stand our will - ing feet.
2. joy and praise to wor - ship there.
3. si - ah's sure and last - ing throne.
4. glad - ness with thy chil - dren dwell.
5. lov - ing care shall nev - er cease. A - men.

Harmony

This tune in a higher key: 286

When God Delivered Israel

Michael Saward, 1973

133

SHEAVES, 7.6.7.7.66

Norman Warren, 1973

1. When God de-liv-ered Is-rael from bond-age long a - go,
2. The god-less na-tions round them could not de-ny his power;
3. O God, re-store our na - tion; come, ir - ri-gate dry souls,

1. they thought that they were dream - ing, but soon they turned to laugh-ing
2. they cried, "O see this mar - vel!" "God's work," re - plied his peo - ple,
3. that those who sow in sad - ness may reap their sheaves with glad - ness

st. 1,2   *st. 3*

1. and sang the song of joy, and sang the song of joy.
2. and so they sang for joy, and so they sang for joy.
3. and sing the song of joy, and sing the song of joy.

Martin Luther; mostly tr. R. Massie, 1854

AUS TIEFER NOTH, 8.7.8.7.88.7

Melody by Martin Luther, 1524

1. Out of the depths to thee I raise the voice of lam-en-ta-tion;
2. To wash a-way the crim-son stain grace, grace a-lone pre-vail-eth;
3. There-fore my trust is in the Lord, and not in mine own mer-it;
4. What though I wait the live-long night, and till the dawn ap-pear-eth,

1. Lord, turn a gra-cious ear to me, and hear my sup-pli-ca-tion;
2. our works, a-las! are all in vain; in much the best life fail-eth:
3. on him my soul shall rest: his word up-holds my faint-ing spir-it;
4. my heart still trust-eth in his might; it doubt-eth not nor fear-eth:

1. if thou shouldst be ex-treme to mark each se-cret sin
2. for none can glo-ry in thy sight; all must a-like
3. his prom-ised mer-cy is my fort, my com-fort, and
4. so let the Is-rael-ite in heart, born of the Spir-

1. and mis-deed dark, O who could stand be-fore thee?
2. con-fess thy might, and live a-lone by mer-cy.
3. my strong sup-port; I wait for it with pa-tience.
4. it, do his part, and wait till God ap-pear-eth.

135
Arise, O King of Grace, Arise

Isaac Watts, 1719; st. 5 attributed to
John Henry Livingston, 1789

BELGRAVE, CM

William Horsley, 1817

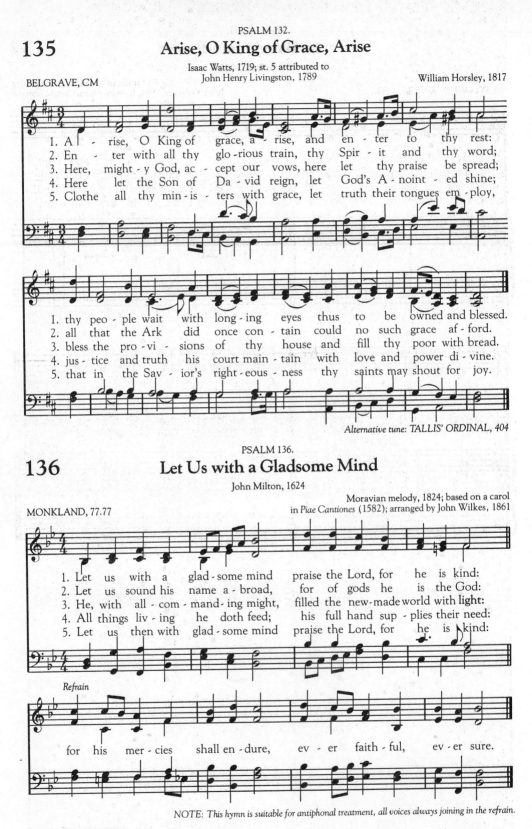

1. A - rise, O King of grace, a - rise, and en - ter to thy rest:
2. En - ter with all thy glo - rious train, thy Spir - it and thy word;
3. Here, might - y God, ac - cept our vows, here let thy praise be spread;
4. Here let the Son of Da - vid reign, let God's A - noint - ed shine;
5. Clothe all thy min - is - ters with grace, let truth their tongues em - ploy,

1. thy peo - ple wait with long - ing eyes thus to be owned and blessed.
2. all that the Ark did once con - tain could no such grace af - ford.
3. bless the pro - vi - sions of thy house and fill thy poor with bread.
4. jus - tice and truth his court main - tain with love and power di - vine.
5. that in the Sav - ior's right - eous - ness thy saints may shout for joy.

Alternative tune: TALLIS' ORDINAL, 404

136
Let Us with a Gladsome Mind

John Milton, 1624

MONKLAND, 77.77

Moravian melody, 1824; based on a carol
in *Piae Cantiones* (1582); arranged by John Wilkes, 1861

1. Let us with a glad - some mind praise the Lord, for he is kind:
2. Let us sound his name a - broad, for of gods he is the God:
3. He, with all - com - mand - ing might, filled the new - made world with light:
4. All things liv - ing he doth feed; his full hand sup - plies their need:
5. Let us then with glad - some mind praise the Lord, for he is kind:

Refrain

for his mer - cies shall en - dure, ev - er faith - ful, ev - er sure.

NOTE: *This hymn is suitable for antiphonal treatment, all voices always joining in the refrain.*

By the Babylonian Rivers

Ewald Bash, 1964

Latvian traditional melody, arranged by
John Ylvisaker, 1964; harmony from *Cantate Domino*

BABYLONIAN RIVERS, 8.7.8.7

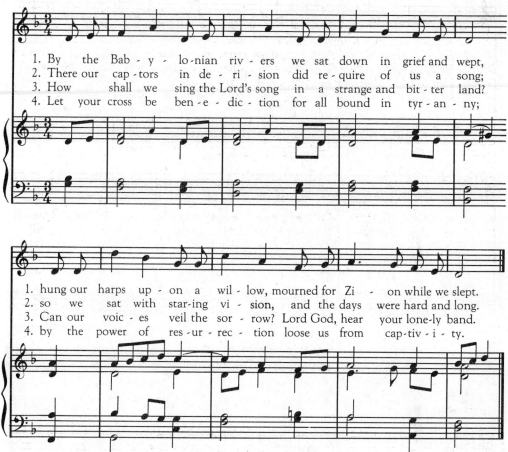

1. By the Bab-y-lo-nian riv-ers we sat down in grief and wept,
2. There our cap-tors in de-ri-sion did re-quire of us a song;
3. How shall we sing the Lord's song in a strange and bit-ter land?
4. Let your cross be ben-e-dic-tion for all bound in tyr-an-ny;

1. hung our harps up-on a wil-low, mourned for Zi-on while we slept.
2. so we sat with star-ing vi-sion, and the days were hard and long.
3. Can our voic-es veil the sor-row? Lord God, hear your lone-ly band.
4. by the power of res-ur-rec-tion loose us from cap-tiv-i-ty.

138

Thou Art Before Me, Lord

Ian Pitt-Watson, 1973

SURSUM CORDA, 10.10. 10.10

Alfred Morton Smith, 1940

1. Thou art be - fore me, Lord, thou art be - hind, and
2. Then whith - er from thy Spir - it shall I go; and
3. If I should take my flight in - to the dawn, if
4. If I should say, "Dark - ness will cov - er me, and

1. thou a - bove me hast spread out thy hand; such
2. whith - er from thy pres - ence shall I flee? If
3. I should dwell on o - cean's far - thest shore, thy
4. I shall hide with - in the veil of night," sure -

1. knowl - edge is too won - der - ful for me, too
2. I as - cend to heav - en, thou art there, and
3. might - y hand would rest up - on me still, and
4. ly the dark - ness is not dark with thee: the

1. high to grasp, too great to un - der - stand.
2. in the low - est depths I meet with thee.
3. thy right hand would guard me ev - er - more.
4. night is as the day, the dark - ness light.

5. Search me, O God, search me and know my heart;
   try me, O God, my mind and spirit try;
   keep me from any path that gives thee pain,
   and lead me in the everlasting way.

PSALMS PRAISE HIM

My God, My King, Thy Various Praise

139

Isaac Watts, 1719

ST. BARTHOLOMEW, LM

Henry Duncalf, 1762

1. My God, my King, thy var - ious praise shall fill the
2. The wings of ev - 'ry hour shall bear some thank - ful
3. Thy truth and jus - tice I'll pro - claim; thy boun - ty
4. Let dis - tant times and na - tions raise the long suc -
5. But who can speak thy won - drous deeds? Thy great - ness

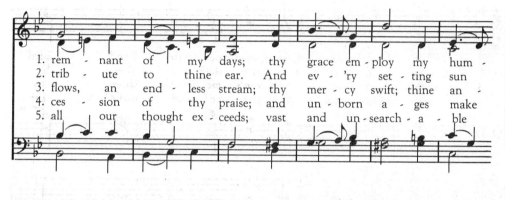

1. rem - nant of my days; thy grace em - ploy my hum -
2. trib - ute to thine ear. And ev - 'ry set - ting sun
3. flows, an end - less stream; thy mer - cy swift; thine an -
4. ces - sion of thy praise; and un - born a - ges make
5. all our thought ex - ceeds; vast and un - search - a - ble

1. ble tongue, till death and glo - ry raise the song.
2. shall see new works of du - ty done for thee.
3. ger slow, but dread - ful to the stub - born foe.
4. my song the joy and la - bor of their tongue.
5. thy ways: vast and im - mor - tal be thy praise!

140 I'll Praise My Maker While I've Breath

Isaac Watts, 1674–1748; alt'd by John Wesley, 1703–1791

Strasburger Kirchenamt (1525);
probably by Matthaus Greiter c. 1500–1552;
harmonized by V. Earle Copes

OLD 113th, 88.8.88.8

1. I'll praise my Mak - er while I've breath; and when my voice is lost in death,
2. Hap - py the one whose hopes re - ly on Is - rael's God; he made the sky
3. The Lord pours eye - sight on the blind; the Lord sup-ports the faint-ing mind;
4. I'll praise him while he lends me breath; and when my voice is lost in death,

1. praise shall em - ploy my no - bler powers. My days of praise shall ne'er be past,
2. and earth and seas, with all their train. His truth for - ev - er stands se - cure,
3. he sends the la - boring con-science peace. He helps the strang-er in dis - tress,
4. praise shall em - ploy my no - bler powers. My days of praise shall ne'er be past,

1. while life, and thought, and be - ing last, or im - mor - tal - i - ty en - dures.
2. he saves th'op-pressed, he feeds the poor, and none shall find his prom-ise vain.
3. the wid - ow and the fa - ther - less, and grants the pris-oner sweet re - lease.
4. while life, and thought, and be - ing last, or im - mor - tal - i - ty en - dures.

Praise Ye, Praise Ye the Lord

141

The Psalter (1912)

AMHERST, 6.6.6.6.88

Melody by William Billings, 1770

1. Praise ye, praise ye the Lord in yon - der heav'n - ly height;
2. Praise him, ye high - est heav'ns, praise him, ye clouds that roll,
3. Ye crea - tures in the sea and crea - tures on the earth,
4. Ye hills and moun - tains, praise: each tree and beast and bird;
5. By all let God be praised for he a - lone is great;

1. ye an - gels, all his hosts, in joy - ful praise u - nite.
2. cre - at - ed by his power and un - der his con - trol,
3. your might - y Mak - er praise, and tell his match - less worth.
4. ye kings and realms of earth, now let your praise be heard;
5. a - bove the earth and heaven he reigns in glo - rious state.

1. O sun and moon, de - clare his might; show forth his praise, ye stars of light.
2. ye heav'ns that stand e - ter - nal - ly, es - tab - lished by his firm de - cree.
3. Praise him, ye storm - y winds that blow, ye fire and hail, ye rains and snow.
4. by high and low, by young and old, be all his praise and glo - ry told.
5. Praise him, ye saints who know his grace, and ev - er dwell be - fore his face.

142   Praise the Lord! His Glories Show

H. F. Lyte, 1834

LLANFAIR, 77.77 with Alleluias

Robert Williams, 1817

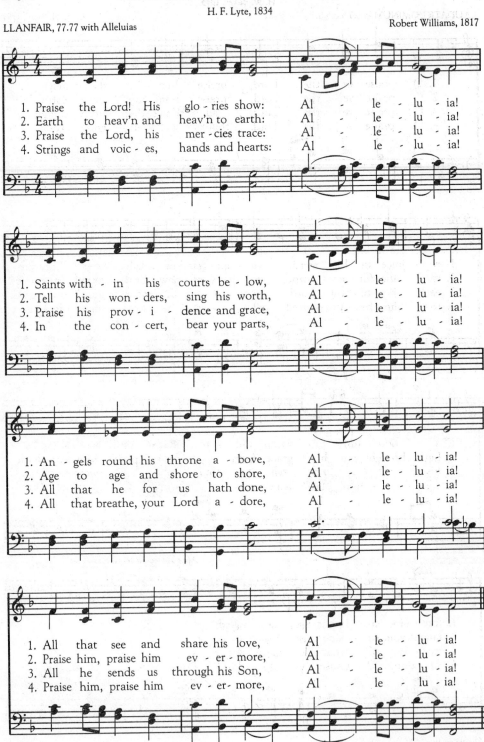

1. Praise the Lord! His glo-ries show: Al - le - lu - ia!
2. Earth to heav'n and heav'n to earth: Al - le - lu - ia!
3. Praise the Lord, his mer-cies trace: Al - le - lu - ia!
4. Strings and voic-es, hands and hearts: Al - le - lu - ia!

1. Saints with - in his courts be - low, Al - le - lu - ia!
2. Tell his won - ders, sing his worth, Al - le - lu - ia!
3. Praise his prov-i - dence and grace, Al - le - lu - ia!
4. In the con - cert, bear your parts, Al - le - lu - ia!

1. An - gels round his throne a - bove, Al - le - lu - ia!
2. Age to age and shore to shore, Al - le - lu - ia!
3. All that he for us hath done, Al - le - lu - ia!
4. All that breathe, your Lord a - dore, Al - le - lu - ia!

1. All that see and share his love, Al - le - lu - ia!
2. Praise him, praise him ev - er - more, Al - le - lu - ia!
3. All he sends us through his Son, Al - le - lu - ia!
4. Praise him, praise him ev - er - more, Al - le - lu - ia!

This tune in a higher key: 331

PSALMS PRAISE HIM

O Praise Ye the Lord

143

H. W. Baker, 1875

LAUDATE DOMINUM, 5.5.5.5.6.5.6.5

C. H. H. Parry, 1897

1. O praise ye the Lord, praise him in the height;
2. O praise ye the Lord, praise him up-on earth,
3. O praise ye the Lord, all things that give sound;
4. O praise ye the Lord, thanks-giv-ing and song

1. re - joice in his word, ye an-gels of light; ye heav-ens
2. in tune-ful ac-cord, ye heirs of new birth; praise him who
3. each ju-bi-lant chord re-ech-o a-round; loud or-gans
4. to him be out-poured all a-ges a-long; for love in

1. a - dore him, by whom you were made, and wor-ship be -
2. hath brought you his grace from a - bove, praise him who hath
3. his glo-ry forth-tell in deep tone, and sweet harp the
4. cre - a - tion, for heav-en re-stored, for grace of sal -

After last stanza only (SATB)

1. fore him in bright-ness ar - rayed.
2. taught you to sing of his love.
3. sto - ry of what he hath done.
4. va - tion, O praise ye the Lord! Praise ye the Lord!

Alternative tune: LYONS, 598

Praise, My Soul, the King of Heaven

H. F. Lyte, 1834 *(alt'd)*

PRAISE MY SOUL, 8.7.8.7.8.7

John Goss, 1869

1. Praise, my soul, the King of heav - en; to his feet thy trib-ute bring;

1. ransomed, healed, re-stored, for - giv - en, who like thee his praise should sing?

1. Praise him, praise him, praise him, praise him, praise the ev - er - last-ing King.

2. Praise him for his grace and fa - vor to his peo-ple in dis -tress;

2. praise him still the same for - ev - er, slow to chide, and swift to bless:

COME, MAGNIFY THE LORD WITH ME

2. praise him, praise him, praise him, praise him, glo-rious in his faith-ful - ness.

3. Fa-ther - like he tends and spares us; well our fee-ble frame he knows.

3. In his hands he gent - ly bears us, res - cues us from all our foes:

3. praise him, praise him, praise him, praise him, wide - ly as his mer - cy flows.

4. Frail as sum-mer's flower we flour - ish, blows the wind and it is gone;

COME, MAGNIFY THE LORD WITH ME

COME, MAGNIFY THE LORD WITH ME

Praise to the Lord, the Almighty

145

Lobe den herren, by Joachim Neander, 1680;
tr. Catherine Winkworth, 1863 (alt'd)

LOBE DEN HERREN, 14 14.47.8

Later form of melody in *Stralsund Gesangbuch* (1665)

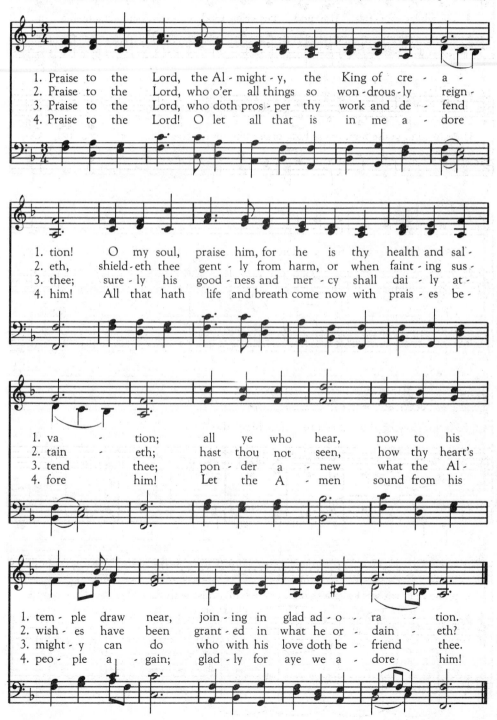

1. Praise to the Lord, the Al - might - y, the King of cre - a - tion! O my soul, praise him, for he is thy health and sal - va - tion; all ye who hear, now to his tem - ple draw near, join - ing in glad ad - o - ra - tion.
2. Praise to the Lord, who o'er all things so won - drous - ly reign - eth, shield - eth thee gent - ly from harm, or when faint - ing sus - tain - eth; hast thou not seen, how thy heart's wish - es have been grant - ed in what he or - dain - eth?
3. Praise to the Lord, who doth pros - per thy work and de - fend thee; sure - ly his good - ness and mer - cy shall dai - ly at - tend thee; pon - der a - new what the Al - might - y can do who with his love doth be - friend thee.
4. Praise to the Lord! O let all that is in me a - dore him! All that hath life and breath come now with prais - es be - fore him! Let the A - men sound from his peo - ple a - gain; glad - ly for aye we a - dore him!

Ps. 103

COME, MAGNIFY THE LORD WITH ME

Sing Praise to God Who Reigns Above

Sei Lob und Ehr, by J. J. Schütz,
1675; tr. Frances E. Cox, 1858

Melody in the hymnbook of the Bohemian
Brethren, 1566; as given in J. B.
Reimann's *Deutsche Geistliche Lieder* (1895)

MIT FREUDEN ZART, 8.7.8.7.88.7

1. Sing praise to God who reigns a-bove, the God of all cre - a - tion,
2. What God's al-might-y power hath made his gra-cious mer-cy keep-eth;
*3. The Lord is nev-er far a-way, but through all grief dis-tress-ing,
*4. Thus all my glad-some way a-long I sing a-loud thy prais-es

1. the God of power, the God of love, the God of our sal - va - tion;
2. by morn-ing glow or eve-ning shade his watch-ful eye ne'er sleep-eth.
3. an ev-er pres-ent help and stay, our peace and joy and bless-ing;
4. that all may hear the grate-ful song my voice un-wea-ried rais-es.

1. with heal-ing balm my soul he fills and ev-'ry faith-less
2. With - in the king-dom of his might, lo! all is just and
3. as with a moth-er's ten-der hand he leads his own, his
4. Be joy-ful in the Lord, my heart, both soul and bod-y

1. mur - mur stills:
2. all is right: } To God all praise and glo - ry!
3. cho - sen band:
4. take your part:

Jer. 51:8

5. O ye who name Christ's holy name,
  give God all praise and glory;
  all ye who own his pow'r proclaim
  around the wondrous story!

Cast each false idol from his throne,
  the Lord is God, and he alone:
To God all praise and glory!

Fill Thou My Life, O Lord My God 147

Horatius Bonar, 1863

ARDEN, CM

George Thalben-Ball, 1951

1. Fill thou my life, O Lord my God, in ev - 'ry part with praise,
2. Not for the lip of praise a - lone, nor e'en the prais - ing heart—
3. Praise in the com - mon things of life, its go - ings out and in,
4. So shalt thou, gra - cious Lord, from me re - ceive the glo - ry due,
5. So shall no part of day or night from sa - cred - ness be free,

1. that my whole be - ing may pro - claim thy be - ing and thy ways.
2. I ask but for a life made up of praise in ev - 'ry part.
3. praise in each du - ty and each deed, how - ev - er small and mean.
4. and so shall I be - gin on earth the song for - ev - er new.
5. but all my life, in ev - 'ry step, be fel - low - ship with thee.

Alternative tune: GRÄFENBERG, 278
This tune in a higher key: 128

148   Commit Thou All Thy Griefs

Befiehl du deine Wegen, Paul Gerhardt, 1676;
tr. John Wesley, 1737
(This and the next two hymns are parts of the same original
and can be sung in series:
the tunes are interchangeable.)

ICH HALTE, SMD   Schemelli *Gesangbuch* (1736)

1. Com - mit thou all thy griefs and ways in - to his hands,
2. Thou on the Lord re - ly, so safe shalt thou go on;

1. to his sure truth and ten - der care who earth and heav'n com - mands,
2. fix on his work thy stead - fast eye, so shall thy work be done.

1. who points the clouds their course, whom winds and seas o - bey:
2. No prof - it canst thou gain from self - con - sum - ing care;

1. he shall di - rect thy wan - d'ring feet, he shall pre - pare thy way.
2. to him com - mend thy cause; his ear at - tends the soft - est prayer.

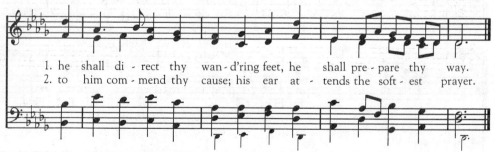

NOTE: *This tune was edited, and possibly composed, by J. S. Bach. It was set to be sung in unison, and the small notes should be played by the organ if the tune is thus sung.*

Give to the Winds Thy Fears

149

(continuation of Hymn 148)

ST. BRIDE, SM

Samuel Howard, 1762

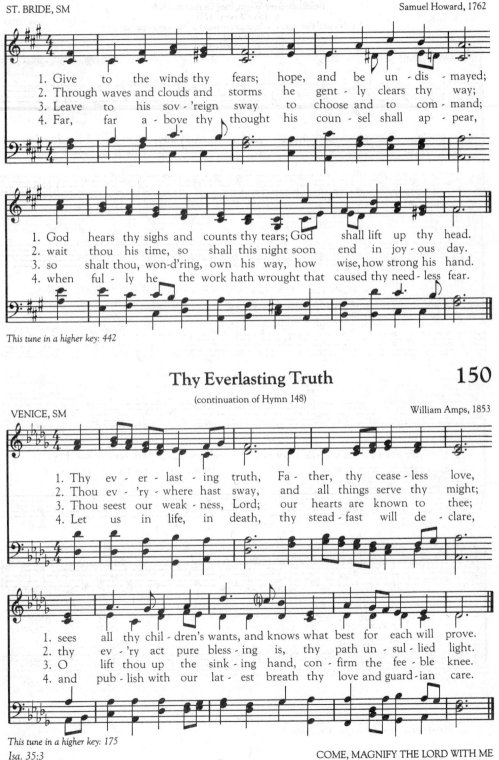

1. Give to the winds thy fears; hope, and be un-dis-mayed;
2. Through waves and clouds and storms he gent-ly clears thy way;
3. Leave to his sov-'reign sway to choose and to com-mand;
4. Far, far a-bove thy thought his coun-sel shall ap-pear,

1. God hears thy sighs and counts thy tears; God shall lift up thy head.
2. wait thou his time, so shall this night soon end in joy-ous day.
3. so shalt thou, won-d'ring, own his way, how wise, how strong his hand.
4. when ful-ly he the work hath wrought that caused thy need-less fear.

This tune in a higher key: 442

Thy Everlasting Truth

150

(continuation of Hymn 148)

VENICE, SM

William Amps, 1853

1. Thy ev-er-last-ing truth, Fa-ther, thy cease-less love,
2. Thou ev-'ry-where hast sway, and all things serve thy might;
3. Thou seest our weak-ness, Lord; our hearts are known to thee;
4. Let us in life, in death, thy stead-fast will de-clare,

1. sees all thy chil-dren's wants, and knows what best for each will prove.
2. thy ev-'ry act pure bless-ing is, thy path un-sul-lied light.
3. O lift thou up the sink-ing hand, con-firm the fee-ble knee.
4. and pub-lish with our lat-est breath thy love and guard-ian care.

This tune in a higher key: 175

Isa. 35:3

COME, MAGNIFY THE LORD WITH ME

If Thou But Trust in God to Guide Thee

Wer nur den lieben Gott, by Georg Neumark, 1657;
tr. Catherine Winkworth, 1863 *(alt'd)*

NEUMARK, 9.8.9.8.88

Georg Neumark, 1657

1. If thou but trust in God to guide thee, and hope in him
2. On-ly be still, and wait his lei-sure in cheer-ful hope,
3. Sing, pray, and keep his ways un-swerv-ing; so do thine own

1. through all thy ways, he'll give thee strength, what-e'er be-tide thee,
2. with heart con-tent to take what-e'er thy Fa-ther's plea-sure
3. part faith-ful-ly; and trust his Word, though un-de-serv-ing.

1. and bear thee through the e-vil days; who trusts in God's
2. and all-dis-cern-ing love hath sent; nor doubt our in-
3. Thou yet shalt find it true for thee. God nev-er yet

1. un-chang-ing love builds on the rock that nought can move.
2. most wants are known to him who chose us for his own.
3. for-sook at need the soul that trust-ed him in-deed.

Alternative tune: MENTZER, 529

Who Trusts in God, a Sure Defense

Wer Gott vertraut, by Joachim Magdeburg, 1572;
tr. B. H. Kennedy, 1863; W. W. How, 1864 (alt'd)

WAS MEIN GOTT WILL, 8.7.8.7 D iambic

Melody attributed to
Claude de Sermisy, d. 1562; arranged by J. S. Bach

152

1. Who trusts in God, a sure de-fense in heaven and earth pos - sess - es;
2. Though Sa - tan's wrath be - set our path and world-ly scorn as - sail us,
3. In all the strife of mor-tal life our feet shall stand se - cure - ly;

1. who looks in love to Christ a - bove, no fear that heart op - press - es.
2. while thou art near we will not fear, thy strength shall nev - er fail us.
3. temp - ta-tion's hour shall lose its power, for thou shalt guard us sure - ly.

1. In thee a - lone, dear Lord, we own sweet hope and con - so - la - tion:
2. Thy rod and staff shall keep us safe, and guide our steps for - ev - er,
3. O God, re - new with heaven-ly dew our bod - y, soul, and spir - it

1. our shield from foes, our balm for woes, our great and sure sal - va - tion.
2. nor shades of death, nor hell be-neath, our souls from thee shall sev - er.
3. un - til we stand at thy right hand, through Je - sus' sav - ing mer - it.

Ps. 23:4; Rom. 8:28–29

TRUST IN THE LORD

153 Whate'er My God Ordains Is Right

Was Gott thut, Samuel Rodigast, 1675;
tr. Catherine Winkworth, 1863

Severus Gastorius, 1681
(later form of melody)

WAS GOTT THUT, 8.7.8.7.44.88

1. What-e'er my God or-dains is right; his ho-ly will a-bid-eth;
2. What-e'er my God or-dains is right; he nev-er will de-ceive me;
3. What-e'er my God or-dains is right; here shall my stand be tak-en;

1. I will be still, what-e'er he doth, and fol-low where he guid-eth.
2. he leads me by the prop-er path; I know he will not leave me,
3. though sor-row, need, or death be mine, yet am I not for-sak-en;

1. He is my God; though dark the road, he holds me that
2. and take, con-tent, what he hath sent; his hand can turn
3. my Fa-ther's care is round me there; he holds me that

1. I shall not fall, where-fore to him I leave it all.
2. my griefs a-way, and pa-tient-ly I wait his day.
3. I shall not fall, and so to him I leave it all.

Be Still, My Soul

Stille, mein Wille; by Katharina von Schlegel, 1752;
tr. Jane Borthwick, 1855

Melody by Jean Sibelius, 1899;
arranged by David Hugh Jones, 1955

FINLANDIA, 10.10.10.10.10 10

154

1. Be still, my soul: the Lord is on thy side; bear pa-tient-
2. Be still, my soul: thy God doth un-der-take to guide the
3. Be still, my soul: the hour is has-tening on when we shall

1. ly the cross of grief or pain; leave to thy God to
2. fu-ture as he has the past. Thy hope, thy con-fi-
3. be for-ev-er with the Lord, when dis-ap-point-ment,

1. or-der and pro-vide; in ev-ery change he
2. dence, let noth-ing shake; all now mys-te-rious
3. grief, and fear are gone, sor-row for-got, love's

1. faith-ful will re-main. Be still, my soul: thy best, thy heaven-ly
2. shall be bright at last. Be still, my soul: the waves and winds still
3. pur-est joys re-stored. Be still, my soul: when change and tears are

1. Friend through thorn-y ways leads to a joy-ful end.
2. know his voice who ruled them while he dwelt be-low.
3. past, all safe and bless-ed we shall meet at last.

Ps. 46:10

This tune in a lower key: 497

TRUST IN THE LORD

155 Great Is Thy Faithfulness

Thomas O. Chisholm, 1923

FAITHFULNESS, 11.10.11.10 D dactylic

William M. Runyan, 1923;
arranged by Erik Routley, 1982

1. Great is thy faith - ful - ness, O God my Fa - ther,
3. Par - don for sin and a peace that en - dur - eth,

1. there is no shad - ow of turn - ing with thee;
3. thy own dear pres - ence to cheer and to guide;

1. thou chang - est not, thy com - pas - sions they fail not;
3. strength for to - day and bright hope for to - mor - row,

1. as thou hast been, thou for - ev - er wilt be.
3. bless - ings all mine, with ten thou - sand be - side.

TRUST IN THE LORD

2. Sum - mer and win - ter and spring - time and har - vest,
4. Great is thy faith - ful - ness, great is thy faith - ful - ness,

2. sun, moon, and stars in their cours - es a - bove
4. morn - ing by morn - ing new mer - cies I see;

2. join with all na - ture in man - i - fold wit - ness
4. all I have need - ed thy hand hath pro - vid - ed—

2. to thy great faith - ful - ness, mer - cy, and love.
4. great is thy faith - ful - ness, Lord, un - to me!

NOTE: *This hymn can be sung using st. 4 as a chorus after st. 1-3, and using the music of st. 1 for st. 1-3.*

Ps. 36:5; Lam. 3:23   TRUST IN THE LORD

156 All My Hope on God Is Founded

Robert Seymour Bridges, 1844–1930;
based on a hymn by Joachim Neander, 1650–1680 (alt'd)
First Tune

MEINE HOFFNUNG, 8.7.8.7.33.7

J. Neander, 1680

1. All my hope on God is found-ed; he doth still my trust re - new.
2. Hu - man pride and earth-ly glo - ry, sword and crown be - tray his trust.
3. God's great good-ness aye en - dur-eth; deep his wis - dom, pass-ing thought.
4. Dai - ly doth th'al - might - y Giv - er boun-teous gifts on us be-stow;
5. Still from earth to God e - ter - nal sac - ri - fice of praise be done,

1. Me through change and chance he guid-eth, on - ly good and on - ly true.
2. What with care and toil we fash-ion, tower and tem - ple, fall to dust.
3. Splen-dor, light, and life at - tend him; beau - ty spring-eth out of nought.
4. his de - sire our soul de-light-eth; plea - sure leads us where we go.
5. high a - bove all prais-es prais-ing for the gift of Christ his Son.

1. God un-known, he a - lone calls my heart to be his own.
2. But God's power, hour by hour, is my tem - ple and my tower.
3. Ev - er - more from his store new - born worlds rise and a - dore.
4. Love doth stand at his hand; joy doth wait on his com-mand.
5. Christ doth call one and all: ye who fol - low shall not fall.

♯ last time only

TRUST IN THE LORD

All My Hope on God Is Founded

Second Tune

MICHAEL, 8.7.8.7.33.7

Herbert Howells, 1930, 1977

1. All my hope on God is found - ed; he doth still my trust re - new.
2. Hu - man pride and earth-ly glo - ry, sword and crown be - tray his trust.
3. God's great good-ness aye en - dur - eth, deep his wis - dom, pass - ing thought.
4. Dai - ly doth th'al - might - y Giv - er boun - te-ous gifts on us be - stow;
5. Still from earth to God e - ter - nal sac - ri-fice of praise be done,

1. Me through change and chance he guid - eth, on - ly good and on - ly true.
2. What with care and toil we fash - ion, tower and tem - ple, fall to dust.
3. Splen - dor, light, and life at tend him; beau - ty spring-eth out of nought.
4. his de - sire our soul de - light - eth; plea - sure leads us where we go.
5. high a - bove all prais - es prais - ing for the gift of Christ his Son.

1. God un - known, he a lone calls my heart to be his own.
2. But God's power, hour by hour, is my tem - ple and my tower.
3. Ev - er - more from his store new-born words rise and a - dore.
4. Love doth stand at his hand; joy doth wait on his com - mand.
5. Christ doth call one and all: ye who fol - low shall not fall.

TRUST IN THE LORD

158

Lord, Take My Hand and Lead Me

So nimm denn meine Hände, Julie von Hausmann, 1825–1901;
tr. *Lutheran Book of Worship* (1978)

LORD, TAKE MY HAND, 7.4.7.4 D iambic

F. Silcher, 1842

1. Lord, take my hand and lead me up-on life's way;
2. Lord, when the tem-pest rag-es I need not fear,
3. Lord, when the shad-ows length-en and night has come,

1. di-rect, pro-tect, and feed me from day to day.
2. for you, the Rock of A-ges, are al-ways near.
3. I know that you will strength-en my steps toward home,

1. With-out your grace and fa-vor I go a-stray,
2. Close by your side a-bid-ing, I fear no foe,
3. and noth-ing can im-pede me, O bless-ed Friend!

1. so take my hand, O Sav-ior, and lead the way.
2. for when your hand is guid-ing, in peace I go.
3. So, take my hand and lead me un-to the end.

TRUST IN THE LORD

Ps. 46:2–3

Sometimes a Light Surprises †

159

William Cowper, 1779

Melody adapted from the offertory in
a mass by Michael Haydn, 1737–1806

OFFERTORIUM, 7.6.7.6 D

†1. Some-times a light sur - pris - es the Chris-tian while he sings:
2. In ho - ly con - tem - pla - tion we sweet - ly then pur - sue
3. It can bring with it noth - ing but he will bear us through;
4. Though vine nor fig - tree nei - ther their wont - ed fruit should bear,

1. it is the Lord, who ris - es with heal - ing in his wings;
2. the theme of God's sal - va - tion, and find it ev - er new;
3. who gives the lil - ies cloth - ing will clothe his peo - ple too;
4. though all the fields should with - er, nor flocks nor herds be there,

1. when com - forts are de - clin - ing, he grants the soul a - gain
2. set free from pres - ent sor - row we cheer-ful - ly can say,
3. be - neath the spread-ing heav - ens no crea-ture but is fed;
4. yet God the same a - bid - ing, his praise shall tune my voice,

1. a sea - son of clear shin - ing to cheer it af - ter rain.
2. e'en let the un-known mor - row bring with it what it may.
3. and he who feeds the ra - vens will give his chil - dren bread.
4. for while in him con - fid - ing I can - not but re - joice.

Hab. 3:17; Mt. 6:28

TRUST IN THE LORD

160   From Noon of Joy to Night of Doubt

John Campbell Shairp, 1871

NOEL, CMD

Arthur Sullivan, 1874;
based on a traditional carol tune

1. From noon of joy to night of doubt our feel-ings come and go;
2. I grasp thy strength, make it my own, my heart with peace is bless'd;
3. Thy pur-pose of e-ter-nal good let me but sure-ly know;

1. our best es-tate is toss'd a-bout in cease-less ebb and flow;
2. I lose my hold, and then comes down dark-ness and cold un-rest.
3. on this I'll lean, let chang-ing mood and feel-ing come and go;

1. no mood of feel-ing, form of thought, is con-stant for a day,
2. Let me no more my com-fort draw from my frail grasp of thee:
3. glad when thy sun-shine fills my soul, not sad when clouds o'er-cast,

1. but thou, O Lord, thou chang-est not; the same thou art al-way.
2. in this a-lone re-joice with awe, thy might-y grasp of me.
3. since thou with-in thy sure con-trol of love dost hold me fast.

TRUST IN THE LORD

He Leadeth Me

Joseph H. Gilmore, 1862

AUGHTON, LM with refrain

William B. Bradbury, 1864

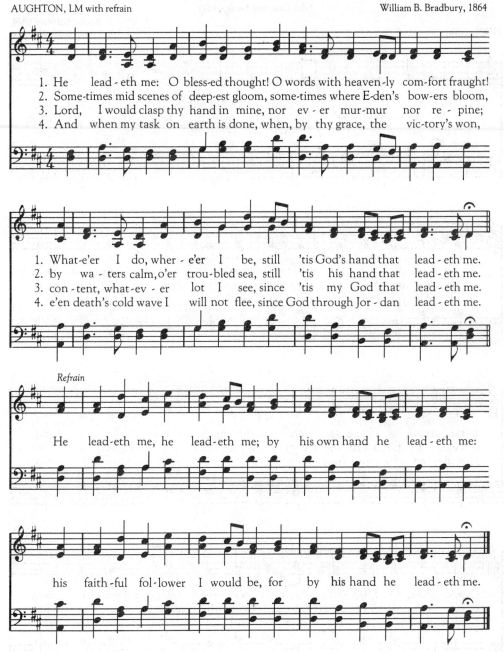

1. He lead-eth me: O bless-ed thought! O words with heaven-ly com-fort fraught!
2. Some-times mid scenes of deep-est gloom, some-times where E-den's bow-ers bloom,
3. Lord, I would clasp thy hand in mine, nor ev - er mur-mur nor re - pine;
4. And when my task on earth is done, when, by thy grace, the vic-tory's won,

1. What-e'er I do, wher - e'er I be, still 'tis God's hand that lead - eth me.
2. by wa - ters calm, o'er trou-bled sea, still 'tis his hand that lead - eth me.
3. con - tent, what-ev - er lot I see, since 'tis my God that lead - eth me.
4. e'en death's cold wave I will not flee, since God through Jor - dan lead - eth me.

Refrain

He lead-eth me, he lead-eth me; by his own hand he lead - eth me:

his faith-ful fol-lower I would be, for by his hand he lead - eth me.

Ps. 23:2

TRUST IN THE LORD

I Sought the Lord

Anonymous, in the *Pilgrim Hymnal* (1904)

The Revivalist (1869);
arranged by George Brandon, 1958

PEACE, 10.10.10.6

1. I sought the Lord, and af-ter-ward I knew
2. Thou didst reach forth thy hand and mine en-fold;
3. I find, I walk, I love, but O the whole

1. he moved my soul to seek him, seek-ing me; it was not I that
2. I walked and sank not on the storm-vexed sea; 'twas not so much that
3. of love is but my an-swer, Lord, to thee! For thou wast long be-

1. found, O Sav-ior true; no, I was found of thee.
2. love on thee took hold as thou, dear Lord, on me.
3. fore-hand with my soul; al-ways thou lov-edst me.

TRUST IN THE LORD

Mt. 14:28ff

Wherever I May Wander

163

Ann B. Snow, 1959

NEW ENGLAND, 7.6.8.6 D

New England folk melody

1. Wher-ev-er I may wan-der, wher-ev-er I may be,
2. Through-out God's whole cre-a-tion I see his lov-ing care

1. I'm cer-tain of my Fa-ther's love; God's care is o-ver me. He
2. for ev-'ry-one in ev-'ry land, God's chil-dren ev-'ry-where. Wher-

1. made the great high moun-tains; he made the wide blue sea;
2. ev-er I may wan-der, wher-ev-er I may be,

1. he made the sky where air-planes fly; he made the world, and me.
2. I'm cer-tain of my Fa-ther's love; God's care is o-ver me.

TRUST IN THE LORD

164

Father, Lead Me Day by Day

John Page Hopps, 1877

POSEN, 77.77

Georg C. Strattner, 1691

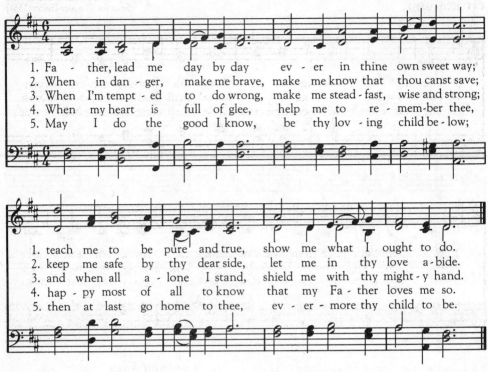

1. Fa - ther, lead me day by day ev - er in thine own sweet way;
2. When in dan - ger, make me brave, make me know that thou canst save;
3. When I'm tempt - ed to do wrong, make me stead - fast, wise and strong;
4. When my heart is full of glee, help me to re - mem - ber thee,
5. May I do the good I know, be thy lov - ing child be - low;

1. teach me to be pure and true, show me what I ought to do.
2. keep me safe by thy dear side, let me in thy love a - bide.
3. and when all a - lone I stand, shield me with thy might - y hand.
4. hap - py most of all to know that my Fa - ther loves me so.
5. then at last go home to thee, ev - er - more thy child to be.

TRUST IN THE LORD

The Lord Will Come and Not Be Slow

John Milton, 1648

Adapted in *Scottish Psalter* (1565);
from the *Genevan Psalter* (1551)

OLD 107th, CMD

1. The Lord will come and not be slow; his foot-steps can-not err;
2. Truth from the earth, like to a flower, shall bud and blos-som fresh,
3. The na - tions, all whom thou hast made, shall come and all shall frame

1. be - fore him righ-teous-ness shall go, his roy-al har-bin' - ger.
2. and jus - tice from her heav'n-ly bower look down on mor - tal flesh.
3. to bow them low be - fore thee, Lord, and glo - ri - fy thy name.

1. Mer - cy and truth that long were missed, now joy-ful-ly are met;
2. Rise, God, judge thou the earth in might; this wick-ed earth re-dress,
3. For great thou art, and won - ders great by thy strong hand are done;

1. sweet peace and righ-teous-ness have kissed, and hand in hand is set.
2. for thou art he that shall by right the na-tions all pos - sess.
3. thou in thy ev - er - last - ing seat re-main-est God a - lone.

Alternative tune: ST. ANNE, 1

Pss. 85, 86, 82

THUS SAYS THE LORD

166
Behold the Mountain of the Lord

Varied from *Scottish Paraphrases* (1781)

GLASGOW, CM

Moore's *Companion* (1756)

1. Be - hold, the moun-tain of the Lord in lat - ter days shall rise
2. The beam that shines from Zi - on's hill shall glad - den ev - 'ry land;
3. A - mong the na - tions he shall judge; his judg-ments truth shall guide;
4. No strife shall vex Mes - si - ah's reign, nor mar the peace-ful years;

1. a - bove the moun - tains and the hills, and draw the won-d'ring eyes.
2. the Might - y God, the Prince of Peace, shall all the world com-mand.
3. his scep - ter shall pro - tect the just, and quell the sin - ner's pride.
4. to plough-shares soon they beat their swords, to prun-ing hooks their spears.

5. No longer hosts encountering hosts,
   their carnage they deplore;
   the tools of death they lay aside,
   and study war no more.

6. Come then, O come from every land
   to worship at his shrine,
   and walking in the light of God,
   with holy beauties shine.

THUS SAYS THE LORD

Isa. 2:2–5

The Race That Long in Darkness Pined

John Morison, 1781

PISGAH, CM

American folk hymn, attributed to J. C. Lowry, 1818;
adapted and harmonized in *Songs of Praise* (1925)

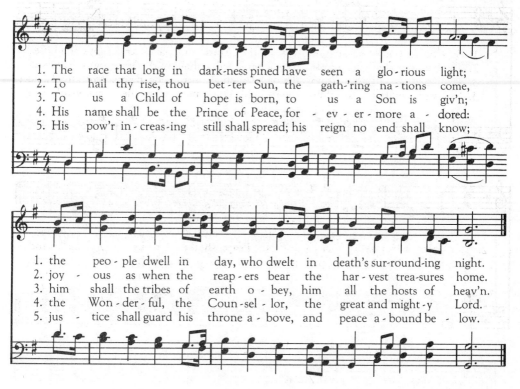

1. The race that long in dark-ness pined have seen a glo-rious light;
2. To hail thy rise, thou bet-ter Sun, the gath-'ring na-tions come,
3. To us a Child of hope is born, to us a Son is giv'n;
4. His name shall be the Prince of Peace, for - ev - er - more a - dored:
5. His pow'r in - creas-ing still shall spread; his reign no end shall know;

1. the peo - ple dwell in day, who dwelt in death's sur-round-ing night.
2. joy - ous as when the reap - ers bear the har - vest trea-sures home.
3. him shall the tribes of earth o - bey, him all the hosts of heav'n.
4. the Won - der - ful, the Coun - sel - or, the great and might - y Lord.
5. jus - tice shall guard his throne a - bove, and peace a - bound be - low.

Isa. 9:2–7

THUS SAYS THE LORD

Watchman, Tell Us of the Night

John Bowring, 1825

WATCHMAN, 7.7.7.7 D

Melody by Lowell Mason, 1830

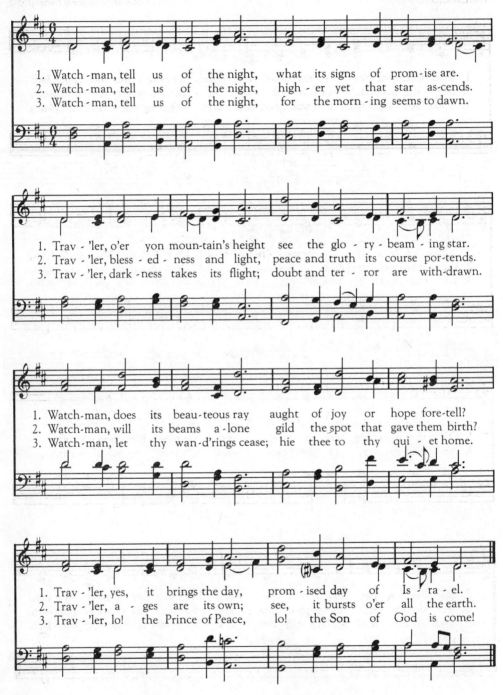

1. Watch-man, tell us of the night, what its signs of prom-ise are.
2. Watch-man, tell us of the night, high-er yet that star as-cends.
3. Watch-man, tell us of the night, for the morn-ing seems to dawn.

1. Trav-'ler, o'er yon moun-tain's height see the glo-ry-beam-ing star.
2. Trav-'ler, bless-ed-ness and light, peace and truth its course por-tends.
3. Trav-'ler, dark-ness takes its flight; doubt and ter-ror are with-drawn.

1. Watch-man, does its beau-teous ray aught of joy or hope fore-tell?
2. Watch-man, will its beams a-lone gild the spot that gave them birth?
3. Watch-man, let thy wan-d'rings cease; hie thee to thy qui-et home.

1. Trav-'ler, yes, it brings the day, prom-ised day of Is-ra-el.
2. Trav-'ler, a-ges are its own; see, it bursts o'er all the earth.
3. Trav-'ler, lo! the Prince of Peace, lo! the Son of God is come!

NOTE: *This hymn may be sung antiphonally, in which case the tune should be sung in unison.*

THUS SAYS THE LORD

Isa. 21:11–12

Comfort, Comfort Ye, My People

Trostet, Trostet, by J. Olearius;
tr. Catherine Winkworth, 1863

PSALM 42, 8.7.8.7.77.88

Melody in *Genevan Psalter* (1551)

1. Com-fort, com-fort ye, my peo-ple; speak ye peace: thus saith your God;
2. For the her-ald's voice is call-ing, in the des-ert far and near,
3. Make ye straight what long was crook-ed; make the rough-er plac-es plain;

1. com-fort those who sit in dark-ness, bowed be-neath op-pres-sion's load;
2. bid-ding all to make re-pen-tance, since the king-dom now is here.
3. let your hearts be true and hum-ble, as be-fits his ho-ly reign.

1. of the peace that waits for them speak ye to Je-ru-sa-lem;
2. O that warn-ing cry o-bey! Now pre-pare for him a way;
3. For the glo-ry of the Lord now o'er earth is shed a-broad,

1. tell her that her sins I cov-er, and her war-fare now is o-ver.
2. let the val-leys rise to meet him, and the hills bow down to greet him.
3. and all flesh shall see the to-ken that his word is nev-er bro-ken.

Isa. 40:1–5

THUS SAYS THE LORD

170   Hast Thou Not Known, Hast Thou Not Heard?

Scottish Paraphrases (1781)

LONDON NEW, CM

Playford's Psalms (1671)

1. Hast thou not known, hast thou not heard, that firm re-mains on high
2. Art thou a-fraid his pow'r shall fail when comes thy e-vil day?
3. Su-preme in wis-dom as in pow'r, the Rock of A-ges stands,
4. He gives the con-quest to the weak, sup-ports the faint-ing heart,

1. the ev-er-last-ing throne of him who formed the earth and sky?
2. And can an all-cre-at-ing arm grow wea-ry or de-cay?
3. though him thou canst not see, nor trace the work-ing of his hands.
4. and cour-age in the e-vil hour his heav'n-ly aids im-part.

Alternative tune: DUNDEE, 572

This tune in a lower key: 36

5. Mere human power shall fast decay,
    and youthful vigor cease;
but they who wait upon the Lord
    in strength shall still increase.

6. They with unwearied feet shall tread
    the path of life divine,
with growing ardor onward move,
    with growing brightness shine.

THUS SAYS THE LORD

Isa. 40:28–31

Paul Inwood, 1972

WOODLANDS, 10.10.10.10   Walter Greatorex, 1919

1. The voice of God goes out to all the world; his glo-ry
2. The Lord has said, "Re-ceive my mes-sen-ger, my prom-ise
3. "The bro-ken reed he will not tram-ple down, nor set his
4. "A-noint-ed with the Spir-it and with power, he comes to

1. speaks a-cross the u-ni-verse. The great King's her-ald cries from star to
2. to the world, my pledge made fresh, a lamp to ev-ery na-tion, light from
3. heel up-on the dy-ing flame. He binds the wounds, and health is in his
4. crown with com-fort all the weak, to show the face of jus-tice to the

1. star: "With power, with jus-tice, he will walk his way!"
2. light: with power, with jus-tice, he will walk his way!
3. hand: with power, with jus-tice, he will walk his way!
4. poor: with power, with jus-tice, he will walk his way!

Alternative tune:
SHELDONIAN, 269

5. "His touch will bless the eyes that darkness held,
   the lame shall run, the halting tongue shall sing,
   and prisoners laugh in light and liberty:
   with power, with justice, he will walk his way!"

Isa. 42:3; Isa. 51:1–3   THUS SAYS THE LORD

How Firm a Foundation

Anon., c. 1787 (alt'd)

FOUNDATION, 11 11.11 11 anapaestic

American folk hymn

1. How firm a foun-da-tion, you saints of the Lord,
2. "Fear not, I am with you; O be not dis-mayed,
3. "When through the deep wa-ters I call you to go,
4. "When through fi-ery tri-als your path-way shall lie,

1. is laid for your faith in his ex-cel-lent word:
2. for I am your God and will still give you aid:
3. the riv-ers of sor-row shall not o-ver-flow,
4. my grace all-suf-fi-cient shall be your sup-ply;

1. what more can he say than to you he hath said,
2. I'll strength-en you, help you, and cause you to stand,
3. for I will be with you in trou-ble to bless
4. the flame shall not hurt you, my on-ly de-sign

1. to you who for ref-uge to Je-sus have fled?
2. up-held by my right-eous, om-nip-o-tent hand.
3. and sanc-ti-fy to you your deep-est dis-tress.
4. your dross to con-sume and your gold to re-fine."

5. The soul that on Jesus has leaned for repose
he will not, he cannot desert to its foes;
that soul, though all hell should endeavor to shake,
he never will leave, he will never forsake.

Alternative tune:
ADESTE FIDELES, 195

COMFORT! COMFORT! MY PEOPLE

Isa. 28:16; Isa. 43:2; Mal. 3:2

Rejoice, O Land, in God Thy Might

Robert Bridges, 1899

WAREHAM, LM

William Knapp, 1738

Descant, st. 2, by Eric H. Thiman

2. Glad shalt thou be, with bless - ing crowned; with joy and

1. Re - joice, O land, in God thy might; his will o -
2. Glad shalt thou be, with bless - ing crowned; with joy and
3. He shall for - give thy sins un - told; re - mem - ber

2. peace thou shalt a - bound; yea, love with thee shall

1. bey, him serve a - right; for thee the saints up -
2. peace thou shalt a - bound; yea, love with thee shall
3. thou his love of old; walk in his way, his

2. make its home, un - til thou see God's king - dom come.

1. lift their voice; fear not, O land, in God re - joice.
2. make its home, un - til thou see God's king - dom come.
3. word a - dore, and keep his truth for - ev - er - more.

This tune in a lower key: 57

Joel 2:21

COMFORT! COMFORT! MY PEOPLE

174   Awake, Awake, Put On Thy Strength, O Zion

Ronald A. Knox and C. A. Alington, 1918

Adapted from a melody by
Henry Smart, 1868

PILGRIMS, 11.10.11.10 with refrain

1. A-wake, a - wake,   put on thy strength, O Zi - on;
2. O ye that thirst,   the pleas - ant foun - tains wait you;
3. For now the low   es - tate of his hand - maid - en
4. A - rise and shine: thy bat - tle - ments are shin - ing;

1. God's pur - pose tar - ries,   but his will stands fast;
2. ye that are poor,   ye shall be free - ly fed.
3. God hath re - gard - ed,   and she shall be blest;
4. up - on thee breaks the   glo - ry of the Lord;

1. of Ju - dah's tribe   is born the might - y Li - on,
2. Why give ye gold   for wine that can - not sate you?
3. hear him that saith,   "Come, all ye heav - y lad - en,
4. and from the east,   thy roy - al - ty di - vin - ing,

1. and he shall bruise the   ser - pent's head at last.
2. Why strive your hands for   that which is not bread?
3. come un - to me, and   I will give you rest."
4. the Gen - tiles come to   see thy peace re - stored.

Gen. 49:9; Lk. 1:46–48; Mt. 11:28–29

COMFORT! COMFORT! MY PEOPLE

plus texts on next page

Refrain

Prom - ise and cov - e - nant God sure - ly keeps:

he watch - ing o'er us slum - bers not, nor sleeps.

Isa. 52:1; Isa. 55:1-2; Isa. 60:1-3; Ps. 121:4

How Beauteous Are Their Feet 175

Isaac Watts, 1707

VENICE, SM

William Amps, 1858

1. How beau-teous are their feet who stand on Zi-on's hill,
2. How charm-ing is their voice, how sweet the tid-ings are!
3. How bless-ed are our eyes that see this heav'n-ly light;
4. The Lord makes bare his arm through all the earth a-broad;

1. who bring sal - va - tion on their tongues, and words of peace re - veal.
2. Zi - on, be - hold thy Sav - ior King; he reigns and tri - umphs here.
3. proph - ets and kings de - sired it long, but died with-out the sight.
4. let ev - 'ry na - tion now be - hold their Sav - ior and their God!

This tune in a lower key: 150

Isa. 52:7–10

COMFORT! COMFORT! MY PEOPLE

176 What Does the Lord Require?

Albert Bayly, 1950

SHARPTHORNE, 6.6.6.6.33.6

Erik Routley, 1969

1. What does the Lord re - quire for praise and of - fer - ing?
2. Rul - ers of earth, give ear! should you not jus - tice know?
3. Still down the a - ges ring the proph - et's stern com - mands;
4. How shall our life ful - fill God's law so hard and high?

1. What sac - ri - fice, de - sire, or trib - ute bid thee bring? Do just - ly,
2. Will God your pleading hear while crime and cruel - ty grow? Do just - ly,
3. to mer-chant, work-er, king, he brings God's high com-mands: Do just - ly,
4. Let Christ endue our will with grace to for - ti - fy. Then just - ly,

st. 1, 2, 3   st. 4

1. love mer - cy, walk hum-bly with your God.
2. love mer - cy, walk hum-bly with your God.
3. love mer - cy, walk hum-bly with your God.
4. in mer - cy, we'll   4. hum-bly walk with God.

Mic. 6:6–8

177 How Blest Are They, O Lord

Cento from A. Toplady, 1772

SONG 20, SM

Melody and bass by Orlando Gibbons, 1623

1. How blest are they, O Lord, who stay them-selves on thee;
2. When we in dark-ness walk, nor feel the heav'n - ly flame,
3. Soon shall our doubts and fears sub - side at his con - trol:
4. Wait till the shad-ows flee; wait thy ap - point - ed hour;
5. His grace will to the end strong - er and bright - er shine,

COMFORT! COMFORT! MY PEOPLE

1. who wait for thy sal - va - tion, Lord, shall thy sal - va - tion see.
2. then is the time to trust our God, and call up - on his name.
3. his lov - ing - kind - ness shall break thro' the mid - night of the soul.
4. wait till the Bride-groom of thy soul re - veals his love with power.
5. nor pres - ent things, nor things to come shall quench the spark di - vine.

Alternative tune: ST. THOMAS, 409

Ps. 1; Ps. 27:14; Rom. 8:38–39

O Day of God, Draw Nigh

178

Robert B. Y. Scott, 1958

TYTHERTON, SM

Louis R. West, 1790

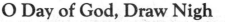

1. O day of God, draw nigh in beau - ty and in power;
2. Bring to our trou - bled minds, un - cer - tain and a - fraid,
3. Bring jus - tice to our land, that all may dwell se - cure,
4. Bring to our world of strife thy sov - 'reign word of peace,
5. O day of God, draw nigh, as at cre - a - tion's birth;

1. come with thy time-less judg-ment now to match our pres - ent hour.
2. the qui - et of a stead-fast faith, calm of a call o - beyed.
3. and fine - ly build for days to come foun - da - tions that en - dure.
4. that war may haunt the earth no more, and des - o - la - tion cease.
5. let there be light a - gain, and set thy judg-ments in the earth.

Alternative tune: ST. MICHAEL, 540

Gen. 1:3; Ps. 105:7

COMFORT! COMFORT! MY PEOPLE

179

A Mighty Fortress Is Our God

Ein' Feste Burg, by Martin Luther, c. 1528;
tr. F. H. Hedge, 1853

EIN' FESTE BURG, 8.7.8.7.66.66.7

Later form of melody by
Martin Luther, c. 1528

1. A mighty fortress is our God, a bulwark never failing;
2. Did we in our own strength confide, our striving would be losing;
3. And though this world, with devils filled, should threaten to undo us,
4. That word above all earthly powers, no thanks to them, abideth;

1. our helper he amid the flood of mortal ills prevailing.
2. were not the right man on our side, the man of God's own choosing.
3. we will not fear, for God hath willed his truth to triumph through us.
4. the Spirit and the gifts are ours through him who with us sideth;

1. For still our ancient foe doth seek to work us woe; his craft and power are
2. Dost ask who that may be? Christ Jesus, it is he; Lord Sabaoth his
3. The prince of darkness grim, we tremble not for him; his rage we can en-
4. let goods and kindred go, this mortal life also; the body they may

1. great; and, armed with cruel hate, on earth is not his equal.
2. name, from age to age the same, and he must win the battle.
3. dure, for lo! his doom is sure; one little word shall fell him.
4. kill; God's truth abideth still; his kingdom is for ever.

COMFORT! COMFORT! MY PEOPLE

Ps. 46:1

Hail to the Brightness of Zion's Glad Morning

Thomas Hastings, 1832

WESLEY, 11.10.11.10

Melody by Lowell Mason, 1833

1. Hail to the bright-ness of Zi-on's glad morn-ing!
2. Lo, in the des-ert rich flow-ers are spring-ing;
3. Hear, from all lands, from the isles of the o-cean,

1. Joy to the lands that in dark-ness have lain!
2. streams ev-er co-pious are glid-ing a-long;
3. praise to the Sav-ior as-cend-ing on high;

1. Hushed be the ac-cents of sor-row and mourn-ing;
2. loud from the moun-tain-tops ech-oes are ring-ing;
3. fall-en the en-gines of war and com-mo-tion;

1. Zi-on in tri-umph be-gins her mild reign.
2. wastes rise in ver-dure and min-gle in song.
3. shouts of sal-va-tion are rend-ing the sky.

Isa. 35:1

COMFORT! COMFORT! MY PEOPLE

181

Christ Is the World's True Light

G. W. Briggs, 1931 (alt'd)

THACKERAY, 6.7.6.7.6.6.6.6   Deborah Holden, 1980

1. Christ is the world's true light, our Cap-tain of sal - va - tion,
2. In Christ all rac - es meet, their an - cient feuds for - get - ting,
3. One Lord, in one great name u - nite us all who own thee;

1. our Day - star clear and bright, De - sire of ev - 'ry na - tion.
2. the whole round world com - plete from sun - rise to its set - ting.
3. cast out our pride and shame that hin - der to en - throne thee.

1. New life, new hope a - wakes for all who own his sway; free - dom her
2. When Christ is throned as Lord all shall for - sake their fear, to plough - share
3. The world has wait - ed long, has tra - vailed long in pain; to heal its

st. 1,2   st. 3

1. bond - age breaks and night is turned to day.
2. beat the sword, to prun - ing - hook the spear.
3. an - cient wrong, come, Prince of Peace, and reign.

COMFORT! COMFORT! MY PEOPLE   Mic. 4:1–5

Tell Out, My Soul, the Greatness of the Lord 182

Timothy Dudley-Smith, 1962

WOODLANDS, 10.10.10.10   Walter Greatorex, 1919

1. Tell out, my soul, the greatness of the Lord: unnumbered blessings give my spirit voice; tender to me the promise of his word; in God my Savior shall my heart rejoice.

2. Tell out, my soul, the greatness of his name: make known his might, the deeds his arm has done; his mercy sure, from age to age the same; his holy name, the Lord, the Mighty One.

3. Tell out, my soul, the greatness of his might: pow'rs and dominions lay their glory by; proud hearts and stubborn wills are put to flight, the hungry fed, the humble lifted high.

4. Tell out, my soul, the glories of his word: firm is his promise, and his mercy sure. Tell out, my soul, the greatness of the Lord to children's children and forevermore.

Alternative tune: SHELDONIAN, 269

Lk. 1:46ff   COMFORT! COMFORT! MY PEOPLE

183 Come, Thou Long-Expected Jesus

Charles Wesley, 1744

STUTTGART, 8.7.8.7

Melody by C. F. Witt, 1715 (later form)

Descant, st. 4, by John Wilson

4. By thine own e - ter - nal Spir-it rule in all our hearts a-lone;

1. Come, thou long - ex - pect-ed Je -sus, born to set thy peo-ple free;
2. Is - rael's strength and con - so - la -tion, hope of all the earth thou art,
3. Born thy peo - ple to de - liv - er, born a child and yet a king,
4. By thine own e - ter - nal Spir -it, rule in all our hearts a - lone;

4. by thine all - suf - fi - cient mer - it raise us to thy glo - rious throne.

1. from our fears and sins re - lease us; let us find our rest in thee.
2. dear de - sire of ev - 'ry na - tion, joy of ev - 'ry long-ing heart.
3. born to reign in us for - ev - er, now thy gra-cious king-dom bring.
4. by thine all - suf - fi - cient mer - it raise us to thy glo-rious throne.

Alternative tunes (in two stanzas): BLAENWERN, 115, HYFRYDOL, 346   Hag. 2:7

184 O Come, O Come, Immanuel

Medieval Latin antiphons; tr. composite

VENI IMMANUEL, 88.88.88

14th-century melody, adapted

1. O come, O come, Im - man - u -el, and ran-som cap-tive Is - ra - el

ADVENT

1. that mourns in lone-ly ex - ile here un - til the Son of God ap-pear.

Refrain

1. Re - joice! Re-joice! Im - man - u - el shall come to thee, O Is - ra - el.

*2. O come, thou Wisdom from on high,
who ord'rest all things mightily;
to us the path of knowledge show
and teach us in her ways to go.
      Rejoice! Rejoice! Immanuel
      shall come to thee, O Israel.

3. O come, O come, thou Lord of might,
who to thy tribes on Sinai's height
in ancient times didst give the law
in cloud and majesty and awe.
      Rejoice! Rejoice! Immanuel
      shall come to thee, O Israel.

*4. O come, thou Rod of Jesse's stem;
from every foe deliver them
that trust thy mighty power to save,
and give them victory o'er the grave.
      Rejoice! Rejoice! Immanuel
      shall come to thee, O Israel.

5. O come, thou Key of David, come
and open wide our heavenly home;
make safe the way that leads on high,
and close the path to misery.
      Rejoice! Rejoice! Immanuel
      shall come to thee, O Israel.

*6. O come, thou Dayspring, come and cheer
our spirits by thine advent here;
disperse the gloomy clouds of night,
and death's dark shadows put to flight.
      Rejoice! Rejoice! Immanuel
      shall come to thee, O Israel.

7. O come, Desire of nations, bind
all peoples in one heart and mind:
bid thou our sad divisions cease,
and be thyself our King of Peace.
      Rejoice! Rejoice! Immanuel
      shall come to thee, O Israel!

Isa. 11:1ff

ADVENT

185

Lift Up Your Heads, Ye Mighty Gates

Macht hoch die Thur, by Georg Weissel, 1590–1635;
tr. Catherine Winkworth, 1862 (alt'd)

TRURO, LM

Melody in *Psalmodia Evangelica* (1789)

1. Lift up your heads, ye might-y gates; be-hold the King of Glo-ry waits;
2. O blest the land, the cit-y blest, where Christ the Rul-er is con-fess'd!
3. Fling wide the por-tals of your heart; make it a tem-ple set a-part
4. Re-deem-er, come! We o-pen wide our hearts to thee; here, Lord, a-bide!
5. Thy Ho-ly Spir-it lead us on un-til our glo-rious goal is won;

1. the King of kings is draw-ing near; the Sav-ior of the world is here.
2. O hap-py hearts and hap-py homes to whom this King in tri-umph comes!
3. from earth-ly use for heav'n's em-ploy, a-dorned with prayer and love and joy.
4. Let us thy in-ner pres-ence feel; thy grace and love in us re-veal.
5. e-ter-nal praise, e-ter-nal fame be of-fered, Sav-ior, to thy name!

This tune in a higher key: 99

Ps. 24:7ff

186

Hail, Jesus! Israel's Hope and Light!

Henry Harbaugh, 1860

LLEDROD, LM

Canaiadau y Cyssegr (1839)

1. Hail, Je-sus! Is-rael's hope and light! Proph-ets and priests pre-pared thy way;
2. Thine ad-vent, Lord, re-vives the world; thy life shall wait-ing na-tions know;
3. Those vales, where dark-ness lin-gers last, now kin-dle in pro-phet-ic light;
4. Hail, glo-rious ad-vent, heav'n-ly birth! Shout, saints, in tri-umph! Christ ap-pears;

ADVENT

1. thy peo-ple through the break-ing night with wait-ing joy fore-saw thy day.
2. the ban-ner of thy truth un-furled shall glo-rious on the moun-tains glow.
3. the morn-ing breaks, for-ev-er past the fear-ful reign of an-cient night.
4. good will to all, and peace on earth reign on through-out the gold-en years!

Isa. 9:2

This tune in a higher key: 413

On Jordan's Bank the Baptist's Cry   187

Jordanis oras praevia, by Charles Coffin, 1736;
tr. composite, based on J. Chandler, 1837

WINCHESTER NEW, LM

Later form (1847) of melody in
Musicalisches Handbuch (Hamburg, 1690)

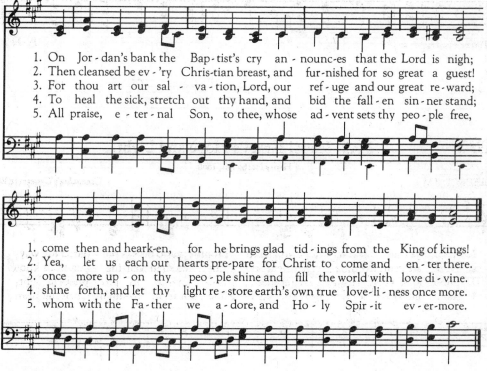

1. On Jor-dan's bank the Bap-tist's cry an-nounc-es that the Lord is nigh;
2. Then cleansed be ev-'ry Chris-tian breast, and fur-nished for so great a guest!
3. For thou art our sal-va-tion, Lord, our ref-uge and our great re-ward;
4. To heal the sick, stretch out thy hand, and bid the fall-en sin-ner stand;
5. All praise, e-ter-nal Son, to thee, whose ad-vent sets thy peo-ple free,

1. come then and heark-en, for he brings glad tid-ings from the King of kings!
2. Yea, let us each our hearts pre-pare for Christ to come and en-ter there.
3. once more up-on thy peo-ple shine and fill the world with love di-vine.
4. shine forth, and let thy light re-store earth's own true love-li-ness once more.
5. whom with the Fa-ther we a-dore, and Ho-ly Spir-it ev-er-more.

Alternative tune: TUGWOOD, 542

This tune in a higher key: 378

Mt. 3:1–3

ADVENT

188 Let All Mortal Flesh Keep Silence

Greek original from the Liturgy of St. James, 4th century;
tr. Gerard Moultrie, 1829–1885

French carol melody, arranged
by R. Vaughan Williams, 1872–1958

PICARDY, 8.7.8.7.8.7

Unsion

1. Let all mor-tal flesh keep si-lence, and with fear and trem-bling stand;
2. King of kings, yet born of Mar-y, as of old on earth he stood,
3. Rank on rank the host of heav-en spreads its van-guard on the way,
4. At his feet the six-winged ser-aph; cher-u-bim, with sleep-less eye,

1. pon-der noth-ing earth-ly - mind-ed, for with bless-ing in his hand,
2. Lord of lords, in hu-man ves-ture, in the bod-y and the blood,
3. as the Light of light de-scend-eth from the realms of end-less day,
4. veil their fac-es to the pres-ence, as with cease-less voice they cry,

1. Christ our Lord to earth de - scend - eth, our full hom-age to de - mand.
2. he will give to all the faith - ful his own self for heaven-ly food.
3. that the powers of hell may van - ish as the dark-ness clears a - way.
4. Al - le - lu - ia! Al - le - lu - ia! Al - le - lu - ia, Lord most high!"

Hab. 2:20

Savior of the Nations, Come

Nun Komm, der Heiden Heiland, Luther's paraphase of
Veni Redemptor, ascribed to Ambrose, 4th century;
tr. based on that of W. M. Reynolds, 1850

NUN KOMM, 77.77

Melody in *Enchiridion* (Erfurt, 1524)

1. Sav - ior of the na-tions, come; vir - gin's son, make here your home.
2. From the Fa - ther forth you came, soon re - turn - ing to the same,
3. You, the Fa-ther's on - ly son, have o'er sin the vic - tory won.
4. Bright-ly does your man - ger shine; glo - rious is its light di - vine.

1. Mar - vel now, O heav'n and earth, that the Lord chose such a birth.
2. cap - tive lead - ing death and hell. Let the song of tri-umph swell!
3. Bound-less shall your king-dom be; when shall we its glo - ries see?
4. Let not sin o'er - cloud this light; ev - er be our faith thus bright.

190 Of the Father's Love Begotten

Aurelius Clemens Prudentius, 348–413;
tr. John Mason Neale, 1854, and Henry W. Baker, 1859

DIVINUM MYSTERIUM, 8.7.8.7.8.7.7

12th-century plainsong (Mode V); arranged
by Charles Winfred Douglas, 1916

1. Of the Fa-ther's love be-got - ten, ere the worlds be-
2. O ye heights of heaven, a-dore him; an-gel hosts, his
3. Christ, to thee with God the Fa - ther, and, O Ho - ly

1. gan to be, he is Al - pha and O - me - ga,
2. prais - es sing; powers, do-min-ions, bow be-fore him,
3. Ghost, to thee, hymn and chant and high thanks-giv - ing

1. he the Source, the End - ing he; of the things that are, that have——been,
2. and ex-tol our God and King; let no tongue on earth be si - lent;
3. and un-wea-ried prais - es be; hon-or, glo-ry, and do-min - ion,

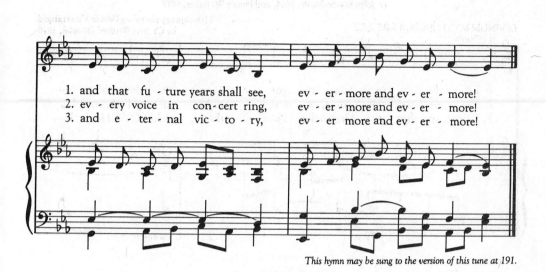

1. and that fu - ture years shall see, ev - er - more and ev - er - more!
2. ev - ery voice in con - cert ring, ev - er - more and ev - er - more!
3. and e - ter - nal vic - to - ry, ev - er more and ev - er - more!

This hymn may be sung to the version of this tune at 191.

191   Of the Father's Heart Begotten

(Christmas version)
Corde natus, by Prudentius, b. 348; tr. R. F. Davis, 1906

DIVINUM MYSTERIUM, 8.7.8.7.8.7.7   *Piae Cantiones* (1582)

Unison

1. Of the Fa-ther's heart be-got-ten, ere the world from cha-os
*2. By his word was all cre-at-ed; he com-mand-ed, and 'twas
*3. He as-sumed this mor-tal bod-y, frail and fee-ble, doomed to
4. O how blest that won-drous birth-day, when the Maid the curse re-

1. rose, He is Al-pha; from that foun-tain all that is and
2. done: earth and sky and bound-less o-cean, u-ni-verse of
3. die, that the race, from dust cre-at-ed might not per-ish
4. trieved, brought to birth the world's sal-va-tion by the Ho-ly

1. hath been flows. He of all things is O-me-ga
2. three in one, all that sees the moon's soft ra-diance,
3. ut-ter-ly, which the an-cient law had sen-tenced
4. Ghost con-ceived; and the Babe, the world's Re-deem-er

1. yet to come the mys-tic close, ev-er-more and ev-er-more....
2. all that breathes be-neath the sun, ev-er-more and ev-er-more....
3. in the depths of hell to lie, ev-er-more and ev-er-more....
4. in her lov-ing arms re-ceived—ev-er-more and ev-er-more....

Note: St. 2–5 may be sung antiphonally; if by women and men, st. 2 and 4 are for the women and 3 and 5 for the men.

NATIVITY   Ps. 33:9; Rev. 1:8

5. This is he, whom seer and sybil
     sang in ages long gone by;
   this is he of old reveal-ed
     in the page of prophecy;
   lo! he comes, the promised Savior;
     let the world his praises cry
     evermore and evermore.

6. Sing, ye heights of heav'n, his praises;
     angels and archangels, sing!
   Wheresoe'er ye be, ye faithful,
     let your joyous anthems ring,
   ev'ry tongue his name confessing,
     countless voices answering,
     evermore and evermore!

Alternative tune: 190

From East to West, from Shore to Shore 192

A solis ortus cardine, by Coelius Sedulius, c. 450;
tr. John Ellerton (version as in *Hymns for Church and School*, 1964)

THIS ENDRIS NYGHT, CM

English carol tune, c. 15th century;
harmonized by R. Vaughan Williams, 1906

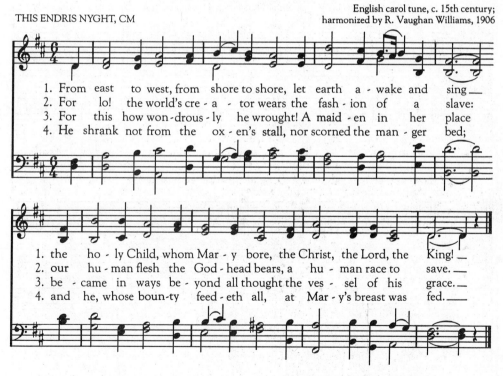

1. From east to west, from shore to shore, let earth a - wake and sing
2. For lo! the world's cre - a - tor wears the fash - ion of a slave:
3. For this how won-drous-ly he wrought! A maid - en in her place
4. He shrank not from the ox - en's stall, nor scorned the man - ger bed;

1. the ho - ly Child, whom Mar - y bore, the Christ, the Lord, the King!
2. our hu - man flesh the God - head bears, a hu - man race to save.
3. be - came in ways be - yond all thought the ves - sel of his grace.
4. and he, whose boun-ty feed - eth all, at Mar - y's breast was fed.

5. To shepherds poor the Lord most high,
     Great Shepherd, was revealed
   While angel choirs sang joyously
     above the midnight field:

6. "All glory be to God above,
     and on the earth be peace
   to all who long to taste his love,
     till time itself shall cease."

Phil. 2:7

193

O Little Town of Bethlehem

Phillips Brooks, 1868
First Tune

FOREST GREEN, CMD Irregular

English folk song, arranged by R. Vaughan Williams, 1906

1. O lit - tle town of Beth - le - hem, how still we see thee lie;
2. For Christ is born of Mar - y, and gath - ered all a - bove,
3. How si - lent - ly, how si - lent - ly the won - drous gift is given!
4. O ho - ly Child of Beth - le - hem, de - scend to us, we pray;

1. a - bove thy deep and dream - less sleep the si - lent stars go by.
2. while mor - tals sleep the an - gels keep their watch of won - d'ring love.
3. So God im - parts to hu - man hearts the bless - ings of his heaven.
4. cast out our sin and en - ter in, be born in us to - day.

1. Yet in thy dark streets shin - eth the ev - er - last - ing light;
2. O morn - ing stars to - geth - er pro - claim the ho - ly Birth;
3. No ear may hear his com - ing, but in this world of sin,
4. We hear the Christ - mas an - gels the great glad tid - ings tell;

1. the hopes and fears of all the years are met in thee to - night.
2. and prais - es sing to God the King, and peace to all on earth.
3. where meek souls will re - ceive him still, the dear Christ en - ters in.
4. O come to us, a - bide with us, our Lord, Im - man - u - el!

This tune in a higher key: 9

O Little Town of Bethlehem

Second Tune

ST. LOUIS, CMD Irregular

Lewis H. Redner, 1868

1. O lit - tle town of Beth - le - hem, how still we see thee lie;
2. For Christ is born of Mar - y, and gath-ered all a - bove,
3. How si - lent-ly, how si - lent-ly the won-drous gift is given!
4. O ho - ly Child of Beth - le - hem, de - scend to us, we pray;

1. a - bove thy deep and dream-less sleep the si - lent stars go by.
2. while mor - tals sleep, the an - gels keep their watch of won - d'ring love.
3. So God im-parts to hu - man hearts the bless-ings of his heaven.
4. cast out our sin and en - ter in, be born in us to - day.

1. Yet in thy dark streets shin - eth the ev - er - last - ing Light;
2. O morn - ing stars, to - geth - er pro - claim the ho - ly birth;
3. No ear may hear his com - ing, but in this world of sin,
4. We hear the Christmas an - gels the great glad tid - ings tell;

1. the hopes and fears of all the years are met in thee to - night.
2. and prais - es sing to God the King, and peace to all on earth.
3. where meek souls will re - ceive him still, the dear Christ en - ters in.
4. O come to us, a - bide with us, our Lord Im - man - u - el!

NATIVITY

195 O Come, All Ye Faithful

Latin, 18th century; tr. Frederick Oakeley, 1841 (alt'd)

J. F. Wade, 1711–1786

ADESTE FIDELES, 6.6.10.5.6 with refrain

St. 1 only

1 O come, all ye faith-ful, joy-ful and tri-um-phant; O
2. Sing, choirs of an-gels, sing in ex-ul-ta-tion;
3. Yea, Lord, we greet thee, born that hap-py morn-ing;

1. come ye, O come ye to Beth-le-hem.
2. sing, all ye cit-i-zens of heav'n a-bove:
3. Je-sus, to thee be all glo-ry giv'n,

Refrain

1. Come and be-hold him born the King of an-gels: O
2. "Glo-ry to God, in the high-est!" O
3. Word of the Fa-ther, now in flesh ap-pear-ing: O

come, let us a-dore him; O come, let us a-dore him; O

come, let us a-dore him, Christ the Lord!

Hark, the Herald Angels Sing

Charles Wesley, 1739 (text of 1753, alt'd)

MENDELSSOHN, 77.77 D with refrain

from a melody by F. Mendelssohn-Bartholdy, 1840;
arranged by W. H. Cummings, 1856

1. Hark, the her-ald an-gels sing, "Glo-ry to the new-born King.
2. Christ, by high-est heav'n a-dored, Christ, the ev-er-last-ing Lord,
3. Hail, the heav'n-born Prince of Peace, hail, the Sun of Righ-teous-ness!

1. Peace on earth and mer-cy mild, God and sin-ners rec-on-ciled."
2. late in time be-hold him come, off-spring of a vir-gin's womb.
3. Light and life to all he brings, ris'n with heal-ing in his wings.

1. Joy-ful all ye na-tions rise, join the tri-umph of the skies,
2. Veiled in flesh, the God-head see; hail, th'in-car-nate De-i-ty;
3. Mild he lays his glo-ry by, born that we no more may die,

1. with th'an-gel-ic host pro-claim, "Christ is born in Beth-le-hem."
2. pleased in flesh with us to dwell, Je-sus, our Im-man-u-el.
3. born to raise us from the earth, born to give us sec-ond birth.

Unison

Hark, the her-ald an-gels sing, "Glo-ry to the new-born King!"

NATIVITY

197

Christians, Awake!

John Byrom, 1749

STOCKPORT, 10 10.10 10.10 10

John Wainwright, 1750

1. Chris - tians, a - wake! Sa - lute the hap - py morn where - on the
2. Then to the watch - ful shep-herds it was told, who heard th' an-
3. He spake, and straight - way the ce - les - tial choir in hymns of
*4. O may we keep and pon - der in our mind God's won - drous
*5. Then may we hope th' an - gel - ic thrones a - mong to sing, re -

1. Sav - ior of the world was born; rise to a - dore the mys - ter - y of
2. gel - ic her - ald's voice: "Be - hold, I bring good tid - ings of a Sav - ior's
3. joy un-known be - fore con - spire; the prais - es of re - deem-ing love they
4. love in sav - ing hu - man - kind. Trace we the Babe, who hath re-trieved our
5. deemed, a glad tri - um - phal song; he that was born up - on that joy - ful

1. love, which hosts of an-gels chant-ed from a - bove; with them the joy - ful
2. birth to you and all the na-tions up - on earth; this day hath God ful -
3. sang, and heav'n's whole orb with al - le - lu - ias rang: God's high-est glo - ry
4. loss, from his poor man-ger to his bit - ter cross; tread in his steps, as -
5. day a - round us all his glo - ry shall dis - play; saved by his love, in -

1. tid - ings first be - gun, of God in - car-nate and the vir - gin's Son.
2. filled his prom - ised word; this day is born a Sav - ior, Christ the Lord."
3. was their an - them still, "Peace up - on earth and un - to all good - will."
4. sist - ed by his grace, till our first heav'n-ly state a - gain takes place.
5. ces - sant we shall sing e - ter - nal praise to heav'n's Al - might - y King.

NOTE: St. 4 and 5 may be used as a doxology throughout Epiphany.

NATIVITY

Lk. 2:8-20

Joy to the World !

198

Isaac Watts, 1719

ANTIOCH, CM

Lowell Mason, 1832

1. Joy to the world! the Lord is come: let earth re - ceive her King;
2. Joy to the world! the Sav - ior reigns: let us our songs em - ploy;
3. No more let sins and sor - rows grow, nor thorns in - fest the ground;
4. He rules the world with truth and grace, and makes the na - tions prove

1. let ev - ery heart pre - pare him room, and heaven and na - ture sing,
2. while fields and floods, rocks, hills, and plains re - peat the sound - ing joy,
3. he comes to make his bless - ings flow far as the curse is found,
4. the glo - ries of his right - teous - ness, and won - ders of his love,

and heaven and na -

1. and heaven and na - ture sing, and heaven, and heaven and na - ture sing.
2. re - peat the sound - ing joy, re - peat, re - peat the sound - ing joy.
3. far as the curse is found, far as, far as the curse is found.
4. and won - ders of his love, and won - ders, won - ders of his love.

ture sing,

and heaven and na - ture sing.

Ps. 98

NATIVITY

199 While Shepherds Watched Their Flocks

Nahum Tate, 1700
First Tune

WINCHESTER OLD, CM

Melody in *Este's Psalter* (1592)

Descant, st. 6, by Alan Gray

6. "All glo-ry be to God on high, and to the earth be peace:

1. While shep-herds watched their flocks by night, all seat-ed on the ground,
2. "Fear not," said he (for might-y dread had seized their trou-bled mind);
3. "To you in Da-vid's town this day is born of Da-vid's line
4. "The heav'n-ly babe you there shall find to hu-man view dis-played,

6. good will to all from high-est heaven be - gin and nev-er cease."

1. the an-gel of the Lord came down, and glo-ry shone a - round.
2. "glad tid-ings of great joy I bring to you and hu-man-kind.
3. a Sav-ior, who is Christ the Lord, and this shall be the sign:
4. all mean-ly wrapped in swath-ing bands, and in a man-ger laid."

5. Thus spake the seraph, and forthwith
appeared a shining throng
of angels praising God, who thus
addressed their joyful song:

6. "All glory be to God on high,
and to the earth be peace:
good will to all from highest heaven
begin and never cease."

NATIVITY

Lk. 2:8–15

While Shepherds Watched Their Flocks

Second Tune

CHRISTMAS, CM

Arranged by Lowell Mason (1821) from
an air in *Siroe*, by G. F. Handel

1. While shep-herds watched their flocks by night, all seat-ed on the
2. "Fear not," said he (for might-y dread had seized their trou-bled
3. "To you in Da-vid's town this day is born of Da-vid's
4. "The heaven-ly babe you there shall find to hu-man view dis-

1. ground, the an-gel of the Lord came down, and
2. mind); "glad tid-ings of great joy I bring to
3. line the Sav-ior, who is Christ the Lord, and
4. played, all mean-ly wrapped in swath-ing bands, and

1. glo-ry shone a-round, and glo-ry shone a-round.
2. you and hu-man-kind, to you and hu-man-kind.
3. this shall be the sign: and this shall be the sign:
4. in a man-ger laid, and in a man-ger laid."

5. Thus spake the seraph, and forthwith
   appeared a shining throng
   of angels praising God, who thus
   addressed their joyful song:
   addressed their joyful song:

6. "All glory be to God on high,
   and to the earth be peace:
   good will to all from highest heaven
   begin and never cease!
   Begin and never cease!"

NATIVITY

201

Once in Royal David's City

Cecil Frances Alexander, 1848

H. J. Gauntlett, 1858;
harmony by A. H. Mann, 1919

IRBY, 8.7.8.7.77

1. Once in roy-al Da-vid's cit-y stood a low-ly cat-tle shed
2. He came down to earth from heav-en, who is God and Lord of all,
3. Je-sus is our child-hood's pat-tern: day by day like us he grew;
4. And our eyes at last shall see him, through his own re-deem-ing love,
*5. Not in that poor low-ly sta-ble with the ox-en stand-ing by

1. where a moth-er laid her ba-by in a man-ger for his bed.
2. and his shel-ter was a sta-ble, and his cra-dle was a stall;
3. he was lit-tle, weak, and help-less; tears and smiles like us he knew;
4. for that Child, so dear and gen-tle, is our Lord in heav'n a-bove,
5. we shall see him, but in heav-en, set at God's right hand on high,

1. Mar-y was that moth-er mild, Je-sus Christ her lit-tle child.
2. with the poor and mean and low-ly lived on earth our Sav-ior ho-ly.
3. and he feel-eth for our sad-ness, and he shar-eth in our glad-ness.
4. and he leads his chil-dren on to the place where he is gone.
5. where, like stars, his chil-dren crowned, all in white shall wait a-round.

NATIVITY

Lk. 2:3–7

All My Heart This Night Rejoices

Fröhlich soll, by Paulus Gerhardt, 1653;
tr. Catherine Winkworth, 1863

BONN (FRÖHLICH SOLL), 8.33.6 D

Melody by J. G. Ebeling, 1666

1. All my heart this night re-joic-es as I hear, far and near,
2. Hark, a voice from yon-der man-ger; soft and sweet doth en-treat,
3. Come, then, let us has-ten yon-der; here let all, great and small,
*4. Bless-ed Sav-ior, let me find thee! Keep thou me close to thee;
*5. Thee, O Lord, with care I'll cher-ish; live to thee, and with thee

1. sweet-est an-gel voic-es: "Christ is born," their choirs are sing-ing,
2. "Flee from woe and dan-ger; peo-ple come: from all doth grieve you,
3. kneel in awe and won-der. Love him who with love is yearn-ing,
4. cast me not be-hind thee! Life of life, my heart thou still-est;
5. dy-ing, shall not per-ish; but shall dwell with thee for-ev-er,

1. till the air ev-'ry-where now with joy is ring-ing.
2. you are freed; all you need I will sure-ly give you."
3. hail the star that from far bright with hope is burn-ing.
4. calm I rest on thy breast: all this void thou fill-est.
5. far on high in the joy that can al-ter nev-er.

NOTE: *The last two stanzas of this hymn can be detached and used on other occasions.*

Mt. 1:21

NATIVITY

203 What Adam's Disobedience Cost

Fred Pratt Green, 1978

Melody and bass by Jeremiah Clarke, 1707;
arranged by John Wilson, 1978

HERMON, 8.6.8.6.6

1. What Ad-am's dis-o-be-dience cost, let Ho-ly
2. An Ark of mer-cy rode the flood, but we, where
3. A lit-tle Child is Ad-am's heir, is Ad-am's
4. Re-gained is Ad-am's bless-ed-ness: the an-gels

1. Scrip-ture say: our-selves es-tranged, an E-den lost,
2. wa-ters swirled, re-built, im-pa-tient of the good,
3. hope and Lord, Sing joy-ful car-ols ev-'ry-where,
4. sheathe their swords; in joy-ful car-ols all con-fess

st. 1,2,3   st. 4

1. and then a judg-ment day: each day a judg-ment day.
2. an-oth-er fall-en world: an un-re-pen-tant world.
3. that E-den is re-stored: in Je-sus is re-stored.
4. the King-dom is the Lord's: the glo-ry is the Lord's!

NOTE: *A choral setting of this can be found in* Sixteen Hymns of Today for Use as Simple Anthems, *ed. John Wilson (Addington Press, 1978).*

NATIVITY

Gen. 3:7–9; Gen. 3:23; Rom. 5:19

Lo, How a Rose E'er Blooming

204

Es ist ein' Ros' entsprungen, German carol, c. 15th century;
st. 1-2 tr. Theodore Baker, 1894; st. 3 tr. *The Hymnal—1940*

ES IST EIN' ROS', 7.6.7.6.6.7.6   Traditional melody, harmonized by M. Praetorius, 1609

1. Lo, how a rose e'er bloom-ing from ten-der stem hath sprung, of
2. I - sa-iah 'twas fore-told it, the rose I have in mind; with
3. O flow'r whose fra-grance ten-der with sweet-ness fills the air, dis-

1. Jes-se's lin-eage com-ing by faith-ful proph-ets sung; it came a flow'ret
2. Mar-y we be-hold it, the vir-gin moth-er kind. To show God's love a-
3. pel in glo-rious splen-dor our dark-ness ev-'ry-where. Hu-man, yet ver-y

1. bright, a - mid the cold of win-ter when half spent was the night.
2. right she bore for us a Sav-ior when half spent was the night.
3. God, from sin and death now save us and share our ev-'ry load.

NOTE: *If this song is performed by the choir alone, F or G would be a better key.*

Isa. 11:1; Isa. 35:1   NATIVITY

205

A Stable Lamp Is Lighted

Richard Wilbur, 1961

Traditional melody; harmonized
by M. Praetorius, 1609

ES IST EIN' ROS', 7.6.7.6.6.7.6

1. A sta - ble lamp is light - ed whose glow shall wake the sky; the stars shall
2. This child through Da - vid's cit - y shall ride in tri - umph by; the palm shall
3. Yet he shall be for - sak - en and yield - ed up to die; the sky shall
4. But now as at the end - ing the low is lift - ed high: the stars shall

1. bend their voic - es, and ev - ery stone shall cry, and straw like gold shall shine;
2. strew its branch - es, and ev - ery stone shall cry though hea - vy, cold and dumb,
3. groan and dark - en, and ev - ery stone shall cry for ston - y hearts he's slain;
4. bend their voic - es, and ev - ery stone shall cry in prais - es of the Child

1. a barn shall har - bor heav - en, a stall be - come a shrine.
2. and lie with - in the road - way to pave God's king - dom come.
3. God's blood up - on the spear - head, God's blood re - fused a - gain.
4. by whose de - scent a - mong us the worlds are rec - on - ciled.

NATIVITY

Lk. 2:7; Lk. 20:40; Lk. 19:36–40; Mk. 15:33–39

Angels We Have Heard on High

Anon., 19th century

GLORIA, 7.7.7.7 with refrain

French carol melody; arranged by Edward Shippen Barnes, 1937

1. An - gels we have heard on high,   sing - ing sweet - ly through the night,
2. Shep-herds,why this ju - bi - lee?   Why these songs of hap - py cheer?
3. Come to Beth - le - hem and see   him whose birth the an - gels sing;
4. See him in a man-ger laid   whom the an - gels praise a - bove;

1. and the moun - tains, in re - ply,   ech - o - ing their brave de - light.
2. What great bright - ness did you see?   What glad tid - ings did you hear?
3. come, a - dore, on bend - ed knee,   Christ, the Lord, the new - born King.
4. Mar - y, Jos - eph, lend your aid,   while we raise our hearts in love.

Refrain

Glo - - - - - - ri - a

in ex - cel - sis De - o, Glo - - - - - - ri - a in ex - cel - sis De - o.

Lk. 2:15

NATIVITY

207 From Heaven High I Come to Earth

Vom Himmel hoch, by Martin Luther, 1541;
tr. Roland H. Bainton, 1948

Melody by Martin Luther;
second version from J. S. Bach's *Christmas Oratorio*

VOM HIMMEL HOCH, LM

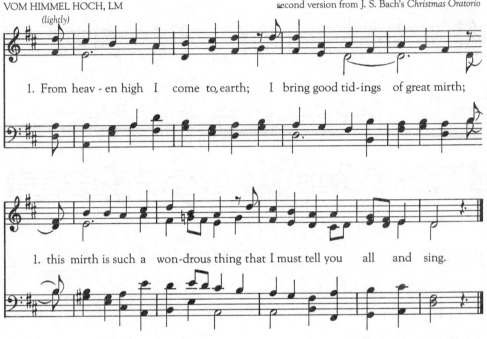

1. From heav-en high I come to earth; I bring good tid-ings of great mirth;

1. this mirth is such a won-drous thing that I must tell you all and sing.

2. A little child for you this morn
has from a chosen maid been born,
a little child so tender, sweet,
that you should skip upon your feet.

3. How glad we'll be that this is so!
With all the shepherds let us go
to see what God for us has done
in sending us his own dear Son.

4. Look, look, my heart, and let me peek.
Whom in the manger do you seek?
Who is that lovely little one?
The baby Jesus, God's own Son.

5. Be welcome, Lord; be now our guest.
By you poor sinners have been blessed.
In nakedness and cold you lie.
How can I thank you; how can I?

6. You wanted so to make me know
that you had let all great things go.
You had a palace in the sky;
you left it there for such as I.

7. And if the world were twice as wide,
with gold and precious jewels inside,
still such a cradle would not do
to hold a babe as great as you.

NOTE: *The carol should begin with a solo voice, preferably that of a child; as it passes through st. 2–6 more voices should gradually be added, and then everybody present should join in the last stanza as set on the next page, fortissimo.*

8. To God who sent his on-ly Son be glo-ry, laud, and hon-or done.

8. Let all the choir of heav'n re-joice, the new ring in with heart and voice.

Lk. 2:10

Shepherds Came, Their Praises Bringing 208

Quem Pastores laudavere, German carol, 14th century;
tr. G. B. Caird, 1951

QUEM PASTORES, 88.8.7   Traditional melody; harmonized by R. Vaughan Williams, 1906

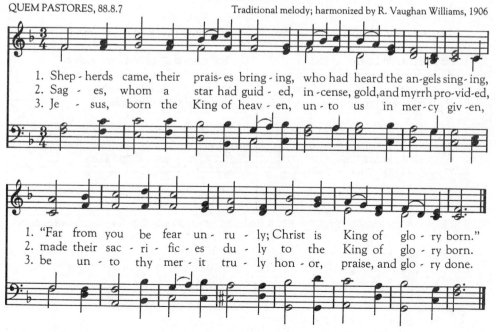

1. Shep-herds came, their prais-es bring-ing, who had heard the an-gels sing-ing,
2. Sag - es, whom a star had guid - ed, in-cense, gold, and myrrh pro-vid-ed,
3. Je - sus, born the King of heav - en, un-to us in mer-cy giv-en,

1. "Far from you be fear un - ru - ly; Christ is King of glo - ry born."
2. made their sac - ri - fic - es du - ly to the King of glo - ry born.
3. be un - to thy mer - it tru - ly hon - or, praise, and glo - ry done.

Lk. 2:8ff; Mt. 2:11

God Rest You Merry, Gentlemen †

English carol, 18th century

Traditional melody; harmonized in Bramley & Stainer,
Christmas Carols Old and New (1871)

GOD REST YOU MERRY, Irregular, with refrain

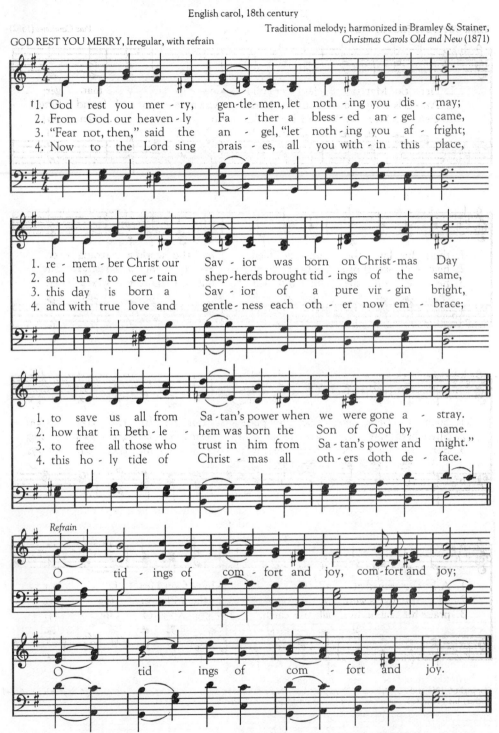

†1. God rest you mer - ry, gen - tle- men, let noth - ing you dis - may;
2. From God our heaven - ly Fa - ther a bless - ed an - gel came,
3. "Fear not, then," said the an - gel, "let noth - ing you af - fright;
4. Now to the Lord sing prais - es, all you with - in this place,

1. re - mem - ber Christ our Sav - ior was born on Christ -mas Day
2. and un - to cer - tain shep-herds brought tid - ings of the same,
3. this day is born a Sav - ior of a pure vir - gin bright,
4. and with true love and gentle-ness each oth - er now em - brace;

1. to save us all from Sa - tan's power when we were gone a - stray.
2. how that in Beth - le - hem was born the Son of God by name.
3. to free all those who trust in him from Sa - tan's power and might."
4. this ho - ly tide of Christ - mas all oth - ers doth de - face.

Refrain

O tid - ings of com - fort and joy, com-fort and joy;

O tid - ings of com - fort and joy.

NOTE: *No attempt has been made to alter the traditional language of this sociable song. Those who wish to avoid "gentlemen"
in the opening line may sing "Christians all."*

NATIVITY

Lk. 2:9–10

Gentle Mary Laid Her Child

Joseph Simpson Cook, 1919

TEMPUS ADEST FLORIDUM, 7.6.7.6 D trochaic

Piae Cantiones (1582)

1. Gen - tle Mar - y laid her child low - ly in a man - ger;
2. An - gels sang a - bout his birth; wise men sought and found him;
3. Gen - tle Mar - y laid her child low - ly in a man - ger;

1. there he lay, the un - de - filed, to the world a strang - er.
2. heav - en's star shone bright - ly forth, glo - ry all a - round him.
3. he is still the un - de - filed, but no more a strang - er.

1. Such a Babe in such a place — can he be the Sav - ior?
2. Shep - herds saw the won - drous sight, heard the an - gels sing - ing;
3. Son of God, of hum - ble birth, beau - ti - ful the sto - ry;

1. Ask the saved of all the race, who have found his fa - vor.
2. all the plains were lit that night, all the hills were ring - ing.
3. praise his name in all the earth, hail the King of Glo - ry!

Lk. 2:7–8

NATIVITY

211

Sheep Fast Asleep

Genzō Miwa, 1907; tr. John Moss, 1957 (alt'd)

KŌRIN, 87.8.7.87.8.6

Chûgorò Torii, 1941

1. Sheep fast a-sleep, there on a hill; grass for their bed, all is still.
2. Star in the sky, shin-ing so bright, si-lent and pure, won-drous light!
3. Glo-ry to God! Praise him on high! Sing ye "No-el!" Day is nigh!

1. Cold win-ter night, the frost ap-pears; shep-herds keep watch by their fire.
2. What tid-ings brings it Is-ra-el? Can we new hope in it find?
3. All ye who dwell on earth be-low, peace be to you, and good will.

1. Soft there a sound, far, far a-way; is it the stream? winds at play?
2. Good news it brings! "Fear not, I pray! Born is God's son, born to-day!
3. Come, let us go to Beth-le-hem; fol-low the star, seek-ing him.

1. Nay, friend, it is the heav'n-ly choir, sing-ing through-out the spheres.
2. God's gift of love to all the earth, our Lord, Im-man-u-el."
3: let us a-dore and wor-ship still, in love and joy to grow.

NATIVITY

Lk. 2:8–14; Mt. 2:10–11

On This Day Earth Shall Ring

Piae Cantiones (1582); tr. Jane M. Joseph, c. 1894–1929

PERSONENT HODIE, 666.66 with refrain   *Piae Cantiones* (1582); arranged by Gustav Holst, 1925

Unison

1. On this day earth shall ring with the song
2. His the doom, ours the mirth when he came
3. God's bright star o'er his head, wise men three
4. On this day an-gels sing, with their song

1. chil-dren sing to the Lord Christ our King, born on earth to
2. down to earth, Beth-le-hem saw his birth; ox and ass be-
3. to him led, kneel-ing low by his bed, lay their gifts be-
4. earth shall ring, prais-ing Christ, heav-en's King, born on earth to

1. save us, him the Fa-ther gave us:
2. side him from the cold would hide him:
3. fore him, praise him and a-dore him:
4. save us, peace and love he gave us:

*I - de - o -

org.

o - o. I-de-o - o - o, I-de-o glo-ri-a in ex-cel-sis De-o!

The word ideo (pronounced ee-day-o) is Latin for therefore.

Mt. 2:11   NATIVITY

213

Away in a Manger

Anon., Philadelphia, 1885; st. 3, 1892
First Tune

MUELLER, 11 11.11 11

Anon., Philadelphia, 1887

1. A - way in a man - ger, no crib for his bed, the lit - tle Lord
2. The cat - tle are low - ing, the poor Ba - by wakes, but lit - tle Lord
3. Be near me, Lord Je - sus; I ask thee to stay close by me for -

1. Je - sus laid down his sweet head. The stars in the sky looked
2. Je - sus, no cry - ing he makes. I love thee, Lord Je - sus; look
3. ev - er and love me, I pray. Bless all the dear chil - dren in

1. down where he lay, the lit - tle Lord Je - sus, a - sleep on the hay.
2. down from the sky, and stay by my side un - til morn - ing is nigh.
3. thy ten - der care, and fit us for heav - en to live with thee there.

Lk. 2:7

214

Away in a Manger

Second Tune

AWAY IN A MANGER

W. J. Kirkpatrick, 1895

Unison

1. A - way in a man - ger, no crib for his bed, the lit - tle Lord
2. The cat - tle are low - ing, the poor Ba - by wakes, but lit - tle Lord
3. Be near me, Lord Je - sus; I ask thee to stay close by me for -

NATIVITY

1. Je - sus laid down his sweet head. The stars in the sky looked
2. Je - sus, no cry - ing he makes. I love thee, Lord Je - sus; look
3. ev - er and love me, I pray. Bless all the dear chil - dren in

1. down where he lay, the lit - tle Lord Je - sus, a - sleep on the hay.
2. down from the sky, and stay by my side un - til morn - ing is nigh.
3. thy ten - der care, and fit us for heav - en to live with thee there.

Child in the Manger  215

Leanabh an aigh, Gaelic song by Mary Macdonald of Mull,
19th century; tr. Lachlan McBean, 1888

BUNESSAN, 5.5.5.3 D   Hebridean melody from the Isle of Mull

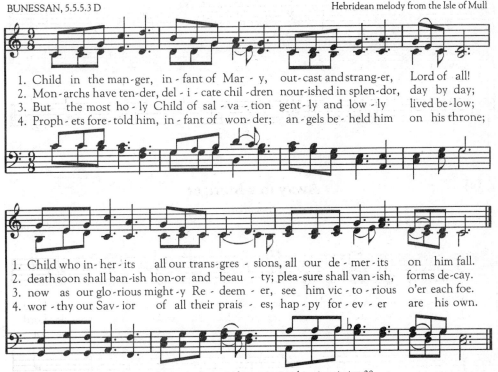

1. Child in the man - ger, in - fant of Mar - y, out - cast and strang - er, Lord of all!
2. Mon - archs have ten - der, del - i - cate chil - dren nour - ished in splen - dor, day by day;
3. But the most ho - ly Child of sal - va - tion gent - ly and low - ly lived be - low;
4. Proph - ets fore - told him, in - fant of won - der; an - gels be - held him on his throne;

1. Child who in - her - its all our trans - gres - sions, all our de - mer - its on him fall.
2. death soon shall ban - ish hon - or and beau - ty; plea - sure shall van - ish, forms de - cay.
3. now as our glo - rious might - y Re - deem - er, see him vic - to - rious o'er each foe.
4. wor - thy our Sav - ior of all their prais - es; hap - py for - ev - er are his own.

NOTE: This is the original association of the tune; alternative harmonization, for unison singing: 20.

216 Silent Night!

Stille Nacht, by Joseph Mohr, 1818; tr. anon., c. 1850

SILENT NIGHT (*Stille Nacht*), Irregular

F. Gruber, 1818

1. Si - lent night! ho - ly night! All is calm, all is bright, round yon
2. Si - lent night! ho - ly night! Shep-herds quake at the sight, glo - ries
3. Si - lent night! ho - ly night! Son of God, love's pure light ra - diant
4. Si - lent night! ho - ly night! Won-drous star, lend thy light; with the

1. vir - gin moth-er and child! Ho - ly In-fant, so ten-der and mild,
2. stream from heav-en a - far, heaven-ly hosts sing: "Al - le - lu - ia;
3. beams from thy ho-ly face, with the dawn of re - deem - ing grace.
4. an - gels let us sing, Al - le - lu - ia to our King;

1. sleep in heav - en - ly peace, sleep in heav - en - ly peace.
2. Christ the Sav - ior is born, Christ the Sav - ior is born."
3. Je - sus, Lord, at thy birth, Je - sus, Lord, at thy birth.
4. Christ the Sav - ior is born, Christ the Sav - ior is born.

What Child Is This?

William Chatterton Dix, 1871

GREENSLEEVES, 8.7.8.7 with refrain

English melody, c. 16th century

1. What Child is this, who, laid to rest, on Mar-y's lap is sleep-ing?
2. Why lies he in such mean es-tate where ox and ass are feed-ing?
3. So bring him in-cense,gold, and myrrh, come, peas-ant, king, to own him;

1. Whom an-gels greet with an-thems sweet, while shep-herds watch are keep-ing?
2. Good Chris-tian, fear: for sin-ners here the si-lent word is plead-ing.
3. the King of kings sal-va-tion brings, let lov-ing hearts en-throne him.

Refrain

This, this is Christ the King, whom shep-herds guard and an-gels sing:

haste, haste to bring him laud, the babe, the son of Mar-y.

NOTE: *This tune can be performed in the original mode by sharping all Cs in the treble and alto parts (but those in the bass in measures 3 and 11 should be unaltered).*

218

Good Christian Friends, Rejoice

In dulci Jubilo, medieval carol; paraphrased by J. M. Neale, 1853 (alt'd)

Medieval melody, arranged in *Christmas Carols, Old and New* (1871);

IN DULCI JUBILO, 66.77.78.55

restored to original form, 1953

1. Good Chris - tian friends, re - joice with heart, and soul, and voice;
2. Good Chris - tian friends, re - joice with heart, and soul, and voice;
3. Good Chris - tian friends, re - joice with heart, and soul, and voice;

1. give ye heed to what we say: Je - sus Christ is born to - day;
2. now ye hear of end - less bliss: Je - sus Christ was born for this!
3. now ye need not fear the grave: Je - sus Christ was born to save!

1. ox and ass be - fore him bow, and he is in the man - ger now.
2. He has oped the heaven - ly door, and we are bless - ed ev - er - more.
3. Calls you one and calls you all, to gain his ev - er - last - ing hall.

1. Christ is born to - day! Christ is born to - day!
2. Christ was born for this! Christ was born for this!
3. Christ was born to save! Christ was born to save!

NATIVITY

Mt. 2:1–11

See in Yonder Manger Low

Edward Caswall, 1858

HUMILITY, 77.77 D

John Goss, 1871

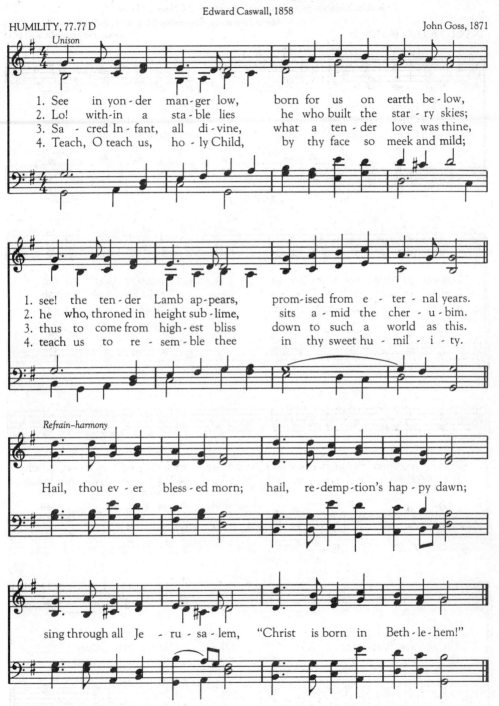

1. See in yon-der man-ger low, born for us on earth be-low,
2. Lo! with-in a sta-ble lies he who built the star-ry skies;
3. Sa-cred In-fant, all di-vine, what a ten-der love was thine,
4. Teach, O teach us, ho-ly Child, by thy face so meek and mild;

1. see! the ten-der Lamb ap-pears, prom-ised from e-ter-nal years.
2. he who, throned in height sub-lime, sits a-mid the cher-u-bim.
3. thus to come from high-est bliss down to such a world as this.
4. teach us to re-sem-ble thee in thy sweet hu-mil-i-ty.

Hail, thou ev-er bless-ed morn; hail, re-demp-tion's hap-py dawn;

sing through all Je-ru-sa-lem, "Christ is born in Beth-le-hem!"

Jn. 1:1–3

NATIVITY

220 Welcome, Child of Mary

English version from the Dutch; st. 4 added by Elizabeth Poston

NU ZIJT WELLECOME, Irregular

Theodotus's *Paradys der Gheestelycke en Kerckelycke Lofsangen* (1627); harmonized by Adriaan Engels

1. Wel - come, Child of Mar - y, com - ing from a - far,
2. Shep - herds on the hill - side saw the heav - enly light
3. There to pay their trib - ute, come three east - ern kings;
4. Ky - ri - e e - lei - son, Christ - mas Babe, we sing;

1. on earth with us to so - journ be - neath thy star.
2. and heard the an - gels' song. "He is born this night;
3. sweet gifts of gold and spic - es now each one brings;
4. with Ky - ri - e e - lei - son we greet our King.

1. From the heav - ens' glo - ry thou in grace dost now de - scend,
2. fear not," was their mes - sage; "now to Da - vid's cit - y go;
3. kneel - ing, they a - dore him, as their earth - ly crowns they bow,
4. Pray we to the ho - ly In - fant: he will bless our way;

1. know - ing all our sto - ry and come to be our friend: Ky - rie e - leis.
2. seek God in a man - ger, as yon - der star will show." Ky - rie e - leis.
3. maj - es - ty sa - lut - ing be - fore a man - ger low: Ky - rie e - leis.
4. Ky - ri - e e - lei - son in all the world we say: Ky - rie e - leis.

NATIVITY

Infant Holy

W żłobie leży, Polish carol;
paraphrased by Edith M. G. Reed, c. 1925

INFANT HOLY, 44.7.44.7.4444.7

Traditional Polish tune; harmonized by David Hugh Jones, 1953

1. In - fant ho - ly, in - fant low - ly, for his bed a cat - tle stall;
2. Flocks were sleep - ing; shep - herds keep - ing vig - il till the morn - ing new

1. ox - en low - ing, lit - tle know - ing Christ the babe is Lord of all.
2. saw the glo - ry, heard the sto - ry, tid - ings of a gos - pel true.

1. Swift are wing - ing an - gels sing - ing, no - els ring - ing,
2. Thus re - joic - ing, free from sor - row, prais - es voic - ing,

1. tid - ings bring - ing: Christ the babe is Lord of all.
2. greet the mor - row: Christ the babe was born for you.

Lk. 2:8

NATIVITY

222

To Us in Bethlem City

Percy Dearmer; based on a carol in *Cölner Psalter* (1638)

BETHLEM CITY, 7.6.7.6.4.6

Melody in *Cölner Psalter* (1638)

1. To us in Beth-lem cit - y was born a lit - tle Son;
2. And all our love and for - tune lie in his might-y hands;
3. O Shep-herd, ev - er near us, we'll go where thou dost lead;
4. No grief shall part us from thee, how - ev - er sharp the edge;

1. in him all gen-tle grac - es were gath-ered in - to one:
2. our sor-rows, joys, and fail - ures he sees and un-der - stands:
3. no mat - ter where the pas - ture, with thee at hand to feed:
4. we'll serve and do thy bid - ding — O take our hearts in pledge!

1. *Ei - a: ei - a; were gath-ered in - to one.
2. Ei - a: ei - a; he sees and un - der - stands.
3. Ei - a: ei - a; with thee at hand to feed.
4. Ei - a: ei - a; O take our hearts in pledge!

*Eia, eia (pronounced ay-ah, ay-ah) is the original version; "O joy: glad joy!" can also be sung here.

Lk. 2; Ps. 23:1–3

The First Nowell*

English traditional carol

THE FIRST NOWELL,
Irregular with refrain

Traditional melody;
harmonized in Bramley and Stainer, *Christmas Carols Old and New* (1871)

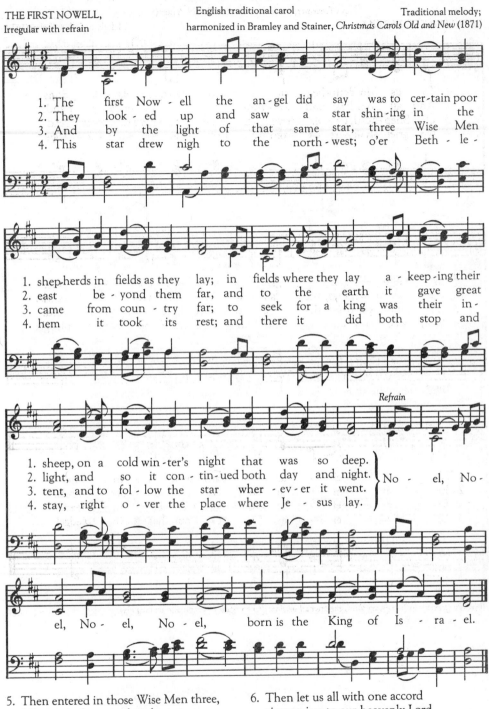

1. The first Now-ell the an-gel did say was to cer-tain poor
2. They look-ed up and saw a star shin-ing in the
3. And by the light of that same star, three Wise Men
4. This star drew nigh to the north-west; o'er Beth-le-

1. shep-herds in fields as they lay; in fields where they lay a-keep-ing their
2. east be-yond them far, and to the earth it gave great
3. came from coun-try far; to seek for a king was their in-
4. hem it took its rest; and there it did both stop and

Refrain

1. sheep, on a cold win-ter's night that was so deep.
2. light, and so it con-tin-ued both day and night. } No-el, No-
3. tent, and to fol-low the star wher-ev-er it went.
4. stay, right o-ver the place where Je-sus lay.

el, No-el, No-el, born is the King of Is-ra-el.

5. Then entered in those Wise Men three,
   fell reverently upon their knee,
   and offered there in his presence,
   their gold, and myrrh, and frankincense.

6. Then let us all with one accord
   sing praises to our heavenly Lord,
   that hath made heaven and earth of nought,
   and with his blood our life hath bought.

NOTE: In this carol, Nowell (Latin novellae) means news, and Noel (Latin natalis) means birthday.

Mt. 2:1–11

NATIVITY

Go, Tell It on the Mountain

Anon. American folk hymn, 19th century

GO TELL IT ON THE MOUNTAIN, Irregular

American folk tune

Refrain

Go, tell it on the moun - tain o - ver the hills and ev - ery - where;

go, tell it on the moun - tain that Je - sus Christ is born!

1. While shep - herds kept their watch - ing o'er si - lent flocks by night,
2. The shep - herds feared and trem - bled when lo! a - bove the earth
3. Down in a low - ly man - ger the hum - ble Christ was born,

1. be - hold through - out the heav - ens there shone a ho - ly light.
2. rang out the an - gel cho - rus that hailed our Sav - ior's birth.
3. and God sent us sal - va - tion that bless - ed Christ - mas morn.

NATIVITY

We Three Kings of Orient Are

Words and music by John H. Hopkins, 1857 (alt'd)

KINGS OF ORIENT, 88.8.6 with refrain

1. We three kings of O-ri-ent are; bear-ing gifts, we trav-erse a-far
2. Born a King on Beth-le-hem's plain, gold I bring to crown him a-gain,
3. Frank-in-cense to of-fer have I; in-cense owns a De-i-ty nigh;
4. Myrrh is mine: its bit-ter per-fume breathes a life of gath-er-ing gloom;
5. Glo-rious now be-hold him a-rise, King and God and Sac-ri-fice;

1. field and foun-tain, moor and moun-tain, fol-low-ing yon-der star.
2. King for-ev-er, ceas-ing nev-er o-ver us all to reign.
3. prayer and prais-ing, voic-es rais-ing, wor-ship him, God on high.
4. sor-rowing, sigh-ing, bleed-ing, dy-ing, sealed in the stone-cold tomb.
5. Al-le-lu-ia, Al-le-lu-ia! Peals through the earth and skies.

Refrain *a tempo*

O star of won-der, star of night, star with roy-al beau-ty bright,

west-ward lead-ing, still pro-ceed-ing, guide us to thy per-fect light.

Mt. 2:1–11

NATIVITY

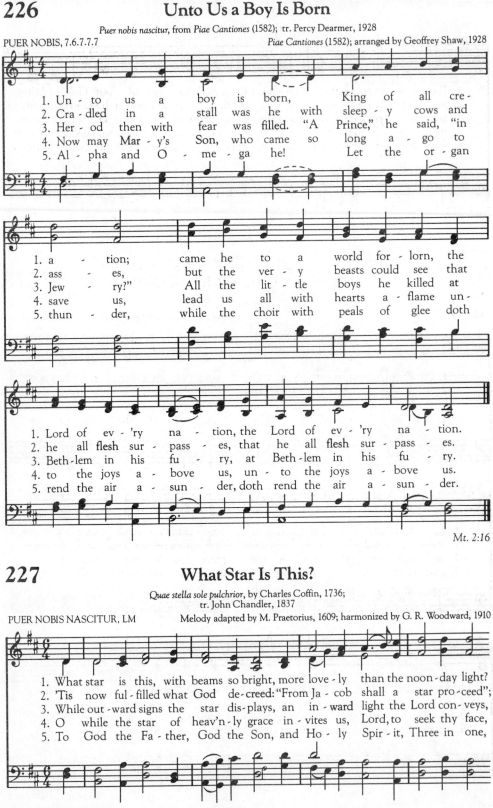

226

Unto Us a Boy Is Born

Puer nobis nascitur, from Piae Cantiones (1582); tr. Percy Dearmer, 1928

PUER NOBIS, 7.6.7.7.7   *Piae Cantiones* (1582); arranged by Geoffrey Shaw, 1928

1. Un - to us a boy is born, King of all cre -
a - tion; came he to a world for - lorn, the
Lord of ev - 'ry na - tion, the Lord of ev - 'ry na - tion.

2. Cra - dled in a stall was he with sleep - y cows and
ass - es, but the ver - y beasts could see that
he all flesh sur - pass - es, that he all flesh sur - pass - es.

3. Her - od then with fear was filled. "A Prince," he said, "in
Jew - ry?" All the lit - tle boys he killed at
Beth - lem in his fu - ry, at Beth - lem in his fu - ry.

4. Now may Mar - y's Son, who came so long a - go to
save us, lead us all with hearts a - flame un -
to the joys a - bove us, un - to the joys a - bove us.

5. Al - pha and O - me - ga he! Let the or - gan
thun - der, while the choir with peals of glee doth
rend the air a - sun - der, doth rend the air a - sun - der.

Mt. 2:16

227

What Star Is This?

Quae stella sole pulchrior, by Charles Coffin, 1736;
tr. John Chandler, 1837

PUER NOBIS NASCITUR, LM   Melody adapted by M. Praetorius, 1609; harmonized by G. R. Woodward, 1910

1. What star is this, with beams so bright, more love - ly than the noon - day light?
2. 'Tis now ful - filled what God de - creed: "From Ja - cob shall a star pro - ceed";
3. While out - ward signs the star dis - plays, an in - ward light the Lord con - veys,
4. O while the star of heav'n - ly grace in - vites us, Lord, to seek thy face,
5. To God the Fa - ther, God the Son, and Ho - ly Spir - it, Three in one,

EPIPHANY AND YOUTH

1. 'Tis sent to an-nounce a new-born King, glad tid-ings of our God to bring.
2. and lo! the east-ern sag-es stand, to read in heav'n the Lord's com-mand.
3. and urg-es them, with force be-nign, to seek the Giv-er of the sign.
4. may we no more that grace re-pel, or quench that light which shines so well.
5. may ev-'ry tongue and na-tion raise an end-less song of thank-ful praise.

Num. 24:17

As with Gladness Men of Old

228

W. Chatterton Dix, 1860

DIX, 77.77.77

Adapted (1861) from a chorale by Conrad Kocher, 1838

1. As with glad-ness men of old did the guid-ing star be-hold;
2. As with joy-ful steps they sped to that low-ly man-ger bed,
3. As they of-fered gifts most rare at that man-ger rude and bare;
4. Ho-ly Je-sus, ev-ery day keep us in the nar-row way;

1. as with joy they hailed its light, lead-ing on-ward, beam-ing bright;
2. there to bend the knee be-fore him whom heaven and earth a-dore;
3. so may we with ho-ly joy, pure, and free from sin's al-loy,
4. and, when earth-ly things are past, bring our ran-somed souls at last

1. so, most gra-cious Lord, may we ev-er-more be led to thee.
2. so may we with will-ing feet ev-er seek thy mer-cy seat.
3. all our cost-liest trea-sures bring, Christ, to thee, our heaven-ly King.
4. where they need no star to guide, where no clouds thy glo-ry hide.

This tune in a lower key: 5

Mt. 2:1–11

EPIPHANY AND YOUTH

229 Angels, from the Realms of Glory

James Montgomery, 1816, 1825

REGENT SQUARE, 8.7.8.7.8.7

Henry Smart, 1867

1. An - gels, from the realms of glo - ry, wing your flight o'er all the earth;
2. Shep-herds, in the fields a - bid - ing, watch-ing o'er your flocks by night,
3. Sag - es, leave your con - tem-pla-tions, bright-er vi - sions beam a - far;
4. Saints, be - fore the al - tar bend-ing, watch-ing long in hope and fear,

1. ye who sang cre - a - tion's sto - ry now pro-claim Mes - si - ah's birth:
2. God with us is now re - sid - ing, yon-der shines the in - fant Light:
3. seek the great De - sire of Na - tions; ye have seen his na - tal star:
4. sud - den - ly the Lord, de-scend-ing, in his tem - ple shall ap- pear:

1. come and wor - ship, come and wor - ship, wor-ship Christ, the new-born King!
2. come and wor - ship, come and wor - ship, wor-ship Christ, the new-born King!
3. come and wor - ship, come and wor - ship, wor-ship Christ, the new-born King!
4. come and wor - ship, come and wor - ship, wor-ship Christ, the new-born King!

EPIPHANY AND YOUTH

Lk. 2:15ff; Mt. 2:1ff

Brightest and Best
of the Sons of the Morning

Reginald Heber, 1793–1826

230

MORNING STAR, 11.10.11.10 dactylic

J. P. Harding, 1892

1. Bright - est and best of the Sons of the Morn - ing,
2. Cold on his cra - dle the dew - drops are shin - ing;
3. Shall we not yield him in cost - ly de - vo - tion,
4. Vain - ly we of - fer each am - ple ob - la - tion,

1. dawn on our dark - ness and lend us thine aid;
2. low lies his head with the beasts of the stall:
3. o - dors of E - dom and of - ferings di - vine,
4. vain - ly with gifts would his fa - vor se - cure:

1. star of the East, the ho - ri - zon a - dorn - ing,
2. an - gels a - dore him in slum - ber re - clin - ing,
3. gems of the moun - tain and pearls of the o - cean,
4. rich - er by far is the heart's ad - o - ra - tion,

1. guide where our in - fant Re - deem - er is laid.
2. Mak - er and Mon - arch and Sav - ior of all!
3. myrrh from the for - est, or gold from the mine?
4. dear - er to God are the prayers of the poor.

Isa. 60:6

EPIPHANY AND YOUTH

231 Songs of Thankfulness and Praise

Christopher Wordsworth, 1862

SALZBURG, 77.77 D

Melody by Jakob Hintze, 1678 (alt'd); harmony by J. S. Bach

1. Songs of thank-ful - ness and praise, Je - sus, Lord, to thee we raise,
2. Man - i - fest at Jor - dan's stream, Proph-et, Priest, and King su-preme,
3. Man - i - fest in mak-ing whole pal - sied limbs and faint-ing soul,
4. Grant us grace to see thee, Lord, mir-rored in thy ho - ly Word;

1. man - i - fest-ed by the star to the sag - es from a - far;
2. and at Ca - na, wed-ding guest in thy God - head man - i - fest,
3. man - i - fest in va - liant fight, quell-ing all the dev - il's might,
4. may we im - i - tate thee now, and be pure, as pure art thou,

1. branch of roy - al Da - vid's stem in thy birth at Beth - le - hem,
2. man - i - fest in pow'r di - vine, chang-ing wa - ter in - to wine,
3. man - i - fest in gra-cious will, ev - er bring-ing good from ill,
4. that we like to thee may be at thy great e - piph - a - ny,

1. an - thems be to thee ad-dressed, word in flesh made man - i - fest.
2. an - thems be to thee ad-dressed, God on earth made man - i - fest.
3. an - thems be to thee ad-dressed, God for us made man - i - fest.
4. and may praise thee, ev - er blest, God for all made man - i - fest.

EPIPHANY AND YOUTH

Mt. 2:1ff; Jn. 2:1ff; Mt. 4:1ff

Hail to the Lord's Anointed

232

James Montgomery, 1822

ROCKPORT, 7.6.7.6 D

T. Tertius Noble, 1938

1. Hail to the Lord's a - noint - ed, great Da - vid's great - er son!
2. Kings shall fall down be - fore him, and gold and in - cense bring;
3. He shall come down like show - ers up - on the fruit - ful earth,
4. O'er ev - ery foe vic - to - rious, he on his throne shall rest,

1. Hail, in the time ap - point - ed, his reign on earth be - gun!
2. all na - tions shall a - dore him, his praise all peo - ple sing;
3. and love, joy, hope, like flow - ers, spring in his path to birth;
4. from age to age more glo - rious, all bless - ing and all blest;

1. He comes to break op - pres - sion, to set the cap - tive free,
2. for he shall have do - min - ion o'er riv - er, sea, and shore,
3. be - fore him on the moun - tains shall peace, the her - ald, go;
4. the tide of time shall nev - er his cov - e - nant re - move;

1. to take a - way trans - gres - sion, and rule in eq - ui - ty.
2. far as the ea - gle's pin - ion or dove's light wing can soar.
3. and righ - teous - ness in foun - tains from hill to val - ley flow.
4. his name shall stand for - ev - er; that name to us is Love.

233

Jesus Shall Reign

Isaac Watts, 1719

DUKE STREET, LM

John Hatton, 1793

Descant, st. 5, by Erik Routley

5. Let ev-'ry crea-ture rise and bring pe-cu-liar hon-ors to our King;

1. Je-sus shall reign wher-e'er the sun does its suc-ces-sive jour-neys run;
2. To him shall end-less prayer be made, and prais-es throng to crown his head;
3. Peo-ple and realms of ev-'ry tongue dwell on his love with sweet-est song;
4. Bless-ings a-bound wher-e'er he reigns; the pris-'ners leap to lose their chains,
5. Let ev-'ry crea-ture rise and bring pe-cu-liar hon-ors to our King;

5. an-gels de-scend with songs a-gain, and earth re-peat the loud A-men.

1. his king-dom stretch from shore to shore till moons shall wax and wane no more.
2. his name like sweet per-fume shall rise with ev-'ry morn-ing sac-ri-fice.
3. and in-fant voic-es shall pro-claim their ear-ly bless-ings on his name.
4. the wea-ry find e-ter-nal rest, and all who suf-fer want are bless'd.
5. an-gels de-scend with songs a-gain, and earth re-peat the loud A-men.

Ps. 72

234

Bless'd Are the Pure in Heart

John Keble, 1827

FIFTH TUNE, SMD

Thomas Tallis, c. 1557

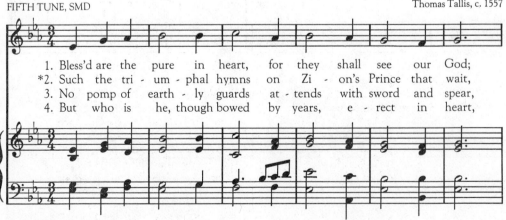

1. Bless'd are the pure in heart, for they shall see our God;
*2. Such the tri-um-phal hymns on Zi-on's Prince that wait,
3. No pomp of earth-ly guards at-tends with sword and spear,
4. But who is he, though bowed by years, e-rect in heart,

EPIPHANY AND YOUTH

1. the se - cret of the Lord is theirs; their soul is Christ's a - bode.
2. in high pro - ces - sion pass - ing on to - wards his tem - ple gate.
3. and all de - fy - ing, daunt - less, look their mon - arch's way to clear:
4. whose prayers are strug - gling with his tears? "Lord, let me now de - part:

1. Might mor - tal thought pre - sume to guess an an - gel's lay,
2. Give ear, ye kings; bow down, ye rul - ers of the earth —
3. yet are there more with him than all that are with you —
4. now hath thy ser - vant seen thy sav - ing health, O Lord:

1. such are the notes that ech - o through the courts of heav'n to - day.
2. this, this is he, your priest by grace, your God and King by birth.
3. the ar - mies of the high - est heav'n, all righ - teous, good, and true.
4. 'tis time that I de - part in peace, ac - cord - ing to thy word."

*5. Yet swells the pomp: one more
   comes forth to bless her God:
full four-score years, meek widow, she
   her heav'nward way hath trod:
she who to earthly joys
   so long had giv'n farewell,
now sees, unlooked for, heav'n on earth,
   Christ in his Israel.

6. Wide open from that hour
   the temple gates are set,
and still the saints rejoicing there
   the holy Child have met.
Still to the lowly soul
   he doth himself impart,
and for his cradle and his throne
   chooseth the pure in heart.

Lk. 2:22–37

EPIPHANY AND YOUTH

235

Faithful Vigil Ended

Timothy Dudley-Smith, 1969

PASTOR, 6.5.6.5

F. Silcher, 1841

1. Faith-ful vig-il end-ed, watch-ing, wait-ing cease;
2. All thy Spir-it prom-ised, all the Fa-ther willed,
3. This thy great de-liv-'rance sets thy peo-ple free;
4. Christ, thy peo-ple's glo-ry! Watch-ing, doubt-ing cease;

1. "Mas-ter, grant thy ser-vant his dis-charge in peace."
2. now these eyes be-held it per-fect-ly ful-filled.
3. Christ their light up-lift-ed all the na-tions see.
4. grant to us thy ser-vants their dis-charge in peace.

Lk. 2:29–32

236

Blest Are the Pure in Heart

Mitre Hymn Book (1836); based on John Keble

FRANCONIA, SM

W. H. Havergal, 1847; based on a chorale by J. B. König, 1738

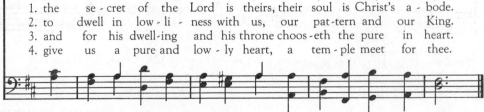

1. Blest are the pure in heart, for they shall see our God;
2. The Lord, who left the heavens, our life and peace to bring,
3. Still to the low-ly soul he doth him-self im-part,
4. Lord, we thy pres-ence seek; may ours this bless-ing be:

1. the se-cret of the Lord is theirs, their soul is Christ's a-bode.
2. to dwell in low-li-ness with us, our pat-tern and our King.
3. and for his dwell-ing and his throne choos-eth the pure in heart.
4. give us a pure and low-ly heart, a tem-ple meet for thee.

This tune in a higher key: 531

Mt. 5:3

Joy and Gladness!

237

George W. Bethune, 1847

KANSFIELD, 8.4.8.4.888.4

Erik Routley, 1982

1. Joy and glad-ness! Joy and glad-ness! O hap-py day!
2. Son of Mar-y (bless-ed moth-er!), thy love we claim;
3. In thy ho-ly foot-steps tread-ing, guide, lest we stray;

1. Ev-'ry thought of sin and sad-ness chase, chase a-way.
2. Son of God, our el-der broth-er (O gen-tle name!),
3. from thy word of prom-ise shed-ding light on our way,

1. Heard ye not the an-gels tell-ing, Christ the Lord of might ex-cel-ling
2. to thy Fa-ther's throne as-cend-ed, with thine own his glo-ry blend-ed,
3. nev-er leave us nor for-sake us; like thy-self in mer-cy make us,

1. on the earth with us is dwell-ing, clad in our clay?
2. thou art, all thy tri-als end-ed, ev-er the same.
3. and at last to glo-ry take us, Je-sus, we pray.

Lk. 2:15; Heb. 4:14

EPIPHANY AND YOUTH

238　O Master Workman of the Race

Jay T. Stocking, 1912

SEDGWICK, CMD

Lee Hastings Bristol, Jr., 1951

1. O　Mas-ter Work-man　of　the race, thou Man of Gal-i-lee,
2. O　Car-pen-ter　of　Naz-a-reth, build-er　of　life di-vine,
3. O　thou who dost the　vi-sion send and　giv-est each their task,

1. who　with the eyes　of　ear-ly youth e-ter-nal things did　see,
2. who　shap-est us　to　God's own law, thy-self the fair de-sign,
3. and　with the task suf-fi-cient strength, show us　thy will, we　ask;

1. we　thank thee for　thy　boy-hood faith that shone thy whole　life through;
2. build　us　a　tower of Christ-like height that　we　thy land may view
3. give　us　a　con-science bold and good, give us　a　pur-pose true,

1. "Did　ye　not know it　is　my work my　Fa-ther's work to　do?"
2. and　see, like thee, our　no-blest work our　Fa-ther's work to　do.
3. that　it　may be our　high-est joy our　Fa-ther's work to　do.

Son of the Lord Most High †

G. W. Briggs, 1930

LAWES' PSALM 47, 6.6.6.6.88

Melody and bass by Henry Lawes, 1637

†1. Son of the Lord most high, who gave the worlds their birth,
2. Born in so low es-tate, schooled in a work-er's trade,
3. Then, when his time was come, he heard his Fa-ther's call,
4. Toil-ing by night and day, him-self oft bur-dened sore,
5. O low-ly maj-es-ty! Lof-ty in low-li-ness!

1. he came to live and die, the Son of Man on earth.
2. not with the high and great his home the High-est made;
3. and, leav-ing friends and home, he gave him-self for all,
4. where hearts in bond-age lay, him-self their bur-den bore,
5. Bless'd Sav-iour, who am I to share thy bless-ed-ness?

1. ·In Beth-lem's sta-ble born was he, and hum-bly bred in Gal-i-lee.
2. but, lab-'ring by his com-rades' side, life's com-mon lot he glo-ri-fied.
3. glad news to bring, the lost to find, to heal the sick, the lame, the blind.
4. till, scorned by those he came to save, him-self in death, as life, he gave.
5. Yet thou hast called me, e-ven me, ser-vant di-vine, to fol-low thee.

Lk. 2:52

EPIPHANY AND YOUTH

240

Son of the Living God!

St. 1, anon.; st. 2–5, Charles Wesley, 1746

EPSOM, CM

William Tans'ur, 1734

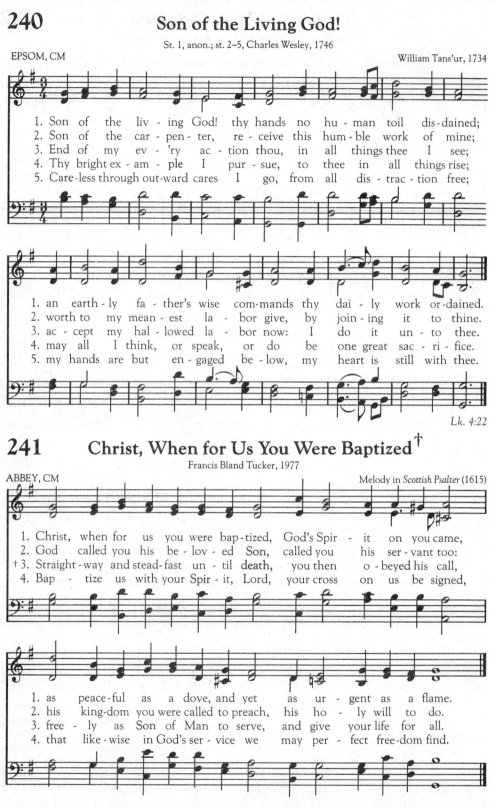

1. Son of the liv - ing God! thy hands no hu - man toil dis-dained;
2. Son of the car - pen - ter, re - ceive this hum - ble work of mine;
3. End of my ev - 'ry ac - tion thou, in all things thee I see;
4. Thy bright ex - am - ple I pur - sue, to thee in all things rise;
5. Care-less through out-ward cares I go, from all dis - trac - tion free;

1. an earth - ly fa - ther's wise com-mands thy dai - ly work or-dained.
2. worth to my mean - est la - bor give, by join-ing it to thine.
3. ac - cept my hal - lowed la - bor now: I do it un - to thee.
4. may all I think, or speak, or do be one great sac - ri - fice.
5. my hands are but en - gaged be - low, my heart is still with thee.

Lk. 4:22

241

Christ, When for Us You Were Baptized†

Francis Bland Tucker, 1977

ABBEY, CM

Melody in *Scottish Psalter* (1615)

1. Christ, when for us you were bap-tized, God's Spir - it on you came,
2. God called you his be - lov - ed Son, called you his ser - vant too:
† 3. Straight-way and stead-fast un - til **death**, you then o - beyed his call,
4. Bap - tize us with your Spir - it, Lord, your cross on us be signed,

1. as peace-ful as a dove, and yet as ur - gent as a flame.
2. his king-dom you were called to preach, his ho - ly will to do.
3. free - ly as Son of Man to serve, and give your life for all.
4. that like-wise in God's ser - vice we may per - fect free-dom find.

MINISTRY

Mk. 1:9–11

The Glory of These Forty Days

242

Clarum decus jejunii, attributed to Gregory the Great, d. 604;
tr. M. F. Bell, 1906

ERHALT'UNS, HERR, LM

Melody from Klug's *Geistliche Lieder* (1543); arranged by J. S. Bach

1. The glo-ry of these for-ty days we cel-e-brate with songs of praise,
2. A-lone and fast-ing, Mo-ses saw the lov-ing God, who gave the Law,
3. So Dan-iel trained his mys-tic sight, de-liv-ered from the li-ons' might,
4. Then grant us, Lord, like these to be full oft in fast and prayer with thee;

1. for Christ, by whom all things were made, him-self has fast-ed and has prayed.
2. and to E-li-jah, fast-ing, came the steeds and char-i-ots of flame.
3. and John, the Bride-groom's friend, be-came the her-ald of Mes-si-ah's name.
4. our spir-its strength-en with thy grace and give us joy to see thy face.

Ex. 19:20; II Kgs. 2:11, Dan. 6:16ff; Mt. 1:12–13; Mt. 3:4

Older version of this tune: 615

My Dear Redeemer and My Lord

243

INVITATION, LM

Isaac Watts, 1707

Jacob Kimball, 1793

1. My dear Re-deem-er and my Lord, I read my du-ty in thy word,
2. Such was thy truth and such thy zeal, such def-'rence to thy Fa-ther's will,
3. Cold moun-tains and the mid-night air wit-nessed the fer-vor of thy prayer;
4. Be thou my pat-tern; make me bear more of thy gra-cious i-mage here;

1. but in thy life the law ap-pears drawn out in liv-ing char-ac-ters.
2. such love, and meek-ness so di-vine, I would tran-scribe and make them mine.
3. the des-ert thy temp-ta-tions knew, thy con-flict, and thy vic-t'ry too.
4. then God, the Judge, shall own my name a-mongst the fol-l'wers of the Lamb.

Alternative tune: FESTUS, 505
Lk. 4:1ff

MINISTRY

244 With Joy We Contemplate the Grace

CONTEMPLATION, CM   Isaac Watts, 1707   F. A. G. Ouseley, 1889

1. With joy we con-tem-plate the grace of our High Priest a-bove;
2. Touched with a sym-pa-thy with-in, he knows our fee-ble frame;
3. But spot-less, in-no-cent, and pure the great Re-deem-er stood
4. He'll nev-er quench the smok-ing flax, but raise it to a flame;
5. Then let our hum-ble faith ad-dress his mer-cy and his pow'r;

1. his heart is made of ten-der-ness; it o-ver-flows with love.
2. he knows what sore temp-ta-tions mean, for he has felt the same.
3. while Sa-tan's fi-ery darts he bore, and did re-sist to blood.
4. the bruis-ed reed he nev-er breaks, nor scorns the mean-est name.
5. we shall ob-tain de-liv-'ring grace in ev-'ry need-ful hour.

This tune in a higher key: 358   *Isa. 42:3; Heb. 4:15ff; Heb. 12:4; Eph. 6:16*

245 Shepherd Divine, Our Wants Relieve

BEDENS BROOK, CM   Charles Wesley, 1739   Erik Routley, 1979

1. Shep-herd di-vine, our wants re-lieve in this, our e-vil day;
2. Long as our fi-ery tri-als last, long as the cross we bear,
3. Thy Spir-it's in-ter-ced-ing grace give us in faith to claim,
4. Till thou thy per-fect love im-part, till thou thy-self be-stow,

Bb last st.

1. to all thy tempt-ed fol-l'wers give the power to watch and pray.
2. O let our souls on thee be cast in nev-er ceas-ing prayer.
3. to wres-tle till we see thy face, and know thy hid-den name.
4. be this the cry of ev-'ry heart: "I will not let thee go!

Small notes for organ, last stanza

5. "I will not let thee go unless
   thou tell thy name to me,
   with all thy great salvation bless,
   and make me all like thee."

6. Then let me on the mountaintop
   behold thine open face
   where faith in sight is swallowed up,
   and prayer in endless praise.

MINISTRY   *Gen. 32:26-29; Mk. 9:2-7*

O Happy Band of Pilgrims

J. M. Neale, 1862 (alt'd)

DU MEINE SEELE SINGEN, 7.6.7.6 D

J. G. Ebeling, 1666

1. O hap-py band of pil-grims, if on-ward you will tread,
2. The faith by which you see him, the hope in which you yearn,
3. The tri-als that be-set you, the sor-rows you en-dure,
4. The cross that Je-sus car-ried, he car-ried as your due;

1. with Je-sus as your fel-low, to Je-sus as your head!
2. the love that through all trou-bles to him a-lone will turn —
3. the man-i-fold temp-ta-tions that death a-lone can cure —
4. the crown that Je-sus wear-eth, he wear-eth it for you.

1. O hap-py if you la-bor as Je-sus did for all,
2. what are they but fore-run-ners, to lead you to his sight?
3. what are they but his jew-els of right ce-les-tial worth?
4. O hap-py band of pil-grims, look up-ward to the skies,

1. if, pray-ing, fast-ing, lis-t'ning, you hear the Sav-ior's call!
2. What are they but the ef-fluence of un-cre-at-ed light?
3. What are they but the lad-der set up to heav'n on earth?
4. where such a light af-flic-tion shall win so great a prize!

247

In the Hour of Trial

James Montgomery, 1834

WARUM SIND DER THRÄNEN, 6.5.6.5 D

J. A. P. Schulz, 1785

1. In the hour of tri - al, Je - sus, plead for me, lest by base de -
2. With for - bid - den plea - sures should this vain world charm, or its tempt - ing
3. If with sore af - flic - tion thou in love chas - tise, pour thy ben - e -
4. When in dust and ash - es to the grave I sink, while heav'n's glo - ry

1. ni - al I de - part from thee; when thou see'st me wa - ver,
2. trea - sures spread to work me harm, bring to my re - mem - brance
3. dic - tion on the sac - ri - fice; then, up - on the al - tar,
4. flash - es o'er the shelv - ing brink, on thy truth re - ly - ing

1. with a look re - call, nor for fear or fa - vor suf - fer me to fall.
2. sad Geth-sem-a - ne, or in dark - er sem-blance, cross-crowned Cal-va-ry.
3. free - ly of - fered up, though the flesh may fal - ter, faith shall drink the cup.
4. through that mor-tal strife, Lord, re - ceive me, dy - ing, to e - ter-nal life.

Mk. 14:66ff

248

Lord Jesus, Think on Me

Greek poem by Synesius, 4th century; tr. A. W. Chatfield, 1876

SOUTHWELL, SM

Varied from *Daman's Psalter* (1579)

1. Lord Je - sus, think on me, and purge a - way my sin;
2. Lord Je - sus, think on me, nor let me go a - stray;
3. Lord Je - sus, think on me, when flows the tem - pest high;
4. Lord Je - sus, think on me, that, when the flood is past,

Gen. 8:13

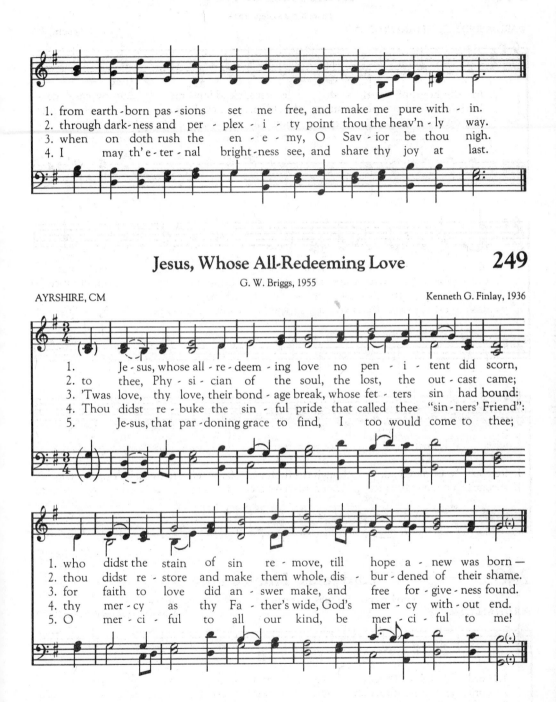

1. from earth-born pas-sions set me free, and make me pure with - in.
2. through dark-ness and per - plex - i - ty point thou the heav'n - ly way.
3. when on doth rush the en - e - my, O Sav - ior be thou nigh.
4. I may th' e-ter - nal bright-ness see, and share thy joy at last.

Jesus, Whose All-Redeeming Love 249

G. W. Briggs, 1955

AYRSHIRE, CM

Kenneth G. Finlay, 1936

1. Je - sus, whose all - re - deem - ing love no pen - i - tent did scorn,
2. to thee, Phy - si - cian of the soul, the lost, the out - cast came;
3. 'Twas love, thy love, their bond - age break, whose fet - ters sin had bound:
4. Thou didst re - buke the sin - ful pride that called thee "sin - ners' Friend":
5. Je - sus, that par - doning grace to find, I too would come to thee;

1. who didst the stain of sin re - move, till hope a - new was born—
2. thou didst re - store and make them whole, dis - bur - dened of their shame.
3. for faith to love did an - swer make, and free for - give - ness found.
4. thy mer - cy as thy Fa - ther's wide, God's mer - cy with - out end.
5. O mer - ci - ful to all our kind, be mer - ci - ful to me!

250   We Would See Jesus; Lo! His Star Is Shining

J. Edgar Park, 1913

FOREST HILL, 11.10.11.10

University of Wales, 1923

1. We would see Jesus; lo! his star is shining, above the stable while the angels sing; in manger humble on the hay reclining, haste, let us lay our gifts before the King.

2. We would see Jesus; Mary's Son most holy, Light of the village life from day to day; he shines revealed through ev'ry task most lowly, the Christ of God, the Life, the Truth, the Way.

3. We would see Jesus; on the mountain teaching, with all the list'ning people gathered round; while birds and flow'rs and sky above are preaching the bless-ed-ness which simple trust has found.

4. We would see Jesus; in his work of healing, that joyful evening when the sun was set; divine and human, in his deep revealing of God made flesh in loving service meet.

5. We would see Jesus; in the early morning,
still, as of old, he calleth, "Follow me";
let us arise, all meaner service scorning;
Lord, we are thine: we give ourselves to thee.

Hark, the Glad Sound! The Savior Comes

251

Philip Doddridge, 1702–1751

BRISTOL, CM

Melody and bass from *Ravenscroft's Psalter* (1621)

1. Hark, the glad sound! The Sav - ior comes: the Sav - ior prom - ised long!
2. He comes the pris - 'ners to re - lease, in Sa - tan's bond - age held;
3. He comes the bro - ken heart to bind, the bleed - ing soul to cure,
4. Our glad ho - san - nas, Prince of peace, thy wel - come shall pro - claim,

1. Let ev - 'ry heart pre - pare a throne, and ev - 'ry voice a song.
2. the gates of brass be - fore him burst, the i - ron fet - ters yield.
3. and with the trea - sures of his grace to en - rich the hum - ble poor.
4. and heav'n's e - ter - nal arch - es ring with thy be - lov - ed name.

Lk. 4:18ff

Alternative tune: RICHMOND, 362

At Even, When the Sun Was Set †

252

Henry Twells, 1868

ANGELUS, LM

Adapted (1868) from a melody by G. Scheffler, 1657

1. At e - ven, when the sun was set, the sick, O Lord, a - round thee lay;
2. Once more 'tis e - ven - tide, and we, op - pressed with var - ious ills, draw near:
3. O Sav - ior Christ, our woes dis - pel: for some are sick, and some are sad,
† 4. O Sav - ior Christ, thou too art man; thou hast been trou - bled, tempt - ed, tried;
5. Thy touch has still its an - cient power; no word from thee can fruit - less fall:

1. O in what di - vers pains they met! O with what joy they went a - way!
2. what if thy form we can - not see? We know and feel that thou art here.
3. and some have nev - er loved thee well, and some have lost the love they had.
4. thy kind but search - ing glance can scan the ver - y wounds that shame would hide.
5. hear in this sol - emn eve - ning hour, and in thy mer - cy heal us all.

Mk. 1:32

MINISTRY

253　O Where Is He That Trod the Sea?

T. T. Lynch, 1856

SHEPHERD'S PIPES, CMD

Annabeth McClelland Gay, 1958

1. O where is he that trod the sea? O where is he that spake
2. O where is he that trod the sea? O where is he that spake
3. O where is he that trod the sea? 'Tis on-ly he can save;
4. O where is he that trod the sea? My soul, the Lord is here!

1. and de-mons from their vic-tims flee, the dead their slum-bers break,
2. and pierc-ing words of lib-er-ty the deaf ears o-pen shake,
3. to thou-sands hun-g'ring wea-ri-ly a won-drous meal he gave;
4. Let all thy fears be hushed in thee; be thine to look, to hear:

1. the pal-sied rise in free-dom strong, the speech-less talk and sing,
2. and mild-est words ar-rest the haste of fe-ver's dead-ly fire,
3. full soon with bread from heav-en fed, their rus-tic fare they take;
4. he all thy needs will sat-is-fy. Art thou dis-eased or dumb,

1. and from blind eyes be-night-ed long bright beams of morn-ing spring?
2. and strong ones heal the weak who waste their lives in sad de-sire?
3. 'twas spring-tide when he bless'd the bread, and har-vest when he brake.
4. or dost thou in thy hun-ger cry? "I come," saith Christ, "I come!"

Alternative tune: FOREST GREEN, 9

Mt. 14:25

Immortal Love, Forever Full

J. G. Whittier, 1856

BISHOPTHORPE, CM

Select Portions of the Psalms of David (1786)

1. Im - mor - tal love, for - ev - er full, for - ev - er flow - ing free,
2. Our out - ward lips con - fess the name all oth - er names a - bove;
3. We may not climb the heav'n-ly steeps to bring the Lord Christ down;
4. But warm, sweet, ten-der e - ven yet, a pres - ent help is he;

1. for - ev - er shared, for - ev - er whole, a nev - er ebb - ing sea.
2. love on - ly know - eth whence it came, and com - pre - hend - eth love.
3. in vain we search the low - est deeps, for him no depths can drown.
4. and faith has still its Ol - i - vet, and love its Gal - i - lee.

5. The healing of his seamless dress
   is by our beds of pain;
   we touch him in life's throng and press,
   and we are whole again.

6. Alone, O love ineffable,
   thy saving name is given;
   to turn aside from thee is hell;
   to walk with thee is heaven.

255   Heal Us, Immanuel, Hear Our Prayer

William Cowper, 1779

WIGTON, CM

Scottish Psalter (1635)

1. Heal us, Im - man - uel, hear our prayer; we wait to feel thy touch;
2. Our faith is fee - ble, we con - fess; we faint - ly trust thy word;
3. Re - mem - ber him who once ap - plied with trem - bling for re - lief:
4. She, too, who touched thee in the press, and heal - ing vir - tue stole,
5. Like her, with hopes and fears we come to touch thee if we may;

1. deep-wound-ed souls to thee re - pair, and, Sav - ior, we are such.
2. but wilt thou pit - y us the less? Be that far from thee, Lord!
3. "Lord, I be - lieve," with tears he cried; "O help my un - be - lief."
4. was an-swered, "Daughter, go in peace: thy faith hath made thee whole."
5. O send us not de - spair - ing home, send none un - healed a - way.

This tune in a lower key: 584

Mk. 9:24

256   O Wondrous Sight, O Vision Fair

Caelestis formam gloriae, 15th century;
tr. J. Neale, 1851; text of 1861 (alt'd)

DEO GRACIAS (AGINCOURT SONG), LM

15th-century English melody

1. O won-drous sight, O vi-sion fair of glo - ry that the Church shall share,
2. From age to age the tale de - clares how with the three dis - ci - ples there,
3. The law and proph-ets there have place, two cho-sen wit-ness - es of grace;
4. With shin - ing face and bright ar - ray Christ deigns to man - i - fest that day
5. And faith - ful hearts are raised on high by this great vi - sion's mys - ter - y,

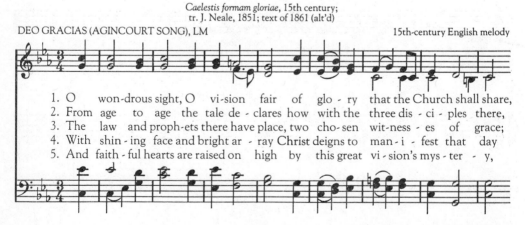

MINISTRY

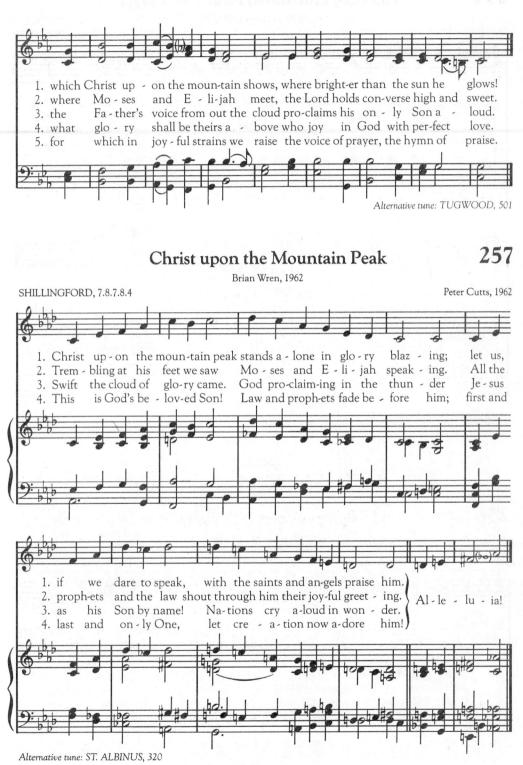

1. which Christ up - on the moun-tain shows, where bright-er than the sun he glows!
2. where Mo - ses and E - li-jah meet, the Lord holds con-verse high and sweet.
3. the Fa - ther's voice from out the cloud pro-claims his on - ly Son a - loud.
4. what glo - ry shall be theirs a - bove who joy in God with per-fect love.
5. for which in joy - ful strains we raise the voice of prayer, the hymn of praise.

Alternative tune: TUGWOOD, 501

Christ upon the Mountain Peak 257

Brian Wren, 1962

SHILLINGFORD, 7.8.7.8.4   Peter Cutts, 1962

1. Christ up - on the moun-tain peak stands a - lone in glo-ry blaz - ing; let us,
2. Trem - bling at his feet we saw Mo - ses and E - li-jah speak - ing. All the
3. Swift the cloud of glo-ry came. God pro-claim-ing in the thun - der Je - sus
4. This is God's be - lov-ed Son! Law and proph-ets fade be - fore him; first and

1. if we dare to speak, with the saints and an-gels praise him.
2. proph-ets and the law shout through him their joy-ful greet - ing. } Al - le - lu - ia!
3. as his Son by name! Na-tions cry a-loud in won - der.
4. last and on - ly One, let cre - a - tion now a-dore him!

Alternative tune: ST. ALBINUS, 320

Copyright © 1977 by Hope Publishing Company, Carol Stream, IL 60188. All Rights Reserved. Used by Permission.

Mk. 9:2ff   MINISTRY

258

Jesus Calls Us

SUSSEX, 8.7.8.7

Cecil Frances Alexander, 1852
First Tune

English folk song;
adapted by R. Vaughan Williams, 1906

1. Je - sus calls us: o'er the tu - mult of our life's wild, rest - less sea,
2. Je - sus calls us from the wor - ship of the vain world's gold - en store,
3. In our joys and in our sor - rows, days of toil and hours of ease,
4. Je - sus calls us: by thy mer - cies, Sav - ior, may we hear thy call,

1. day by day his sweet voice sound - eth, say - ing, "Chris - tian, fol - low me."
2. from each i - dol that would keep us, say - ing, "Chris - tian, love me more."
3. still he calls, in cares and plea - sures, "Chris - tian, love me more than these."
4. give our hearts to thine o - be - dience, serve and love thee best of all.

Mk. 1:16–18; Jn. 21:15

259

Jesus Calls Us

GALILEE, 8.7.8.7

Second Tune

W. H. Jude, 1887

1. Je - sus calls us: o'er the tu - mult of our life's wild, rest - less sea,
2. Je - sus calls us from the wor - ship of the vain world's gold - en store,
3. In our joys and in our sor - rows, days of toil and hours of ease,
4. Je - sus calls us: by thy mer - cies, Sav - ior, may we hear thy call,

1. day by day his sweet voice sound - eth, say - ing, "Chris - tian, fol - low me."
2. from each i - dol that would keep us, say - ing, "Chris - tian love me more."
3. still he calls, in cares and plea - sures, "Chris - tian, love me more than these."
4. give our hearts to thine o - be - dience, serve and love thee best of all.

MINISTRY

Blessed Are the Poor in Spirit

CARCANT, 8.7.8.7 D   Norman Elliott, 1967   Erik Routley, 1967

Gently

1. Bless-ed are the poor in spir-it, claim-ing noth-ing as their own,
2. Bless-ed are the strong but gen-tle, trained to serve a high-er will,
3. Blest are they who show their mer-cy to the guil-ty and the poor,
4. Bless-ed are the brave and peace-ful, bring-ing peace wher-e'er they live,

1. but as giv'n them by their Fa-ther that his good-ness may be shown.
2. wise to know the e-ter-nal pur-pose which their Fa-ther shall ful-fill.
3. for to them, set free from judg-ment, shall be o-pened heav-en's door.
4. God shall own them as his chil-dren and through them his peace will give.

1. Blest are they who share the sor-row of their God's un-chang-ing love;
2. Blest are they who with true pas-sion strive to make the right pre - vail,
3. Bless-ed, the sin - cere and truth-ful from the lie's de-cep-tion free,
4. All for love and truth who suf-fer in your God re-joice and sing;

1. they shall know his pres-ence with them and his prom-ised com-fort prove.
2. for the earth is God's pos - ses - sion and his pur-pose will not fail.
3. for the God of truth and beau-ty they in joy will sure-ly see.
4. he, the end of all your striv-ing, he, your Fa-ther, Lord and King.

Mk. 5:3ff   MINISTRY

261   Lord, Teach Us How to Pray Aright

James Montgomery, 1823

GLENLUCE, CM

Scottish Psalter (1635)

1. Lord, teach us how to pray a-right, with rev-'rence and with fear;
2. We per-ish if we cease from prayer: O grant us power to pray;
3. Give deep hu-mil-i-ty, the sense of god-ly sor-row give;
4. faith in the on-ly sac-ri-fice that can for sin a-tone,

1. though weak and sin-ful in thy sight, we may, we must draw near.
2. and when to meet thee we pre-pare, Lord, meet us by the way.
3. a strong de-sir-ing con-fi-dence to hear thy voice and live;
4. to cast our hopes, to fix our eyes on Christ, on Christ a-lone;

5. patience to watch, and wait, and weep
   though mercy long delay;
  courage, our fainting souls to keep
  and trust thee though thou slay:

6. give these — and then thy will be done;
   thus strengthened with all might,
  we by thy Spirit and thy Son
  shall pray, and pray aright.

Lk.11:1; Ps. 119:175; Job 13:15

262   Our Heav'nly Father

James Montgomery, 1825

Arranged by William Crotch, 1836,
from Psalm 101 in the *Genevan Psalter* (1551)

ST. MICHAEL, SM

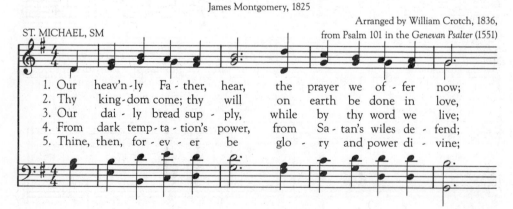

1. Our heav'n-ly Fa-ther, hear, the prayer we of-fer now;
2. Thy king-dom come; thy will on earth be done in love,
3. Our dai-ly bread sup-ply, while by thy word we live;
4. From dark temp-ta-tion's power, from Sa-tan's wiles de-fend;
5. Thine, then, for-ev-er be glo-ry and power di-vine;

1. thy name be hal-lowed far and near, to thee all na-tions bow.
2. as saints and ser-a-phim ful-fill thy per-fect law a-bove.
3. the guilt of our in-iq-ui-ty for-give as we for-give.
4. de-liv-er in the e-vil hour and guide us to the end.
5. the scep-ter, throne and maj-es-ty, of heav'n and earth are thine.

Mt. 6:9–13

Alternative tune: TYTHERTON, 178

"Seek Ye First the Kingdom"   263

CRANHAM, 6.5.6.5 D   Norman Elliott, 1951   Gustav Holst, 1906

1. "Seek ye first the king-dom: 'tis your Fa-ther's will" — so the voice of
2. As for hid-den trea-sure or for match-less pearl, when at last dis-
3. As the si-lent leav-en works its se-cret way, or as grows the
4. As the ten-der seed-ling grows up tall and strong and the birds of
5. Hum-blest shall be great-est, poor in spir-it reign; home shall come the

1. Je-sus bids us fol-low still.   Sav-ior, we would hear thee,
2. cov-ered, some will sell their all;   so, when breaks the vi-sion
3. seed grain through the night and day;   Lord, so be the in-crease
4. heav-en to its branch-es throng,   so shall all God's chil-dren,
5. child-like, born thro' thee a-gain;   ea-ger hearts ar-rive there

1. fol-low, find, and see,   and in life's ad-ven-ture thy dis-ci-ples be.
2. of that king-dom fair,   ours shall be its rich-es and its beau-ty rare.
3. peace-a-ble but sure,   of thy word with-in us, and thy king-dom's power.
4. from the east and west,   gath-er to his king-dom, in its shad-ow rest.
5. on the pil-grim's road.   Hail! the king-dom glo-rious of the liv-ing God!

Mt. 6:33   MINISTRY

264

Lord, Who Shall Sit Beside Thee?

William Romanis, 1878

CHRISTUS DER IST MEIN LEBEN, 7.6.7.6

M. Vulpius, 1609; harmonized by J. S. Bach

1. Lord, who shall sit be - side thee, en-throned on ei - ther hand,
2. Who drinks the cup of sor - row the Fa - ther gave to thee
3. Who on thy pas - sion think - ing can find in loss a gain,
4. O Je - sus, form with - in us thy like - ness clear and true;
5. This law it - self ful - fill - eth; Christ-like to Christ is nigh;

1. when clouds no long - er hide thee 'mid all thy faith - ful band?
2. 'neath shad - ows of the mor - row in dark Geth - sem - a - ne?
3. and dare to meet un - shrink - ing thy bap - ti - sm of pain?
4. by thine ex - am - ple win us to suf - fer and to do.
5. who - e'er the Fa - ther will - eth shall sit with Christ on high.

A simpler form of this tune, in a lower key: 95

Mt. 20:20–28

265

He Sat to Watch O'er Customs Paid

William Bright, 1824–1901

BROCKHAM, LM

Melody and bass by Jeremiah Clarke, 1701;
mean parts by John Wilson

1. He sat to watch o'er cus-toms paid, a man of scorned and hard-'ning trade;
2. But grace with - in his heart had stirred; there need - ed but the time - ly word;
3. E - nough, when thou wast pass-ing by, to hear thy voice, to meet thine eye:
*4. O wise ex-change! with these to part, and lay up trea-sures in the heart;

1. a - like the sym - bol and the tool of for - eign mas - ters' hat - ed rule.
2. it came, true Lord of souls, from thee, that roy - al sum-mons, "Fol - low me!"
3. he rose, re - spon-sive to the call and left his task, his gains, his all.
4. let them of Mat-thew's wealth par-take, who yield up all for Je - sus' sake.

MINISTRY

Mt. 9:9

The King of Love My Shepherd Is

H. W. Baker, 1868

DOMINUS REGIT ME, 8.7.8.7 iambic

J. B. Dykes, 1868

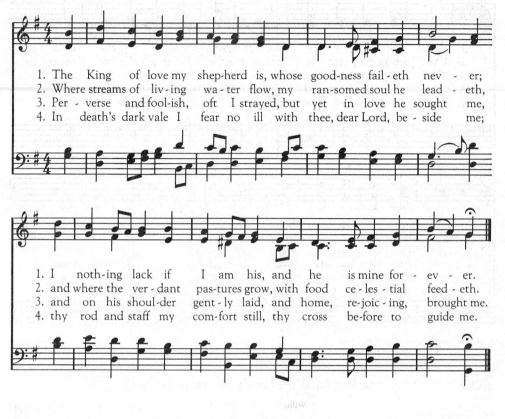

1. The King of love my shep-herd is, whose good-ness fail-eth nev - er;
2. Where streams of liv-ing wa-ter flow, my ran-somed soul he lead - eth,
3. Per - verse and fool-ish, oft I strayed, but yet in love he sought me,
4. In death's dark vale I fear no ill with thee, dear Lord, be - side me;

1. I noth-ing lack if I am his, and he is mine for - ev - er.
2. and where the ver - dant pas-tures grow, with food ce - les - tial feed - eth.
3. and on his shoul-der gent - ly laid, and home, re-joic-ing, brought me.
4. thy rod and staff my com-fort still, thy cross be-fore to guide me.

5. Thou spread'st a table in my sight;
   thy unction grace bestoweth:
   and oh, what transport of delight
   from thy pure chalice floweth!

6. And so, through all the length of days
   thy goodness faileth never;
   Good Shepherd, may I sing thy praise
   within thy house forever.

Ps. 23; Mt. 18:12

MINISTRY

267
The King of Love My Shepherd Is
Second Tune

ST. COLUMBA, 8.7.8.7 iambic

Irish traditional hymn tune; harmonized by C. V. Stanford

1. The King of love my shep-herd is, whose good-ness fail-eth nev - er;
2. Where streams of liv-ing wa - ter flow, my ran-somed soul he lead - eth,
3. Per - verse and fool-ish, oft I strayed, but yet in love he sought me,
4. In death's dark vale I fear no ill with thee, dear Lord, be - side me;

1. I noth-ing lack if I am his, and he is mine for - ev - er.
2. and where the ver-dant pas-tures grow, with food ce - les - tial feed - eth.
3. and on his shoul-der gent - ly laid, and home, re - joic-ing, brought me.
4. thy rod and staff my com-fort still, thy cross be-fore to guide me.

5. Thou spread'st a table in my sight;
thy unction grace bestoweth:
and oh, what transport of delight
from thy pure chalice floweth!

6. And so, through all the length of days
thy goodness faileth never;
Good Shepherd, may I sing thy praise
within thy house forever.

This tune in a higher key: 350. Alternative tune: TALLIS' ORDINAL, 404

Ps. 23; Mt. 18:12

268
"Take Up Thy Cross," the Savior Said

C. W. Everest, 1833

Melody by F. Mendelssohn-Bartholdy;
adapted from a tune in *As Hymnodus Sacer* (Leipzig, 1625)

BRESLAU, LM

1. "Take up thy cross," the Sav - ior said; "if thou wouldst my dis - ci - ple be,
2. Take up thy cross, let not its weight fill thy weak spir - it with a-larm;
3. Take up thy cross, nor heed the shame, and let thy fool-ish pride be still;
4. Take up thy cross and fol - low Christ, nor think till death to lay it down,

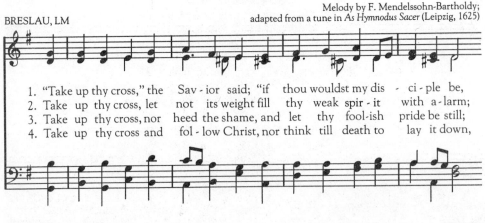

MINISTRY

Mk. 8:34

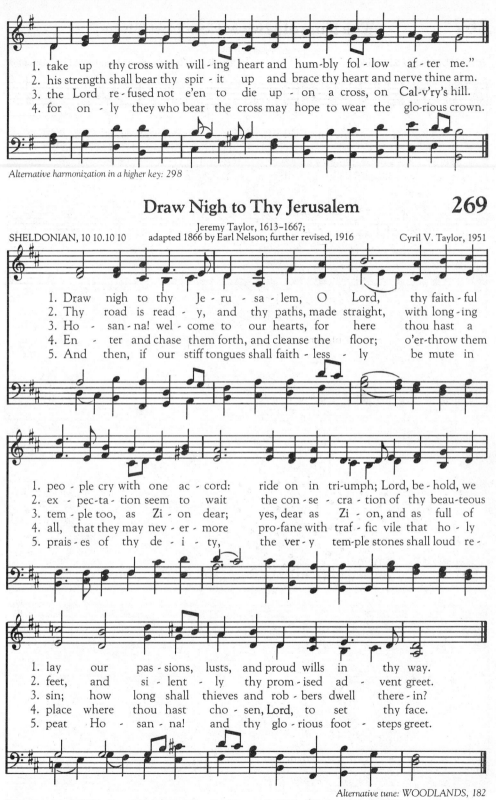

1. take up thy cross with will-ing heart and hum-bly fol-low af-ter me."
2. his strength shall bear thy spir-it up and brace thy heart and nerve thine arm.
3. the Lord re-fused not e'en to die up-on a cross, on Cal-v'ry's hill.
4. for on-ly they who bear the cross may hope to wear the glo-rious crown.

Alternative harmonization in a higher key: 298

Draw Nigh to Thy Jerusalem 269

Jeremy Taylor, 1613–1667;
adapted 1866 by Earl Nelson; further revised, 1916

SHELDONIAN, 10 10.10 10

Cyril V. Taylor, 1951

1. Draw nigh to thy Je-ru-sa-lem, O Lord, thy faith-ful
2. Thy road is read-y, and thy paths, made straight, with long-ing
3. Ho-san-na! wel-come to our hearts, for here thou hast a
4. En-ter and chase them forth, and cleanse the floor; o'er-throw them
5. And then, if our stiff tongues shall faith-less-ly be mute in

1. peo-ple cry with one ac-cord: ride on in tri-umph; Lord, be-hold, we
2. ex-pec-ta-tion seem to wait the con-se-cra-tion of thy beau-teous
3. tem-ple too, as Zi-on dear; yes, dear as Zi-on, and as full of
4. all, that they may nev-er-more pro-fane with traf-fic vile that ho-ly
5. prais-es of thy de-i-ty, the ver-y tem-ple stones shall loud re-

1. lay our pas-sions, lusts, and proud wills in thy way.
2. feet, and si-lent-ly thy prom-ised ad-vent greet.
3. sin; how long shall thieves and rob-bers dwell there-in?
4. place where thou hast cho-sen, Lord, to set thy face.
5. peat Ho-san-na! and thy glo-rious foot-steps greet.

Alternative tune: WOODLANDS, 182

Mk. 11:15–17

MINISTRY

270

Jesus, My Lord, How Rich Thy Grace

Philip Doddridge, 1702–1751 (alt'd)

GEORGETOWN, CM

David McK. Williams, 1941

Unison

1. Je - sus, my Lord, how rich thy grace; thy boun-ties, how com - plete!
2. High on a throne of ra-diant light dost thou ex - alt - ed shine;
3. But lo, our world's for-got-ten poor are part-ners of thy grace;
4. In them thou may'st be clothed and fed, and vis - it - ed and cheered,
5. Thy face with rev - 'rence and with love I in thy poor would see;

1. How shall I count the match-less sum, or pay the might - y debt?
2. what can my pov - er - ty be-stow, when all the worlds are thine?
3. thou wilt con - fess their hum-ble names be - fore thy Fa - ther's face.
4. and in their ac - cents of dis - tress my Sav - ior's voice is heard.
5. O let me rath - er beg my bread than hold it back from thee.

Alternative tune: GRÄFENBERG, 278

Mt. 25:31*ff*

271

Lift Up Your Heads, Rejoice

TALLIS' SEVENTH TUNE, 6.6.6.6 D

T. T. Lynch, 1856

Thomas Tallis, c. 1557

1. Lift up your heads, re - joice: re - demp - tion draw-eth nigh;
2. Lift up your heads, re - joice: re - demp - tion draw-eth nigh;
3. Lift up your heads, re - joice: re - demp - tion draw-eth nigh;
4. He comes, the wide world's King; he comes, the true heart's friend,

1. now breathes a soft - er air, now shines a mild - er sky;
2. now mount the lead - en clouds, now flames the dark - 'ning sky;
3. O note the vary - ing signs of earth and air and sky;
4. new glad - ness to be - gin, and an - cient wrong to end;

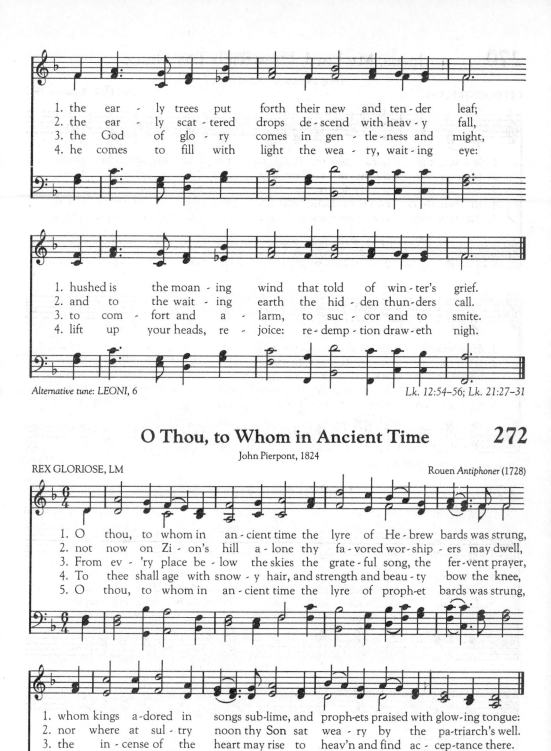

1. the ear - ly trees put forth their new and ten - der leaf;
2. the ear - ly scat - tered drops de - scend with heav - y fall,
3. the God of glo - ry comes in gen - tle - ness and might,
4. he comes to fill with light the wea - ry, wait - ing eye:

1. hushed is the moan - ing wind that told of win - ter's grief.
2. and to the wait - ing earth the hid - den thun - ders call.
3. to com - fort and a - larm, to suc - cor and to smite.
4. lift up your heads, re - joice: re - demp - tion draw - eth nigh.

Alternative tune: LEONI, 6

Lk. 12:54–56; Lk. 21:27–31

O Thou, to Whom in Ancient Time 272

John Pierpont, 1824

REX GLORIOSE, LM

Rouen *Antiphoner* (1728)

1. O thou, to whom in an - cient time the lyre of He - brew bards was strung,
2. not now on Zi - on's hill a - lone thy fa - vored wor - ship - ers may dwell,
3. From ev - 'ry place be - low the skies the grate - ful song, the fer - vent prayer,
4. To thee shall age with snow - y hair, and strength and beau - ty bow the knee,
5. O thou, to whom in an - cient time the lyre of proph - et bards was strung,

1. whom kings a - dored in songs sub - lime, and proph - ets praised with glow - ing tongue:
2. nor where at sul - try noon thy Son sat wea - ry by the pa - triarch's well.
3. the in - cense of the heart may rise to heav'n and find ac - cep - tance there.
4. and child - hood lisp with rev - 'rent air its prais - es and its prayers to thee.
5. to thee at last in ev - 'ry clime shall tem - ples rise and praise be sung.

Jn. 4:5–6, 21–24

MINISTRY

273

Jesus, Thou Joy of Loving Hearts

Jesu dulcedo cordium, anonymous Latin poem, c. 1200; tr. Ray Palmer, 1858 (alt'd)

From an original tune by J. S. Bach in Schemelli's *Gesangbuch*;
arranged by John Wilson, 1936

NURNBERG, LM

1. Je - sus, thou joy of lov - ing hearts, thou fount of life, thou light of all,
2. Thy truth un - changed hath ev - er stood; thou sav - est those that on thee call;
3. We taste thee, O thou liv - ing bread, and long to feast up - on thee still;
4. Our rest - less spir - its yearn for thee, wher - e'er our change - ful lot is cast,
5. O Je - sus, ev - er with us stay; make all our mo - ments calm and bright;

1. from the best bliss that earth im - parts we turn, un - filled, to heed thy call.
2. to them that seek thee thou art good, to them that find thee all in all.
3. we drink of thee the foun - tain - head and thirst our souls from thee to fill.
4. glad when thy gra - cious smile we see, blest when our faith can hold thee fast.
5. chase the dark night of sin a - way; shed o'er the world thy ho - ly light.

Jn. 6:35ff

274

Thou Art the Way

George Washington Doane, 1824

American folk hymn;
attributed to Lucius Chapin, 1813

TWENTY-FOURTH, CM

1. Thou art the Way: to thee a - lone from sin and death we flee;
2. Thou art the Truth: thy word a - lone true wis - dom can im - part;
3. Thou art the Life: the rend - ing tomb pro - claims thy con - qu'ring arm;
4. Thou art the Way, the Truth, the Life; grant us that way to know,

1. and all who would the Fa - ther seek must seek him, Lord, by thee.
2. thou on - ly canst in - form the mind and pu - ri - fy the heart.
3. and those who put their trust in thee nor death nor hell can harm.
4. that truth to keep, that life to win, whose joys e - ter - nal flow.

Lord Christ, the Father's Mighty Son

275

Brian Wren, 1962

EAST MEADS, 88.5.8.6

John W. Wilson, 1980

4. We will not ques-tion nor re-fuse the way you work, the

1. Lord Christ, the Fa-ther's might-y Son, whose work up-on the
2. To make us one your prayers were said, to make us one you
3. Lord Christ, for-give us, make us new! What our de-signs could
4. We will not ques-tion nor re-fuse the way you work, the

4. means you choose, the pat-tern you weave; but rec-on-cile our

1. cross was done to give and re-ceive, make all our scat-tered
2. broke the bread, for all to re-ceive; its piec-es scat-ter
3. nev-er do your love can a-chieve. Our prayers, our work, we
4. means you choose, the pat-tern you weave; but rec-on-cile our

4. war-ring views, that the world may be-lieve.

1. church-es one, that the world may be-lieve.
2. us in-stead: how can oth-ers be-lieve?
3. bring to you, that the world may be-lieve.
4. war-ring views, that the world may be-lieve.

Jn. 17:21

MINISTRY

276 Come, My Way

George Herbert, 1593–1633
First Tune

COME, MY WAY, 7.7.7.7

Alexander Brent Smith, c. 1925

1. Come, my Way, my Truth, my Life: such a way, as gives us breath;
2. Come, my Light, my Feast, my Strength: such a light, as shows a feast;

1. such a truth, as ends all strife; such a life, as kill-eth death.
2. such a feast, as mends in length; such a strength, as makes his guest.

Congregation

3. Come, my Joy, my Love, my Heart: such a joy as none can move;

Organ

* such a joy,

3. such a joy as none can move;

3. such a love, as none can part; such a heart, as joys in love.
   such a love,

3. such a love, as none can part; such a heart, as joys in love.

*Choir descant begins here; all other choir voices sing with the congregation.
NOTE: All three stanzas can be sung to the music of st. 1-2.

MINISTRY

Come, My Way

Second Tune

THE CALL, 7.7.7.7

R. Vaughan Williams, 1911

1. Come, my Way, my Truth, my Life: such a way as gives us breath;
2. Come, my Light, my Feast, my Strength: such a light as shows a feast;
3. Come, my Joy, my Love, my Heart: such a joy as none can move;

1. such a truth as ends all strife; such a life as kill - - - eth death.
2. such a feast as mends in length; such a strength as makes_____ his guest.
3. such a love as none can part; such a heart as joys_____ in love.

278

Jesus, These Eyes Have Never Seen

Ray Palmer, 1858

NUN DANKET ALL' (GRÄFENBERG), CM

Praxis Pietatis (1653)

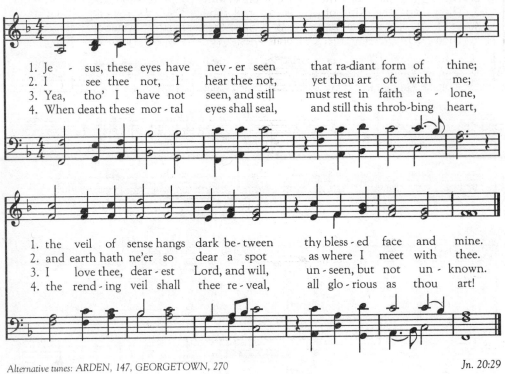

1. Je - sus, these eyes have nev - er seen that ra-diant form of thine;
2. I see thee not, I hear thee not, yet thou art oft with me;
3. Yea, tho' I have not seen, and still must rest in faith a - lone,
4. When death these mor - tal eyes shall seal, and still this throb-bing heart,

1. the veil of sense hangs dark be - tween thy bless - ed face and mine.
2. and earth hath ne'er so dear a spot as where I meet with thee.
3. I love thee, dear - est Lord, and will, un - seen, but not un - known.
4. the rend - ing veil shall thee re - veal, all glo - rious as thou art!

Alternative tunes: ARDEN, 147, GEORGETOWN, 270

Jn. 20:29

279

All Glory, Laud, and Honor

Gloria, laus et honor, by Theodulph of Orleans, d. 821;
tr. J. M. Neale, 1851

ST. THEODULPH, 7.6.7.6 D

Melody by M. Teschner, 1615; arranged in this form, 1861

Refrain (before st. 2 and after all stanzas)   Fine

1. All glo - ry, laud, and hon - or to thee, Re - deem - er, king,
1. to whom the lips of chil - dren made sweet ho - san - nas ring.

PASSION AND DEATH

Mt. 21:1ff

2. The peo-ple of the He-brews with palms be-fore thee went;
3. Thou art the King of Is-rael, thou Da-vid's roy-al Son,
4. To thee, be-fore thy pas-sion, they sang their hymns of praise;
5. Thou didst ac-cept their prais-es; ac-cept the prayers we bring,

2. our praise and prayer and an-thems be-fore thee we pre-sent.
3. who in the Lord's name com-est, the King and bless-ed One!
4. to thee, now high ex-alt-ed, our mel-o-dy we raise.
5. who in all good de-light-est, thou good and gra-cious King!

NOTE: *When this hymn is sung to other tunes (e.g., 368, 394), it should be sung straight through without treating the first stanza as a refrain.*

Alternative tunes:
AURELIA, 394, HELDER, 368

Ride On! Ride On in Majesty! 280

THE KING'S MAJESTY, LM

H. H. Milman, 1827
First Tune

Graham George, 1938

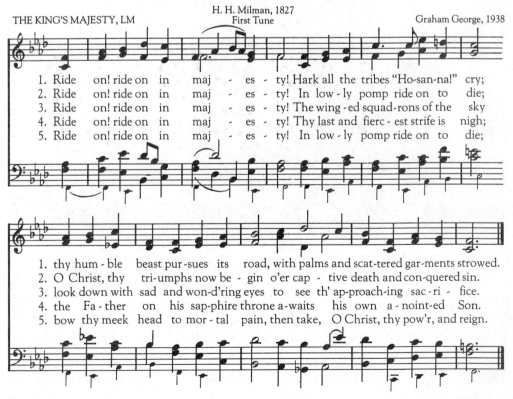

1. Ride on! ride on in maj-es-ty! Hark all the tribes "Ho-san-na!" cry;
2. Ride on! ride on in maj-es-ty! In low-ly pomp ride on to die;
3. Ride on! ride on in maj-es-ty! The wing-ed squad-rons of the sky
4. Ride on! ride on in maj-es-ty! Thy last and fierc-est strife is nigh;
5. Ride on! ride on in maj-es-ty! In low-ly pomp ride on to die;

1. thy hum-ble beast pur-sues its road, with palms and scat-tered gar-ments strowed.
2. O Christ, thy tri-umphs now be-gin o'er cap-tive death and con-quered sin.
3. look down with sad and won-d'ring eyes to see th' ap-proach-ing sac-ri-fice.
4. the Fa-ther on his sap-phire throne a-waits his own a-noint-ed Son.
5. bow thy meek head to mor-tal pain, then take, O Christ, thy pow'r, and reign.

Mt. 21:1ff

PASSION AND DEATH

281

Ride On! Ride On in Majesty!

Second Tune

ST. BARTHOLOMEW, LM — Henry Duncalf, 1762

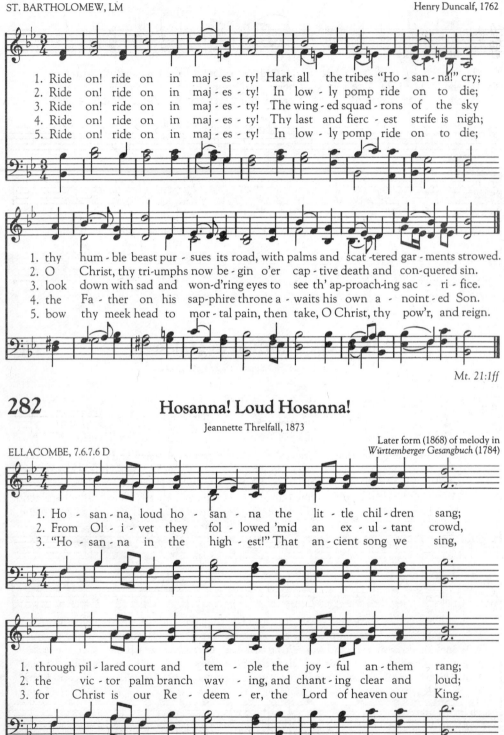

1. Ride on! ride on in maj-es-ty! Hark all the tribes "Ho-san-na!" cry;
2. Ride on! ride on in maj-es-ty! In low-ly pomp ride on to die;
3. Ride on! ride on in maj-es-ty! The wing-ed squad-rons of the sky
4. Ride on! ride on in maj-es-ty! Thy last and fierc-est strife is nigh;
5. Ride on! ride on in maj-es-ty! In low-ly pomp ride on to die;

1. thy hum-ble beast pur-sues its road, with palms and scat-tered gar-ments strowed.
2. O Christ, thy tri-umphs now be-gin o'er cap-tive death and con-quered sin.
3. look down with sad and won-d'ring eyes to see th' ap-proach-ing sac-ri-fice.
4. the Fa-ther on his sap-phire throne a-waits his own a-noint-ed Son.
5. bow thy meek head to mor-tal pain, then take, O Christ, thy pow'r, and reign.

Mt. 21:1ff

282

Hosanna! Loud Hosanna!

Jeannette Threlfall, 1873

ELLACOMBE, 7.6.7.6 D — Later form (1868) of melody in *Württemberger Gesangbuch* (1784)

1. Ho-san-na, loud ho-san-na the lit-tle chil-dren sang;
2. From Ol-i-vet they fol-lowed 'mid an ex-ul-tant crowd,
3. "Ho-san-na in the high-est!" That an-cient song we sing,

1. through pil-lared court and tem-ple the joy-ful an-them rang;
2. the vic-tor palm branch wav-ing, and chant-ing clear and loud;
3. for Christ is our Re-deem-er, the Lord of heaven our King.

1. to Je - sus, who had blessed them close fold - ed to his breast,
2. the Lord of earth and heav - en rode on in low - ly state,
3. O may we ev - er praise him with heart and life and voice,

1. the chil - dren sang their prais - es, the sim - plest and the best.
2. nor scorned that lit - tle chil - dren should on his bid - ding wait.
3. and in his bliss - ful pres - ence e - ter - nal - ly re - joice.

It Happened on That Fateful Night 283

Lutheran Book of Worship (1978); based on Isaac Watts

TALLIS' CANON, LM

Thomas Tallis, c. 1557

1. It hap-pened on that fate - ful night when pow'rs of earth and hell a - rose
2. Be - fore the bit - ter scene be - gan, he took the bread and blessed and broke.
3. "My bod - y bro - ken for your sin re - ceive and eat as liv - ing food."
4. "Do this," he said, "till time shall end, re - mem - ber - ing your dy - ing Friend;
5. O Lord, your feast we cel - e - brate: we show your death, we sing your name

1. a - gainst the Son, our God's De - light, and friends be - trayed him to his foes.
2. What love through all his ac - tions ran! What won - drous words of love he spoke!
3. He took the cup and blessed the wine: "Share this new tes - ta - ment, my blood!"
4. meet at my ta - ble and re - cord the full o - be - dience of the Lord."
5. till you re - turn, when we shall eat the mar - riage sup - per of the Lamb.

This tune in a lower key: 591

Mk. 14:22-24

PASSION AND DEATH

284

My Song Is Love Unknown

Samuel Crossman, 1664

LOVE UNKNOWN, 6.6.6.6.4.44.4

John Ireland, 1918

1. My song is love un-known, my Sav-ior's love to me,
2. He came from his blest throne sal-va-tion to be-stow,
3. Some-times they strew his way and his sweet prais-es sing,
4. Why, what hath my Lord done? What makes this rage and spite?
5. They rise, and needs will have my dear Lord made a-way;

1. love to the love-less shown, that they might love-ly be.
2. but all made strange, and none the longed-for Christ would know.
3. re-sound-ing all the way Ho-san-nas to their King.
4. He made the lame to run, he gave the blind their sight.
5. a mur-der-er they save, the Prince of life they slay.

1. O who am I, that for my sake my Lord should take frail flesh, and die?
2. But, O, my Friend, my Friend in-deed, who at my need his life did spend!
3. Then "Cru-ci-fy!" is all their breath, and for his death they thirst and cry.
4. Sweet in-ju-ries! Yet they at these them-selves dis-please and 'gainst him rise.
5. Yet cheer-ful he to suf-f'ring goes that he his foes from thence might free.

6. In life, no house, no home
   my Lord on earth might have;
   in death, no friendly tomb,
   but what a stranger gave.
   What may I say?
   Heaven was his home,
   but mine the tomb
   wherein he lay.

7. Here might I stay and sing
   no story so divine:
   never was love, dear King,
   never was grief like thine.
   This is my Friend,
   in whose sweet praise
   I all my days
   would gladly spend.

Alternative tune: RHOSYMEDRE, 522, repeating the fifth line of words (+ .... +)

PASSION AND DEATH

Acts 3:14–15

Ah, Holy Jesus, How Hast Thou Offended? 285

Herzliebster Jesu, by Johann Heermann, 1630; tr. Robert Bridges, 1899 (alt'd)

HERZLIEBSTER JESU, 11 11.11 5

Johann Crüger, 1640

1. Ah, holy Jesus, how hast thou offended, that some to judge thee have in hate pretended? By foes derided, by thine own rejected, O most afflicted!

2. Who was the guilty? Who brought this upon thee? Alas, my treason, Jesus hath undone thee. 'Twas I, Lord Jesus, I it was denied thee: I crucified thee.

3. Lo, the good Shepherd for the sheep is offered: the slave hath sinned, and the Son hath suffered for our atonement; while we nothing heeded, God interceded.

4. For me, kind Jesus, was thy incarnation, thy mortal sorrow, and thy life's oblation; thy death of anguish and thy bitter passion, for my salvation.

5. Therefore, kind Jesus, since I cannot pay thee, I do adore thee, and will ever pray thee; think on thy pity and thy love unswerving, not my deserving.

286 The Royal Banners Forward Go

Vexilla Regis prodeunt, by Venantius Fortunatus, c. 574
translation anonymous, c. 1685; first two lines, J. M. Neale

GONFALON ROYAL, LM   First Tune   Percy C. Buck, 1918

1. The roy-al ban-ners for-ward go, _____ the cross shines
2. That which the proph-et King of old _____ hath in mys-
3. Blest tree, most sa-cred and di-vine, _____ which dost in
4. Blest tree, whose hap-py branch-es bore _____ the wealth that
5. Blest Trin-i-ty, life's source and spring, _____ may ev-'ry

1. forth in mys-tic glow; up-on it life did death en-dure,
2. te-rious verse fore-told is now ac-com-plished while we see
3. roy-al pur-ple shine, sup-port-ing an in-car-nate God,
4. did the world re-store, the bal-ance which the price did weigh
5. soul thy prais-es sing! Let those ob-tain a crown in heav'n

1. and yet by death did life pro-cure. ___
2. that God is reign-ing from a tree! ___
3. and ren-dered ho-ly by thy load! ___
4. that spoiled the spoil-er of his prey! ___
5. to whom the cross has con-quest giv'n! ___ A - - men!

Harmony

Antiphon verse (all voices)

That which the proph-et King of old ___ hath in mys-te-rious verse fore-told
is now ac-com-plished while we see that God is reign-ing from a tree. ___

PASSION AND DEATH   *This tune in a lower key: 132*   Ps. 96:10

The Royal Banners Forward Go

287

Second Tune

NOTE: *The whole hymn may be sung as set opposite, to the tune GONFALON ROYAL, or the stanzas printed below may be sung by a soloist or the choir to the plainsong tune, in which case the antiphon stanza (st. 2 opposite) should be sung by the whole congregation at the beginning and after each stanza (or after st. 2 and 4), with "Amen" at the end, as in the score opposite.*

VEXILLA REGIS (to be sung by a cantor, or antiphonally by small groups)

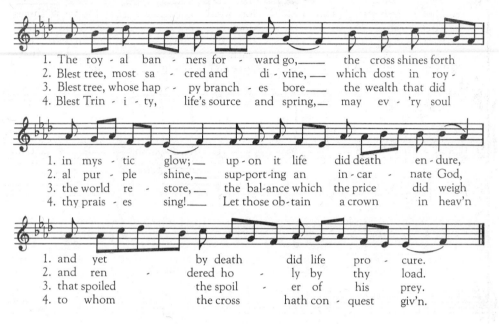

1. The roy - al ban - ners for - ward go,___ the cross shines forth
2. Blest tree, most sa - cred and di - vine, ___ which dost in roy -
3. Blest tree, whose hap - py branch - es bore___ the wealth that did
4. Blest Trin - i - ty, life's source and spring,___ may ev - 'ry soul

1. in mys - tic glow; ___ up-on it life did death en - dure,
2. al pur - ple shine,___ sup-port-ing an in - car - nate God,
3. the world re - store, ___ the bal-ance which the price did weigh
4. thy prais - es sing! ___ Let those ob-tain a crown in heav'n

1. and yet by death did life pro - cure.
2. and ren - dered ho - ly by thy load.
3. that spoiled the spoil - er of his prey.
4. to whom the cross hath con - quest giv'n.

Alone Thou Goest Forth, O Lord

288

Peter Abélard, 1079–1142; tr. F. Bland Tucker, 1940

Melody from W. Tans'ur's *Compleat Melody* (1735);
harmonized by John Wilson, 1964

BANGOR, CM

1. A - lone thou go - est forth, O Lord, in sac - ri - fice to die;
2. Our sins, not thine, thou bear-est, Lord; make us thy sor - row feel,
3. This is earth's dark-est hour, but thou dost light and life re - store;
4. Give us com - pas-sion for thee, Lord, that, as we share this hour,

1. is this thy sor - row naught to us who pass un - heed-ing by?
2. till through our pit - y and our shame love an-swers love's ap - peal.
3. then let all praise be giv - en thee who liv - est ev - er - more!
4. thy cross may bring us to thy joy and res - ur - rec - tion power.

Alternative tune: WALSALL, 26

Mk. 14:50

PASSION AND DEATH

Sing, My Tongue, How Glorious Battle

Pange lingua, by Venantius Fortunatus, c. 530–609; tr. composite

PICARDY, 8.7.8.7.8.7   French carol melody; arranged by R. Vaughan Williams, 1872–1958

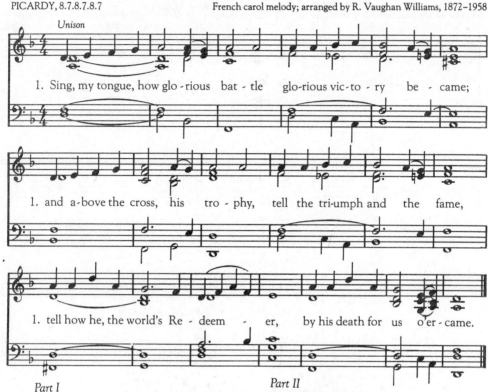

Unison

1. Sing, my tongue, how glo-rious bat-tle glo-rious vic-to-ry be-came;

1. and a-bove the cross, his tro-phy, tell the tri-umph and the fame,

1. tell how he, the world's Re-deem - er, by his death for us o'er-came.

Part I

1. Sing, my tongue, how glorious battle
   glorious victory became;
   and above the cross, his trophy,
   tell the triumph and the fame,
   tell how he, the world's Redeemer,
   by his death for us o'ercame.

2. God in pity saw us fallen,
   shamed and sunk in misery,
   when we fell on death by tasting
   fruit of the forbidden tree:
   then another tree was chosen
   which the world from death should free.

3. Thus the scheme of our salvation
   was of old in order laid,
   that the manifold deceiver's
   art by art might be outweighed,
   and the lure the foe put forward
   into means of healing made.

4. Therefore, when the appointed fullness
   of the holy time was come,
   he was sent, who maketh all things,
   forth from God's eternal home;
   thus he came to earth incarnate,
   offspring of a virgin's womb.

Part II
(begin with st. 1 and continue with st. 5–8)

5. Thirty years among us dwelling,
   his appointed time fulfilled,
   born for this, he meets his Passion,
   for that this he freely willed,
   on the cross the Lamb is lifted
   where his life-blood shall be spilled.

6. Faithful cross! above all other,
   one and only noble tree!
   None in foliage, none in blossom,
   none in fruit thy peer may be!
   Sweetest wood and sweetest iron!
   Sweetest weight is hung on thee.

7. Thou alone wast counted worthy
   this world's ransom to uphold;
   for a shipwrecked race preparing
   harbor, like the ark of old;
   with the sacred blood anointed
   from the smitten Lamb that rolled.

8. To the Trinity be glory
   everlasting, as is meet;
   equal to the Father, equal
   to the Son and Paraclete:
   Trinal Unity, whose praises
   all created things repeat.

PASSION AND DEATH

Sing, My Tongue, How Glorious Battle

A liturgical version for Passiontide

J. F. Wade, 1751

ST. THOMAS (HOLYWOOD), 8.7.8.7.8.7.

NOTE: The congregation sings this stanza first and after each of the cantor's stanzas.

Faith-ful cross! a-bove all oth-er, one and on-ly no-ble tree,

none in fo-liage, none in blos-som, none in fruit thy peer may be.

Sweet-est wood and sweet-est i-ron! Sweet-est weight is hung on thee.

NOTE: This and the plainsong tune may be sung a half-tone lower.

PANGE LINGUA

Traditional plainsong, Mode III transposed

Cantor or choir

1. Sing, my tongue, how glo-rious bat-tle glo-rious vic-to-ry be-came,___
2. Thir-ty years a-mong us dwell-ing, his ap-point-ed time ful-filled,___
3. Thou a-lone wast count-ed wor-thy this world's ran-som to up-hold;___
4. Un-to God be laud and hon-or, to the Fa-ther, to the Son,___

1. and a-bove the cross, his tro-phy, tell the tri-umph and the fame,___
2. born for this, he meets his Pas-sion, for that this he free-ly willed,___
3. for a ship-wrecked race pre-par-ing har-bor, like the ark of old;___
4. to the might-y Spir-it, glo-ry, ev-er Three and ev-er One;___

1. tell how he, the world's Re-deem-er, by his death for us o'er-came.
2. on the cross the Lamb is lift-ed where his life-blood shall be spilled.
3. with the sa-cred blood a-noint-ed from the smit-ten Lamb that rolled.
4. pow'r and glo-ry in the high-est while e-ter-nal a-ges run.

PASSION AND DEATH

291 **Behold, the Lamb of God!**

WIGAN, 6.66.4.88.4   Matthew Bridges, 1848 (alt'd)   S. S. Wesley, 1872

1. Be - hold, the Lamb of God! O thou for sin - ners slain,
2. Be - hold, the Lamb of God! All hail, in - car - nate Word!
3. Be - hold, the Lamb of God! Wor - thy is he a - lone

1. let it not be in vain that thou hast died. Thee for my Sav - ior
2. Thou ev - er - last-ing Lord, thou Sav - ior blest! Fill us with love that
3. to sit up - on the throne of God a - bove, one with the An - cient

1. let me take. My on - ly ref - uge let me make thy pierc - ed side.
2. nev - er faints. Grant us with all thy bless-ed saints e - ter - nal rest.
3. of All Days, one with the Com-fort - er in praise, all light, all love!

Jn. 1:29

292 **When I Survey the Wondrous Cross**

Isaac Watts, 1707
First Tune

ROCKINGHAM, LM   Later version of a tune by E. Miller;
this version mostly from S. Webbe, 1830

1. When I sur - vey the won-drous cross on which the Prince of glo - ry died,
2. For - bid it, Lord, that I should boast, save in the death of Christ my God;
3. See, from his head, his hands, his feet, sor - row and love flow min - gled down;
*4. His dy - ing crim - son, like a robe, spreads o'er his bod - y on the tree;
5. Were the whole realm of na - ture mine, that were a pres - ent far too small;

PASSION AND DEATH

1. my rich - est gain I count but loss, and pour con-tempt on all my pride.
2. all the vain things that charm me most, I sac - ri - fice them to his blood.
3. did e'er such love and sor - row meet, or thorns com-pose so rich a crown?
4. then am I dead to all the globe, and all the globe is dead to me.
5. love so a - maz - ing, so di - vine, de-mands my soul, my life, my all.

This tune in a higher key with familiar harmonies: 544

Gal. 6:14

When I Survey the Wondrous Cross 293

Second Tune

HAMBURG, LM

Lowell Mason, 1824

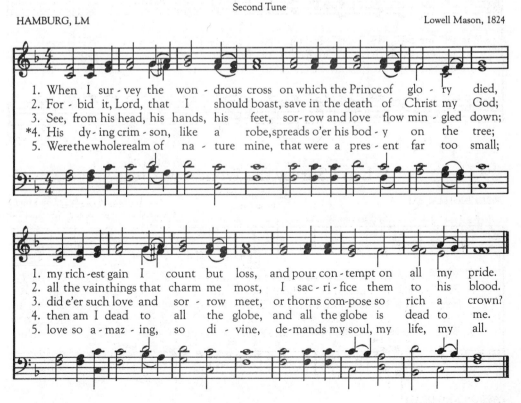

1. When I sur - vey the won - drous cross on which the Prince of glo - ry died,
2. For - bid it, Lord, that I should boast, save in the death of Christ my God;
3. See, from his head, his hands, his feet, sor - row and love flow min - gled down;
*4. His dy - ing crim - son, like a robe, spreads o'er his bod - y on the tree;
5. Were the whole realm of na - ture mine, that were a pres - ent far too small;

1. my rich -est gain I count but loss, and pour con - tempt on all my pride.
2. all the vain things that charm me most, I sac - ri - fice them to his blood.
3. did e'er such love and sor - row meet, or thorns com-pose so rich a crown?
4. then am I dead to all the globe, and all the globe is dead to me.
5. love so a - maz - ing, so di - vine, de-mands my soul, my life, my all.

PASSION AND DEATH

294

Nature with Open Volume Stands

Isaac Watts, 1707
First Tune

Melody in N. Gawthorn's
Harmonia Perfecta (1730);
harmony by S. S. Wesley, 1872

ELTHAM, LM

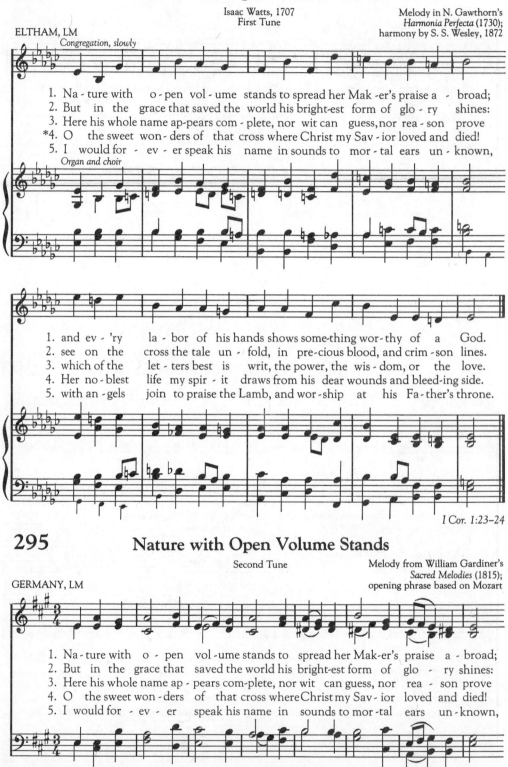

1. Na-ture with o-pen vol-ume stands to spread her Mak-er's praise a - broad;
2. But in the grace that saved the world his bright-est form of glo - ry shines:
3. Here his whole name ap-pears com - plete, nor wit can guess, nor rea - son prove
*4. O the sweet won - ders of that cross where Christ my Sav - ior loved and died!
5. I would for - ev - er speak his name in sounds to mor - tal ears un - known,

1. and ev - 'ry la - bor of his hands shows some-thing wor - thy of a God.
2. see on the cross the tale un - fold, in pre-cious blood, and crim - son lines.
3. which of the let - ters best is writ, the power, the wis - dom, or the love.
4. Her no - blest life my spir - it draws from his dear wounds and bleed-ing side.
5. with an - gels join to praise the Lamb, and wor - ship at his Fa-ther's throne.

I Cor. 1:23–24

295

Nature with Open Volume Stands

Second Tune

Melody from William Gardiner's
Sacred Melodies (1815);
opening phrase based on Mozart

GERMANY, LM

1. Na-ture with o-pen vol-ume stands to spread her Mak-er's praise a - broad;
2. But in the grace that saved the world his bright-est form of glo - ry shines:
3. Here his whole name ap - pears com-plete, nor wit can guess, nor rea - son prove
4. O the sweet won - ders of that cross where Christ my Sav - ior loved and died!
5. I would for - ev - er speak his name in sounds to mor-tal ears un - known,

PASSION AND DEATH

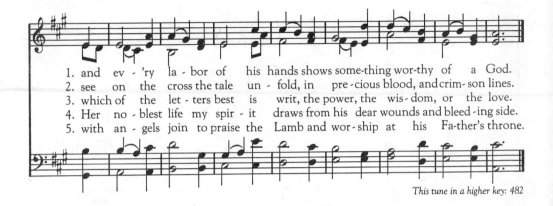

1. and ev - 'ry la - bor of his hands shows some-thing wor-thy of a God.
2. see on the cross the tale un - fold, in pre-cious blood, and crim-son lines.
3. which of the let - ters best is writ, the power, the wis-dom, or the love.
4. Her no - blest life my spir - it draws from his dear wounds and bleed-ing side.
5. with an - gels join to praise the Lamb and wor-ship at his Fa-ther's throne.

This tune in a higher key: 482

We Sing the Praise of Him Who Died 296

Thomas Kelly, 1815; adapted from Samuel Medley, 1738–1799 (alt'd)

Felix Mendelssohn–Bartholdy, 1836;
based on a melody in *As Hymnodus Sacer* (Leipzig, 1625)

BRESLAU, LM

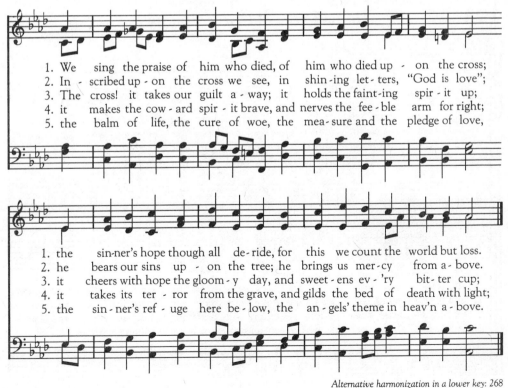

1. We sing the praise of him who died, of him who died up - on the cross;
2. In - scribed up - on the cross we see, in shin-ing let - ters, "God is love";
3. The cross! it takes our guilt a - way; it holds the faint-ing spir - it up;
4. it makes the cow - ard spir - it brave, and nerves the fee - ble arm for right;
5. the balm of life, the cure of woe, the mea - sure and the pledge of love,

1. the sin - ner's hope though all de - ride, for this we count the world but loss.
2. he bears our sins up - on the tree; he brings us mer - cy from a - bove.
3. it cheers with hope the gloom - y day, and sweet - ens ev - 'ry bit - ter cup;
4. it takes its ter - ror from the grave, and gilds the bed of death with light;
5. the sin - ner's ref - uge here be - low, the an - gels' theme in heav'n a - bove.

Alternative harmonization in a lower key: 268

Mk. 15:26

PASSION AND DEATH

297

In the Cross of Christ I Glory

John Bowring, 1825
First Tune

CRUCIFIXION, 8.7.8.7.

John Stainer, 1887

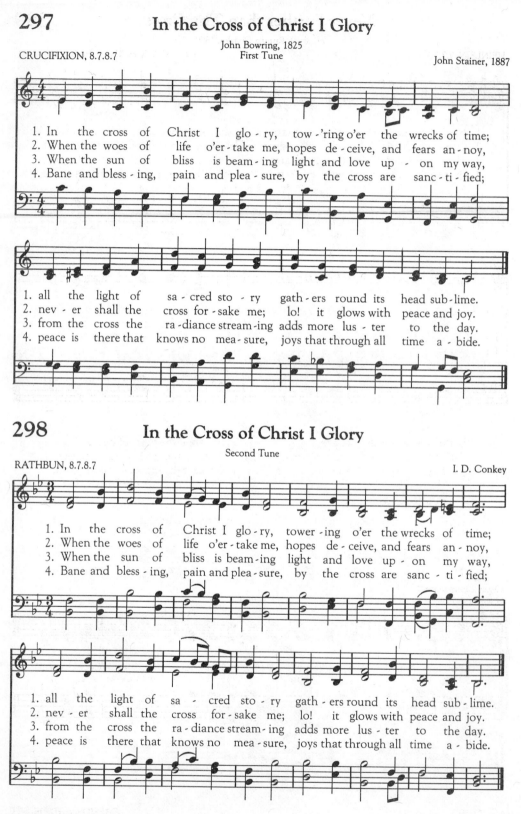

1. In the cross of Christ I glo-ry, tow-'ring o'er the wrecks of time;
2. When the woes of life o'er-take me, hopes de-ceive, and fears an-noy,
3. When the sun of bliss is beam-ing light and love up-on my way,
4. Bane and bless-ing, pain and plea-sure, by the cross are sanc-ti-fied;

1. all the light of sa-cred sto-ry gath-ers round its head sub-lime.
2. nev-er shall the cross for-sake me; lo! it glows with peace and joy.
3. from the cross the ra-diance stream-ing adds more lus-ter to the day.
4. peace is there that knows no mea-sure, joys that through all time a-bide.

298

In the Cross of Christ I Glory

Second Tune

RATHBUN, 8.7.8.7.

I. D. Conkey

1. In the cross of Christ I glo-ry, tower-ing o'er the wrecks of time;
2. When the woes of life o'er-take me, hopes de-ceive, and fears an-noy,
3. When the sun of bliss is beam-ing light and love up-on my way,
4. Bane and bless-ing, pain and plea-sure, by the cross are sanc-ti-fied;

1. all the light of sa-cred sto-ry gath-ers round its head sub-lime.
2. nev-er shall the cross for-sake me; lo! it glows with peace and joy.
3. from the cross the ra-diance stream-ing adds more lus-ter to the day.
4. peace is there that knows no mea-sure, joys that through all time a-bide.

PASSION AND DEATH

Never Further than Thy Cross

Elisabeth Rundle Charles, 1860

HEINLEIN, 7.7.7.7

Melody by Martin Herbst, 1654–1681

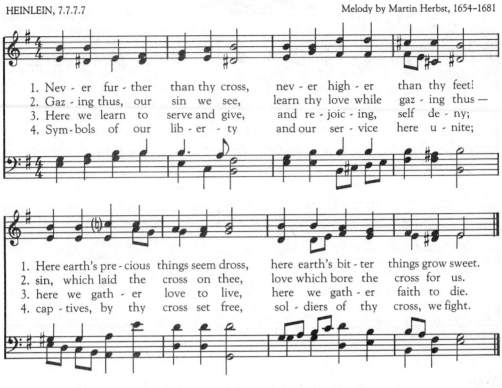

1. Nev - er fur - ther than thy cross, nev - er high - er than thy feet!
2. Gaz - ing thus, our sin we see, learn thy love while gaz - ing thus —
3. Here we learn to serve and give, and re - joic - ing, self de - ny;
4. Sym - bols of our lib - er - ty and our ser - vice here u - nite;

1. Here earth's pre - cious things seem dross, here earth's bit - ter things grow sweet.
2. sin, which laid the cross on thee, love which bore the cross for us.
3. here we gath - er love to live, here we gath - er faith to die.
4. cap - tives, by thy cross set free, sol - diers of thy cross, we fight.

5. Pressing onward as we can,
    still to this our hearts must tend,
   where our earliest hopes began,
    there our last aspirings end,

   [no pause between stanzas]

6. till, amid the hosts of heaven,
    we, in thee redeemed, complete,
   through thy cross all sins forgiven,
    cast our crowns before thy feet.

Organ accompaniment
at join of st. 5 and 6

Start st. 6

End of st. 6

etc.

there our last as - pir - ings end (till, a - mid the) (fore thy feet)

Manual only   ped.   etc.

Mk. 15:40

PASSION AND DEATH

300 O Sacred Head, Now Wounded

Medieval Latin poem, *Salve caput cruentatum;*
tr. in German as *O Haupt voll Blut und Wunden;*
English version by James Waddell Alexander, 1830

PASSION CHORALE, 7.6.7.6 D   Hans Leo Hassler, 1601; arranged by J. S. Bach

1. O sa-cred head, now wound-ed, with grief and shame weighed down,
2. What thou, my Lord, hast suf-fered was all for sin-ners' gain;
3. What lan-guage shall I bor-row to thank thee, dear-est friend,

1. now scorn-ful-ly sur-round-ed with thorns thine on-ly crown:
2. mine, mine was the trans-gres-sion, but thine the dead-ly pain.
3. for this, thy dy-ing sor-row, thy pit-y with-out end?

1. how art thou pale with an-guish, with sore a-buse and scorn,
2. Lo, here I fall, my Sav-ior; 'tis I de-serve thy place;
3. O make me thine for-ev-er, and should I faint-ing be,

1. how does that vis-age lan-guish, which once was bright as morn!
2. look on me with thy fa-vor, as-sist me with thy grace.
3. Lord, let me nev-er, nev-er out-live my love to thee.

PASSION AND DEATH   Mk. 15:17–18

O Dearest Lord, Thy Sacred Head

301

H. E. Hardy, c. 1930

SPRINGDALE, CM

Erik Routley, 1980

Unison

1. O dear-est Lord, thy sa-cred head with thorns was pierced for me;
2. O dear-est Lord, thy sa-cred hands with nails were pierced for me;
3. O dear-est Lord, thy sa-cred feet with nails were pierced for me;
4. O dear-est Lord, thy sa-cred heart with spear was pierced for me;

1. O pour thy bless-ing on my head, that I may think for thee.
2. O shed thy bless-ing on my hands, that they may work for thee.
3. O pour thy bless-ing on my feet, that they may fol - low thee.
4. O pour thy bless-ing on my heart, that I may live for thee.

Mk. 15:17, 24; Jn. 19:34

Come to the Place of Grief and Shame

302

St. 1, compilers; st. 2–4, F. W. Faber, 1849

ST. CROSS, LM

J. B. Dykes, 1861

1. Come to the place of grief and shame; come to the strick-en Sav-ior's side.
2. O break, O break, hard heart of mine! Thy weak self-love and guil-ty pride
3. A bro-ken heart, a fount of tears, ask, and they will not be de-nied.
4. O love of God! O pow'r of sin! In this dread act your strength is tried,

1. A - lone, re-ject-ed, wound-ed, scorned, Je-sus our Lord is cru-ci-fied!
2. his Pi-late and his Ju-das were: Je-sus our Lord is cru-ci-fied!
3. A bro-ken heart love's cra-dle is: Je-sus our Lord is cru-ci-fied!
4. and vic-to-ry re-mains with love: Je-sus our Lord is cru-ci-fied!

Mt. 26:47

PASSION AND DEATH

303   To Mock Your Reign, O Dearest Lord

Fred Pratt Green, 1973
First Tune

TALLIS' THIRD TUNE, CMD   Thomas Tallis, c. 1557; edited by John Wilson, 1978

Unison or harmony

1. To mock your reign, O dear-est Lord, they made a crown of thorns,
2. In mock ac-claim, O gra-cious Lord, they snatched a pur-ple cloak,
3. A scep-tered reed, O pa-tient Lord, they thrust in-to your hand,

1. set you with taunts a-long that road from which no one re-turns.
2. your pas-sion turned, for all they cared, in-to a sol-dier's joke.
3. and act-ed out their grim cha-rade to its ap-point-ed end.

1. They could not know, as we do now, how glo-rious is that crown,
2. They could not know, as we do now, that though we mer-it blame,
3. They could not know, as we do now, though em-pires rise and fall,

1. that thorns would flow'r up-on your brow, your sor-rows heal our own.
2. you will your robe of mer-cy throw a-round our na-ked shame.
3. your king-dom shall not cease to grow till love em-brac-es all.

PASSION AND DEATH   Mk. 15:17–20

To Mock Your Reign

304

Second Tune

(a) WINDSOR, CM
(b) COLESHILL, CM

Daman's Psalter (1591);
Barton's Psalter (1644)

1. To mock your reign, O dear-est Lord, they made a crown of thorns,
2. In mock ac-claim, O gra-cious Lord, they snatched a pur-ple cloak,
3. A scep-tered reed, O pa-tient Lord, they thrust in-to your hand,

1. set you with taunts a - long that road from which no one re - turns.
2. your pas-sion turned, for all they cared, in - to a sol-dier's joke.
3. and act - ed out their grim cha - rade to its ap-point-ed end.

1. They could not know, as we do now, how glo - rious is that crown,
2. They could not know, as we do now, that though we mer - it blame,
3. They could not know, as we do now, though em-pires rise and fall,

1. that thorns would flow'r up - on that brow, your sor - rows heal our own.
2. you will your robe of mer - cy throw a - round our na - ked shame.
3. your king - dom shall not cease to grow till love em - brac - es all.

PASSION AND DEATH

305   There Springs a Fountain

William Cowper, 1779; amended by Nathaniel Micklem, 1888–1976

WINDSOR, CM

Melody in *Daman's Psalter* (1591)

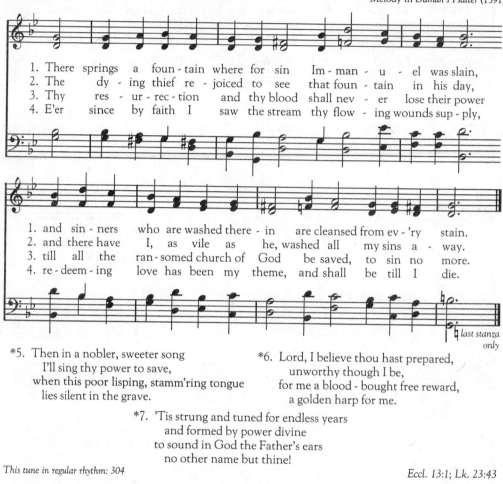

1. There springs a foun-tain where for sin Im-man-u-el was slain,
2. The dy-ing thief re-joiced to see that foun-tain in his day,
3. Thy res-ur-rec-tion and thy blood shall nev-er lose their power
4. E'er since by faith I saw the stream thy flow-ing wounds sup-ply,

1. and sin-ners who are washed there-in are cleansed from ev-'ry stain.
2. and there have I, as vile as he, washed all my sins a-way.
3. till all the ran-somed church of God be saved, to sin no more.
4. re-deem-ing love has been my theme, and shall be till I die.

last stanza only

*5. Then in a nobler, sweeter song
    I'll sing thy power to save,
when this poor lisping, stamm'ring tongue
    lies silent in the grave.

*6. Lord, I believe thou hast prepared,
    unworthy though I be,
for me a blood-bought free reward,
    a golden harp for me.

*7. 'Tis strung and tuned for endless years
    and formed by power divine
    to sound in God the Father's ears
    no other name but thine!

This tune in regular rhythm: 304

Eccl. 13:1; Lk. 23:43

306   There Is a Green Hill Far Away

Cecil Frances Alexander, 1848 (alt'd)

HORSLEY, CM

William Horsley, 1830

1. There is a green hill far a-way out-side a cit-y wall,
2. We may not know, we can-not tell what pains he had to bear,
3. There was no oth-er good e-nough to pay the price of sin;
4. O dear-ly, dear-ly has he loved, and we must love him too,

PASSION AND DEATH

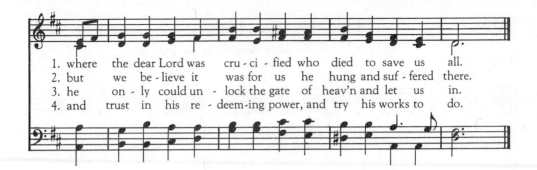

1. where the dear Lord was cru-ci-fied who died to save us all.
2. but we be-lieve it was for us he hung and suf-fered there.
3. he on-ly could un-lock the gate of heav'n and let us in.
4. and trust in his re-deem-ing power, and try his works to do.

There in God's Garden Stands the Tree of Wisdom 307

Based on a hymn in Hungarian by P. K. Imre, 1961
Paraphrased by Erik Routley, 1974

DIVA SERVATRIX, 11.11.11.5

Bayeux Antiphoner (1739)

1. There in God's gar-den stands the Tree of Wis-dom,
2. Its name is Je-sus, name that says, "Our Sav-ior!"
3. Thorns not his own are tan-gled in its fo-liage;
4. See how its branch-es reach to us in wel-come;

1. whose leaves hold forth the heal-ing of the na-tions: Tree of all
2. There on its branch-es see the scars of suf-f'ring; see where the
3. our greed has starved it, our de-spite has choked it. Yet, look! it
4. hear what the Voice says, "Come to me, ye wea-ry! Give me your

1. knowl-edge, Tree of all com-pas-sion, Tree of all beau-ty.
2. ten-drils of our hu-man self-hood feed on its life-blood.
3. lives! its grief has not de-stroyed it nor fire con-sumed it.
4. sick-ness, give me all your sor-row, I will give bless-ing."

5. This is my ending, this my resurrection;
   into your hands, Lord, I commit my spirit.
   This have I searched for;
   now I can possess it.
   This ground is holy.

6. All heav'n is singing,
   "Thanks to Christ whose Passion
   offers in mercy healing, strength, and pardon.
   Peoples and nations, take it, take it freely!"
   Amen! My Master!

Gen. 2:9; Ex. 3:2; Rev. 22:2

PASSION AND DEATH

308 Jesus, Name All Names Above

Greek hymn by Theoktistus, 9th century; tr. J. M. Neale, 1862

WERDE MUNTER, 7.6.7.6.88.77

J. Schop, 1641; arranged by J. S. Bach

1. Je - sus, name all names a - bove, Je - sus, best and dear - est,
2. Thou didst call the prod - i - gal; thou didst par - don Mar - y;
3. Je - sus, o - pen me the gate that the rob - ber en - ter'd,

1. Je - sus, fount of per - fect love, ho - liest, ten - d'rest, near - est,
2. thou whose words can nev - er fall, love can nev - er var - y,
3. who in that most lost es - tate whol - ly on thee ven - tured.

1. Je - sus, source of grace com - plet - est, Je - sus, pur - est, Je - sus, sweet - est,
2. Lord, to heal my lost con - di - tion give (for thou canst give) con - tri - tion;
3. Thou whose wounds are ev - er plead - ing, and thy Pas - sion in - ter - ced - ing,

1. Je - sus, well of pow'r di - vine, make me, keep me, seal me thine!
2. thou canst par - don all my ill if thou wilt; O say, "I will!"
3. from my sins, O let me rise to a home in par - a - dise!

PASSION AND DEATH

Lk. 8:2; Lk. 15:11ff; Lk. 23:43

"It Is Finished!"

Gabriel Gillett, 1906

SEBASTIAN, 7.88.7.8.7.8.7   J. A. Freylinghausen, 1714; bass by J. S. Bach, 1736

309

1. "It is fin-ished!" Christ hath known all the life of our way-far-ing,
2. "It is fin-ished!" Christ is slain on the al-tar of cre-a-tion,
3. "It is fin-ished!" Christ our King wins the vic-tor's crown of glo-ry;

1. hu-man joys and sor-rows shar-ing, mak-ing hu-man needs his own.
2. of-f'ring for a world's sal-va-tion sac-ri-fice of love and pain.
3. sun and stars re-cite his sto-ry, floods and fields his tri-umph sing.

1. Lord, in us thy life re-new-ing, lead us where thy feet have trod,
2. Lord, thy love through pain re-veal-ing, purge our pas-sions, scourge our vice,
3. Lord, whose praise the world is tell-ing, Lord to whom all pow'r is giv'n,

1. till, the way of truth pur-su-ing, hu-man souls find rest in God.
2. till up-on the tree of suf-f'ring self is slain in sac-ri-fice.
3. by thy death hell's ar-mies quell-ing, bring thy saints to reign in heav'n!

Jn. 19:30   PASSION AND DEATH

310

Beneath the Cross of Jesus

Elizabeth C. Clephane, 1830–1869 (alt'd)
First Tune

ST. CHRISTOPHER, 7.6.8.6.8.6.8.6   F. C. Maker, 1881

1. Be - neath the cross of Je - sus I fain would take my stand,
2. Up - on the cross of Je - sus my eyes at times can see
3. I take, O cross, thy shad - ow for my a - bid - ing place:

1. the shad - ow of a might - y rock with - in a wea - ry land,
2. the ver - y dy - ing form of one who suf - fered there for me,
3. I ask no oth - er sun - shine than the sun - shine of thy face;

1. a home with - in the wil - der - ness, a rest up - on the way,
2. and from my hum - bled heart with shame two won - ders I con - fess:
3. con - tent un - to the world to die, to know no gain or loss,

1. from the burn - ing of the noon - tide heat and the bur - den of the day.
2. the won - ders of re - deem - ing love, and my own love - less - ness.
3. my on - ly shame a sin - ful heart, my glo - ry all, the cross.

PASSION AND DEATH   *Isa. 32:2*

Beneath the Cross of Jesus

Second Tune

WOLVERCOTE, 7.6.8.6.8.6.8.6

W. H. Ferguson, c. 1910

1. Be - neath the cross of Je - sus I fain would take my stand,
2. Up - on the cross of Je - sus mine eyes at times can see
3. I take, O cross, thy shad - ow for my a - bid - ing place:

1. the shad - ow of a might - y rock with - in a wea - ry land,
2. the ver - y dy - ing form of one who suf - fered there for me,
3. I ask no oth - er sun-shine than the sun-shine of his face;

1. a home with - in the wil - der - ness, a rest up - on the way,
2. and from my hum - bled heart with shame two won - ders I con - fess:
3. con - tent un - to the world to die, to know no gain or loss,

1. from the burn - ing of the noon - tide heat and the bur - den of the day.
2. the won - ders of re - deem - ing love, and my own love - less - ness.
3. my on - ly shame a sin - ful heart, my glo - ry all, the cross.

PASSION AND DEATH

312

Jesus Christ Is Risen Today

Surrexit Christus Hodie, late medieval Latin carol; this version, 1816

EASTER HYMN, 77.77 with Alleluias   Later form (1741) of melody in *Lyra Davidica* (1708)

1. Je - sus Christ is risen to - day, Al - le - lu - ia!
2. Hymns of praise then let us sing, Al - le - lu - ia!
3. But the pains which he en - dured, Al - le - lu - ia!

1. Our tri - um - phant ho - ly day, Al - le - lu - ia!
2. Un - to Christ, our heaven - ly King, Al - le - lu - ia!
3. Our sal - va - tion have pro - cured; Al - le - lu - ia!

1. Who did once, up - on the cross, Al - le - lu - ia!
2. Who en - dured the cross and grave, Al - le - lu - ia!
3. Now a - bove the sky he's King, Al - le - lu - ia!

1. Suf - fer to re - deem our loss. Al - le - lu - ia!
2. Sin - ners to re - deem and save. Al - le - lu - ia!
3. Where the an - gels ev - er sing. Al - le - lu - ia!

NOTE: *A descant can be formed for this tune if the descant voices sing on the first two Alleluias the music of the fourth, and on the fourth, the music of the first an octave higher. Descanters should join with all other voices on the third.*

That Easter Day with Joy Was Bright 313

Claro paschali gaudio, early medieval Latin hymn;
tr. by the compilers of *Hymns Ancient and Modern*, 1861 (slightly alt'd)

PUER NOBIS NASCITUR, LM

Melody adapted by M. Praetorius, 1609

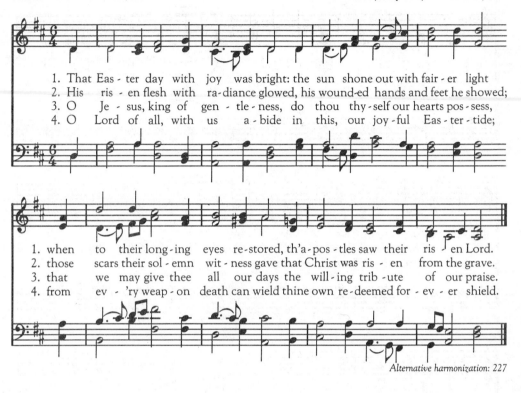

1. That Eas-ter day with joy was bright: the sun shone out with fair-er light
2. His ris-en flesh with ra-diance glowed, his wound-ed hands and feet he showed;
3. O Je-sus, king of gen-tle-ness, do thou thy-self our hearts pos-sess,
4. O Lord of all, with us a-bide in this, our joy-ful Eas-ter-tide;

1. when to their long-ing eyes re-stored, th'a-pos-tles saw their ris-en Lord.
2. those scars their sol-emn wit-ness gave that Christ was ris-en from the grave.
3. that we may give thee all our days the will-ing trib-ute of our praise.
4. from ev-'ry weap-on death can wield thine own re-deemed for-ev-er shield.

Alternative harmonization: 227

The Lamb's High Banquet 314

Latin, 7th century; tr. J. M. Neale and others

(Easter Vigil)

This hymn to be sung to tune above: PUER NOBIS NASCITUR

1. The Lamb's high banquet called to share,
   arrayed in garments white and fair,
   the Red Sea past, we fain would sing
   to Jesus, our triumphant King.

2. Upon the altar of the cross
   his body hath redeemed our loss;
   and, tasting of his precious blood,
   our life is hid with him in God.

3. That paschal eve God's arm was bared,
   the devastating angel spared;
   by strength of hand our hosts went free
   from Pharaoh's ruthless tyranny.

4. Now Christ, our Passover, is slain,
   the Lamb of God without a stain;
   the true oblation offered here,
   our own unleavened bread sincere.

5. Christ rises conqueror from the grave,
   from death returning, strong to save,
   with his right hand the tyrant chains,
   and paradise for us regains.

6. All praise be thine, O risen Lord,
   from death to endless life restored;
   all praise to God the Father be,
   and Holy Ghost eternally.

RESURRECTION AND ASCENSION

315   Come, Ye Faithful, Raise the Strain

Greek hymn by John of Damascus, d. 750; tr. J. M. Neale, 1862
First Tune

ST. KEVIN, 7.6.7.6 D

Arthur S. Sullivan, 1842–1900

1. Come, ye faith - ful, raise the strain of tri - um - phant glad - ness;
2. 'Tis the spring of souls to - day; Christ hath burst his pris - on,
3. Now the queen of sea - sons, bright with the day of splen - dor,
4. Nei - ther might the gates of death, nor the tomb's dark por - tal,

1. God hath brought his Is - ra - el in - to joy from sad - ness;
2. and from three days' sleep in death as a sun hath ris - en.
3. with the roy - al feast of feasts, comes its joy to ren - der;
4. nor the watch - ers, nor the seal hold thee as a mor - tal;

1. loosed from Pha - raoh's bit - ter yoke, Ja - cob's sons and daugh - ters
2. All the win - ter of our sins, long and dark, is fly - ing
3. comes to glad Je - ru - sa - lem, who with true af - fec - tion
4. but to - day a - midst thine own thou didst stand, be - stow - ing

1. led them, with un - moist - ened foot through the Red Sea wa - ters.
2. from his light, to whom we give laud and praise un - dy - ing.
3. wel - comes in un - wea - ried strains Je - sus' res - ur - rec - tion.
4. thine own peace which ev - er - more pass - eth hu - man know - ing.

RESURRECTION AND ASCENSION

Ex. 14:29; I Cor. 15:20–28

Come, Ye Faithful, Raise the Strain

Second Tune

AVE VIRGO, 7.6.7.6 D

Melody from J. Horn's *Gesangbuch* (1544)

1. Come, ye faith - ful, raise the strain of tri - um - phant glad - ness;
2. 'Tis the spring of souls to - day; Christ hath burst his pris - on,
3. Now the queen of sea - sons, bright with the day of splen - dor,
4. Nei - ther might the gates of death, nor the tomb's dark por - tal,

1. God hath brought his Is - ra - el in - to joy from sad - ness;
2. and from three days' sleep in death as a sun hath ris - en.
3. with the roy - al feast of feasts, comes its joy to ren - der;
4. nor the watch - ers, nor the seal hold thee as a mor - tal;

1. loosed from Pha - raoh's bit - ter yoke, Ja - cob's sons and daugh - ters
2. All the win - ter of our sins, long and dark, is fly - ing
3. comes to glad Je - ru - sa - lem, who with true af - fec - tion
4. but to - day a - midst thine own thou didst stand, be - stow - ing

1. led them, with un - moist - ened foot through the Red Sea wa - ters.
2. from his light, to whom we give laud and praise un - dy - ing.
3. wel - comes in un - wea - ried strains Je - sus' res - ur - rec - tion.
4. thine own peace which ev - er - more pass - eth hu - man know - ing.

RESURRECTION AND ASCENSION

317
The Day of Resurrection!

Greek hymn by John of Damascus; tr. J. M. Neale, 1862

LANCASHIRE, 7.6.7.6 D

Henry Smart, 1836

1. The day of res - ur - rec - tion! Earth, tell it out a - broad;
2. Our hearts be pure from e - vil, that we may see a - right
3. Now let the heavens be joy - ful, let earth her song be - gin;

1. the Pass - o - ver of glad - ness, the Pass - o - ver of God.
2. the Lord in rays e - ter - nal of res - ur - rec - tion light;
3. let the round world keep tri - umph, and all that is there - in;

1. From death to life e - ter - nal, from this world to the sky,
2. and, lis - tening to his ac - cents, may hear, so calm and plain,
3. let all things seen and un - seen their notes of glad - ness blend,

1. our Christ hath brought us o - ver with hymns of vic - to - ry.
2. his own "All hail!" and, hear - ing, may raise the vic - tor strain.
3. for Christ the Lord hath ris - en, our joy that hath no end.

This tune in a lower key: 423
Alternative tune: LLANGLOFFAN, 80

Ye Sons and Daughters of the King

O filii et filiae, J. Tisserand, d. 1494; tr. J. M. Neale, 1851

O FILII ET FILIAE, 888 with Alleluias

Melody c. 15th century

Before first stanza only
Unison

All stanzas begin here

Al - le - lu - ia! Al - le - lu - ia! Al - le - lu - ia!

1. Ye sons and daugh-ters
2. On that first morn-ing
3. An an - gel bade their
4. That night th' a - pos - tles

1. of the King whom heav'n - ly hosts in glo - ry sing, to -
2. of the week the Mar - ys went their Lord to seek be -
3. sor - row flee, for thus he spoke un - to the three: "Your
4. met in fear; a - midst them came their Lord most dear, and

1. day the grave hath lost its sting.
2. fore the day be - gan to break.
3. Lord is gone to Gal - i - lee."
4. said, "Peace be un - to you here."

Al - le - lu - ia!

*5. What Thomas afterwards had heard
that Jesus had fulfilled his word,
he doubted if it were the Lord. Alleluia!

*6. "Thomas, behold my side," said he;
"my hands, my feet, my body see,
and doubt not, but believing be." Alleluia!

*7. No longer Thomas then denied;
he saw the feet, the hands, the side.
"Thou art my Lord and God," he cried.
Alleluia!

8. How blest are they who have not seen,
and yet whose faith had constant been;
in life eternal they shall reign. Alleluia!

9. On this most holy day of days
to God your hearts and voices raise
in laud and jubilee and praise. Alleluia!

NOTE: When St. Thomas appears in the Lectionary, st. 1–2, 4–7 are suitable.

Jn. 20:26:29

RESURRECTION AND ASCENSION

The Strife Is O'er

Finita iam sunt proelia, Latin hymn in *Symphonia Serenum Selectarum* (1695);
tr. based on that of F. Pott, 1861

VICTORY, 888 with Alleluia

W. H. Monk, 1861; based on a *Gloria* of Palestrina, 1591

1. The strife is o'er, the bat - tle done; the vic-to - ry of life is won;
2. The powers of death have done their worst, but Christ their le - gions hath dis - persed;
3. The three sad days have quick - ly sped; he ris - es glo - rious from the dead;
4. He closed the yawn - ing gates of hell; the bars from heaven's high por - tals fell;
5. Lord, by the stripes which wound-ed thee, from death's dread sting thy ser-vants free,

1. the song of tri - umph has be - gun. Al - le - lu - ia!
2. let shouts of ho - ly joy out - burst. Al - le - lu - ia!
3. all glo - ry to our ris - en Head! Al - le - lu - ia!
4. yet hymns of praise his tri - umphs tell. Al - le - lu - ia!
5. that we may live and sing to thee! Al - le - lu - ia!

Rev. 1:18

Jesus Lives!

Jesus Lebt, by C. F. Gellert, 1757; tr. Frances E. Cox, 1841 (rev.)

ST. ALBINUS, 7.8.7.8.4

H. J. Gauntlett, 1852

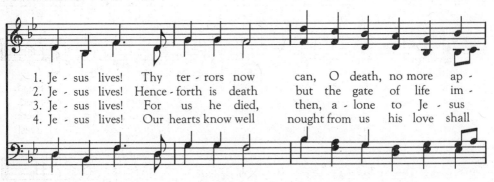

1. Je - sus lives! Thy ter - rors now can, O death, no more ap -
2. Je - sus lives! Hence - forth is death but the gate of life im -
3. Je - sus lives! For us he died, then, a - lone to Je - sus
4. Je - sus lives! Our hearts know well nought from us his love shall

RESURRECTION AND ASCENSION

1. pal us; Je - sus lives! By this we know thou, O grave, canst
2. mor - tal; this shall calm our trem-bling breath when we pass its
3. liv - ing, pure in heart may we a - bide, glo - ry to our
4. sev - er; life, nor death, nor pow'rs of hell tear us from his

1. not en - thral us. Al - le - lu - ia!
2. gloom - y por - tal. Al - le - lu - ia!
3. Sav - ior giv - ing. Al - le - lu - ia!
4. keep - ing ev - er. Al - le - lu - ia! A - men!

Alternative tune: SHILLINGFORD, 257
Rom. 6:3ff; Rom. 8:38–39

No fermata in last stanza

I Know That My Redeemer Lives 321

Samuel Medley, 1775

ST. BARTHOLOMEW, LM

Henry Duncalf, 1762

1. I know that my Re - deem-er lives—what joy the blest as - sur-ance gives!
2. He lives, to bless me with his love; he lives, to plead for me a - bove;
3. He lives, and grants me dai - ly breath; he lives, and I shall con-quer death;
4. He lives; all glo - ry to his name; he lives, my Sav - ior still the same;

1. He lives, he lives who once was dead; he lives, my ev - er - last - ing Head.
2. he lives, my hun - gry soul to feed; he lives, to help in time of need.
3. he lives, my man - sion to pre - pare; he lives, to lead me safe - ly there.
4. what joy the blest as - sur-ance gives: I know that my Re - deem - er lives!

Job 19:25; Rom. 6:3ff

RESURRECTION AND ASCENSION

322

Jesus Lives! The Victory's Won!

Jesus lebt, as hymn 320; tr. in *Lutheran Book of Worship* (1978)

JESUS MEINE ZUVERSICHT, 7.8.7.8.77

Melody by J. Crüger, 1653; arranged by J. S. Bach;
harmony simplified

1. Je - sus lives! the vic-tory's won! Death no long - er can ap-pal me.
2. Je - sus lives! to him the throne there a - bove all things is giv - en.
3. Je - sus lives! for me he died, hence will I, to Je - sus liv - ing,
4. Je - sus lives! and I am sure nei - ther death nor life shall sev - er
5. Je - sus lives! and now is death but the gate of life im - mor - tal;

1. Je - sus lives! death's reign is done: from the grave will Christ re-call me.
2. I shall go where he is gone, live and reign with him in heav - en.
3. pure in heart and act a - bide praise to him and glo - ry giv - ing.
4. me from him. I shall en - dure in his love, thro' death, for - ev - er.
5. this shall calm my trem - bling breath when I pass its gloom - y por - tal.

1. Bright-er scenes shall then com-mence; this shall be my con - fi - dence.
2. All I need will God dis - pense; this shall be my con - fi - dence.
3. God is faith - ful; doubt-ings, hence! this shall be my con - fi - dence.
4. God will be my sure de - fense; this shall be my con - fi - dence.
5. Faith shall cry, as fails each sense, "Je - sus is my con - fi - dence!"

RESURRECTION AND ASCENSION

I Cor. 15:51–56

Christ the Lord Is Risen Again

323

Christus ist erstanden, M. Weisse, 1531;
tr. Catherine Winkworth, 1855

ANTIPHON: *to be sung at the beginning by the choir, then by the congregation and after st. 4; after any other stanza as desired.*

Al - le - lu - ia! Al - le - lu - ia! Al - le - lu - ia!

last time only

CHRISTUS IST ERSTANDEN, 77.77 with Alleluias

Medieval German melody

1. Christ the Lord is ris'n a - gain; Christ hath bro - ken ev - 'ry chain;
2. He who gave for us his life, who for us en - dured the strife,
3. He who bore all pain and loss com - fort - less up - on the cross,
4. He who slum - bered in the grave is ex - alt - ed now to save;

1. hark, the an - gels shout for joy, sing - ing ev - er - more on high, "Al - le - lu - ia!"
2. is our Pas - chal Lamb to - day; we too sing for joy and say, "Al - le - lu - ia!"
3. lives in glo - ry now on high, pleads for us and hears our cry: "Al - le - lu - ia!"
4. now thro' Chris - ten - dom it rings that the Lamb is King of kings, Al - le - lu - ia!

324   Christ Jesus Lay in Death's Strong Bands

Christ lag in Todes Banden, by Martin Luther, 1524;
tr. Richard Massie, 1858 (alt'd)

CHRIST LAG IN TODESBANDEN, 8.7.8.7.78.7.4   Medieval melody arranged by J. Walther, 1524

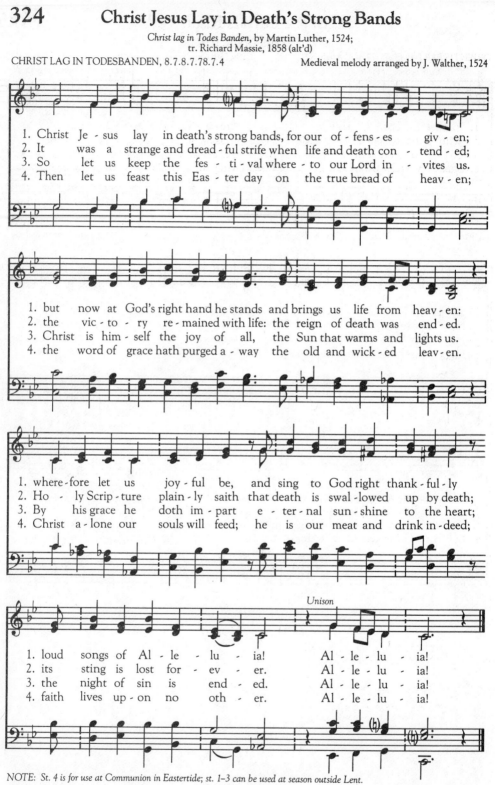

1. Christ Jesus lay in death's strong bands, for our offenses given;
2. It was a strange and dreadful strife when life and death contended;
3. So let us keep the festival whereto our Lord invites us.
4. Then let us feast this Easter day on the true bread of heaven;

1. but now at God's right hand he stands and brings us life from heaven:
2. the victory remained with life: the reign of death was ended.
3. Christ is himself the joy of all, the Sun that warms and lights us.
4. the word of grace hath purged away the old and wicked leaven.

1. wherefore let us joyful be, and sing to God right thankfully
2. Holy Scripture plainly saith that death is swallowed up by death;
3. By his grace he doth impart eternal sunshine to the heart;
4. Christ alone our souls will feed; he is our meat and drink indeed;

Unison

1. loud songs of Alleluia! Alleluia!
2. its sting is lost forever. Alleluia!
3. the night of sin is ended. Alleluia!
4. faith lives upon no other. Alleluia!

NOTE: St. 4 is for use at Communion in Eastertide; st. 1–3 can be used at season outside Lent.

RESURRECTION AND ASCENSION   Isa. 25:8; I Cor. 5:7–8; I Cor. 15:26–28

"Christ the Lord Is Risen Today"

Charles Wesley, 1739

ORIENTIS PARTIBUS, 77.77 with Alleluia   Early 13th century; harmonized by R. Vaughan Williams, 1906

1. "Christ the Lord is ris'n to-day," all cre-a-tion joins to say; raise your songs
2. Vain   the stone, the watch, the seal: Christ has burst the gates of hell! Death in   vain
3. Lives   a-gain our glo-rious King; where, O death, is now thy sting? Dy-ing once,
4. Soar   we now where Christ has led, fol-l'wing our ex-alt-ed Head; made like him,

1. and   tri-umphs high; sing, ye heav'ns, and earth re-ply:
2. for-bids his rise; Christ has o-pened Par-a-dise!   } Al-le-lu-ia!
3. he   all doth save; where thy vic-to-ry, O grave?
4. like him we rise; ours the cross, the grave, the skies!

Alternative tune: EASTER HYMN, 312

5. Hail the Lord of earth and heaven!
   Praise to thee by both be given;
   Thee we greet triumphant now;
   Hail the Resurrection thou!
   Alleluia!

6. King of glory, soul of bliss
   everlasting life is this:
   thee to know, thy power to prove,
   thus to sing, and thus to love!
   Alleluia!

Mt. 27:66   RESURRECTION AND ASCENSION

326   Good Christians All, Rejoice and Sing!

C. A. Alington, 1925

GELOBT SEI GOTT, 888 with Alleluias   Melody by Melchior Vulpius, c. 1560–1616

1. Good Chris-tians all, re-joice and sing! Now is the tri - umph
2. The Lord of life is ris'n for aye; bring flowers of song to
3. Praise we in songs of vic-to - ry that love, that life which
4. Thy name we bless, O ris - en Lord, and sing to-day with

1. of our King! To all the world glad news we bring:
2. strew his way; let ev - 'ry tongue re - joice and say:
3. can-not die, and sing with hearts up - lift - ed high:
4. one ac - cord the life laid down, the life re - stored:

Al - le - lu - ia! Al - le - lu - ia! Al - le - lu - ia!

This tune in a lower key: 396

Thine Be the Glory

A toi la gloire, by Edmond Budry, 1884; tr. R. Birch Hoyle, 1923

MACCABAEUS, 5.5.6.5.6.5.6.5 with refrain   Air from *Judas Maccabaeus*, by G. F. Handel, 1747

1. Thine be the glo - ry, ris - en, con-qu'ring Son; end - less is the vic - t'ry
2. Lo! Je - sus meets us, ris - en from the tomb; lov - ing - ly he greets us,
3. No more we doubt thee, glo - rious Prince of life! Life is nought with-out thee;

1. thou o'er death hast won. An - gels in bright rai - ment rolled the stone a - way,
2. scat - ters fear and gloom. Let his church with glad - ness hymns of tri - umph sing,
3. aid us in our strife. Make us more than conqu'-rors thro' thy death - less love;

Refrain

1. kept the fold - ed grave clothes where thy bod - y lay.
2. for the Lord now liv - eth; death has lost its sting. } Thine be the glo - ry,
3. bring us safe thro' Jor - dan to thy home a - bove.

ris - en, con -qu'ring Son: end - less is the vic - t'ry thou o'er death hast won.

Mt. 28:9   RESURRECTION AND ASCENSION

This Joyful Eastertide

G. R. Woodward, 1894

VRUCHTEN, 6.7.6.7 D

Melody in *David's Psalmen*, J. Oudaen (Amsterdam, 1685)

1. This joy-ful Eas-ter-tide, a-way with sin and sor - row;
2. My flesh in hope shall rest and for a sea-son slum - ber,
3. Death's flood has lost its chill since Je-sus crossed the riv - er;

1. my Love, the Cru-ci-fied, hath sprung to life this mor - row.
2. till trump from East to West shall wake the dead in num - ber.
3. Lov-er of souls, from ill my pass-ing soul de-liv - er.

Refrain

Had Christ, that once was slain, ne'er burst his three-day pris - on,

our faith had been in vain: but now is Christ a-ris - en,

a - ris - en, a - ris - en, a - ris - en!

How Rich, at Eastertide 329

Hoe Groot de Vruchtenzijn, by Joachim Oudaen, 1685; tr. Fred Pratt Green, 1981
(This is a translation of the Dutch song originally associated with the tune VRUCHTEN.)

1. How rich, at Eastertide,
    the harvest we are reaping,
   for Christ, the Crucified,
    gives comfort to the weeping.
   Saved by his bitter death,
    with all our sins forgiven,
   we learn to live by faith,
    for now is Christ arisen.

2. As first - gifts hallow all
    if offered in thanksgiving,
   so Christ has died for all,
    the First of all the living.
   Wherefore, the blessed dead,
    who else had vainly striven,
   are one with him, their Head,
    for Christ is now arisen.

3. The Lord, who taught the way
    of dying and forsaking,
   shall bring us to that day
    of our complete awaking.
   Then let no ill destroy
    the hope we have of heaven;
   come, serve our God with joy,
    for now is Christ arisen.

The Lord Ascendeth Up on High 330

ASCENDIT DEUS, 88.7.88.7   Arthur T. Russell, 1851   J. G. Schicht, 1819

1. The Lord as - cend -eth   up on high, the   Lord hath tri - umphed glo - rious - ly,
2. The heavens with joy re - ceive their Lord, by   saints, by an - gel hosts a - dored;
3. Our great High Priest hath gone be - fore, now   on his church his grace to pour,

1. in   power and might ex - cel - ling; the   grave and hell are cap - tive led,
2. O   day of ex - ul - ta - tion! O   earth, a - dore thy glo - rious King!
3. and   still his love he giv - eth; O   may our hearts to him as - cend;

1. lo!   he re - turns, our   glo - rious Head, to   his e - ter - nal dwell - ing.
2. His   ris - ing, his as - cen - sion sing with   grate - ful ad - o - ra - tion!
3. may   all with - in us   up - ward tend to   him who ev - er liv - eth!

Heb. 4:14   RESURRECTION AND ASCENSION

331   Hail the Day That Sees Him Rise

Charles Wesley, 1739 (alt'd)

LLANFAIR, 77.77 with Alleluias

Robert Williams, 1817

1. Hail the day that sees him rise, Al - le - lu - ia! to his throne a-
bove the skies, Al - le - lu - ia! Christ, a - while to mor - tals giv'n,
Al - le - lu - ia! en - ters now his na - tive heav'n, Al - le - lu - ia!

2. See, he lifts his hands a - bove! Al - le - lu - ia! See, he shows the
prints of love! Al - le - lu - ia! Hark, his gra - cious lips be - stow,
Al - le - lu - ia! bless - ings on his church be - low, Al - le - lu - ia!

3. Still for us he in - ter - cedes, Al - le - lu - ia! His pre - vail - ing
death he pleads; Al - le - lu - ia! near him - self pre - pares our place,
Al - le - lu - ia! he the first fruits of our race, Al - le - lu - ia!

4. Mas - ter (we will ev - er say), Al - le - lu - ia! tak - en from our
sight to - day, Al - le - lu - ia! see thy faith - ful ser - vants, see,
Al - le - lu - ia! ev - er gaz - ing up to thee, Al - le - lu - ia!

This tune in a lower key: 142

5. Grant, though parted from our sight, Alleluia!
high above yon azure height . . .
grant our hearts may thither rise,
following thee beyond the skies.

6. There we shall with thee remain,
partners of thy endless reign,
there thy face unclouded see,
find our heaven of heavens in thee.

RESURRECTION AND ASCENSION   Acts 1:9–11

A Hymn of Glory Let Us Sing

332

Hymnum canamus gloriae, the Venerable Bede, 673–735;
tr. B. Webb and J. M. Neale, 1851 (alt'd)

ST. PATRICK, LMD

Irish traditional melody; harmonized by Erik Routley

1. A hymn of glo-ry let us sing; new hymns through-out the world shall ring:
2. To them the an-gels, draw-ing nigh: "Why stand and gaze up-on the sky?
3. O grant us thith-er-ward to tend, and with un-wea-ried hearts as-cend

1. Christ by a road be-fore un-trod as-cend-eth to the throne of God.
2. This is the Sav-ior," thus they say; "this is his no-ble tri-umph day.
3. to-ward thy king-dom's throne, where thou, as is our faith, art seat-ed now.

1. The ho-ly ap-os-tol-ic band up-on the Mount of O-lives stand,
2. A-gain shall ye be-hold him, so as ye to-day have seen him go:
3. Be thou our joy and strong de-fense, who art our fu-ture rec-om-pense:

1. and with the vir-gin moth-er see their Lord's re-splen-dent maj-es-ty.
2. in glo-rious pomp as-cend-ing high up to the por-tals of the sky."
3. so shall the light that springs from thee be ours through all e-ter-ni-ty.

♮ *last time only*

RESURRECTION AND ASCENSION

333

Hail, Thou Once-Despised Jesus

John Bakewell, 1757 (alt'd)

IN BABILONE, 8.7.8.7 D

Traditional Dutch melody, c. 1710:
arranged by J. Röntgen, 1855–1932, and edited by Erik Routley

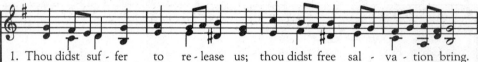

1. Hail, thou once-de-spis-ed Je-sus; hail, thou Gal-i-le-an King!
2. Pas-chal Lamb, by God ap-point-ed, all our sins were on thee laid;
3. Je-sus, hail! en-throned in glo-ry, there for-ev-er to a-bide;
4. Wor-ship, hon-or, power, and bless-ing thou art wor-thy to re-ceive;

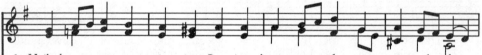

1. Thou didst suf-fer to re-lease us; thou didst free sal-va-tion bring.
2. by al-might-y love a-noint-ed, thou hast full a-tone-ment made:
3. all the heav'n-ly hosts a-dore thee, seat-ed at thy Fa-ther's side.
4. loud-est prais-es with-out ceas-ing meet it is for us to give.

1. Hail, thou ag-o-niz-ing Sav-ior, bear-er of our sin and shame,
2. all thy peo-ple are for-giv-en through the vir-tue of thy blood;
3. There for sin-ners thou art plead-ing; there thou dost our place pre-pare,
4. Help, ye bright an-gel-ic spir-its, bring your sweet-est, no-blest lays;

1. by thy mer-its we find fa-vor; life is giv-en through thy name.
2. o-pened is the gate of heav-en; rec-on-ciled are we with God.
3. ev-er for us in-ter-ced-ing, till in glo-ry we ap-pear.
4. help to sing our Sav-ior's mer-its; help to chant Im-man-uel's praise!

See, the Conqueror Mounts in Triumph 334

Christopher Wordsworth, 1862

EBENEZER, 8.7.8.7 D

Thomas J. Williams, 1890

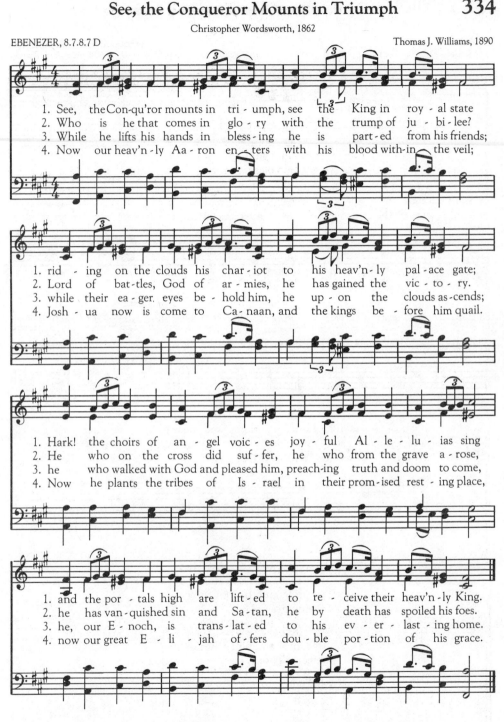

1. See, the Con-qu'ror mounts in tri - umph, see the King in roy - al state
2. Who is he that comes in glo - ry with the trump of ju - bi - lee?
3. While he lifts his hands in bless - ing he is part - ed from his friends;
4. Now our heav'n - ly Aa - ron en - ters with his blood with-in the veil;

1. rid - ing on the clouds his char - iot to his heav'n - ly pal - ace gate;
2. Lord of bat - tles, God of ar - mies, he has gained the vic - to - ry.
3. while their ea - ger eyes be - hold him, he up - on the clouds as - cends;
4. Josh - ua now is come to Ca - naan, and the kings be - fore him quail.

1. Hark! the choirs of an - gel voic - es joy - ful Al - le - lu - ias sing
2. He who on the cross did suf - fer, he who from the grave a - rose,
3. he who walked with God and pleased him, preach-ing truth and doom to come,
4. Now he plants the tribes of Is - rael in their prom - ised rest - ing place,

1. and the por - tals high are lift - ed to re - ceive their heav'n - ly King.
2. he has van - quished sin and Sa - tan, he by death has spoiled his foes.
3. he, our E - noch, is trans - lat - ed to his ev - er - last - ing home.
4. now our great E - li - jah of - fers dou - ble por - tion of his grace.

5. He has raised our human nature
   on the clouds to God's right hand;
   there we sit in heav'nly places,
   there with him in glory stand;

Jesus reigns, adored by angels,
   God's own son is on the throne;
   mighty Lord, in thine Ascension
   we by faith behold our own.

Ps. 24:7; Ps. 98:2; Lk. 24:50–51; Gen. 5:24; Heb. 5:4;
Josh. 5:1; II Kgs. 2:9–11; Heb. 1:5–8

RESURRECTION AND ASCENSION

335 The Head That Once Was Crowned with Thorns

Thomas Kelly, 1825

ST. MAGNUS, CM

Attributed to Jeremiah Clarke, 1701

Descant, st. 6

6. The cross he bore is life and health, though shame and death to him;

1. The head that once was crowned with thorns is crowned with glo - ry now:
2. The high-est place that heav'n af - fords is his, is his by right,
3. the joy of all who dwell a - bove, the joy of all be - low,
4. To them the cross with all its shame, with all its grace, is giv'n,

rit.

6. his peo - ple's hope, his peo - ple's wealth, their ev - er - last - ing theme!

1. a roy - al di - a - dem a - dorns the might - y Vic - tor's brow.
2. the King of kings and Lord of lords, and heav'n's e - ter - nal light —
3. to whom he man - i - fests his love, and grants his name to know.
4. their name, an ev - er - last - ing name, their joy, the joy of heav'n.

5. They suffer with their Lord below,
   they reign with him above,
   their profit and their joy to know
   the mystery of his love.

6. The cross he bore is life and health,
   though shame and death to him;
   his people's hope, his people's wealth,
   their everlasting theme!

WORTHY IS THE LAMB

II Tim. 2:12

At the Name of Jesus

Caroline M. Noel, 1870 (alt'd)

KING'S WESTON, 6.5.6.5 D

R. Vaughan Williams, 1925

1. At the name of Je - sus ev - 'ry knee shall bow, ev - 'ry tongue con-
2. Hum-bled for a sea - son to re-ceive a name from the lips of
3. bore it up tri - um - phant with its hu - man light, through all ranks of
4. In your hearts en - throne him; there let him sub - due all that is not

1. fess him King of glo - ry now; 'tis the Fa - ther's plea - sure
2. sin - ners un - to whom he came, faith - ful - ly he bore it,
3. crea - tures to the cen - tral height, to the throne of God - head,
4. ho - ly, all that is not true; crown him as your Cap - tain

1. we should call him Lord, who from the be - gin - ning was the might - y Word.
2. spot - less to the last, brought it back vic - to - rious when from death he passed,
3. to the Fa - ther's breast, filled it with the glo - ry of that per - fect rest.
4. in temp - ta - tion's hour; let his will en - fold you in its light and power.

5. Christians, this Lord Jesus shall return again,
   with his Father's glory, with his angel - train,
   for all wreaths of empire meet upon his brow,
   and our hearts confess him King of glory now.

*Whenever this repeated figure occurs in the bass, the organist should tie the eighth notes in the bass part.

Phil. 2:11–12

WORTHY IS THE LAMB

337

Christ Is the World's Redeemer

Christus cum Deo sederat, attributed to Columba, 521–597;
tr. Duncan MacGregor, 1897

Adapted from a melody in the *Fitzwilliam Virginal Book* (c. 1622);
also found in the *Augsburg Gesangbuch* (1609)

FITZWILLIAM, 7.6.7.6 D

1. Christ is the world's Re - deem - er, the lov - er of the pure,
2. Christ hath our host sur - round - ed with clouds of mar - tyrs bright,
3. Down in the realms of dark - ness he lay a cap - tive bound,
4. Glo - ry to God the Fa - ther, the un - be - got - ten one;

1. the fount of heav'n - ly wis - dom, our trust and hope se - cure,
2. who wave their palms in tri - umph and fire us for the fight.
3. but at the hour ap - point - ed he rose, a vic - tor crowned;
4. all hon - or be to Je - sus, his sole be - got - ten Son;

1. the ar - mor of his sol - diers, the Lord of earth and sky,
2. This Christ the cross as - cend - ed to save a world un - done,
3. and now, to heav'n as - cend - ed he sits up - on the throne
4. and to the Ho - ly Spir - it, the per - fect Trin - i - ty:

1. our health while we are liv - ing, our life when we shall die.
2. and, suf - f'ring for the sin - ful, our full re - demp - tion won.
3. in glo - ri - ous do - min - ion, his Fa - ther's and his own.
4. let all the worlds give an - swer: "A - men: so let it be!"

WORTHY IS THE LAMB

Heb. 12:1

O Love of God, How Strong and True

338

Horatius Bonar, 1858

MERTHYR TYDFIL, LMD

Joseph Parry, 1870

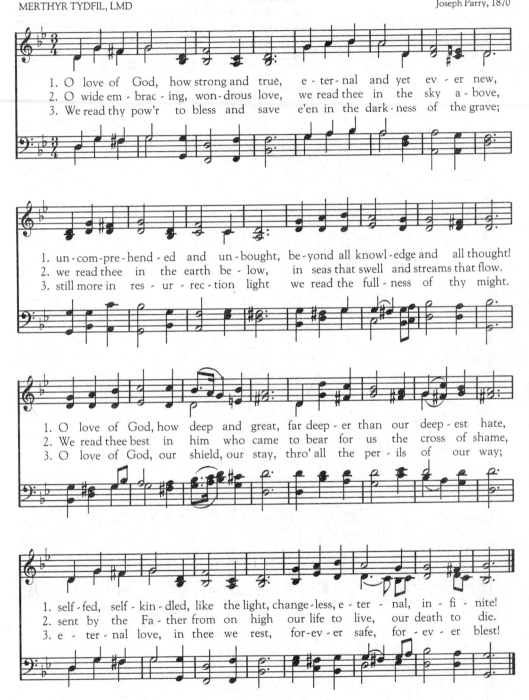

1. O love of God, how strong and true, e - ter - nal and yet ev - er new,
2. O wide em - brac - ing, won - drous love, we read thee in the sky a - bove,
3. We read thy pow'r to bless and save e'en in the dark - ness of the grave;

1. un - com - pre - hend - ed and un - bought, be - yond all knowl - edge and all thought!
2. we read thee in the earth be - low, in seas that swell and streams that flow.
3. still more in res - ur - rec - tion light we read the full - ness of thy might.

1. O love of God, how deep and great, far deep - er than our deep - est hate,
2. We read thee best in him who came to bear for us the cross of shame,
3. O love of God, our shield, our stay, thro' all the per - ils of our way;

1. self - fed, self - kin - dled, like the light, change - less, e - ter - nal, in - fi - nite!
2. sent by the Fa - ther from on high our life to live, our death to die.
3. e - ter - nal love, in thee we rest, for - ev - er safe, for - ev - er blest!

339   Ye, Who the Name of Jesus Bear

Scottish Paraphrases (1754, 1781)

DUNFERMLINE, CM

Scottish Psalter (1615, 1635); harmony by Thomas Tompkins, 1621

May be sung in unison

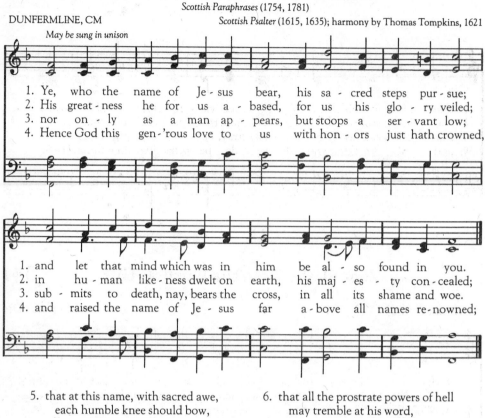

1. Ye, who the name of Je - sus bear, his sa - cred steps pur - sue;
2. His great - ness he for us a - based, for us his glo - ry veiled;
3. nor on - ly as a man ap - pears, but stoops a ser - vant low;
4. Hence God this gen - 'rous love to us with hon - ors just hath crowned,

1. and let that mind which was in him be al - so found in you.
2. in hu - man like - ness dwelt on earth, his maj - es - ty con - cealed;
3. sub - mits to death, nay, bears the cross, in all its shame and woe.
4. and raised the name of Je - sus far a - bove all names re - nowned;

5. that at this name, with sacred awe,
   each humble knee should bow,
of hosts immortal in the skies
and nations spread below;

[no pause between stanzas]

6. that all the prostrate powers of hell
   may tremble at his word,
and every tribe and every tongue
confess that he is Lord.

Phil. 2:5–11

---

340   Father of Peace and God of Love

Scottish Paraphrases (1781); based on Philip Doddridge, 1740

ST. PAUL, CM

J. Chalmers's Collection (1749)

1. Fa - ther of peace, and God of love, we own thy power to save,
2. Him from the dead thou brought'st a - gain, when by his sa - cred blood
3. O may thy Spir - it seal our souls, and mold them to thy will,
4. that to per - fec - tion's sa - cred height we near - er still may rise,

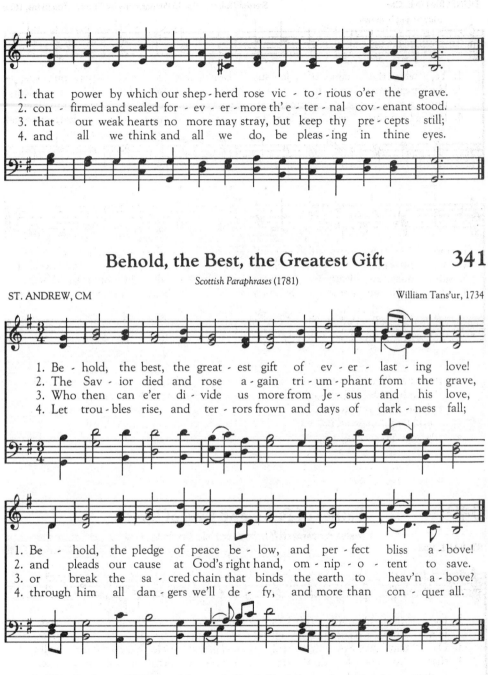

1. that power by which our shep-herd rose vic-to-rious o'er the grave.
2. con-firmed and sealed for-ev-er-more th' e-ter-nal cov-enant stood.
3. that our weak hearts no more may stray, but keep thy pre-cepts still;
4. and all we think and all we do, be pleas-ing in thine eyes.

Behold, the Best, the Greatest Gift 341

Scottish Paraphrases (1781)

ST. ANDREW, CM

William Tans'ur, 1734

1. Be-hold, the best, the great-est gift of ev-er-last-ing love!
2. The Sav-ior died and rose a-gain tri-um-phant from the grave,
3. Who then can e'er di-vide us more from Je-sus and his love,
4. Let trou-bles rise, and ter-rors frown and days of dark-ness fall;

1. Be-hold, the pledge of peace be-low, and per-fect bliss a-bove!
2. and pleads our cause at God's right hand, om-nip-o-tent to save.
3. or break the sa-cred chain that binds the earth to heav'n a-bove?
4. through him all dan-gers we'll de-fy, and more than con-quer all.

5. Nor death, nor life, nor earth, nor hell,
   nor time's destroying sway
   can e'er efface us from his heart
   or make his love decay.

6. Each future hour that love will bless
   as it has blessed the past:
   he loved us from the first of time;
   he loves us to the last.

Rom. 8:31–39 WORTHY IS THE LAMB

342   O Love, How Deep, How Broad, How High

O amor quam ecstaticus, attributed to Thomas à Kempis, 1380–1471;
tr. Benjamin Webb and J. M. Neale, 1851 (alt'd)
First Tune

DEO GRACIAS (AGINCOURT SONG), LM   15th-century English melody

1. O Love, how deep, how broad, how high, how pass-ing thought and fan-ta-sy, that God, the Son of God, should take our mor-tal form for mor-tals' sake.
2. For us bap-tized, for us he bore his ho-ly fast and hun-gered sore; for us temp-ta-tions sharp he knew, for us the tempt-er o-ver-threw.
3. For us he prayed, for us he taught, for us his dai-ly works he wrought, by words and signs and ac-tions, thus still seek-ing not him-self, but us.
4. For us to e-vil pow'r be-trayed, scourged, mocked, in pur-ple robe ar-rayed, he bore the shame-ful cross and death, for us gave up his dy-ing breath.

Alternative tune: TUGWOOD, 501

5. For us he rose from death again;
for us he went on high to reign;
for us he sent his Spirit here
to guide, to comfort, and to cheer.

6. All glory to our Lord and God
for love so deep, so high, so broad —
the Trinity whom we adore
forever and forevermore.

NOTE: *The whole hymn may be sung to either the first or second tune, or st. 1-4 may be sung to the first tune (DEO GRACIAS) and st. 5-6 to the second tune (DEUS TUORUM MILITUM) in unison.*

WORTHY IS THE LAMB

O Love, How Deep, How Broad, How High   343

Second Tune

DEUS TUORUM MILITUM, LM

Melody from *Grenoble Antiphoner* (1753)

1. O Love, how deep, how broad, how high, how pass - ing thought and fan - ta - sy, that God, the Son of God, should take our mor - tal form for mor - tals' sake.
2. For us bap - tized, for us he bore his ho - ly fast and hun - gered sore; for us temp - ta - tions sharp he knew, for us the tempt - er o - ver - threw.
3. For us he prayed, for us he taught, for us his dai - ly works he wrought, by words and signs and ac - tions, thus still seek - ing not him - self, but us.
4. For us to e - vil pow'r be - trayed, scourged, mocked, in pur - ple robe ar - rayed, he bore the shame - ful cross and death, for us gave up his dy - ing breath.

This tune in a lower key: 372

5. For us he rose from death again;
   for us he went on high to reign;
   for us he sent his Spirit here
   to guide, to comfort, and to cheer.

6. All glory to our Lord and God
   for love so deep, so high, so broad —
   the Trinity whom we adore
   forever and forevermore.

WORTHY IS THE LAMB

344 Eternal, Unchanging, We Sing to Thy Praise

R. B. Y. Scott, 1938

ST. BASIL, 11 11.11 11

Healey Willan, 1930

1. E - ter - nal, un - chang - ing, we sing to thy praise: thy mer - cies are
2. A - gain we re - joice in the world thou hast made, thy might - y cre -
3. We praise thee for Je - sus, our Mas - ter and Lord, the might of his

1. end - less, and righ - teous thy ways; thy ser - vants pro - claim the re -
2. a - tion in beau - ty ar - rayed; we thank thee for life, and we
3. Spir - it, the truth of his Word, his com - fort in sor - row, his

1. nown of thy name, who rul - est om - nip - o - tent, ev - er the same.
2. praise thee for joy, for love and for hope that no pow'r can de - stroy.
3. pa - tience in pain, the faith sure and stead - fast that Je - sus shall reign.

Alternative tune: ST. DENIO, 7

Tune © Healey Willan

WORTHY IS THE LAMB

All Praise to Thee, for Thou, O King Divine 345

F. Bland Tucker, 1940

ENGELBERG, 10 10 10.4

C. V. Stanford, 1904

1. All praise to thee, for thou, O King di - vine, didst yield the glo - ry that of right was thine, that in our dark - ened hearts thy grace might shine.
2. Thou cam'st to us in low - li - ness of thought; by thee the out - cast and the poor were sought, and by thy death was God's sal - va - tion wrought.
3. Let this mind be in us which was in thee, who wast a ser - vant that we might be free, hum - bling thy - self to death on Cal - va - ry.
4. Where - fore by God's e - ter - nal pur - pose thou art high ex - alt - ed o'er all crea - tures now and giv'n the name to which all crea - tures bow:
5. Let ev - 'ry tongue con - fess with one ac - cord in heav'n and earth that Je - sus Christ is Lord, and God the Fa - ther be by all a - dored.

st. 1,2,3,4 / st.5

Al - le - lu - ia! Al - le - lu - ia!

This tune in a higher key: 508; alternative tune: SINE NOMINE, 397

Phil. 2:5–11

WORTHY IS THE LAMB

346 Alleluia! Sing to Jesus

W. Chatterton Dix, 1867

HYFRYDOL, 8.7.8.7 D

R. H. Prichard, 1831

1. Alleluia! Sing to Jesus; his the sceptre, his the throne!
2. Alleluia! Not as orphans are we left in sorrow now.
3. Alleluia! Bread of angels, thou on earth our food, our stay.
4. Alleluia! King eternal, thee the Lord of lords we own.

1. Alleluia! His the triumph, his the victory alone.
2. Alleluia! He is near us; faith believes, nor questions how.
3. Alleluia! Here the sinful flee to thee from day to day.
4. Alleluia! Born of Mary, earth thy footstool, heav'n thy throne.

1. Hark! the songs of peaceful Zion thunder like a mighty flood;
2. Though the cloud from sight received him when the forty days were o'er,
3. Intercessor, friend of sinners, earth's Redeemer, plead for me,
4. Thou within the veil hast entered, robed in flesh, our great High Priest—

1. Jesus out of ev'ry nation hath redeemed us by his blood.
2. shall our hearts forget his promise, "I am with you evermore"?
3. where the songs of all the sinless sweep across the crystal sea.
4. thou on earth both priest and victim in the eucharistic feast.

Alternative tunes: BLAENWERN, 115, STUTTGART, 183

WORTHY IS THE LAMB

Lk. 24:50–53; Jn. 6:41–59; Heb. 9:11–14

Give to Our God Immortal Praise

347

Isaac Watts, 1719

WARRINGTON, LM

Ralph Harrison, 1748–1810

1. Give to our God im - mor - tal praise: mer - cy and truth are all his ways;
2. Give to the Lord of lords re - nown: the King of kings with glo - ry crown;
3. He built the earth, he spread the sky, and fixed the star - ry lights on high:
4. He fills the sun with morn - ing light; he bids the moon di - rect the night;

Descant, st. 4 and 6

4. His mer - cies ev - er shall en - dure, when suns and moons shall shine no more.
6. His mer - cies ev - er shall en - dure, when this vain world shall be no more.

1. won - ders of grace to God be - long; re - peat his mer - cies in your song.
2. his mer - cies ev - er shall en - dure, when lords and kings are known no more.
3. won - ders of grace to God be - long; re - peat his mer - cies in your song.
4. his mer - cies ev - er shall en - dure, when suns and moons shall shine no more.

5. He sent his Son with power to save
from guilt and darkness and the grave;
wonders of grace to God belong;
repeat his mercies in your song.

6. Through this vain world he guides our feet,
and leads us to his heavenly seat;
his mercies ever shall endure,
when this vain world shall be no more.

Ps. 136

WORTHY IS THE LAMB

348 Mighty God, While Angels Bless Thee

Robert Robinson, 1774; R. W. Dale, 1879; and others

RUSTINGTON, 8.7.8.7 D

C. H. H. Parry, 1897

1. Might-y God, while an-gels bless thee, may a mor-tal sing thy name?
2. For the gran-deur of thy na-ture, grand be-yond a ser-aph's thought;
3. But thy rich, thy free re-demp-tion, dark through bright-ness all a-long;
4. From the high-est throne of glo-ry to the cross of deep-est woe,

1. Lord of earth as well as an-gels, thou art ev-'ry crea-ture's theme;
2. for the won-ders of cre-a-tion, works with skill and kind-ness wrought;
3. thought is poor, and poor ex-pres-sion: who dare sing that won-drous song?
4. all to ran-som guil-ty cap-tives! Flow my praise, for-ev-er flow.

1. Lord of ev-'ry land and na-tion, An-cient of E-ter-nal Days,
2. for thy prov-i-dence that gov-erns through thine em-pire's wide do-main,
3. Bright-ness of the Fa-ther's glo-ry, shall thy praise un-ut-tered lie?
4. Go, re-turn, im-mor-tal Sav-ior; leave thy foot-stool, claim thy throne;

1. sound-ed through the wide cre-a-tion be thy just and end-less praise.
2. wings an an-gel, guides a spar-row: bless-ed be thy gen-tle reign.
3. Break, my tongue, such guil-ty si-lence; sing the Lord who came to die.
4. thence re-turn, and reign for-ev-er; be the king-dom all thine own!

Alternative tune: AUSTRIA, 3

WORTHY IS THE LAMB

Heb. 1:8–13

There's a Wideness in God's Mercy

349

CROSS OF JESUS, 8.7.8.7   F. W. Faber, 1849   John Stainer, 1887

1. There's a wide-ness in God's mer-cy like the wide-ness of the sea;
2. There is no place where earth's sor-rows are more felt than up in heav'n;
3. There is grace e-nough for thou-sands of new worlds as great as this;
4. There is plen-ti-ful re-demp-tion in the blood that has been shed;
5. If our love were but more sim-ple we should take him at his word,

1. there's a kind-ness in his jus-tice which is more than lib-er-ty.
2. there is no place where earth's fail-ings have such kind-ly judg-ment giv'n.
3. there is room for fresh cre-a-tions in that up-per home of bliss.
4. there is joy for all the mem-bers in the sor-rows of the Head.
5. and our lives would be all sun-shine in the sweet-ness of our Lord.

Alternative tune: KINGDOM, 547

The Great Creator of the Worlds

350

Francis Bland Tucker, 1939; based on the Epistle of Diognetus, c. 150

ST. COLUMBA, CM   Irish hymn melody; harmonized by H. Walford Davies, 1923

1. The great Cre-a-tor of the worlds, the sov-'reign God of heav'n,
2. He sent no an-gel of his host to bear this might-y word,
3. He sent him not in wrath and pow'r, but grace and peace to bring
4. He sent him down as send-ing God; in hu-man flesh he came;

1. his ho-ly and im-mor-tal truth to all on earth hath giv'n.
2. but him through whom the worlds were made, the ev-er-last-ing Lord.
3. in kind-ness, as a king might send his son, him-self a king.
4. as one with us he dwelt with us, and died and lived a-gain.

This tune in a lower key: 267

Alternative tune: TALLIS' ORDINAL, 404

Mk. 12:1–11   WORTHY IS THE LAMB

351 Morning Glory

W. H. Vanstone, 1980

LEW TRENCHARD, 7.7.7.7

Melody adapted in the *English Hymnal* (1906); from *Receuil Noté* (1871)

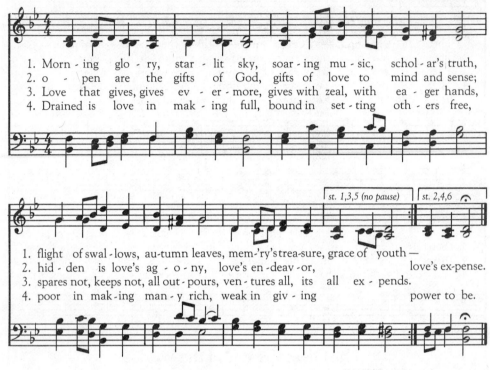

1. Morn - ing glo - ry, star - lit sky, soar - ing mu - sic, schol - ar's truth,
2. o - pen are the gifts of God, gifts of love to mind and sense;
3. Love that gives, gives ev - er - more, gives with zeal, with ea - ger hands,
4. Drained is love in mak - ing full, bound in set - ting oth - ers free,

st. 1,3,5 (no pause) | *st. 2,4,6*

1. flight of swal - lows, au - tumn leaves, mem - 'ry's trea - sure, grace of youth —
2. hid - den is love's ag - o - ny, love's en - deav - or,   love's ex - pense.
3. spares not, keeps not, all out - pours, ven - tures all, its all ex - pends.
4. poor in mak - ing man - y rich, weak in giv - ing   power to be.

5. Therefore he who shows us God
   helpless hangs upon the tree;
   and the nails and crown of thorns
   tell of what God's love must be.

6. Here is God: no monarch he,
   throned in easy state to reign;
   here is God, whose arms of love,
   aching, spent, the world sustain.

I Cor. 13:7

352 Jesus, Good Above All Other

Percy Dearmer, 1906

QUEM PASTORES, 888.7

Arranged from a 14th-century German carol

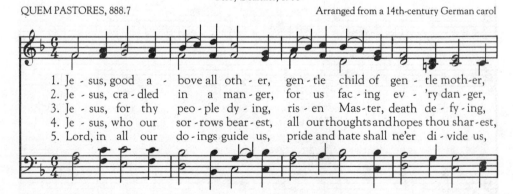

1. Je - sus, good a - bove all oth - er, gen - tle child of gen - tle moth - er,
2. Je - sus, cra - dled in a man - ger, for us fac - ing ev - 'ry dan - ger,
3. Je - sus, for thy peo - ple dy - ing, ris - en Mas - ter, death de - fy - ing,
4. Je - sus, who our sor - rows bear - est, all our thoughts and hopes thou shar - est,
5. Lord, in all our do - ings guide us, pride and hate shall ne'er di - vide us,

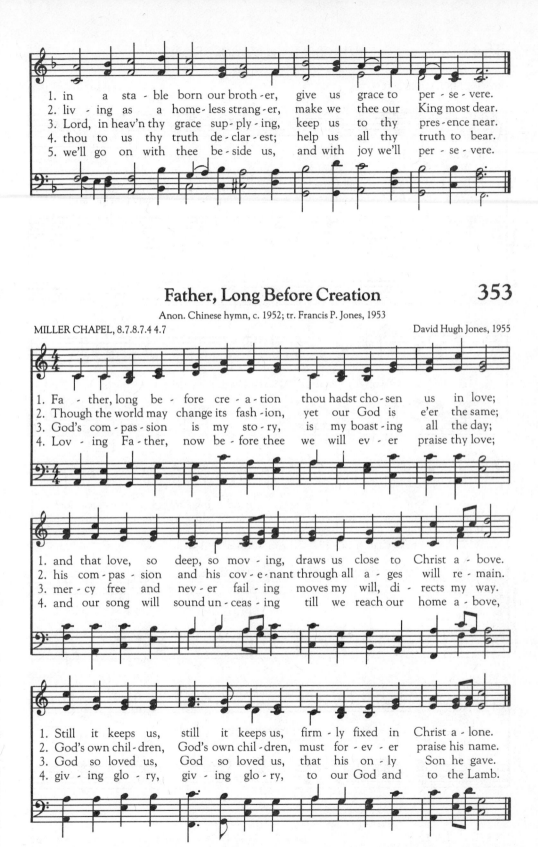

1. in a sta-ble born our broth-er, give us grace to per-se-vere.
2. liv-ing as a home-less strang-er, make we thee our King most dear.
3. Lord, in heav'n thy grace sup-ply-ing, keep us to thy pres-ence near.
4. thou to us thy truth de-clar-est, help us all thy truth to bear.
5. we'll go on with thee be-side us, and with joy we'll per-se-vere.

Father, Long Before Creation 353

Anon. Chinese hymn, c. 1952; tr. Francis P. Jones, 1953

MILLER CHAPEL, 8.7.8.7.4 4.7   David Hugh Jones, 1955

1. Fa - ther, long be - fore cre - a - tion thou hadst cho - sen us in love;
2. Though the world may change its fash - ion, yet our God is e'er the same;
3. God's com - pas - sion is my sto - ry, is my boast - ing all the day;
4. Lov - ing Fa - ther, now be - fore thee we will ev - er praise thy love;

1. and that love, so deep, so mov - ing, draws us close to Christ a - bove.
2. his com - pas - sion and his cov - e - nant through all a - ges will re - main.
3. mer - cy free and nev - er fail - ing moves my will, di - rects my way.
4. and our song will sound un - ceas - ing till we reach our home a - bove,

1. Still it keeps us, still it keeps us, firm - ly fixed in Christ a - lone.
2. God's own chil - dren, God's own chil - dren, must for - ev - er praise his name.
3. God so loved us, God so loved us, that his on - ly Son he gave.
4. giv - ing glo - ry, giv - ing glo - ry, to our God and to the Lamb.

WORTHY IS THE LAMB

354

Who Is He in Yonder Stall?

B. Russell Hanby

RESONET IN LAUDIBUS, Irregular

Melody from *Piae Cantiones* (1582)

Solo

1. Who is he in yon-der stall at whose feet the shep-herds fall?
2. Who is he in deep dis-tress pray-ing in the wil-der-ness?
3. Lo, at mid-night who is he prays in dark Geth-sem-a-ne?
4. Who is he that from the grave comes to heal and help and save?

All

'Tis the Lord, O won-drous sto-ry! 'Tis the Lord, the Christ, the King of glo-ry!

Solo

1. Who is he in yon-der cot, bend-ing to his toil-some lot?
2. Who is he who stands and weeps at the grave where Laz-'rus sleeps?
3. Who is he in Cal-vary's throes asks for bless-ing on his foes?
4. Who is he that from his throne rules the world of light a-lone?

All

'Tis the Lord, the Christ, the King of glo-ry!

WORTHY IS THE LAMB

Lk. 2:8; 4:2; Jn. 11:35; Mt. 26:36; Lk. 23:34; 34:1; Acts 7:56

All—after st. 4 only

At his feet we hum-bly fall, the Lord of all. Crown him,

crown him! This is Christ the Lord, the King of glo - ry.

To God Be the Glory, Great Things He Hath Done 355

Fanny Crosby, 1875

MONTGOMERY, 11 11.11 11

Attributed to S. Jarvis, 1762

1. To God be the glo - ry, great things he hath done; so loved he the
2. O per - fect re - demp-tion, the pur-chase of blood, to ev - 'ry be -
3. Great things he hath taught us, great things he hath done, and great our re -

1. world that he gave us his Son, who yield - ed his life an a -
2. liev - er the prom - ise of God; the vil - est of - fend - er who
3. joic - ing through Je - sus the Son; but pur - er and high - er and

1. tone - ment for sin, and o - pened heav'n's gate-way that all might go in.
2. tru - ly be - lieves that mo - ment from Je - sus a par - don re - ceives.
3. great - er will be the won - der, the beau - ty, when Je - sus we see.

Jn. 3:16

WORTHY IS THE LAMB

356   ### O Sing a Song of Bethlehem

Louis F. Benson, 1899

KINGSFOLD, CMD

English folk song; arranged by R. Vaughan Williams, 1906

1. O sing a song of Beth-le-hem, of shep-herds watch-ing there,
2. O sing a song of Naz-a-reth, of sun-ny days of joy,
3. O sing a song of Gal-i-lee, of lake and woods and hill,
4. O sing a song of Cal-va-ry, its glo-ry and dis-may;

1. and of the news that came to them from an-gels in the air:
2. O sing of fra-grant flow-ers' breath, and of the sin-less boy:
3. of him who walked up-on the sea and bade its waves be still:
4. of him who hung up-on the tree, and took our sins a-way:

1. the light that shone on Beth-le-hem fills all the world to-day;
2. for now the flowers of Naz-a-reth in ev-ery heart may grow;
3. for though, like waves on Gal-i-lee, dark seas of trou-ble roll,
4. for he who died on Cal-va-ry is ris-en from the grave,

1. of Je-sus' birth and peace on earth the an-gels sing al-way.
2. now spreads the fame of his dear name on all the winds that blow.
3. when faith has heard the Mas-ter's word, falls peace up-on the soul.
4. and Christ, our Lord, by heaven a-dored, is might-y now to save.

WORTHY IS THE LAMB   *Lk. 2:32; Mt. 14:24*

Come, Christians, Join to Sing

C. H. Bateman, 1843

357

MADRID, 6.6.6.6 D mixed

Anon. melody (Philadelphia, 1824)

Descant, st. 3

3. Al - le - lu - ia,

1. Come, Chris-tians, join to sing   Al - le - lu - ia,   A - men!   loud praise to
2. Come, lift your hearts on high;   Al - le - lu - ia,   A - men!   let prais - es
3. Praise yet our Christ a - gain;   Al - le - lu - ia,   A - men!   life shall not

3. Al - le - lu - ia!   Al - le - lu - ia,   A - men.

1. Christ our King; Al - le - lu - ia,   A - men!   let all with heart and voice
2. fill the sky; Al - le - lu - ia,   A - men!   he is our guide and friend;
3. end the strain; Al - le - lu - ia,   A - men!   on heav - en's bliss - ful shore

3. Al - le - lu - ia,   A - men.   Al - le - lu - ia,   A - men.

1. be - fore his throne re - joice; praise is his gra-cious choice: Al - le - lu - ia,   A - men!
2. to us he'll con-de-scend; his love shall nev - er end,   Al - le - lu - ia,   A - men!
3. his good-ness we'll a-dore, sing - ing for - ev - er-more, Al - le - lu - ia,   A - men!

358   O Lord and Master of Us All

CONTEMPLATION, CM   J. G. Whittier, 1856   F. A. G. Ouseley, 1889

1. O Lord and Mas - ter of us all, what - e'er our name or sign,
*2. Thou judg-est us; thy pu - ri - ty doth all our lusts con - demn;
3. Yet weak and blind - ed though we be, thou dost our ser - vice own;
4. A - part from thee all gain is loss, all la - bor vain - ly done;
5. We faint - ly hear, we dim - ly see, in dif - f'ring phrase we pray;

1. we own thy sway, we hear thy call, we test our lives by thine.
2. the love that draws us near - er thee is hot with wrath to them.
3. we bring our vary - ing gifts to thee, and thou re - ject - est none.
4. the sol - emn shad - ow of the cross is bet - ter than the sun.
5. but, dim or clear, we own in thee the Life, the Truth, the Way.

This tune in a lower key: 244   Ps. 139:1; Jn. 14:6

359   Jesus, Thy Mercies Are Untold

ST. AGNES, CM

Amor, Jesu dulcissime and *Dulcis Jesu Memoria*, anon., 12th century;
tr. Edward Caswall, 1849   J. B. Dykes, 1866

1. Je - sus, thy mer - cies are un - told through each re - turn - ing day;
2. O hope of ev - 'ry con - trite heart, O joy of all the meek,
3. But what to those who find? Ah, this nor tongue nor pen can show;
4. Je - sus, our on - ly joy be thou, as thou our prize wilt be;

1. thy love ex - ceeds a thou - sand - fold what - ev - er we can say.
2. to those who ask, how kind thou art, how good to those who seek!
3. the love of Je - sus, what it is none but his loved ones know.
4. in thee be all our glo - ry now and through e - ter - ni - ty.

JESUS CHRIST IS LORD   *Alternative tune: LAND OF REST, 360*

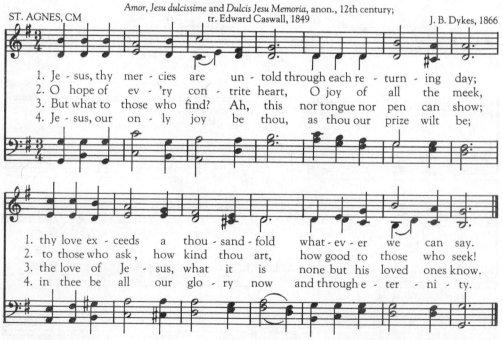

O Jesus, King Most Wonderful 360

LAND OF REST, CM

Jesu, rex admirabile, medieval Latin lyric; tr. E. Caswall, 1849

American folk melody

1. O Je-sus, King most won-der-ful, thou Con-quer-or re-nowned,
2. when once thou vis-it-est the heart, then truth be-gins to shine,
3. May ev-'ry heart con-fess thy name, and ev-er thee a-dore,
4. Thee may our tongues for-ev-er bless, thee may we love a-lone,

Org.

1. thou sweet-ness most in-ef-fa-ble, in whom all joys are found,
2. then earth-ly van-i-ties de-part, then kin-dles love di-vine.
3. and, seek-ing thee, it-self in-flame to seek thee more and more.
4. and ev-er in our lives express the im-age of thine own.

Alternative tune: ST. AGNES, 359

This tune in a lower key: 534

O Jesus, When I Think of Thee 361

George W. Bethune, 1847

CAPEL, CM

English carol melody

1. O Je-sus, when I think of thee, thy man-ger, cross, and throne,
2. I see thee in thy weak-ness first; then, glo-rious from thy shame,
3. Oh, let me share thy ho-ly birth, thy faith, thy death to sin,
4. Then shall I know what means the strain tri-um-phant of Saint Paul,

1. my spir-it trusts ex-ult-ing-ly in thee, and thee a-lone.
2. I see thee death's strong fet-ters burst and reach heav'n's might-iest name.
3. and, strong a-midst the toils of earth, my heav'n-ly life be-gin.
4. "To live is Christ, to die is gain: Christ is my All in All!"

Phil. 1:21

JESUS CHRIST IS LORD

362

O for a Thousand Tongues to Sing

Charles Wesley, 1740
First Tune

RICHMOND, CM

Later form of melody by T. Haweis, 1794

Descant, st. 6, by C. S. Lang

6. My gra-cious Mas - ter and my God, as - sist me to pro-claim,

1. O for a thou - sand tongues to sing my dear Re - deem - er's praise,
2. Je - sus, the name that charms our fears, that bids our sor - rows cease,
3. He speaks, and lis - t'ning to his voice, new life the dead re - ceive,
4. Hear him, ye deaf; his praise, ye dumb, your loos - ened tongues employ;

6. and spread thro' all the earth a - broad the hon - ors of thy name.

1. the glo - ries of my God and King, the tri - umphs of his grace!
2. 'tis mu - sic in the sin - ner's ears, 'tis life, and health, and peace.
3. the mourn - ful, bro - ken hearts re - joice, the hum - ble poor be - lieve.
4. ye blind, be - hold your Sav - ior come; and leap, ye lame, for joy.

5. Look unto him, ye nations: own
   your God, ye fallen race;
   look, and be saved by faith alone;
   be justified by grace.

6. My gracious Master and my God,
   assist me to proclaim,
   and spread through all the earth abroad
   the honors of thy name.

This tune in a lower key: 571
Alternative tune: BRISTOL, 251

Heb. 2:4; Rom. 1:17; Rom. 5:1

363

O for a Thousand Tongues to Sing

Second Tune

AZMON, CM

Melody by Carl G. Glaser, 1784–1829; adapted by Lowell Mason, 1839

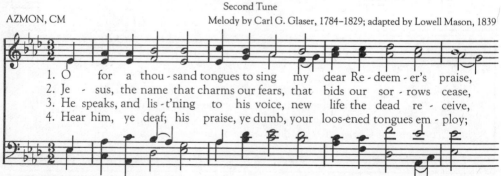

1. O for a thou - sand tongues to sing my dear Re - deem - er's praise,
2. Je - sus, the name that charms our fears, that bids our sor - rows cease,
3. He speaks, and lis - t'ning to his voice, new life the dead re - ceive,
4. Hear him, ye deaf; his praise, ye dumb, your loos-ened tongues em - ploy;

JESUS CHRIST IS LORD

1. the glo - ries of my God and King, the tri - umphs of his grace!
2. 'tis mu - sic in the sin - ner's ears, 'tis life, and health, and peace.
3. the mourn - ful, bro - ken hearts re - joice, the hum - ble poor be - lieve.
4. ye blind, be - hold your Sav - ior come; and leap, ye lame, for joy.

5. Look unto him, ye nations: own
   your God, ye fallen race;
   look, and be saved by faith alone;
   be justified by grace.

6. My gracious Master and my God,
   assist me to proclaim,
   and spread through all the earth abroad
   the honors of thy name.

How Sweet the Name of Jesus Sounds 364

John Newton, 1779

ST. PETER, CM

A. R. Reinagle, 1830

1. How sweet the name of Je - sus sounds in a be - liev - er's ear!
2. It makes the wound - ed spir - it whole, and calms the trou - bled breast;
3. Dear name! the rock on which I build, my shield and hid - ing place,
4. Je - sus, my Shep - herd, Guar - dian, Friend, my Proph - et, Priest, and King,
5. Weak is the ef - fort of my heart, and cold my warm - est thought;

1. It soothes my sor - rows, heals my wounds, and drives a - way my fear.
2. 'tis man - na to the hun - gry soul, and to the wea - ry rest.
3. my nev - er - fail - ing trea - sury, filled with bound - less stores of grace;
4. my Lord, my Life, my Way, my End, ac - cept the praise I bring.
5. but when I see thee as thou art, I'll praise thee as I ought.

Alternative tune: STRACATHRO, 48

JESUS CHRIST IS LORD

365   When Morning Gilds the Skies

Beim' Fruhen Morgenlicht, anon. German, 18th century;
tr. E. Caswall, 1849, and others

LAUDES DOMINI, 66.6.66.6

Joseph Barnby, 1868

5. In heav'n's eternal bliss
the loveliest strain is this:
"May Jesus Christ be praised!"
Let air and sea and sky
from depth to height reply:
"May Jesus Christ be praised!"

6. Be this, while life is mine,
my canticle divine:
"May Jesus Christ be praised!"
Be this th' eternal song
through all the ages long:
"May Jesus Christ be praised!"

JESUS CHRIST IS LORD

I Greet Thee, Who My Sure Redeemer Art 366

Je te salue, mon certain Redempteur, anon. in *Strasbourg Psalter* (1553);
tr. Elizabeth L. Smith, 1868 (alt'd)

TOULON, 10 10.10 10   Abridged (c. 1860) from Psalm 124 in the *Genevan Psalter* (1551)

1. I greet thee, who my sure Re-deem-er art,
   my on-ly trust and Sav-ior of my heart,
   who pain didst un-der-go for my poor sake;
   I pray thee from our hearts all cares to take.

2. Thou art the King of mer-cy and of grace,
   reign-ing om-nip-o-tent in ev-'ry place:
   so come, O King, and our whole be-ing sway;
   shine on us with the light of thy pure day.

3. Thou art the Life, by which a-lone we live,
   and all our sub-stance and our strength re-ceive;
   sus-tain us by thy faith and by thy power,
   and give us strength in ev-'ry try-ing hour.

4. Thou hast the true and per-fect gen-tle-ness,
   no harsh-ness hast thou and no bit-ter-ness:
   O grant to us the grace we find in thee,
   that we may dwell in per-fect u-ni-ty.

5. Our hope is in no other save in thee;
   our faith is built upon thy promise free;
   Lord, give us peace and make us calm and sure,
   that in thy strength we evermore endure.

Alternative tune: JULIUS, 430   JESUS CHRIST IS LORD

367

O Morning Star

Wie schön leuchtet, by Philipp Nicolai, 1598;
tr. in the *Lutheran Book of Worship* (1978)

WIE SCHÖN LEUCHTET, 88.7.88.7.4.8.48   P. Nicolai, 1598; harmony and rhythm chiefly from J. S. Bach

1. O Morn - ing Star, how fair and bright you shine with God's own truth and light,
2. Lord, when you look on us in love, at once there falls from God a - bove
3. What joy to know, when life is past, the Lord we love is first and last,

1. a - glow with grace and mer - cy! Of Ja - cob's race, King Da - vid's Son,
2. a ray of pur - est pleas - sure. Your word and Spir - it, flesh and blood
3. the end and the be - gin - ning! He will one day, oh glo - rious grace!

1. our Lord and Mas - ter, you have won our hearts to serve you on - ly.
2. re - fresh our souls with heav'n - ly food. You are our dear - est trea - sure.
3. trans - port us to that hap - py place be - yond all tears and sin - ning!

1. Low - ly, ho - ly! great and glo - rious, all vic - to - rious,
2. Let your mer - cy warm and cheer us! Oh, draw near us!
3. A - men, A - men! Come, Lord Je - sus! Crown of glad - ness!

1. rich in bless - ing! Rule and might o'er all pos - sess - ing.
2. For you teach us God's own love through you can reach us.
3. We are yearn - ing for the day of your re - turn - ing.

JESUS CHRIST IS LORD   *Rev. 22:16*

O Lord, How Shall I Meet Thee?

368

Wie soll ich dich empfangen, by Paulus Gerhardt, 1653;
tr. Catherine Winkworth, 1863, and others

HELDER, 7.6.7.6 D

Melody by B. Helder, 1648

1. O Lord, how shall I meet thee, how wel-come thee a - right?
2. Love caused thine in-car - na - tion, love brought thee down to me;
3. A glo - ry thou didst give me, a trea-sure safe on high,

1. Thy peo - ple long to greet thee, my hope, my heart's de - light!
2. thy thirst for my sal - va - tion pro - cured my lib - er - ty.
3. that will not fail nor leave me as earth - ly rich - es fly.

1. O kin - dle, Lord most ho - ly, a lamp with - in my breast,
2. O love be - yond all tell - ing, that led thee to em - brace
3. My heart shall bloom for - ev - er for thee with prais - es new,

1. to do in spir - it low - ly all that may please thee best.
2. in love all love ex - cel - ling our lost and fall - en race.
3. and from thy name shall nev - er with - hold the hon - or due.

Alternative tune: ST. THEODULPH, 279

JESUS CHRIST IS LORD

369

Join All the Glorious Names

Isaac Watts, 1707

CROFT'S 136th, 6.6.6.6.88

William Croft, 1708

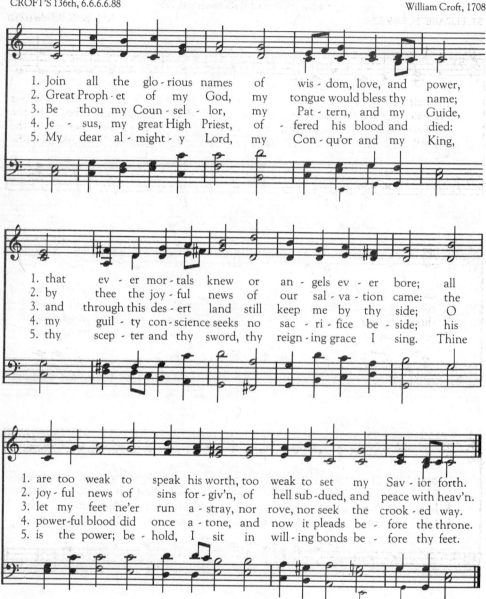

1. Join all the glo-rious names of wis-dom, love, and power,
2. Great Proph-et of my God, my tongue would bless thy name;
3. Be thou my Coun-sel-or, my Pat-tern, and my Guide,
4. Je-sus, my great High Priest, of-fered his blood and died:
5. My dear al-might-y Lord, my Con-qu'or and my King,

1. that ev-er mor-tals knew or an-gels ev-er bore; all
2. by thee the joy-ful news of our sal-va-tion came: the
3. and through this des-ert land still keep me by thy side; O
4. my guil-ty con-science seeks no sac-ri-fice be-side; his
5. thy scep-ter and thy sword, thy reign-ing grace I sing. Thine

1. are too weak to speak his worth, too weak to set my Sav-ior forth.
2. joy-ful news of sins for-giv'n, of hell sub-dued, and peace with heav'n.
3. let my feet ne'er run a-stray, nor rove, nor seek the crook-ed way.
4. power-ful blood did once a-tone, and now it pleads be-fore the throne.
5. is the power; be-hold, I sit in will-ing bonds be-fore thy feet.

JESUS CHRIST IS LORD

Heb. 4:14

Fairest Lord Jesus

Schönster Herr Jesu, anon. German, 1677;
tr. anon., 1850; rev. Isabella Stevenson, 1924

ST. ELIZABETH, 5.6.9.5.5.8

Schlesiger Volkslieder (1842)

1. Fair-est Lord Je-sus, Lord of all cre-a-tion, Son of our
2. Fair are the mead-ows, fair-er still the wood-lands, robed in the
3. Fair is the moon-light, fair-er still the sun-shine, fair is the
4. All fair-est beau-ty, heav-en-ly and earth-ly, won-drous-ly,

1. God who from heav'n came down; thee will I cher-ish,
2. col-ors and bloom of spring. Je-sus is fair-er,
3. shim-m'ring star-ry sky; Je-sus shines bright-er,
4. Je-sus, is found in thee; none can be near-er,

1. thee will I hon-or, O thou my soul's de-light and crown.
2. Je-sus is pur-er; he makes the sad-dest heart to sing.
3. Je-sus shines clear-er than all the heav'n-ly host on high.
4. fair-er, or dear-er than thou, my Sav-ior, art to me.

JESUS CHRIST IS LORD

371 Christians, Lift Up Your Hearts

John E. Bowers, 1980

SALVE FESTA DIES, Irregular

R. Vaughan Williams, 1906

Descant (any stanza after first)

Refrain
Chris-tians, lift up your hearts, and make this a day of re - joic - ing;

Refrain
1. Chris-tians, lift up your hearts, and make this a day of re - joic - ing;

God is our strength and song: glo - ry to his name!

1. God is our strength and song: glo - ry and praise to his name! name!

B
2. Praise for the Spir - it of God, who came to the wait-ing dis - ci - ples;
4. Praise that his love o - ver -flowed in the hearts of all who re - ceived him,
6. Come, Ho-ly Spir - it, to us who live by your pres-ence with- in us;

NOTE: *In performance the organ introduction should consist only of the measures marked st. 1. The choir should then sing the refrain, and the congregation should repeat it after them. This applies only to the beginning of the hymn; thereafter the refrain is sung by all after each stanza.*

PENTECOST

2. there   in   the wind and the fire   God gave new life to   his   own:
4. join - ing   to - geth - er in peace   those once di - vid - ed   by   sin:
6. come   to   di - rect   our course,   give   us your life and your power:

Repeat refrain

C (this part may be sung by the choir alone)

3. God's might-y power was re - vealed   when those   who   once   were so
5. strength-ened by God's might-y power, the dis - ci - ples went out   to all
7. Spir - it   of   God, send us   out   to   live   to your praise   and your

Repeat refrain

3. fear - ful   now could be seen by the world   wit - ness - ing brave - ly   for   Christ:
5. na - tions, preach-ing the Gos-pel of Christ, laugh - ing at dan - ger   and   death:
7. glo - ry;   yours is the power and the might;   ours be the cour - age   and   faith:

Repeat refrain

Ps. 118:14; Ps. 100:3; Rom. 6:4–5

PENTECOST

372   Rejoice! the Year upon Its Way

DEUS TUORUM MILITUM, LM

Beata nobis gaudia, c. 5th century;
tr. composite, based on J. M. Neale

Grenoble church melody, 1753

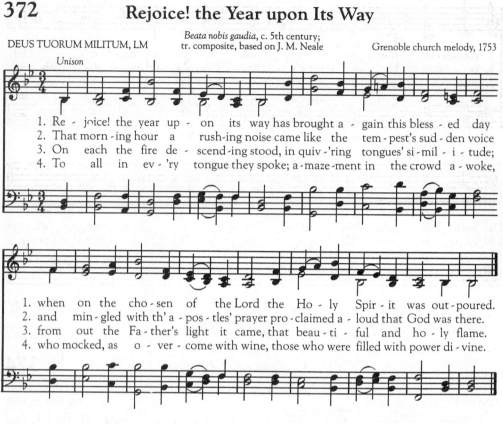

1. Re - joice! the year up - on its way has brought a - gain this bless - ed day
2. That morn - ing hour a rush-ing noise came like the tem - pest's sud - den voice
3. On each the fire de - scend-ing stood, in quiv-'ring tongues' si - mil - i - tude;
4. To all in ev - 'ry tongue they spoke; a - maze-ment in the crowd a - woke,

1. when on the cho - sen of the Lord the Ho - ly Spir - it was out-poured.
2. and min - gled with th' a - pos - tles' prayer pro - claimed a - loud that God was there.
3. from out the Fa - ther's light it came, that beau - ti - ful and ho - ly flame.
4. who mocked, as o - ver - come with wine, those who were filled with power di - vine.

5. As then, O Lord, thou didst fulfill
    each holy heart to do thy will,
    so now do thou our sins forgive,
    and make the world in peace to live.

6. To God the Father, God the Son,
    and God the Spirit, praise be done;
    may Christ the Lord upon us pour
    the Spirit's gifts forevermore.

NOTE: *st. 2–5 may be sung antiphonally by men and women.*
This tune in a higher key: 343

Acts 2:1–11

373   Filled with the Spirit's Power

John R. Peacey, 1969

MAGDA, 10 10.10 10

R. Vaughan Williams, 1925

1. Filled with the Spir - it's power, with one ac - cord the in - fant
2. Now with the mind of Christ set us on fire, that u - ni -
3. Wid - en our love, good Spir - it, to em - brace in your strong

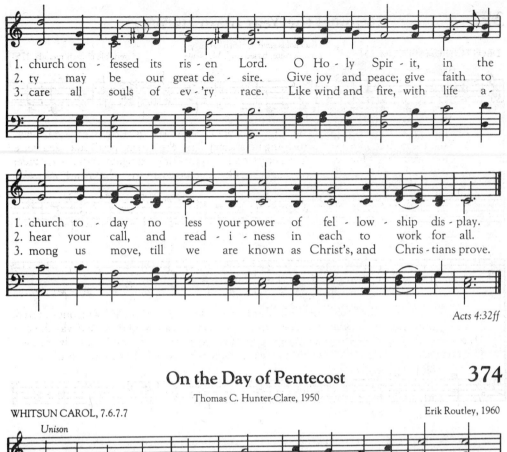

1. church con - fessed its ris - en Lord. O Ho - ly Spir - it, in the
2. ty may be our great de - sire. Give joy and peace; give faith to
3. care all souls of ev - 'ry race. Like wind and fire, with life a -

1. church to - day no less your power of fel - low - ship dis - play.
2. hear your call, and read - i - ness in each to work for all.
3. mong us move, till we are known as Christ's, and Chris - tians prove.

Acts 4:32ff

On the Day of Pentecost

374

Thomas C. Hunter-Clare, 1950

WHITSUN CAROL, 7.6.7.7

Erik Routley, 1960

Unison

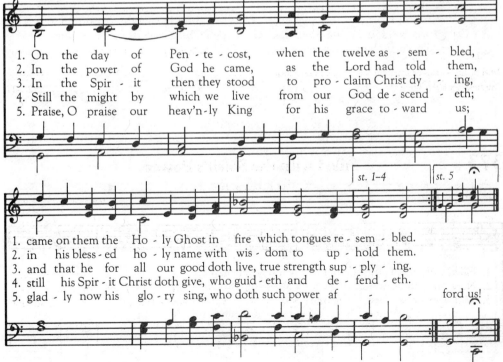

1. On the day of Pen - te - cost, when the twelve as - sem - bled,
2. In the power of God he came, as the Lord had told them,
3. In the Spir - it then they stood to pro - claim Christ dy - ing,
4. Still the might by which we live from our God de - scend - eth;
5. Praise, O praise our heav'n - ly King for his grace to - ward us;

st. 1-4   st. 5

1. came on them the Ho - ly Ghost in fire which tongues re - sem - bled.
2. in his bless - ed ho - ly name with wis - dom to up - hold them.
3. and that he for all our good doth live, true strength sup - ply - ing.
4. still his Spir - it Christ doth give, who guid - eth and de - fend - eth.
5. glad - ly now his glo - ry sing, who doth such power af - ford us!

Acts 2:1–11

PENTECOST

375   Lord God, the Holy Ghost

James Montgomery, 1819, 1825

CAMBERWELL, SM

Anon. melody first noted
by S. S. Wesley, 1872 (alt'd)

1. Lord God the Ho - ly Ghost, in this ac - cept - ed hour,
2. We meet with one ac - cord in our ap - point - ed place,
3. Like might - y rush - ing wind up - on the waves be - neath,
4. The young, the old in - spire with wis - dom from a - bove,

1. as on the day of Pen - te - cost, de - scend with all thy power.
2. and wait the prom - ise of our Lord, the Spir - it of all grace.
3. move with one im - pulse, ev - 'ry mind, one soul, one feel - ing breathe.
4. and give us hearts and tongues of fire to pray and praise and love.

5. Spirit of light, explore
and chase our gloom away,
with lustre shining more and more
unto the perfect day.

6. Spirit of truth, be thou
in life or death our guide;
O Spirit of adoption, now
may we be sanctified.

Acts 2:1–11; Rom. 8:15

376   Put Forth, O Lord, Thy Spirit's Might

CRUCIS VICTORIA, CM

Howard Chandler Robbins, 1937

Myles B. Foster, 1889

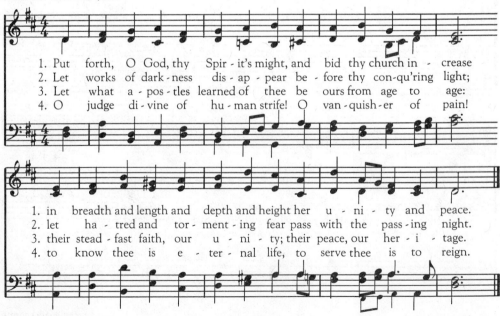

1. Put forth, O God, thy Spir - it's might, and bid thy church in - crease
2. Let works of dark - ness dis - ap - pear be - fore thy con - qu'ring light;
3. Let what a - pos - tles learned of thee be ours from age to age:
4. O judge di - vine of hu - man strife! O van - quish - er of pain!

1. in breadth and length and depth and height her u - ni - ty and peace.
2. let ha - tred and tor - ment - ing fear pass with the pass - ing night.
3. their stead - fast faith, our u - ni - ty; their peace, our her - i - tage.
4. to know thee is e - ter - nal life, to serve thee is to reign.

GIFTS AND POWER

Come, O Creator Spirit, Come

Veni creator Spiritus, medieval Latin; tr. Robert Bridges, 1899

VENI CREATOR SPIRITUS, LM

Plainsong melody, as in
Liber Usualis, mode viii

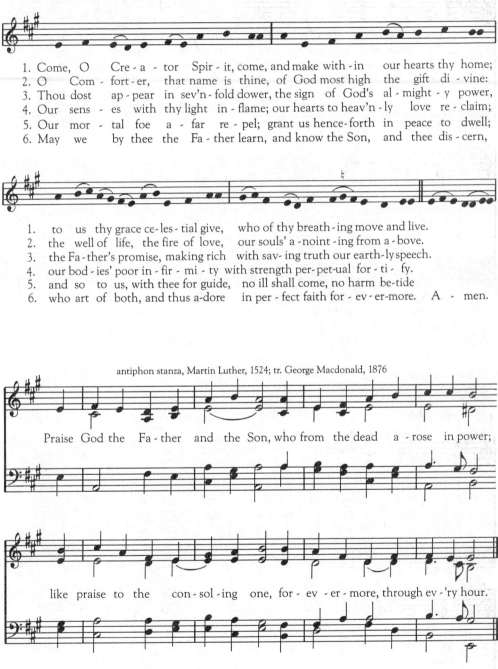

1. Come, O Cre-a-tor Spir-it, come, and make with-in our hearts thy home;
2. O Com-fort-er, that name is thine, of God most high the gift di-vine:
3. Thou dost ap-pear in sev'n-fold dower, the sign of God's al-might-y power,
4. Our sens-es with thy light in-flame; our hearts to heav'n-ly love re-claim;
5. Our mor-tal foe a-far re-pel; grant us hence-forth in peace to dwell;
6. May we by thee the Fa-ther learn, and know the Son, and thee dis-cern,

1. to us thy grace ce-les-tial give, who of thy breath-ing move and live.
2. the well of life, the fire of love, our souls' a-noint-ing from a-bove.
3. the Fa-ther's promise, making rich with sav-ing truth our earth-ly speech.
4. our bod-ies' poor in-fir-mi-ty with strength per-pet-ual for-ti-fy.
5. and so to us, with thee for guide, no ill shall come, no harm be-tide
6. who art of both, and thus a-dore in per-fect faith for-ev-er-more. A-men.

antiphon stanza, Martin Luther, 1524; tr. George Macdonald, 1876

Praise God the Fa-ther and the Son, who from the dead a-rose in power;

like praise to the con-sol-ing one, for-ev-er-more, through ev-'ry hour.

NOTE: *The Plainsong tune should be sung by one or more solo voices or by a small group; the antiphon verse should be sung at the beginning and after st. 2, 4, and 6 by the congregation.*

GIFTS AND POWER

378

O Spirit of the Living God

James Montgomery, 1823

WINCHESTER NEW, LM

Later form (1847) of melody in *Musikalisches Handbuch* (Hamburg, 1690)

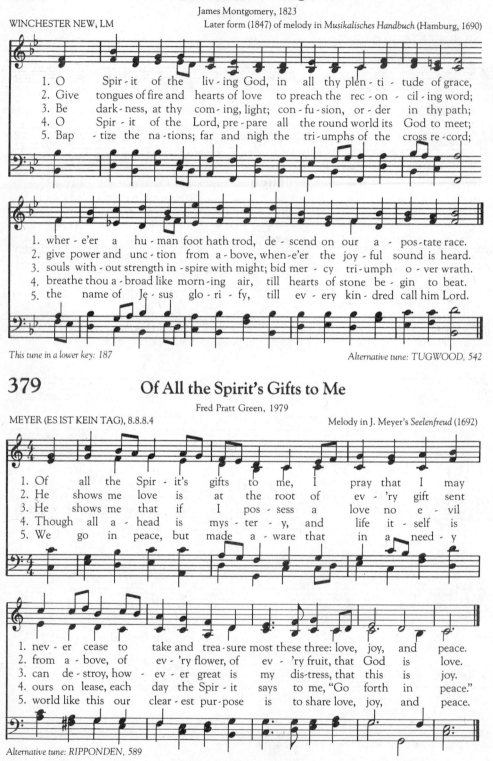

1. O Spir-it of the liv-ing God, in all thy plen-ti-tude of grace,
2. Give tongues of fire and hearts of love to preach the rec-on-cil-ing word;
3. Be dark-ness, at thy com-ing, light; con-fu-sion, or-der in thy path;
4. O Spir-it of the Lord, pre-pare all the round world its God to meet;
5. Bap-tize the na-tions; far and nigh the tri-umphs of the cross re-cord;

1. wher-e'er a hu-man foot hath trod, de-scend on our a-pos-tate race.
2. give power and unc-tion from a-bove, when-e'er the joy-ful sound is heard.
3. souls with-out strength in-spire with might; bid mer-cy tri-umph o-ver wrath.
4. breathe thou a-broad like morn-ing air, till hearts of stone be-gin to beat.
5. the name of Je-sus glo-ri-fy, till ev-ery kin-dred call him Lord.

This tune in a lower key: 187   *Alternative tune: TUGWOOD, 542*

379

Of All the Spirit's Gifts to Me

Fred Pratt Green, 1979

MEYER (ES IST KEIN TAG), 8.8.8.4

Melody in J. Meyer's *Seelenfreud* (1692)

1. Of all the Spir-it's gifts to me, I pray that I may
2. He shows me love is at the root of ev-'ry gift sent
3. He shows me that if I pos-sess a love no e-vil
4. Though all a-head is mys-ter-y, and life it-self is
5. We go in peace, but made a-ware that in a need-y

1. nev-er cease to take and trea-sure most these three: love, joy, and peace.
2. from a-bove, of ev-'ry flower, of ev-'ry fruit, that God is love.
3. can de-stroy, how-ev-er great is my dis-tress, that this is joy.
4. ours on lease, each day the Spir-it says to me, "Go forth in peace."
5. world like this our clear-est pur-pose is to share love, joy, and peace.

Alternative tune: RIPPONDEN, 589

There's a Spirit in the Air

Brian Wren, 1969

LAUDS, 77.77

John Wilson, 1969

Descant for st. 4 and 7
Sopranos (other voices sing unison melody)

Praise ____ the love, ____ Praise ___ the love.

1. There's a spir - it in the air, tell - ing Chris - tians ev - 'ry-where:
2. Lose your shy - ness, find your tongue; tell the world what God has done:
3. When be - liev - ers break the bread, when a hun - gry child is fed:
4. Still his Spir - it leads the fight, see - ing wrong and set - ting right:

Al - le - lu - ia! Al - le - lu - ia!

1. "Praise the love that Christ re - vealed, liv - ing, work - ing in our world."
2. God in Christ has come to stay, we can see his pow'r to - day.
3. praise the love that Christ re -vealed, liv - ing, work-ing in our world.
4. God in Christ has come to stay, we can see his pow'r to - day.

5. When a stranger's not alone
where the homeless find a home,
praise the love that Christ revealed,
living, working in our world.

6. May his Spirit fill our praise,
guide our thoughts and change our ways.
God in Christ has come to stay,
we can see his power today.

7. There's a Spirit in the air,
calling people everywhere:
praise the love that Christ revealed,
living, working in our world.

Mt. 10:42

GIFTS AND POWER

381

Holy Spirit, Ever Dwelling

Timothy Rees, 1922

HOLY MANNA, 8.7.8.7 D

American folk hymn melody

1. Ho - ly Spir - it, ev - er dwell - ing in the ho - liest realms of light;
2. Ho - ly Spir - it, ev - er breath - ing on the church the breath of life;
3. Ho - ly Spir - it, ev - er work - ing through the church's min - is - try —

1. Ho - ly Spir - it, ev - er brood - ing o'er a world of gloom and night;
2. Ho - ly Spir - it, ev - er striv - ing through her in a cease - less strife;
3. quick - 'ning, strength - 'ning, and ab - solv - ing, set - ting cap - tive sin - ners free;

1. Ho - ly Spir - it, ev - er rais - ing earth-bound souls to thrones on high;
2. Ho - ly Spir - it, ev - er form - ing in the church the mind of Christ:
3. Ho - ly Spir - it, ev - er bind - ing age to age and soul to soul

1. liv - ing, life - im - part - ing Spir - it; thee we praise and mag - ni - fy.
2. thee we praise with end - less wor - ship, for thy fruit and gifts un - priced.
3. in a fel - low - ship un - end - ing, thee we wor - ship and ex - tol.

This tune in a higher key: 29

GIFTS AND POWER

For Your Gift of God the Spirit

Margaret Clarkson, 1982

BETHANY, 8.7.8.7 D

Henry Smart, 1867

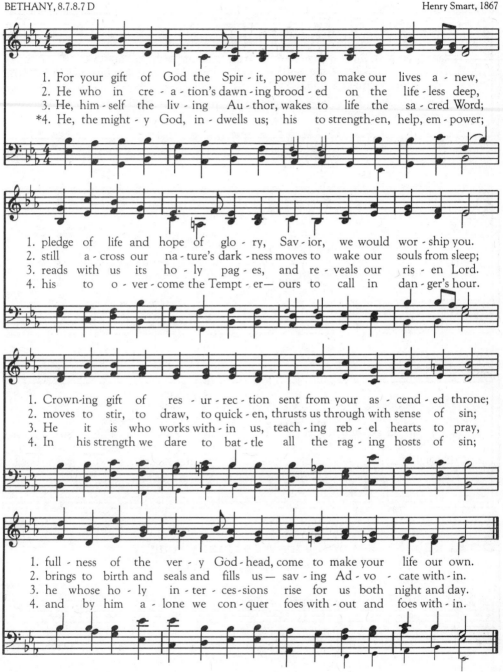

1. For your gift of God the Spir-it, power to make our lives a-new,
2. He who in cre-a-tion's dawn-ing brood-ed on the life-less deep,
3. He, him-self the liv-ing Au-thor, wakes to life the sa-cred Word;
*4. He, the might-y God, in-dwells us; his to strength-en, help, em-power;

1. pledge of life and hope of glo-ry, Sav-ior, we would wor-ship you.
2. still a-cross our na-ture's dark-ness moves to wake our souls from sleep;
3. reads with us its ho-ly pag-es, and re-veals our ris-en Lord.
4. his to o-ver-come the Tempt-er— ours to call in dan-ger's hour.

1. Crown-ing gift of res-ur-rec-tion sent from your as-cend-ed throne;
2. moves to stir, to draw, to quick-en, thrusts us through with sense of sin;
3. He it is who works with-in us, teach-ing reb-el hearts to pray,
4. In his strength we dare to bat-tle all the rag-ing hosts of sin;

1. full-ness of the ver-y God-head, come to make your life our own.
2. brings to birth and seals and fills us— sav-ing Ad-vo-cate with-in.
3. he whose ho-ly in-ter-ces-sions rise for us both night and day.
4. and by him a-lone we con-quer foes with-out and foes with-in.

5. Father, grant your Holy Spirit in our hearts may rule today;
grieved not, quenched not, but unhindered, work in us his sovereign way.
Fill us with your holy fullness, God the Father, Spirit, Son;
in us, through us, then, forever, shall your perfect will be done.

Rom. 8:14

GIFTS AND POWER

383   **Sing to Him in Whom Creation**

FINNIAN, 8.7.8.7.8.7   Michael Hewlett, 1975   Christopher Dearnley, 1975

1. Sing to him in whom creation found its shape and origin:
2. Preacher, singer, priest, and prophet caught his accents, spoke his word;
3. Tell of how th' ascended Jesus armed a people for his own;
4. Pray we then, O Lord the Spirit, on our lives descend in might;
5. Praise, O praise the Holy Spirit, praise the Father, praise the Word,

1. Spirit, moving on the waters troubled by the God within;
2. his the truth behind the wisdoms which as yet knew not our Lord;
3. how a hundred men and women turned the known world upside down,
4. let thy flame break out within us, fire our hearts and clear our sight,
5. Source and Truth and Inspiration, Trinity in deep accord;

1. Source of breath to all things breathing, Life in whom all lives begin.
2. he the love of God eternal which in Christ was seen and heard.
3. to its dark and furthest corners by the wind of Whitsun blown.
4. till, white hot in thy possession, we too set the world alight.
5. through thy voice which speaks within us we thy creatures own thee Lord.

Gen. 1:2–2:7; Acts 17:6

384   **Lord, Thy Word Hath Taught**

Thomas C. Hunter-Clare, b. 1910

SEELENBRÄUTIGAM, 55.88.55   Adam Drese, 1665

1. Lord, thy word hath taught that our deeds are naught;
2. Send thy Spirit down and thy children crown
3. Faith and hope beyond, of true peace the bond,
4. Hear us for his sake, who our flesh did take;

1. if no flame of love doth fire us, nor with god - ly grace in - spire us;
2. with this jew - el best and rar - est, in thy di - a - dem the fair - est,
3. all our vir - tues love u - nit - eth, and thy im - age in us writ - eth;
4. send us love that nev - er fail - eth, love that o'er all foes pre - vail - eth;

1. from thy ho - ly hill, love in us in - still.
2. rich, all gold a - bove, gra - cious, ho - ly love.
3. who hath not its light lives not in thy sight.
4. through thy Son, our Lord, this great gift af - ford.

I Cor. 13:13

This tune in a lower key: 586

Come, Holy Ghost, Our Hearts Inspire   385

METROPOLITAN, CM   Charles Wesley, 1740   Melville Cooke

1. Come, Ho - ly Ghost, our hearts in - spire, let us thine in - fluence prove,
2. Come, Ho - ly Ghost (for moved by thee the proph - ets wrote and spoke),
3. Ex - pand thy wings, Ce - les - tial Dove, brood o'er our na - ture's night;
4. God, through him - self, we then shall know, if thou with - in us shine,

1. source of the old pro - phet - ic fire, foun - tain of life and love.
2. un - lock the truth, thy - self the key, un - seal the sa - cred book.
3. on our dis - or - dered spir - its move, and let there now be light.
4. and sound, with all thy saints be - low, the depths of love di - vine.

This tune in a lower key: 27

Gen. 1:3

SCRIPTURES

386 Thy Strong Word Did Cleave the Darkness

Martin Franzmann, 1969 (alt'd)

LAKELAND, 8.7.8.7 D

Alfred Fedak, 1980

1. Thy strong word did cleave the dark-ness; at thy speak - ing it was done;
2. Thy strong word be-speaks us righ-teous, bright with thine own ho - li - ness;
3. Give us lips to sing thy glo-ry, tongues thy mer - cy to pro-claim,

1. for cre - at - ed light we thank thee, while thy or - dered sea-sons run.
2. glo - rious now, we press t'ward glo - ry, and our lives our hope con - fess.
3. throats that shout the hope that fills us, mouths to speak thy ho - ly name.

1. On a world that dwelt in dark - ness, dark as night and deep as
2. From the cross thy wis - dom shin - ing break-eth forth in con-qu'ring
3. Al - le - lu - ia! Al - le - lu - ia! May the light that thou dost

1. death,   broke the light of thy sal - va - tion,
2. might;   from the cross for - ev - er beam - eth
3. send   fill our songs with al - le - lu - ias,

Optional descant

st. 1,2   st. 3   *rit.*

1. breathed thine own life - giv - ing breath.
2. all thy bright re - deem-ing might.
3. al - le - lu - ias with-out end!

rit.

387   O Word of God Incarnate

William Walsham How, 1867 (alt'd);
chiefly from the *Lutheran Book of Worship* (1978)

Neuvermehrtes Meiningisches Gesangbuch (1693);
adapted by Felix Mendelssohn, 1847

MUNICH, 7.6.7.6 D

1. O Word of God in - car - nate, O Wis - dom from on high,
2. The church from thee, dear Mas - ter, re - ceived the gift di - vine,
3. O make your church, dear Sav - ior, a lamp of bur - nished gold

1. O Truth un - changed, un - chang - ing, O Light of our dark sky:
2. and still that light is lift - ed o'er all the earth to shine.
3. to bear be - fore the na - tions your true light, as of old;

1. we praise you for the ra - diance that from the hal - lowed page,
2. It is the chart and com - pass that, through life's surg - ing sea,
3. O teach your wan - d'ring pil - grims by this their path to trace,

1. a lan - tern to our foot - steps, shines on from age to age.
2. 'mid mists and rocks and quick - sands, still guides, O Christ, to thee.
3. till, clouds and dark - ness end - ed, they see you face to face.

Not Far Beyond the Sea

388

George B. Caird, 1945

GANGES, 88.6 D

American folk song; Wyeth's *Repository*, Part II (1813)

1. Not far be-yond the sea, nor high a - bove the heav'ns, but ver - y nigh thy voice, O God, is heard. For each new step of faith we take thou hast more light and truth to break forth from thy Ho - ly Word.
2. The babes in Christ thy scrip-tures feed with milk suf - fi - cient for their need, the nur - ture of the Lord. Be - neath life's bur - den and its heat the full-grown mind finds strong-er meat in thy un - fail - ing Word.
3. Root - ed and ground - ed in thy love, with saints on earth and saints a - bove, we join in one ac - cord, to grasp the breadth, length, depth, and height, the cru - ci - fied and ris - en might of Christ, th' in - car - nate Word.
4. Help us to press to - ward that mark, and though our vi - sion now is dark, to live by what we see. So, when we see thee face to face, thy truth and light our dwell - ing place for - ev - er - more shall be.

Dt. 30:11–14

SCRIPTURES

389   O God of Light

Sarah E. Taylor, 1952; adapted in the *Lutheran Book of Worship* (1978)

CHARTERHOUSE, 11.10.11.10

David Evans, 1927

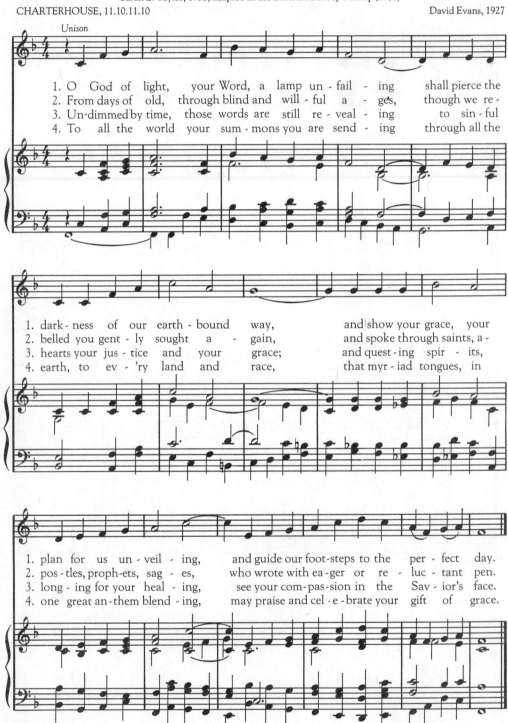

Unison

1. O God of light, your Word, a lamp un-fail-ing shall pierce the
2. From days of old, through blind and will-ful a-ges, though we re-
3. Un-dimmed by time, those words are still re-veal-ing to sin-ful
4. To all the world your sum-mons you are send-ing through all the

1. dark-ness of our earth-bound way, and show your grace, your
2. belled you gent-ly sought a-gain, and spoke through saints, a-
3. hearts your jus-tice and your grace; and quest-ing spir-its,
4. earth, to ev-'ry land and race, that myr-iad tongues, in

1. plan for us un-veil-ing, and guide our foot-steps to the per-fect day.
2. pos-tles, proph-ets, sag-es, who wrote with ea-ger or re-luc-tant pen.
3. long-ing for your heal-ing, see your com-pas-sion in the Sav-ior's face.
4. one great an-them blend-ing, may praise and cel-e-brate your gift of grace.

SCRIPTURES

Ps. 119:105

Thanks to God, Whose Word Was Spoken

R. T. Brooks, 1954

PANTYCELYN, 8.7.8.7.4.7   Erik Routley, 1950

1. Thanks to God, whose word was spo-ken in the deed that made the earth;
2. Thanks to God, whose Word in-car-nate glo-ri-fied the flesh of earth.
3. Thanks to God, whose word was writ-ten in the Bi-ble's sa-cred page,
4. Thanks to God, whose word is pub-lished in the tongues of ev-'ry race:
5. Thanks to God, whose word is an-swered by the Spir-it's voice with-in.

1. his the voice that called a na-tion, his the fires that tried its worth.
2. Deeds and words and death and ris-ing tell of grace and our re-birth.
3. rec-ord of the rev-e-la-tion show-ing God to ev-'ry age.
4. see its glo-ry un-di-min-ished by the change of time or place.
5. Here we drink of joy un-meas-ured, life re-deemed from death and sin.

1. God has spo-ken: praise him for his o-pen word.
2. God has spo-ken: praise him for his o-pen word.
3. God has spo-ken: praise him for his o-pen word.
4. God has spo-ken: praise him for his o-pen word.
5. God is speak-ing: praise him for his o-pen word.

SCRIPTURES

391 A Lamp for Our Feet Has Been Given

Granton Douglas Hay, 1977

CRUGYBAR, 9.8.9.8 D amphibrachic

Welsh hymn melody, 1883

1. A lamp for our feet has been giv-en, a light has been set on a hill;
2. Lord, wor-ship and praise we would of-fer in thanks for the grace we've re-ceived;
3. Lord, grant to us eyes ev-er watch-ful, and ears ev-er o-pen to hear

1. God's word in its truth may be trust-ed by all who sur-ren-der their will
2. your word is our rock and our tow-er; in trust-ing we are not de-ceived.
3. the word that in love you are speak-ing, the word that de-feats all our fear.

1. to or-der the cha-os of dark-ness, give hope in the midst of de-spair,
2. The proph-ets of old had their vi-sions—your word of-ten came in their dreams—
3. In suf-fer-ing love you have claimed us; for-give us for flesh that is weak;

1. to make of our lives new cre-a-tions, and light-en the bur-dens we bear.
2. but we see the word now in-car-nate in Christ and in those he re-deems.
3. you know that our spir-its are will-ing; give strength with the word that you speak.

Christ Is Made the Sure Foundation

Angularis fundamentum, Latin, 7th century; tr. J. M. Neale, 1851

WESTMINSTER ABBEY, 8.7.8.7.8.7

Henry Purcell, 1659–1695

Descant, st. 4

4. Laud and hon-or to the Fa-ther, laud and hon-or to the Son,

1. Christ is made the sure foun-da-tion: Christ the head and cor-ner-stone,
2. To this tem-ple where we call thee, come, O Lord of hosts, to-day;
3. Here vouch-safe to all thy ser-vants what they ask of thee to gain,
4. Laud and hon-or to the Fa-ther, laud and hon-or to the Son,

4. laud and hon-or to the Spir-it, ev-er three and ev-er one:

1. cho-sen of the Lord and pre-cious, bind-ing all the church in one,
2. with thy wont-ed lov-ing-kind-ness, hear thy peo-ple as they pray,
3. what they gain from thee for-ev-er with the bless-ed to re-tain,
4. laud and hon-or to the Spir-it, ev-er three and ev-er one:

4. one in might and one in glo-ry while un-end-ing a-ges run.

1. Ho-ly Zi-on's help for-ev-er and her con-fi-dence a-lone.
2. and thy full-est ben-e-dic-tion shed with-in its walls for aye.
3. and here-af-ter in thy glo-ry ev-er-more with thee to reign.
4. one in might and one in glo-ry while un-end-ing a-ges run.

Alternative tune: REGENT SQUARE, 229

This tune in a higher key, with the composer's original harmonies: 599

I Cor. 3:11

THE CHURCH'S FOUNDING

393 Glorious Things of Thee Are Spoken

John Newton, 1779

ABBOT'S LEIGH, 8.7.8.7 D

Cyril Taylor, 1941

1. Glo - rious things of thee are spo - ken, Zi - on, cit - y of our God;
2. See, the streams of liv - ing wa - ter spring-ing from e - ter - nal love,
*3. Blest in-hab - i - tants of Zi - on, washed in their Re - deem - er's blood,
4. Sav - ior, if of Zi - on's cit - y I through grace a mem - ber am,

1. he, whose word can - not be bro - ken, formed thee for his own a - bode;
2. well sup - ply thy sons and daugh-ters, and all fear of want re - move;
3. Je - sus, whom their souls re - ly on, makes them kings and priests to God.
4. let the world de - ride or pit - y — I will glo - ry in thy name;

1. on the rock of a - ges found-ed, what can shake thy sure re - pose?
2. who can faint while such a riv - er ev - er flows their thirst to as - suage,
3. 'Tis his love his peo - ple rais - es o - ver self to reign as kings,
4. fad - ing are the world-lings' plea-sures, all their boast-ed pomp and show;

1. With sal - va - tion's walls sur-round-ed, thou may'st smile at all thy foes.
2. grace, which, like the Lord, the Giv - er, nev - er fails from age to age.
3. and as priests, his sol - emn prais-es each for a thank - of - f'ring brings.
4. sol - id joys and last - ing trea-sures, none but Zi - on's chil - dren know.

This tune in a higher key: 424; Alternative tune: AUSTRIA, 3

THE CHURCH'S FOUNDING

Ps. 87:3; I Pet. 2:9; Rev. 1:5

The Church's One Foundation

Samuel John Stone, 1866

AURELIA, 7.6.7.6 D

S. S. Wesley, 1864

1. The church's one foun - da - tion is Je - sus Christ her Lord;
2. E - lect from ev - 'ry na - tion, yet one o'er all the earth,
3. Though with a scorn - ful won - der we see her sore op - press'd,
4. 'Mid toil and trib - u - la - tion, and tu - mult of her war,

1. she is his new cre - a - tion by wa - ter and the Word;
2. her char - ter of sal - va - tion, "One Lord, one faith, one birth!"
3. by schi - sms rent a - sun - der, by her - e - sies dis - tress'd,
4. she waits the con - sum - ma - tion of peace for - ev - er - more,

1. from heav'n he came and sought her to be his ho - ly bride;
2. One ho - ly name she bless - es, par - takes one ho - ly food,
3. yet saints their watch are keep - ing, their cry goes up, "How long?"
4. till with the vi - sion glo - rious her long - ing eyes are blest,

1. with his own blood he bought her, and for her life he died.
2. and to one hope she press - es with ev - 'ry grace en - dued.
3. And soon the night of weep - ing shall be the morn of song.
4. and the great church vic - to - rious shall be the church at rest.

*5. Yet she on earth hath union with God, the Three - in - One,
and mystic sweet communion with those whose rest is won;
O happy ones and holy, Lord give us grace that we,
like them, the meek and lowly, on high may dwell with thee.

Alternative tune: ST. THEODULPH, 279

I Cor. 3:11; Eph. 5:26–27

THE CHURCH'S FOUNDING

395   O Faithless, Fearful Army

Der Herr wird für dich streiten, by Heinrich Vogel, 1937; tr. W. A. Whitehouse, 1945

KING'S LYNN, 7.6.7.6 D   English traditional melody; arranged by R. Vaughan Williams, 1906

1. O faith-less, fear-ful ar - my, for you the Lord doth fight;
2. Why down-cast, why de - spair-ing, in face of hos-tile power,
3. His death and res-ur - rec-tion he clothes up-on his folk,

1. for you, through o-ceans storm - y, he cleaves his path of light.
2. as though a-lone you're bear - ing the stress-es of this hour?
3. bound to him in sub - jec-tion by faith and love and hope.

1. De - ter-mined is the is - sue, the cru-cial vic - t'ry past;
2. To death and hell ap-point - ed, see con-qu'ring in your place
3. O war-rior true and glo - rious, thou hast God's bat-tle won!

1. and God, who has re - deemed you, up-holds you to the last.
2. the Son of God, th'A - noint-ed, e - lect by sov-'reign grace!
3. Lord Christ, for us vic - to-rious, thy per-fect work is done.

THE CHURCH'S FOUNDING   *Alternative tune:* LLANGLOFFAN, 80

Christ Is the King! O Friends, Rejoice

G. K. A. Bell, 1930

GELOBT SEI GOTT, 888 with Alleluias

Melody by M. Vulpius, c. 1560–1616

1. Christ is the King! O friends, re - joice; broth - ers and
2. O mag - ni - fy the Lord, and raise an - thems of
3. They with a faith for - ev - er new fol - lowed the
4. O Chris-tian wom - en, Chris - tian men, all the world

1. sis - ters with one voice let the world know he is your choice.
2. joy and ho - ly praise for Christ's brave saints of an - cient days.
3. king, and round him drew thou - sands of ser - vants brave and true.
4. o - ver, seek a - gain the way dis - ci - ples fol-lowed then.

Al - le - lu - ia! Al - le - lu - ia! Al - le - lu - ia!

This tune in a higher key: 326

5. Christ through all ages is the same:
   place the same hope in his great name,
   with the same faith his word proclaim;
   Alleluia! Alleluia! Alleluia!

6. Let love's unconquerable might
   your scattered companies unite
   in service to the Lord of light;
   Alleluia! Alleluia! Alleluia!

397

For All the Saints

William Walsham How, 1867

SINE NOMINE, 10 10 10 with Alleluias

R. Vaughan Williams, 1906 (rev. 1925)

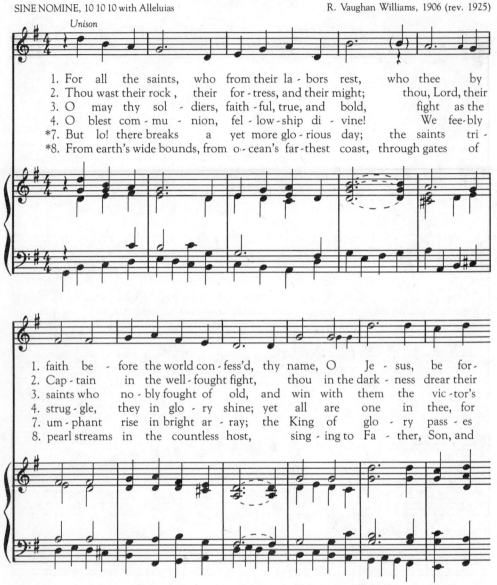

Unison

1. For all the saints, who from their la - bors rest, who thee by
2. Thou wast their rock, their for - tress, and their might; thou, Lord, their
3. O may thy sol - diers, faith - ful, true, and bold, fight as the
4. O blest com - mu - nion, fel - low-ship di - vine! We fee-bly
*7. But lo! there breaks a yet more glo - rious day; the saints tri -
*8. From earth's wide bounds, from o - cean's far-thest coast, through gates of

1. faith be - fore the world con - fess'd, thy name, O Je - sus, be for-
2. Cap - tain in the well - fought fight, thou in the dark - ness drear their
3. saints who no - bly fought of old, and win with them the vic - tor's
4. strug - gle, they in glo - ry shine; yet all are one in thee, for
7. um - phant rise in bright ar - ray; the King of glo - ry pass - es
8. pearl streams in the countless host, sing - ing to Fa - ther, Son, and

NOTE: *The whole hymn is suitable for processional use; for normal use st. 1-4 may be sufficient.*

THE CHURCH'S HISTORY

1. ev - er   bless'd;
2. one   true   light:
3. crown of   gold;
4. all   are   thine:
7. on   his   way:
8. Ho - ly   Ghost;

Al - le - lu - ia!   Al - le - lu - ia!

St. 5 and 6: sing in harmony (more quietly)

*5. And when the strife   is   fierce, the war - fare   long,   steals on the
*6. The gold - en eve - ning bright - ens in the   west;   soon, soon, to

5. ear   the   dis - tant tri - umph   song, and hearts   are   brave a -
6. faith - ful war - riors com - eth   rest: sweet   is the calm of

5. gain, and arms are   strong.} Al - le - lu - ia! Al - le - lu - ia!
6. par - a - dise the   blest.}

Alternative tune: ENGELBERG, 345

Heb. 12:1

THE CHURCH'S HISTORY

398

Rejoice in God's Saints

Fred Pratt Green, 1977

OLD 104th, 10 10.11 11

Melody in *Ravenscroft's Psalter* (1621)

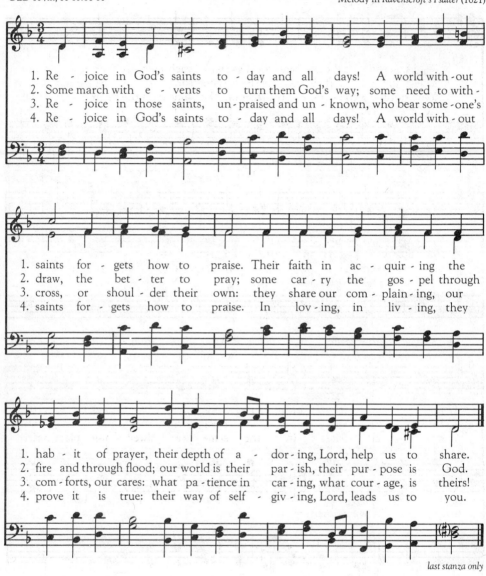

1. Re - joice in God's saints to - day and all days! A world with-out
2. Some march with e - vents to turn them God's way; some need to with -
3. Re - joice in those saints, un - praised and un - known, who bear some-one's
4. Re - joice in God's saints to - day and all days! A world with-out

1. saints for - gets how to praise. Their faith in ac - quir - ing the
2. draw, the bet - ter to pray; some car - ry the gos - pel through
3. cross, or shoul - der their own: they share our com - plain - ing, our
4. saints for - gets how to praise. In lov - ing, in liv - ing, they

1. hab - it of prayer, their depth of a - dor - ing, Lord, help us to share.
2. fire and through flood; our world is their par - ish, their pur - pose is God.
3. com - forts, our cares: what pa - tience in car - ing, what cour - age, is theirs!
4. prove it is true: their way of self - giv - ing, Lord, leads us to you.

last stanza only

We Come unto Our Savior God

Thomas H. Gill, 1868 (alt'd)

NUN FREUT EUCH, 8.7.8.7.8 8.7   English 18th-century form of melody in *Geistliche Lieder* (Wittenberg, 1535)

399

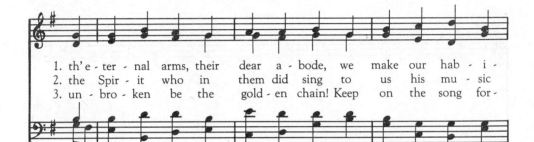

1. We come un-to our Sav-ior God with each past gen-er-a - tion;
2. Their joy un-to their Lord we bring; their song to us de-scend - eth;
3. Ye saints to come, take up the strain, the same great theme en-deav - or;

1. th'e-ter - nal arms, their dear a-bode, we make our hab-i -
2. the Spir - it who in them did sing to us his mu - sic
3. un-bro - ken be the gold-en chain! Keep on the song for-

1. ta - tion. We bring thee, Lord, the praise they brought; we
2. lend - eth; his song in them, in us, is one; we
3. ev - er! Safe in the same dear dwell-ing place, rich

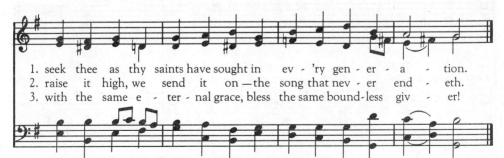

1. seek thee as thy saints have sought in ev - 'ry gen-er-a - tion.
2. raise it high, we send it on —the song that nev - er end - eth.
3. with the same e - ter-nal grace, bless the same bound-less giv - er!

Dt. 33:27

THE CHURCH'S HISTORY

Give Me the Wings of Faith

Isaac Watts, 1707

BEATITUDO, CM

Melody by J. B. Dykes, 1868

1. Give me the wings of faith to rise with-in the veil, and see
2. I ask them whence their vic - t'ry came; they with u - nit - ed breath
3. They marked the foot - steps that he trod— his zeal in - spired their breast—
4. Our glo-rious Lead - er claims our praise for his own pat - tern giv'n,

1. the saints of God, how great their joys, how bright their glo - ries be.
2. as - cribe their con - quest to the Lamb, their tri-umphs to his death.
3. and, fol-l'wing their in - car - nate God, pos - sess the prom - ised rest.
4. while the long cloud of wit - ness - es shows the same path to heaven.

Alternative tune: LIVERPOOL, 437

Heb. 12:1; Rev. 7:13

I Sing a Song of the Saints of God

Lesbia Scott, 1929 (alt'd)

GRAND ISLE, Irregular

J. H. Hopkins, Jr., 1940

1. I sing a song of the saints of God, pa - tient and brave and true,
2. They loved their Lord so dear, so dear, and his love made them strong;
3. They lived not on - ly in a - ges past; there are hun-dreds of thou-sands still;

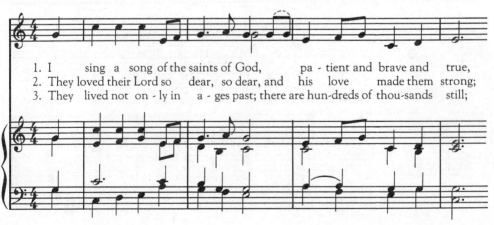

1. who toiled and fought and loved and died for the Lord they loved and knew.
2. and they fol-lowed the right for Je - sus' sake the whole of their good lives long.
3. the world is bright with the joy-ous saints who love to do Je - sus' will.

1. And one was a doc - tor and one was a queen
2. And one was a sol - dier and one was a priest
3. You can meet them in school, on the street, in the store,

1. and one was a shep - herd-ess on the green; they were
2. and one was slain by a fierce wild beast, and there's
3. in church, by the sea, in the house next door; for the

1. all of them saints of God, and I mean, God help-ing, to be one too.
2. not an - y rea - son, no, not the least, why I should-n't be one too.
3. saints of God can be rich or poor, and I mean to be one too.

THE CHURCH'S HISTORY

402　Eternal Ruler of the Ceaseless Round

J. W. Chadwick, 1864

SONG 1, 10.10.10.10.10 10

Melody and bass by Orlando Gibbons, 1623

1. E - ter - nal Rul - er of the cease - less round of cir - cling
2. We are of thee, the chil - dren of thy love, sis - ters and
3. We would be one in ha - tred of all wrong, one in our

1. plan - ets sing - ing on their way, guide of the na - tions
2. broth - ers of thine own dear Son; de - scend, O Ho - ly
3. love of all things sweet and fair, one with the joy that

1. from the night pro - found in - to the glo - ry of the
2. Spir - it, like a dove in - to our hearts, that we may
3. break - eth in - to song, one with the grief that trem - bleth

1. per - fect day, rule in our hearts, that we may ev - er
2. be as one: as one with thee, to whom we ev - er
3. in - to prayer, one in the power that makes the chil - dren

1. be guid - ed and strength - ened and up - held by thee.
2. tend; as one with him, our broth - er and our friend.
3. free to fol - low truth, and thus to fol - low thee.

THE CHURCH'S UNITY AND FELLOWSHIP

O Thou Not Made with Hands

F. T. Palgrave, 1865

OLD 120th, 6.6.6.6.66

Melody from *Damon's Psalter* (1579), and *Este's Psalter* (1592)

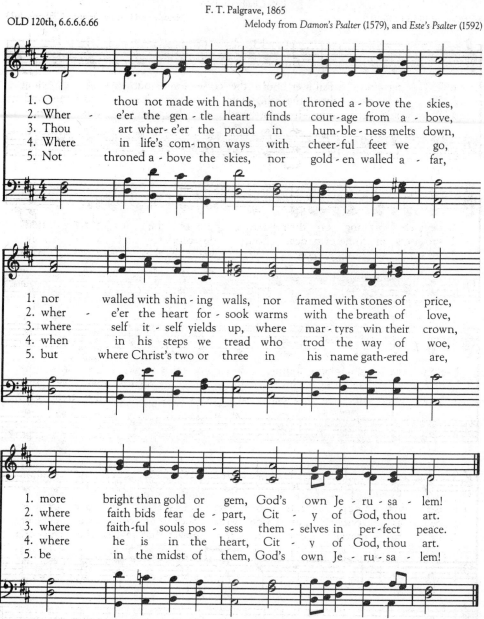

1. O thou not made with hands, not throned a-bove the skies,
2. Wher - e'er the gen - tle heart finds cour -age from a - bove,
3. Thou art wher- e'er the proud in hum-ble - ness melts down,
4. Where in life's com-mon ways with cheer-ful feet we go,
5. Not throned a - bove the skies, nor gold - en walled a - far,

1. nor walled with shin - ing walls, nor framed with stones of price,
2. wher - e'er the heart for - sook warms with the breath of love,
3. where self it - self yields up, where mar - tyrs win their crown,
4. when in his steps we tread who trod the way of woe,
5. but where Christ's two or three in his name gath-ered are,

1. more bright than gold or gem, God's own Je - ru - sa - lem!
2. where faith bids fear de - part, Cit - y of God, thou art.
3. where faith-ful souls pos - sess them - selves in per -fect peace.
4. where he is in the heart, Cit - y of God, thou art.
5. be in the midst of them, God's own Je - ru - sa - lem!

Mt. 18:20

404

O Holy Spirit, Lord of Grace

O fons amoris, Spiritus, C. Coffin, 1736; tr. J. Chandler, 1837

TALLIS' ORDINAL, CM

Thomas Tallis, c. 1557

1. O Ho-ly Spir-it, Lord of grace, e-ter-nal source of love,
2. As thou dost join with ho-liest bonds the Fa-ther and the Son,
3. To God the Fa-ther, God the Son, and God the Ho-ly Ghost,

1. in-flame, we pray, our in-most hearts with fire from heav'n a-bove.
2. so fill thy saints with mu-tual love, and link their hearts in one.
3. e-ter-nal glo-ry be from earth and from the an-gel host.

This tune in a higher key: 527
Alternative tunes: BELGRAVE, 135, ST. COLUMBA, 350

Jn. 17:22

405

Jesus, Lord, We Look to Thee

Cento from Charles Wesley, 1740

VIENNA, 77.77

Melody and bass by J. H. Knecht, 1799

1. Je-sus, Lord, we look to thee; let us in thy name a-gree;
2. Make us of one heart and mind, cour-teous, pit-i-ful, and kind,
3. Let us for each oth-er care, each the oth-er's bur-dens bear;
4. Free from an-ger and from pride, let us thus in God a-bide,
5. Fill us with the Fa-ther's love; nev-er from our souls re-move;

1. show thy-self the Prince of peace; bid all strife for-ev-er cease.
2. low-ly, meek in thought and word, al-to-geth-er like the Lord.
3. to thy church the pat-tern give, show how true be-liev-ers live.
4. all the depths of love ex-press, all the heights of ho-li-ness.
5. dwell in us and we shall be thine through all e-ter-ni-ty.

THE CHURCH'S UNITY AND FELLOWSHIP

God Is Love, and Where True Love Is

406

James Quinn, 1969

UBI CARITAS, 6.6.6.6 D with refrain

Gregory Murray, 1940

Refrain, Unison

God is love, and where true love is God him-self is there.

Harmony

1. Here in Christ we gath - er, love of Christ our call - ing.
2. When we Chris-tians gath - er, mem-bers of one bod - y,
3. Grant us love's ful - fill - ment, joy with all the bless - ed,

1. Christ, our love, is with us, glad-ness be his greet - ing.
2. let there be in us no dis-cord but one spir - it.
3. when we see your face, O Sav - ior, in its glo - ry.

1. Let us fear him, yes, and love him, God e - ter - nal.
2. Ban-ished now be an - ger, strife, and ev - ery quar - rel.
3. Shine on us, O pur - est light of all cre - a - tion,

Repeat refrain after each stanza

1. Lov - ing him, let each love Christ in one an - oth - er.
2. Christ, our God, be al - ways pres - ent here a - mong us.
3. be our bliss while end - less a - ges sing your prais - es.

I Jn. 4:16

THE CHURCH'S UNITY AND FELLOWSHIP

407

Blest Be the Tie That Binds

John Fawcett, 1782 (alt'd)

BOYLESTON, SM
First Tune
Melody by Lowell Mason, 1832

1. Blest be the tie that binds our hearts in Chris-tian love:
2. Be-fore our Fa-ther's throne we pour our ar-dent prayers:
3. We share each oth-er's woes, each oth-er's bur-dens bear,
4. One glo-rious hope re-vives our cour-age by the way,
5. when from all toil and pain and sin we shall be free,

1. the fel-low-ship of kin-dred minds is like to that a - bove.
2. our fears, our hopes, our aims are one, our com-forts and our cares.
3. and of-ten for each oth-er flows the sym-pa-thiz-ing tear.
4. while each in ex-pec-ta-tion lives and longs to see the day —
5. and per-fect love and friend-ship reign through all e-ter-ni-ty.

Gal. 6:2

408

Blest Be the Tie That Binds

Second Tune

DENNIS, SM
Lowell Mason, 1845

1. Blest be the tie that binds our hearts in Chris-tian love:
2. Be fore our Fa-ther's throne we pour our ar-dent prayers:
3. We share each oth-er's woes, each oth-er's bur-dens bear,
4. One glo-rious hope re-vives our cour-age by the way,
5. when from all toil and pain and sin we shall be free,

1. the fel-low-ship of kin-dred minds is like to that a-bove.
2. our fears, our hopes, our aims are one, our com-forts and our cares.
3. and of-ten for each oth-er flows the sym-pa-thiz-ing tear.
4. while each in ex-pec-ta-tion lives and longs to see the day—
5. and per-fect love and friend-ship reign through all e-ter-ni-ty.

Alternative tune: ST. GEORGE, 66

I Love Thy Kingdom, Lord

409

Timothy Dwight, 1801

Adapted from melody in
Aaron Williams' *Psalmody* (1770)

ST. THOMAS, SM

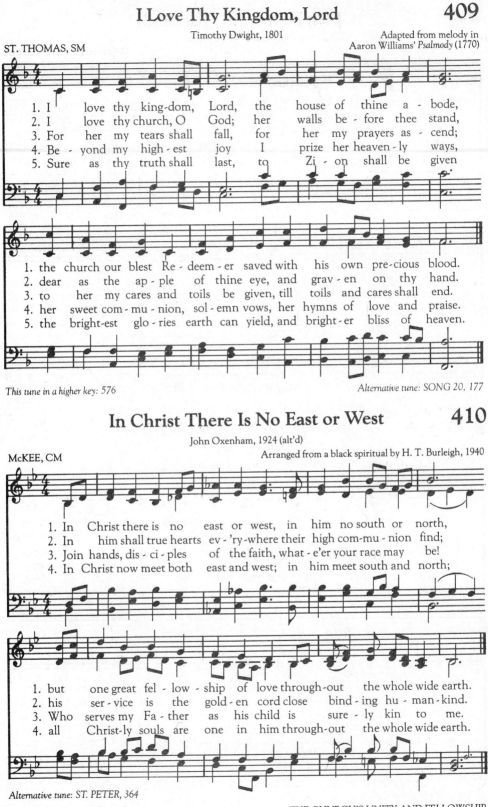

1. I love thy king-dom, Lord, the house of thine a-bode,
2. I love thy church, O God; her walls be-fore thee stand,
3. For her my tears shall fall, for her my prayers as-cend;
4. Be-yond my high-est joy I prize her heaven-ly ways,
5. Sure as thy truth shall last, to Zi-on shall be given

1. the church our blest Re-deem-er saved with his own pre-cious blood.
2. dear as the ap-ple of thine eye, and grav-en on thy hand.
3. to her my cares and toils be given, till toils and cares shall end.
4. her sweet com-mu-nion, sol-emn vows, her hymns of love and praise.
5. the bright-est glo-ries earth can yield, and bright-er bliss of heaven.

This tune in a higher key: 576

Alternative tune: SONG 20, 177

In Christ There Is No East or West

410

John Oxenham, 1924 (alt'd)

Arranged from a black spiritual by H. T. Burleigh, 1940

McKEE, CM

1. In Christ there is no east or west, in him no south or north,
2. In him shall true hearts ev-'ry-where their high com-mu-nion find;
3. Join hands, dis-ci-ples of the faith, what-e'er your race may be!
4. In Christ now meet both east and west; in him meet south and north;

1. but one great fel-low-ship of love through-out the whole wide earth.
2. his ser-vice is the gold-en cord close bind-ing hu-man-kind.
3. Who serves my Fa-ther as his child is sure-ly kin to me.
4. all Christ-ly souls are one in him through-out the whole wide earth.

Alternative tune: ST. PETER, 364

Isa. 49:12; Lk. 13:29

THE CHURCH'S UNITY AND FELLOWSHIP

411 The Heavens Declare Thy Glory, Lord

Isaac Watts, 1707
First Tune

BOULDER, LM

Paul Manz, 1973

1. The heav'ns de-clare thy glo-ry, Lord; in ev-'ry star thy wis-dom shines;
2. Sun, moon, and stars con-vey thy praise round the whole earth and nev-er stand;
3. Nor shall thy spread-ing gos-pel rest till through the world thy truth has run;
4. Great Sun of Righ-teous-ness, a-rise, bless the dark world with heav'n-ly light;
5. Thy no-blest won-ders here we view, in souls re-newed and sins for-giv'n;

1. but when our eyes be-hold thy Word, we read thy name in fair-er lines.
2. so when thy truth be-gan its race it touched and glanced on ev-'ry land.
3. till Christ has all the na-tions bless'd that see the light or feel the sun.
4. thy gos-pel makes the sim-ple wise; thy laws are pure, thy judg-ments right.
5. Lord, cleanse my sins, my soul re-new, and make thy Word my guide to heav'n.

Ps. 19; Mal. 4:2

412 The Heavens Declare Thy Glory, Lord

Second Tune

UXBRIDGE, LM

Melody by Lowell Mason, 1830

1. The heav'ns de-clare thy glo-ry, Lord; in ev-'ry star thy wis-dom shines;
2. Sun, moon, and stars con-vey thy praise round the whole earth and nev-er stand;
3. Nor shall thy spread-ing gos-pel rest till through the world thy truth has run,
4. Great Sun of Righ-teous-ness, a-rise, bless the dark world with heav'n-ly light;
5. Thy no-blest won-ders here we view, in souls re-newed and sins for-giv'n;

1. but when our eyes be-hold thy Word we read thy name in fair-er lines.
2. so when thy truth be-gan its race it touched and glanced on ev-'ry land.
3. till Christ has all the na-tions bless'd that see the light or feel the sun.
4. thy gos-pel makes the sim-ple wise; thy laws are pure, thy judg-ments right.
5. Lord, cleanse my sins, my soul re-new, and make thy Word my guide to heav'n.

Forth in the Peace of Christ We Go   413

James Quinn, 1969

LLEDROD, LM

Canaiadau y Cyssegr (1839)

1. Forth in the peace of Christ we go; Christ to the world with joy we bring;
2. King of our hearts, Christ makes us kings; king-ship with him his ser-vants gain;
3. Priests of the world, Christ sends us forth this world of time to con-se-crate;
4. Christ's are our lips, his word we speak; proph-ets are we whose deeds pro-claim
5. We are the church; Christ bids us show that in his church all na-tions find

1. Christ in our minds, Christ on our lips, Christ in our hearts, the world's true King.
2. with Christ the ser-vant Lord of all, Christ's world we serve to share Christ's reign.
3. this world of sin by grace to heal, Christ's world in Christ to re-cre-ate.
4. Christ's truth in love that we may be Christ in the world, to spread Christ's name.
5. their hearth and home where Christ re-stores true peace, true love to hu-man-kind.

small notes for organ only

This tune in a lower key: 186

414

Hope of the World

Georgia Harkness, 1953

PSALM 12 (DONNE SECOURS), 11.10.11.10   Melody from the *Genevan Psalter* (1551)

May be sung in unison

1. Hope of the world, thou Christ of great com-pas-sion,
2. Hope of the world, God's gift from high-est heav-en,
3. Hope of the world, a-foot on dust-y high-ways,
4. Hope of the world, who by the cross didst save us,

1. speak to our fear-ful hearts, by con-flict rent.
2. bring-ing to hun-gry souls the bread of life,
3. show-ing to wan-d'ring souls the path of light;
4. from death and dark de-spair, from sin and guilt;

1. Save us, thy peo-ple, from con-sum-ing pas-sion,
2. still let thy Spir-it un-to us be giv-en
3. walk thou be-side us lest the tempt-ing by-ways
4. we ren-der back the love thy mer-cy gave us:

1. who by our own false hopes and aims are spent.
2. to heal earth's wounds and end her bit-ter strife.
3. lure us a-way from thee to end-less night.
4. take thou our lives and use them as thou wilt.

♯ *last stanza only*

5. Hope of the world, O Christ, o'er death victorious,
    who by this sign didst conquer grief and pain,
  we would be faithful to thy gospel glorious:
    thou art our Lord! Thou dost forever reign!

THE CHURCH'S MINISTRY AND MISSION

Lift High the Cross

G. W. Kitchin, 1827–1912; rev. M. R. Newbolt, 1916

CRUCIFER, 10 10 with refrain

Sydney H. Nicholson, 1916

Descant (any stanza after first)

1. Lift high the cross, the love of Christ pro - claim,

Refrain

1. Lift high the cross, the love of Christ pro - claim,

1. till all the world a - dore his sa - cred name. *Fine*

1. till all the world a - dore his sa - cred name. *Fine*

Verses (SATB or Unison)

1. Come, friends, and fol - low where our Cap - tain trod,
2. Led on their way by this tri - um - phant sign,
3. This is the sign which Sa - tan's le - gions fear
4. O Lord, once lift - ed on the glo - rious tree,
5. Set up thy throne, that earth's de - spair may cease

Return to refrain

1. our King vic - to - rious, Christ, the Son of God.
2. the hosts of God in con-qu'ring ranks com-bine.
3. and an - gels veil their fac - es to re - vere.
4. as thou hast prom - ised, draw the world to thee.
5. be - neath the shad - ow of its heal-ing peace.

THE CHURCH'S MINISTRY AND MISSION

415

416

God of Grace and God of Glory

Harry Emerson Fosdick, 1930 (alt'd)

CWM RHONDDA, 8.7.8.7.8.7.7

John Hughes, 1907

1. God of grace and God of glo - ry, on thy peo - ple
2. Lo! the hosts of e - vil round us scorn thy Christ, as -
3. Cure thy chil - dren's war - ring mad - ness, bend our pride to
*4. Set our feet on loft - y plac - es; gird our lives that

1. pour thy power; crown thine an - cient church's sto - ry; bring her bud to
2. sail his ways! From the fears that long have bound us free our hearts to
3. thy con - trol; shame our wan - ton, self - ish glad - ness, rich in things and
4. they may be ar-mored with all Christ - like grac - es, pledged to set all

1. glo - rious flower. Grant us wis - dom, grant us cour - age,
2. faith and praise. Grant us wis - dom, grant us cour - age,
3. poor in soul. Grant us wis - dom, grant us cour - age,
4. cap - tives free. Grant us wis - dom, grant us cour - age,

1. for the fac - ing of this hour, for the fac - ing of this hour.
2. for the liv - ing of these days, for the liv - ing of these days.
3. lest we miss thy king-dom's goal, lest we miss thy king-dom's goal.
4. that we fail not them nor thee! That we fail not them nor thee!

5. Save us from weak resignation to the evils we deplore;
   let the gift of thy salvation be our glory evermore.
   Grant us wisdom, grant us courage,
      serving thee whom we adore,
      serving thee whom we adore.

THE CHURCH'S MINISTRY AND MISSION

Ps. 61:2b

Rise Up, O Saints of God! 417

Norman O. Forness, 1978

FESTAL SONG, SM

William H. Walter, 1894

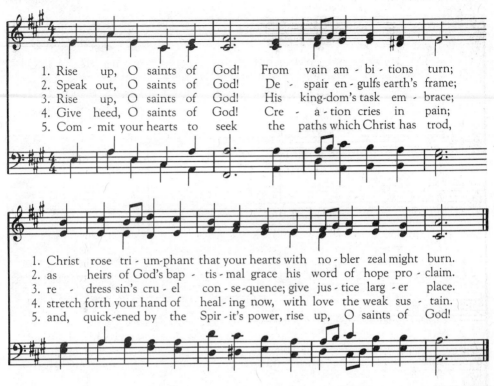

1. Rise up, O saints of God! From vain am-bi-tions turn;
2. Speak out, O saints of God! De-spair en-gulfs earth's frame;
3. Rise up, O saints of God! His king-dom's task em-brace;
4. Give heed, O saints of God! Cre-a-tion cries in pain;
5. Com-mit your hearts to seek the paths which Christ has trod,

1. Christ rose tri-um-phant that your hearts with no-bler zeal might burn.
2. as heirs of God's bap-tis-mal grace his word of hope pro-claim.
3. re-dress sin's cru-el con-se-quence; give jus-tice larg-er place.
4. stretch forth your hand of heal-ing now, with love the weak sus-tain.
5. and, quick-ened by the Spir-it's power, rise up, O saints of God!

Arise, Your Light Is Come! 418

Ruth Duck, 1974

1. Arise, your light is come!
   The Spirit's call obey;
   show forth the glory of your God
   which shines on you today.

2. Arise, your light is come!
   Fling wide the prison door;
   proclaim the captives' liberty,
   good tidings to the poor.

3. Arise, your light is come!
   All you in sorrow born,
   bind up the broken-hearted ones
   and comfort those who mourn.

4. Arise, your light is come!
   The mountains burst in song!
   Rise up like eagles on the wing;
   God's power will make us strong.

Isa. 40:31; Isa. 61:1ff

THE CHURCH'S MINISTRY AND MISSION

419

We Are Your People

Brian Wren, 1973

WHITFIELD, 5.4.5.5.7

John Wilson, 1977

1. We are your peo - ple: Lord, by your grace, you dare to make us
2. How can we dem-on-strate your love and care— speak-ing or lis-t'ning?
3. Called to por-tray you, help us to live clos-er than neigh-bors,
4. Glad of tra-di-tion, help us to see in all life's chang-ing

small note st. 1 only

st. 1,6   *st. 2,3,4,5*

1. Christ to our neigh-bors of ev-'ry na-tion and race.
2. bat - tling or serv-ing? help us to know when and where.
3. o - pen to strang-ers, a - ble to clash and for-give.
4. where you are lead-ing, where our best ef-forts should be.

5. Joined in community,
   breaking your bread,
   may we discover
   gifts in each other,
   willing to lead and be led.

6. Lord, as we minister
   in different ways,
   may all we're doing
   show that you're living,
   meeting your love with our praise.

THE CHURCH'S MINISTRY AND MISSION

Jn. 17:22

Awake, O Spirit of the Watchmen

420

Wach auf, du Geist der ersten Zeugen, 1750;
st. 1, 2, 4 tr. *Lutheran Book of Worship* (1978); st. 3 tr. Catherine Winkworth, 1863

DIR, DIR, JEHOVA, 9.10.9.10.10 10   Melody in J. A. Freylinghausen's *Gesangbuch* (1704)

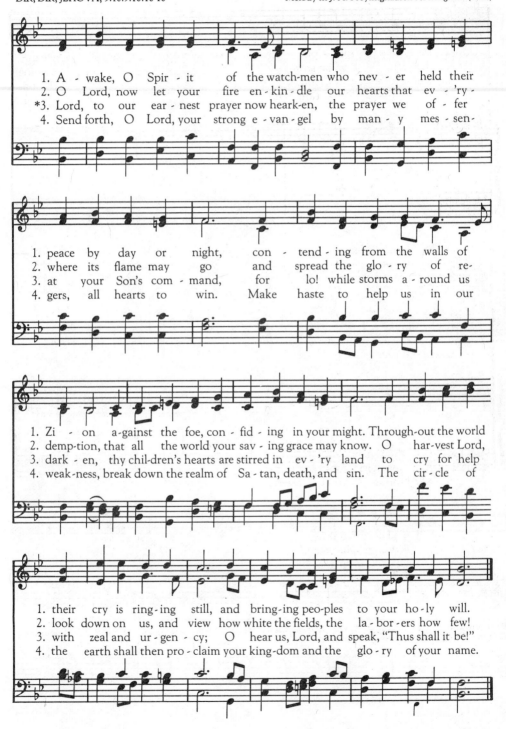

1. A - wake, O Spir - it of the watch-men who nev - er held their
2. O Lord, now let your fire en - kin - dle our hearts that ev - 'ry-
*3. Lord, to our ear - nest prayer now heark-en, the prayer we of - fer
4. Send forth, O Lord, your strong e - van - gel by man - y mes - sen-

1. peace by day or night, con - tend - ing from the walls of
2. where its flame may go and spread the glo - ry of re-
3. at your Son's com - mand, for lo! while storms a - round us
4. gers, all hearts to win. Make haste to help us in our

1. Zi - on a-gainst the foe, con - fid - ing in your might. Through-out the world
2. demp-tion, that all the world your sav - ing grace may know. O har-vest Lord,
3. dark - en, thy chil-dren's hearts are stirred in ev - 'ry land to cry for help
4. weak-ness, break down the realm of Sa - tan, death, and sin. The cir - cle of

1. their cry is ring-ing still, and bring-ing peo-ples to your ho - ly will.
2. look down on us, and view how white the fields, the la - bor - ers how few!
3. with zeal and ur - gen - cy; O hear us, Lord, and speak, "Thus shall it be!"
4. the earth shall then pro - claim your king-dom and the glo - ry of your name.

Isa. 21:8; Mt. 6:10; Mt. 9:37   THE CHURCH'S MINISTRY AND MISSION

421 O Zion Haste, Thy Mission High Fulfilling

Mary Ann Thomson, 1868

TIDINGS, 11.10.11.10 with refrain

James Walch, 1875

1. O Zi - on haste, thy mis - sion high ful - fill - ing, to tell to all the
2. Give of thy strength to bear the mes - sage glo - rious, give of thy wealth to
3. He comes a - gain; O Zi - on, ere thou meet him, make known to ev - 'ry
4. Pro - claim to ev - 'ry peo - ple, ev - 'ry na - tion, that God, in whom they

1. world that God is light, that he who made all na - tions is not will - ing
2. speed it on its way, pour out thy soul for this in prayer vic - to - rious,
3. heart his sav - ing grace; let none whom he hath ran - somed fail to greet him,
4. live and move, is love; tell how he stooped to save his lost cre - a - tion,

1. one soul should per - ish, lost in shades of night.
2. and all thou spend - est Je - sus will re - pay.
3. through thy ne - glect un - fit to see his face.
4. and died on earth that we might live a - bove.

Pub - lish glad tid - ings,

tid - ings of peace, tid - ings of Je - sus, re - demp - tion and re - lease.

THE CHURCH'S MINISTRY AND MISSION

"Christ for the World" We Sing

Samuel Wolcott, 1869

MILTON ABBAS, 66.4.666.4

Eric H. Thiman, 1951

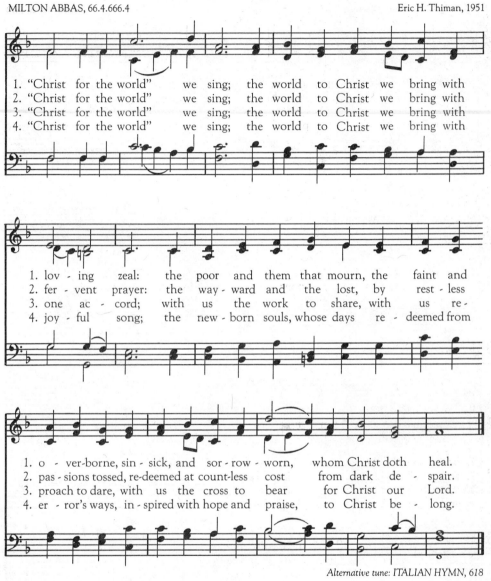

1. "Christ for the world" we sing; the world to Christ we bring with
2. "Christ for the world" we sing; the world to Christ we bring with
3. "Christ for the world" we sing; the world to Christ we bring with
4. "Christ for the world" we sing; the world to Christ we bring with

1. lov - ing zeal: the poor and them that mourn, the faint and
2. fer - vent prayer: the way - ward and the lost, by rest - less
3. one ac - cord; with us the work to share, with us re -
4. joy - ful song; the new - born souls, whose days re - deemed from

1. o - ver-borne, sin - sick, and sor - row - worn, whom Christ doth heal.
2. pas - sions tossed, re-deemed at count-less cost from dark de - spair.
3. proach to dare, with us the cross to bear for Christ our Lord.
4. er - ror's ways, in - spired with hope and praise, to Christ be - long.

Alternative tune: ITALIAN HYMN, 618

422

THE CHURCH'S MINISTRY AND MISSION

423

Lead On, O King Eternal

Ernest Warburton Shurtleff, 1888

LANCASHIRE, 7.6.7.6 D

Henry Smart, 1836

1. Lead on, O King e-ter-nal, the day of march has come;
2. Lead on, O King e-ter-nal, till sin's fierce war shall cease,
3. Lead on, O King e-ter-nal, we fol-low, not with fears,

1. hence-forth in fields of con-quest thy tents shall be our home.
2. and ho-li-ness shall whis-per the sweet a-men of peace.
3. for glad-ness breaks like morn-ing wher-e'er thy face ap-pears.

1. Through days of prep-a-ra-tion thy grace has made us strong,
2. For not with swords' loud clash-ing, nor roll of stir-ring drums,
3. Thy cross is lift-ed o'er us; we jour-ney in its light;

1. and now, O King e-ter-nal, we lift our bat-tle song.
2. but deeds of love and mer-cy, the heaven-ly king-dom comes.
3. the crown a-waits the con-quest; lead on, O God of might.

Alternative tune: LLANGLOFFAN, 80

This tune in a higher key: 317

THE CHURCH'S MINISTRY AND MISSION

You That Know the Lord Is Gracious

424

C. A. Alington, 1950

ABBOT'S LEIGH, 8.7.8.7 D

Cyril V. Taylor, 1941

1. You that know the Lord is gra-cious, you for whom a cor-ner-stone
2. Liv-ing stones by God ap-point-ed each to an al-lot-ted place,
3. Tell the praise of him who called you out of dark-ness in-to light,

1. stands, of God e-lect and pre-cious, laid that you may build there-on,
2. kings and priests, by God a-noint-ed, shall you not de-clare his grace?
3. broke the fet-ters that en-thralled you, gave you free-dom, peace, and sight:

1. see that on that sure foun-da-tion you a liv-ing tem-ple raise,
2. You, a roy-al gen-er-a-tion, tell the tid-ings of your birth,
3. tell the tale of sins for-giv-en, strength re-newed, and hope re-stored,

1. tow-ers that may tell forth sal-va-tion, walls that may re-ech-o praise.
2. tid-ings of a new cre-a-tion to an old and wea-ry earth.
3. till the earth, in tune with heav-en, praise and mag-ni-fy the Lord.

This tune in a lower key: 393

Alternative tune: AUSTRIA, 3

I Pet. 2:4–10

THE CHURCH'S MINISTRY AND MISSION

425

God Is Working His Purpose Out

A. C. Ainger, 1894

PURPOSE, Irregular

Martin Shaw, 1915

1. God is work-ing his pur-pose out as year suc-ceeds to
2. From ut-most east to ut-most west, where hu-man feet have
3. March we forth in the strength of God, with the ban-ner of Christ un-
4. All we can do is noth-ing worth un-less God bless-es. the

1. year: God is work-ing his pur-pose out, and the
2. trod, by the mouth of man-y mes-sen-gers goes
3. furled, that the light of the glo-ri-ous gos-pel of truth may
4. deed; vain-ly we hope for the har-vest-tide till

1. time is draw-ing near; near-er and near-er draws the time,
2. forth the voice of God: "Give ear to me, ye con-ti-nents,
3. shine through-out the world; fight we the fight with sor-row and sin
4. God gives life to the seed; yet near-er and near-er draws the time,

1. the time that shall sure-ly be, when the earth shall be filled with the
2. ye isles, give ear to me," that the earth may be filled with the
3. to set their cap-tives free, that the earth may be filled with the
4. the time that shall sure-ly be, when the earth shall be filled with the

Isa. 11:9; I Cor. 5:18–20

1. glo - ry of God as the wa-ters cov-er the sea.
2. glo - ry of God as the wa-ters cov-er the sea.
3. glo - ry of God as the wa-ters cov-er the sea.
4. glo - ry of God as the wa-ters cov-er the sea.

Thanks Be to God, Whose Church on Earth 426

Caryl Micklem, 1977

GALILEE, LM

Philip Armes, 1889

1. Thanks be to God, whose church on earth has stood the tests of time and place,
2. Thanks be to God, whose Spir - it sent a - pos - tles out up - on his way.
3. Thanks be to God, whose lat - er voice from west to east sent back the Word
4. Thanks be to God, who now would reach his lis - t'ners in more glo - bal ways.
5. Thanks be to God, in whom we share to - day the mis - sion of his Son.

1. and ev - 'ry - where pro - claims new birth through Christ, whose love re - veals God's face.
2. From east to west the mes - sage went: on Greek and Ro - man dawned the day.
3. which, through the ser - vants of his choice, at last in ev - 'ry tongue was heard.
4. Now each will send the news, and each re - ceive and an - swer it in praise.
5. May all the church that time pre - pare when, like the task, the church is one.

427

We Give Thee but Thine Own

William Walsham How, 1858 (alt'd)

SCHUMANN, SM

Cantica Laudis, Lowell Mason and G. J. Webb, 1850

1. We give thee but thine own, what-e'er the gift may be:
2. May we thy boun-ties thus as stew-ards true re - ceive,
3. To com-fort and to bless, to find a balm for woe,
4. The cap-tive to re - lease, to God the lost to bring,
5. And we be - lieve thy word, though dim our faith may be:

1. all that we have is thine a - lone, a trust, O Lord, from thee.
2. and glad - ly, as thou bless-est us, to thee our first-fruits give.
3. to tend the lone and or-phaned ones, is an - gels' work be - low.
4. to teach the way of life and peace, it is a Christ-like thing.
5. what - e'er for thine we do, O Lord, we do it un - to thee.

428

O Master, Let Me Walk with Thee

Washington Gladden, 1879

MARYTON, LM

H. P. Smith, 1874

1. O Mas-ter, let me walk with thee in low-ly paths of ser - vice free;
2. Help me the slow of heart to move by some clear, win - ning word of love;
3. Teach me thy pa-tience; still with thee in clos-er, dear - er com-pa-ny,
4. In hope that sends a shin - ing ray far down the fu - ture's broad-'ning way,

1. tell me thy se - cret, help me bear the strain of toil, the fret of care.
2. teach me the way-ward feet to stay, and guide them in the home-ward way.
3. in work that keeps faith sweet and strong, in trust that tri - umphs o - ver wrong.
4. in peace that on - ly thou canst give, with thee, O Mas - ter, let me live.

THE CHURCH'S MINISTRY AND MISSION

God of the Prophets

Denis Wortman, 1884 (alt'd)

TOULON, 10.10.10.10

Abridged (c. 1860) from Psalm 124 in the *Genevan Psalter* (1551)

1. God of the proph - ets, bless the proph - ets' heirs;
2. A - noint them proph - ets! make their ears at - tend
3. A - noint them priests! strong in - ter - ces - sors they
4. A - noint them rul - ers, gen - tle rul - ers, Lord!

1. E - li - jah's man - tle o'er E - li - sha cast;
2. to thy di - vin - est speech; their hearts a - wake
3. for par - don and for char - i - ty and peace!
4. A - noint them with the Spir - it of thy Son;

1. each age in turn for sol - emn tasks pre - pares;
2. to hu - man need; their lips make el - o - quent
3. O might with them the world, though gone a - stray,
4. theirs not a jew - eled crown, a blood-stained sword;

1. make each one no - bler, strong - er than the last.
2. right to en - throne and ev - 'ry e - vil break.
3. pass in - to Christ's pure life of sac - ri - fice.
4. theirs, by strong love, for Christ a king - dom won.

Alternative tune: JULIUS, 430

5. Send them, apostles, heralds of thy cross;
   forth may they go to tell all realms thy grace;
   inspired of thee, may they count all but loss,
   and stand at last with joy before thy face.

II Kgs. 2:9; Ex. 28:1; I Sam. 16:1, 13; Rom. 1:1–6   THE CHURCH'S MINISTRY AND MISSION

430

Lord of All Good,
Our Gifts We Bring to Thee

Albert Bayly, 1950

JULIUS, 10.10.10.10

Martin Shaw, 1935

1. Lord of all good, our gifts we bring to thee;
2. We give our minds to un-der-stand thy ways,
3. Fa-ther, whose boun-ty all cre-a-tion shows;

1. use them thy ho-ly pur-pose to ful-fill;
2. hands, eyes, and voice to serve thy great de-sign,
3. Christ, by whose will-ing sac-ri-fice we live;

1. to-kens of love and pledg-es they shall be
2. heart with the flame of thine own love a-blaze,
3. Spir-it, from whom all life in full-ness flows:

1. that our whole life is of-fered to thy will.
2. till for thy glo-ry all our pow'rs com-bine.
3. to thee with grate-ful hearts our-selves we give.

Alternative tunes: MAGDA, 373, TOULON, 429

THE CHURCH'S MINISTRY AND MISSION

Hark, the Voice of Jesus Calling

Daniel March, 1868

REX GLORIAE, 8.7.8.7 D

Henry Smart, 1868

431

1. Hark, the voice of Je - sus call - ing, "Who will go to work to - day?
2. If you can - not be the watch - man stand - ing high on Zi - on's wall,
3. Let none hear you i - dly say - ing, "There is noth - ing I can do,"

1. Fields are white and har - vests wait - ing: who will bear the sheaves a - way?"
2. point - ing out the path to heav - en; of - fring life and peace to all,
3. while a hu - man soul is dy - ing, and the Mas - ter calls for you;

1. Loud and long the Mas - ter call - eth; rich re - ward he of - fers free;
2. if you can - not speak like an - gels, if you can - not preach like Paul,
3. take the task he gives you glad - ly; let his work your plea - sure be;

1. who will an - swer glad - ly, say - ing, "Here am I, my Lord, send me"?
2. you can tell the love of Je - sus, you can say, "He died for all."
3. an - swer quick - ly when he call - eth, "Here am I, my Lord, send me."

432

Lord God of Hosts, Whose Purpose, Never Swerving

Shepherd Knapp, 1907

WELWYN, 11.10.11.10

Alfred Scott-Gatty, 1902

1. Lord God of Hosts, whose pur-pose, nev-er swerv-ing,
2. Strong Son of God, whose work was his that sent thee,
3. O Prince of Peace, thou bring-er of good tid-ings,
4. Lord God, whose grace has called us to thy ser-vice,

1. leads toward the day of Je-sus Christ thy Son,
2. one with the Fa-ther, thought and deed and word,
3. teach us to speak thy word of hope and cheer—
4. how good thy thoughts toward us, how great their sum!

1. grant us to march a-mong thy faith-ful le-gions,
2. one make us all, true com-rades in thy ser-vice,
3. rest for the soul, and strength for all our striv-ing,
4. We work with thee, we go where thou wilt lead us,

1. armed with thy cour-age, till the world is won.
2. and make us one in thee with God the Lord.
3. light for the path of life, and God brought near.
4. un-til in all the earth thy King-dom come.

THE CHURCH'S MINISTRY AND MISSION

How Clear Is Our Vocation, Lord

433

Fred Pratt Green, 1981

REPTON, 8.6.88.66

C. H. H. Parry, 1888

1. How clear is our vo-ca-tion, Lord, when once we heed your call:
2. But if, for-get-ful, we should find your yoke is hard to bear,
3. We mark your saints, how they be-came in hin-dranc-es more sure,
4. In what you give us, Lord, to do, to-geth-er or a-lone,

1. to live ac-cord-ing to your word, and dai-ly learn, re-freshed, re-stored,
2. if world-ly pres-sures fray the mind and love it-self can-not un-wind
3. whose joy-ful vir-tues put to shame the cas-ual way we wear your name,
4. in old rou-tines or ven-tures new, may we not cease to look to you,

1. that you are Lord of all, and will not let us fall.
2. its tan-gled skein of care: our in-ward life re-pair.
3. and by our faults ob-scure your power to cleanse and cure.
4. the cross you hung up-on— all you en-deav-ored done.

Heb. 11:32–40

THE CHURCH'S MINISTRY AND MISSION

434   Take Thou Our Minds, Dear Lord

William Hiram Foulkes, 1918

SURSUM CORDA, 10 10.10 10

Melody by George Lomas, 1876; arranged for this book

1. Take thou our minds, dear Lord, we hum-bly pray; give us the
2. Take thou our hearts, O Christ, they are thine own; come thou with-
3. Take thou our wills, Most High! Hold thou full sway; have in our
4. Take thou our-selves, O Lord, mind, heart, and will; through our sur-

1. mind of Christ each pass-ing day; teach us to know the truth that
2. in our souls and claim thy throne; help us to shed a-broad thy
3. in-most souls thy per-fect way; guard thou each sa-cred hour from
4. ren-dered souls thy plan ful-fill. We yield our-selves to thee, time,

1. sets us free; grant us in all our thoughts to hon-or thee.
2. death-less love; use us to make the earth like heav'n a-bove.
3. self-ish ease; guide thou our or-dered lives as thou dost please.
4. tal-ents, all; we hear, and hence-forth heed thy sov-'reign call.

THE CHURCH'S MINISTRY AND MISSION

The Days That Were,
The Days That Are

435

Hywel Elfed Lewis, 1883

CREDITON, CM

Melody by Thomas Clark, c. 1810

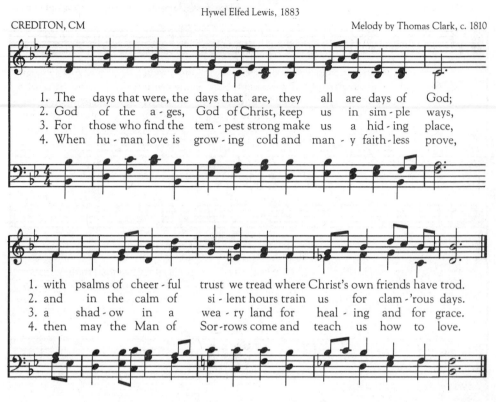

1. The days that were, the days that are, they all are days of God;
2. God of the a-ges, God of Christ, keep us in sim-ple ways,
3. For those who find the tem-pest strong make us a hid-ing place,
4. When hu-man love is grow-ing cold and man-y faith-less prove,

1. with psalms of cheer-ful trust we tread where Christ's own friends have trod.
2. and in the calm of si-lent hours train us for clam-'rous days.
3. a shad-ow in a wea-ry land for heal-ing and for grace.
4. then may the Man of Sor-rows come and teach us how to love.

5. We tarry, Lord, thy leisure still,
   thy best is yet to be;
   nought ever comes too late for us
   that is in time for thee.

6. God of the ages, God of Christ,
   keep us in simple ways;
   and may the toil, the joy, the strife
   be to thy greater praise!

*Isa. 32:2*THE CHURCH'S MINISTRY AND MISSION

436

Lord, Speak to Me

Frances Ridley Havergal, 1872 (alt'd)

WINDHAM, LM

Melody by Daniel Read in *The American Singing Book* (1785)

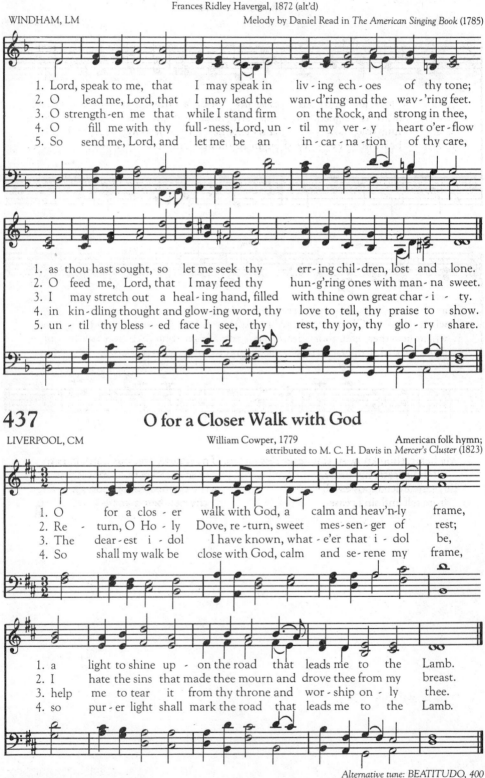

1. Lord, speak to me, that I may speak in liv-ing ech-oes of thy tone;
2. O lead me, Lord, that I may lead the wan-d'ring and the wav-'ring feet.
3. O strength-en me that while I stand firm on the Rock, and strong in thee,
4. O fill me with thy full-ness, Lord, un-til my ver-y heart o'er-flow
5. So send me, Lord, and let me be an in-car-na-tion of thy care,

1. as thou hast sought, so let me seek thy err-ing chil-dren, lost and lone.
2. O feed me, Lord, that I may feed thy hun-g'ring ones with man-na sweet.
3. I may stretch out a heal-ing hand, filled with thine own great char-i-ty.
4. in kin-dling thought and glow-ing word, thy love to tell, thy praise to show.
5. un-til thy bless-ed face I see, thy rest, thy joy, thy glo-ry share.

437

O for a Closer Walk with God

LIVERPOOL, CM

William Cowper, 1779

American folk hymn;
attributed to M. C. H. Davis in *Mercer's Cluster* (1823)

1. O for a clos-er walk with God, a calm and heav'n-ly frame,
2. Re-turn, O Ho-ly Dove, re-turn, sweet mes-sen-ger of rest;
3. The dear-est i-dol I have known, what-e'er that i-dol be,
4. So shall my walk be close with God, calm and se-rene my frame,

1. a light to shine up-on the road that leads me to the Lamb.
2. I hate the sins that made thee mourn and drove thee from my breast.
3. help me to tear it from thy throne and wor-ship on-ly thee.
4. so pur-er light shall mark the road that leads me to the Lamb.

THE CHRISTIAN AS BELIEVER

Alternative tune: BEATITUDO, 400

Gen. 8:10–11

O for a Heart to Praise My God

Charles Wesley, 1742

JACKSON, CM

Thomas Jackson, 1780

1. O for a heart to praise my God, a heart from sin set free! —
2. a heart re-signed, sub-mis-sive, meek, my dear Re-deem-er's throne,
3. a hum-ble, low-ly, con-trite heart, be-liev-ing, true, and clean,
4. a heart in ev-'ry thought re-newed, and full of love di-vine,

1. a heart that al-ways feels thy blood so free-ly spilt for me! —
2. where on-ly Christ is heard to speak, where Je-sus reigns a-lone;
3. which nei-ther life nor death can part from him that dwells with-in;
4. per-fect and right, and pure and good, a cop-y, Lord, of thine!

5. My heart, thou know'st, can never rest
   till thou create my peace,
   till of my Eden repossess'd,
   from self and sin I cease.

6. Thy nature, gracious Lord, impart;
   come quickly from above;
   write thy new name upon my heart,
   thy new best name of love!

Ps. 51:10

THE CHRISTIAN AS BELIEVER

439

O Light That Knew No Dawn

Gregory Nazianzen, c. 329–389 (Greek); tr. J. Brownlie, 1900

EASTVIEW, 6.6.6.6.88

Vernon Lee, c. 1945

1. O Light that knew no dawn, that shines to end-less day,
2. Thy grace, O Fa-ther, give, that I may serve in fear;
3. that cleansed from stain of sin, I may glad hom-age give,
4. In sup-pli-ca-tion meek to thee I bend the knee;
5. Thy grace, O Fa-ther give, I hum-bly thee im-plore;

1. all things in earth and heav'n are lus-tered by thy ray;
2. a-bove all gifts, I pray, grant me thy voice to hear;
3. and, pure in heart, be-hold thy beau-ty while I live,
4. O Christ, when thou shalt come, in love re-mem-ber me,
5. and let thy mer-cy bless thy ser-vant more and more.

1. no eye can to thy throne as-cend, nor mind thy bright-ness com-pre-hend.
2. from sin thy child in mer-cy free, and let me dwell in light with thee,
3. clean hands in ho-ly wor-ship raise, and thee, O Christ my Sav-ior, praise.
4. and in thy king-dom, by thy grace, grant me a hum-ble ser-vant's place.
5. All grace and glo-ry be to thee, from age to age, e-ter-nal-ly.

Abide with Me

H. F. Lyte, 1847

440

EVENTIDE, 10 10. 10 10

W. H. Monk, 1861

1. A - bide with me: fast falls the e - ven - tide;
* 2. Swift to its close ebbs out life's lit - tle day;
3. I need thy pres - ence ev - ery pass - ing hour;
4. I fear no foe, with thee at hand to bless:

1. the dark - ness deep - ens; Lord, with me a - bide!
2. earth's joys grow dim, its glo - ries pass a - way;
3. what but thy grace can foil the tempt - er's power?
4. ills have no weight, and tears no bit - ter - ness.

1. When oth - er help - ers fail, and com - forts flee,
2. change and de - cay in all a - round I see.
3. Who, like thy - self, my guide and stay can be?
4. Where is death's sting? Where, grave, thy vic - to - ry?

1. help of the help - less, O a - bide with me.
2. O thou, who chang - est not, a - bide with me.
3. Through cloud and sun - shine, Lord, a - bide with me.
4. I tri - umph still, if thou a - bide with me.

5. Hold thou thy cross before my closing eyes;
shine through the gloom and point me to the skies.
Heaven's morning breaks, and earth's vain shadows flee;
in life, in death, O Lord, abide with me.

Lk. 24:29; I Cor. 15:55

THE CHRISTIAN AS BELIEVER

441

Jesus, I Live to Thee

Henry Harbaugh, 1850

LAKE ENON, 6.6.44.6

Isaac B. Woodbury, 1856

1. Je - sus, I live to thee, the love - li - est and best;
2. Je - sus, I die to thee, when - ev - er death shall come:
3. Wheth - er to live or die, I know not which is best:
4. Liv - ing or dy - ing, Lord, I ask but to be thine:

1. My life in thee, thy life in me, in thy blest love I rest.
2. to die in thee is life to me, in my e - ter - nal home.
3. to live in thee is bliss to me; to die is end - less rest.
4. My life in thee, thy life in me, makes heav'n for - ev - er mine!

Phil. 1:21

442

Make Me a Captive, Lord

George Matheson, 1890

ST. BRIDE, SM

Samuel Howard, 1762

1. Make me a cap - tive, Lord, and then I shall be free;
2. I sink in life's a - larms when by my - self I stand;
3. My heart is weak and poor un - til it mas - ter find;
4. It can - not free - ly move till thou hast wrought its chain;

1. force me to ren - der up my sword, and I shall con - queror be.
2. im - pris - on me with - in thine arms, and strong shall be my hand.
3. it has no spring of ac - tion sure — it var - ies with the wind.
4. en - slave it with thy match - less love, and death - less it shall reign.

This tune in a lower key: 149

THE CHRISTIAN AS BELIEVER

*5. My will is not my own
   till thou hast made it thine;
   if it would reach a monarch's throne,
   it must its crown resign.

I Need Thee Every Hour

443

Annie S. Hawks, 1872; refrain added by R. Lowry, 1872

NEED, 6.4.6.4 with refrain

Robert S. Lowry, 1872

1. I need thee ev-ery hour, most gra-cious Lord; no oth-er voice but thine
2. I need thee ev-ery hour; stay thou near by; temp-ta-tions lose their power
3. I need thee ev-ery hour; teach me thy will, and thy rich prom-is - es
4. I need thee ev-ery hour, Most Ho - ly One; O make me thine in - deed,

Refrain

1. can peace af - ford.
2. when thou art nigh.
3. in me ful - fill.
4. thou bless - ed Son.

I need thee, O I need thee,

ev - ery hour I need thee! O bless me now, my Sav-ior—I come to thee!

444

Come Down, O Love Divine †

Discendi amor santo, by Bianco of Siena, d. 1434;
tr. R. F. Littledale, 1867

DOWN AMPNEY, 66.11 D

R. Vaughan Williams, 1906

1. Come down, O Love di - vine, seek thou this soul of
2. O let it free - ly burn, till earth - ly pas - sions
† 3. And so the yearn - ing strong with which the soul will

1. mine, and vis - it it with thine own ar - dor glow - ing;
2. turn to dust and ash - es in its heat con - sum - ing;
3. long shall far out - pass the power of hu - man tell - ing;

1. O Com - fort - er, draw near, with - in my heart ap - pear,
2. and let thy glo - rious light shine ev - er on my sight,
3. for none can guess its grace, till he be - come the place

1. and kin - dle it, thy ho - ly flame be - stow - ing.
2. and clothe me round, the while my path il - lum - ing.
3. where - in the Ho - ly Spir - it makes his dwell - ing.

THE CHRISTIAN AS BELIEVER

Spirit of God, Descend upon My Heart

445

Attributed to George Croly, 1867

MORECAMBE, 10.10.10.10

Melody by F. C. Atkinson, 1870

1. Spir - it of God, de - scend up - on my heart;
2. I ask no dream, no proph - et ec - sta - sies,
3. Hast thou not bid us love thee, God and King?
4. Teach me to feel that thou art al - ways nigh;

1. wean it from earth, through all its puls - es move;
2. no sud - den rend - ing of the veil of clay,
3. All, all thine own: soul, heart, and strength and mind;
4. teach me the strug - gles of the soul to bear:

1. stoop to my weak - ness, might - y as thou art,
2. no an - gel vis - i - tant, no open - ing skies,
3. I see thy cross — there teach my heart to cling;
4. to check the ris - ing doubt, the reb - el sigh;

1. and make me love thee as I ought to love.
2. but take the dim - ness of my soul a - way.
3. O let me seek thee, and O let me find!
4. teach me the pa - tience of un - an - swered prayer.

Alternative tune: ELLERS, 517

5. Teach me to love thee as thine angels love:
one holy passion filling all my frame,
the baptism of the heav'n - descended Dove:
my heart an altar, and thy love the flame.

Dt. 6:5; Mt. 22:37

THE CHRISTIAN AS BELIEVER

My Faith Looks Up to Thee

Ray Palmer, 1830

OLIVET, 66.4.666.4

Melody by Lowell Mason, 1830

1. My faith looks up to thee, thou Lamb of Cal-va-ry,
2. May thy rich grace im-part strength to my faint-ing heart,
3. While life's dark maze I tread and griefs a-round me spread,
4. When ends life's tran-sient dream, when death's cold, sul-len stream

1. Sav-ior di-vine; now hear me while I pray; take
2. my zeal in-spire; as thou hast died for me, O
3. be thou my guide; bid dark-ness turn to day, wipe
4. shall o'er me roll, blest Sav-ior, then, in love, fear

1. all my guilt a-way; O let me from this day be whol-ly thine!
2. may my love to thee pure, warm, and change-less be, a liv-ing fire!
3. sor-row's tears a-way, nor let me ev-er stray from thee a-side.
4. and dis-trust re-move; O bear me safe a-bove, a ran-somed soul!

1 Thess. 4:17

Rock of Ages

447

A. M. Toplady, 1776 (alt'd)

REDHEAD 76 (PETRA), 77.77.77

Richard Redhead, 1853

1. Rock of a - ges, cleft for me, let me hide my - self in thee;
2. Should my tears for - ev - er flow, should my zeal no re - spite know,
3. While I draw this fleet - ing breath, when my eye - lids close in death,

1. let the wa - ter and the blood, from thy wound-ed side which flowed,
2. all for sin could not a - tone; thou must save, and thou a - lone;
3. when I rise to worlds un - known, and be - hold thee on thy throne,

1. be of sin the dou - ble cure, cleanse me from its guilt and power.
2. in my hand no price I bring, sim - ply to thy cross I cling.
3. Rock of a - ges, cleft for me, let me hide my - self in thee.

THE CHRISTIAN AS BELIEVER

Jesus, Priceless Treasure

Jesu meine Freude, by Johann Franck, 1650;
tr. Catherine Winkworth, 1863

JESU MEINE FREUDE, 66.5.66.5.7.86

Johann Crüger, *Praxis Pietatis* (1653);
harmonized and adapted by J. S. Bach

1. Je - sus, price - less trea - sure, source of pur - est plea - sure,
2. In thine arm I rest me; foes who would mo - lest me
3. Hence, all thoughts of sad - ness! For the Lord of glad - ness,

1. tru - est friend to me; long my heart hath pant - ed, till it well - nigh
2. can - not reach me here. Though the earth be shak - ing, ev - ery heart be
3. Je - sus, en - ters in: those who love the Fa - ther, though the storms may

1. faint - ed, thirst - ing af - ter thee. Thine I am, O spot - less Lamb,
2. quak - ing, God dis - pels our fear; sin and hell in con - flict fell
3. gath - er, still have peace with - in; yea, what - e'er we here must bear,

1. I will suf - fer nought to hide thee, ask for nought be - side thee.
2. with their heav - iest storms as - sail us: Je - sus will not fail us.
3. still in thee lies pur - est plea - sure, Je - sus, price - less trea - sure!

Jn. 15:15

Come, Thou Fount of Every Blessing

Robert Robinson, c. 1770 (alt'd)

NETTLETON, 8.7.8.7 D

American folk hymn

1. Come, thou Fount of ev-ery bless-ing, tune my heart to sing thy grace;
2. Here I raise my Eb-en-e-zer, hith-er by thy help I'm come;
3. O to grace how great a debt-or dai-ly I'm con-strained to be!

1. streams of mer-cy, nev-er ceas-ing, call for songs of loud-est praise.
2. and I hope, by thy good plea-sure, safe-ly to ar-rive at home.
3. Let that grace, Lord, like a fet-ter, bind my wan-d'ring heart to thee.

1. Teach me some me-lo-dious mea-sure, sung by flam-ing tongues a-bove;
2. Je-sus sought me when a strang-er, wan-d'ring from the fold of God;
3. Prone to wan-der, Lord, I feel it, prone to leave the God I love;

1. O the vast, the bound-less trea-sure of my Lord's un-chang-ing love.
2. he to res-cue me from dan-ger in-ter-posed his pre-cious blood.
3. take my heart, O take and seal it, seal it for thy courts a-bove.

I Sam. 7:12

THE CHRISTIAN AS DISCIPLE

450

And Can It Be That I Should Gain

Charles (or John) Wesley, 1739
First Tune

JENA (DAS NEUGEBORNE KINDELEIN), 8.8.8.8.88

Melody by M. Vulpius, 1609

1. And can it be that I should gain an in-t'rest in the Sav-ior's blood?
*2. 'Tis mys-tery all, th' Im-mor-tal dies: who can ex-plore this strange de-sign?
*3. He left his Fa-ther's throne a-bove (so free, so in-fi-nite his grace!),
4. Long my im-pris-oned spir-it lay fast bound in sin and na-ture's night;
5. No con-dem-na-tion now I dread; Je-sus, and all in him, is mine!

1. Died he for me, who caused his pain— for me, who him to death pur-sued?
2. In vain the first-born ser-aph tries to sound the depths of love di-vine.
3. emp-tied him-self of all but love, and bled for Ad-am's help-less race.
4. thine eye dif-fused a quick-'ning ray; I woke, the dun-geon filled with light!
5. A-live in him, my liv-ing Head, and clothed in righ-teous-ness di-vine,

1. A-maz-ing love! How can it be that thou, my Lord, shouldst die for me?
2. 'Tis mer-cy all! Let earth a-dore, let an-gel minds en-quire no more.
3. 'Tis mer-cy all! im-mense and free! for, O my God, it found out me!
4. My chains fell off; my heart was free; I rose, went forth, and fol-lowed thee.
5. bold I ap-proach th'e-ter-nal throne, and claim the crown, through Christ, my own.

THE CHRISTIAN AS DISCIPLE

Acts 16:25–26

And Can It Be That I Should Gain

Second Tune

SAGINA, 8.8.8.8.88 with refrain

Thomas Campbell, 1825

1. And can it be that I should gain an in-t'rest in the Sav-ior's blood?
2. 'Tis mys-tery all, th' Im-mor-tal dies: who can ex-plore this strange de-sign?
3. He left his Fa-ther's throne a-bove (so free, so in-fi-nite his grace!),
4. Long my im-pris-oned spir-it lay fast bound in sin and na-ture's night;

1. Died he for me, who caused his pain—for me, who him to death pur-sued?
2. In vain the first-born ser-aph tries to sound the depths of love di-vine.
3. emp-tied him-self of all but love, and bled for Ad-am's help-less race.
4. thine eye dif-fused a quick-'ning ray; I woke, the dun-geon filled with light!

1. A-maz-ing love! How can it be that thou, my Lord, shouldst die for me?
2. 'Tis mer-cy all! Let earth a-dore, let an-gel minds en-quire no more.
3. 'Tis mer-cy all! im-mense and free! for, O my God, it found out me.
4. My chains fell off; my heart was free; I rose, went forth, and fol-lowed thee.

Refrain

A-maz-ing love! How can it be that thou, my Lord, shouldst die for me.
A-maz-ing love! How can it be that thou, my Lord,

5. No condemnation now I dread; Jesus, and all in him, is mine!
   Alive in him, my living Head, and clothed in righteousness divine,
   bold I approach th'eternal throne, and claim the crown, through Christ, my own.

THE CHRISTIAN AS DISCIPLE

452

Thou Hidden Love of God

Verborgne Gottesliebe du, by Gerhardt Tersteegen, 1729;
tr. John Wesley, 1737

STELLA, 8.8.8.8.88

Easy Hymns . . . (Newcastle, England, 1852);
harmonized by G. H. Knight, 1950

1. Thou hid-den love of God, whose height, whose depth un-fath-omed
   no one knows, I see from far thy beau-teous light;
   my spir-it longs for thy re-pose; my heart is pained,
   nor can it be at rest till it finds rest in thee.

2. 'Tis mer-cy all that thou hast brought my mind to seek her
   peace in thee; yet while I seek but find thee not,
   no peace my wan-d'ring soul shall see; O when shall all
   my wan-d'rings end, and all my steps to thee-ward tend?

3. Is there a thing be-neath the sun that strives with thee my
   heart to share? Ah! tear it thence, and reign a-lone,
   the Lord of ev-'ry mo-tion there! Then shall my heart
   from sin be free, when it hath found re-pose in thee.

4. Each mo-ment draw from earth a-way my heart that low-ly
   waits thy call; speak to my in-most soul, and say,
   "I am thy Love, thy God, thy All!" To feel thy power,
   to hear thy voice, to taste thy love, be all my choice!

Blessed Assurance

Fanny Crosby, 1873

ASSURANCE, 9 10.99 with refrain

Phoebe P. Knapp, 1873

1. Bless - ed as - sur - ance, Je - sus is mine! O what a fore - taste of glo - ry di -
2. Per - fect sub - mis - sion, per - fect de - light, vi - sions of rap - ture now burst on my
3. Per - fect sub - mis - sion, all is at rest, I in my Sav - ior am hap - py and

1. vine! Heir of sal - va - tion, pur - chase of God, born of his
2. sight; an - gels de - scend - ing, bring from a - bove ech - oes of
3. blest, watch - ing and wait - ing, look - ing a - bove, filled with his

Refrain

1. Spir - it, washed in his blood.
2. mer - cy, whis - pers of love. } This is my sto - ry, this is my
3. good - ness, lost in his love.

song, prais - ing my Sav - ior all the day long; this is my

sto - ry, this is my song, prais - ing my Sav - ior all the day long.

THE CHRISTIAN AS DISCIPLE

454

Jesus, Thy Boundless Love to Me

Paul Gerhardt, 1653; tr. John Wesley, 1739 (alt'd)

Melody by H. F. Hemy and J. G. Walton, 1853;
harmonized by Eric H. Thiman, 1951

ST. CATHERINE, 8.8.8.8.88

1. Je-sus, thy bound-less love to me no thought can reach, no tongue de-clare;
2. O grant that noth-ing in my soul may dwell but thy pure love a - lone;
3. O Love, how cheer-ing is thy ray! All pain be - fore thy pres-ence flies;
4. Still let thy love point out my way, how won-drous things thy love hath wrought;

1. O knit my thank-ful heart to thee, and reign with-out a ri - val there;
2. O may thy love pos-sess me whole, my joy, my trea - sure, and my crown!
3. care, an-guish, sor - row melt a - way wher-e'er thy heal - ing beams a - rise:
4. still lead me lest I go a-stray; di-rect my word, in - spire my thought;

1. thine, whol-ly thine a - lone, I am: Lord, let thy love my heart in - flame.
2. All cold-ness from my heart re - move; my ev-'ry act, word, thought be love.
3. O Je-sus, noth-ing may I see, noth-ing de-sire or seek, but thee.
4. and if I fall, soon may I hear thy voice, and know that love is near.

Alternative tune: GOTTLOB, 114

Christ, of All My Hopes the Ground

Ralph Wardlaw, 1817

SONG 13, 7.7.7.7

Melody and bass by Orlando Gibbons, 1623; rhythm simplified

1. Christ, of all my hopes the ground, Christ, the spring of all my joy,
2. Let thy love my heart in-flame; keep thy fear be - fore my sight;
3. Foun-tain of o'er - flow-ing grace, free - ly from thy full - ness give;
4. Firm - ly trust-ing in thy blood, noth-ing shall my heart con-found;
5. Thus, O thus, an en-trance give to the land of cloud - less sky;

1. still in thee may I be found, still for thee my powers em-ploy.
2. be thy praise my high-est aim; be thy smile my chief de-light.
3. till I close my earth-ly race, may I prove it Christ to live.
4. safe-ly I shall pass the flood, safe-ly reach Im - man-uel's ground.
5. hav-ing known it Christ to live, let me know it gain to die.

Phil. 1:2

Amazing Grace

John Newton, 1779

American folk hymn;
melody arranged by Edwin O. Excell, 1851–1921

NEW BRITAIN, CM

1. A - maz-ing grace! (how sweet the sound!) that saved a wretch like me!
2. 'Twas grace that taught my heart to fear, and grace my fears re - lieved;
3. Through man-y dan-gers, toils, and snares I have al-read-y come:
4. The Lord has prom-ised good to me; his word my hope se - cures;

1. I once was lost, but now am found, was blind, but now I see.
2. how pre-cious did that grace ap-pear the hour I first be - lieved.
3. 'tis grace has brought me safe thus far, and grace will lead me home.
4. he will my shield and por - tion be as long as life en - dures.

Ps. 142:5

THE CHRISTIAN AS DISCIPLE

457

Jesus Loves Me

Anna B. Warner, c. 1865

JESUS LOVES ME, 7 7.7 7 with refrain

W. B. Bradbury, 1861

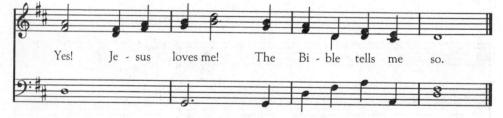

1. Je - sus loves me! This I know, for the Bi - ble tells me so;
2. Je - sus loves me! He who died, heav - en's gate to o - pen wide,
3. Je - sus loves me! He will stay close be - side me all the way;

1. lit - tle ones to him be - long; they are weak, but he is strong.
2. he will wash a - way my sin, let his lit - tle child come in.
3. then his lit - tle child will take up to heav'n for his dear sake.

Refrain

Yes! Je - sus loves me! Yes! Je - sus loves me!

Yes! Je - sus loves me! The Bi - ble tells me so.

THE CHRISTIAN AS DISCIPLE

All the Way My Savior Leads Me

Fanny Crosby, 1875

PLEADING SAVIOR, 8.7.8.7 D

Melody in *Christian Lyre* (1830)

1. All the way my Sav-ior leads me; what have I to fear be-side?
2. All the way my Sav-ior leads me, cheers the wind-ing path I tread,
3. All the way my Sav-ior leads me; O, the full-ness of his love!

1. Can I doubt his ten-der mer-cy who through life has been my Guide?
2. gives me grace for ev-'ry tri-al, feeds me with the liv-ing Bread.
3. Per-fect rest to me is prom-ised in my Fa-ther's house a-bove.

1. Heav'n-ly peace, di-vin-est com-fort, here by faith in him to dwell!
2. Though my wea-ry steps may fal-ter, and my soul a-thirst may be,
3. When my spir-it, clothed, im-mor-tal, wings its flight to end-less day,

1. for I know, what-e'er be-fall me, Je-sus do-eth all things well.
2. gush-ing from the Rock be-fore me, lo, a spring of joy I see.
3. this my song through end-less a-ges: Je-sus led me all the way.

I Cor. 10:4; Jn. 6:35

THE CHRISTIAN AS DISCIPLE

459

My Hope Is Built on Nothing Less

Edward Mote, c. 1834

ST. CATHERINE, 88.88 with refrain

Melody by H. F. Hemy and J. G. Walton, 1853;
harmonized by Eric H. Thiman, 1951

1. My hope is built on noth-ing less than Je-sus' blood and right-teous-ness;
2. When dark-ness veils his love-ly face I rest on his un-chang-ing grace;
3. His oath, his cov-e-nant, his blood sup-port me in the whelm-ing flood;
4. When he shall come with trum-pet sound, O may I then in him be found,

1. I dare not trust the sweet-est frame, but whol-ly lean on Je-sus' name.
2. in ev-'ry high and storm-y gale, my an-chor holds with-in the veil.
3. when all a-round my soul gives way, he then is all my hope and stay.
4. dressed in his right-teous-ness a-lone, fault-less to stand be-fore the throne.

Refrain

On Christ, the sol-id rock, I stand; all oth-er ground is sink-ing sand.

Alternative tune: GOTTLOB, 114

Heb. 6:19

460

My Hope Is Built on Nothing Less

Edward Mote; recast with additions by Norman J. Kansfield, 1982

ELTON, LM

Lowell Mason, 1854

1. My hope is built on noth-ing less than Je-sus' blood and right-teous-ness;
2. When all a-round my soul gives way, he then is all my hope and stay.
3. When dark-ness veils his love-ly face I rest on his un-chang-ing grace;
4. Then he shall come with trum-pet sound, and I will then in him be found,

THE CHRISTIAN AS DISCIPLE

1. on Christ, the sol - id rock, I stand; all oth - er ground is sink - ing sand.
2. His oath, his cov - e - nant, his blood sup - port me in the whelm-ing flood.
3. safe in his sure, un - end - ing love, till gath-ered to his rest a - bove.
4. dressed in his righ-teous-ness a - lone, fault - less to stand be - fore the throne.

Master, Speak!   461

Frances Ridley Havergal, 1867

ALL SAINTS, 8.7.8.7.77   Later form of melody in the Darmstadt *Gesangbuch* (1698)

1. Mas - ter, speak! thy ser - vant hear - eth, wait - ing for thy gra - cious word,
2. Speak to me by name, O Mas - ter; let me know it is to me;
3. Mas - ter, speak, and make me read - y when thy voice is tru - ly heard

1. long - ing for thy voice that cheer - eth; Mas - ter, let it now be heard.
2. speak that I may fol - low fast - er with a step more firm and free,
3. with o - be - dience glad and stead - y still to fol - low ev - 'ry word.

1. I am lis - t'ning, Lord, for thee; what hast thou to say to me?
2. where the Shep - herd leads the flock in the shad - ow of the Rock.
3. I am lis - t'ning, Lord, for thee; Mas - ter, speak, O speak to me!

I Sam. 3:9   THE CHRISTIAN AS DISCIPLE

462 Give to Me, Lord, a Thankful Heart

Caryl Micklem, 1975

GATESCARTH, 8.6.88.6

Caryl Micklem, 1975

1. Give to me, Lord, a thank-ful heart and a dis-cern-ing mind;
2. When in the rush of days my will is hab-it-bound and slow,
3. By your di-vine and ur-gent claim, and by your hu-man face,
4. Je - sus, with all your church I long to see your king-dom come:

1. give, as I play the Christian's part, the strength to fin-ish
2. help me to keep in vi - sion still what love and power and
3. kin - dle our sink - ing hearts to flame, and as you teach the
4. show me your way of right - ing wrong and turn - ing sor - row

1. what I start and act on what I find.
2. peace can fill— a life that trusts in you.
3. world your name, let it be - come your place.
4. in - to song, un - til you bring me home.

Christ, Whose Glory Fills the Skies

Charles Wesley, 1739

RATISBON, 7.7.7.7.77

Freylinghausen's *Gesangbuch* (1704);
revised in Werner's *Gesangbuch* (1815)

1. Christ, whose glo-ry fills the skies, Christ, my true and on-ly Light,
2. Dark and cheer-less is the morn un-ac-com-pa-nied by thee;
3. Vis-it then this soul of mine; pierce the gloom of sin and grief.

1. Sun of Righ-teous-ness, a-rise, tri-umph o'er the shades of night;
2. joy-less is the day's re-turn till thy mer-cy's beams I see,
3. Fill me, ra-dian-cy di-vine; scat-ter all my un-be-lief;

1. Day-spring from on high, be near; Day-star, in my heart ap-pear.
2. till they in-ward light im-part, glad my eyes, and warm my heart.
3. more and more thy-self dis-play, shin-ing to the per-fect day.

Mal. 4:2

THE CHRISTIAN AS DISCIPLE

464
Love Divine, All Loves Excelling

Charles Wesley, 1747

HYFRYDOL, 8.7.8.7 D

R. H. Prichard, 1831

1. Love di - vine, all loves ex - cel - ling, joy of heav'n to earth come down;
2. Come al - might - y to de - liv - er; let us all thy life re - ceive;
3. Fin - ish then thy new cre - a - tion; pure and spot - less let us be;

1. fix in us thy hum - ble dwell-ing, all thy faith - ful mer - cies crown.
2. sud - den - ly re - turn and nev - er, nev - er - more thy tem - ples leave.
3. let us see thy great sal - va - tion per - fect - ly re - stored in thee,

1. Je - sus, thou art all com - pas - sion; pure, un - bound - ed love thou art;
2. Thee we would be al - ways bless-ing, serve thee as thy hosts a - bove,
3. changed from glo - ry in - to glo - ry, till in heav'n we take our place,

1. vis - it us with thy sal - va - tion; en - ter ev - 'ry trem - bling heart.
2. pray and praise thee with - out ceas - ing, glo - ry in thy per - fect love.
3. till we cast our crowns be - fore thee, lost in won - der, love, and praise!

Alternative tune: BEECHER, 479

THE CHRISTIAN AS DISCIPLE

II Cor. 3:18

There Is a Balm in Gilead

North American spiritual

BALM IN GILEAD, *Irregular*

Arranged by Betty Pulkingham

Refrain

There is a balm in Gil-e-ad to make the woun-ded whole. ____

There is a balm in Gil-e-ad to heal the sin-sick soul.

Fine

Verses

1. Some - times I feel dis - cour-aged, and think my work's in vain,
2. If you can-not sing like an - gels, if you can - not preach like Paul,

1. but then the Ho - ly Spir - it re - vives my soul a - gain. ____ There is a
2. you can tell the love of Je - sus and say he died for all. ____

THE CHRISTIAN AS DISCIPLE

466

O Mighty God!

Erik Routley, 1982

O STORE GUD, 11.10.11.10.10.8.10.8

Swedish hymn melody;
harmonized by Erik Routley, 1982

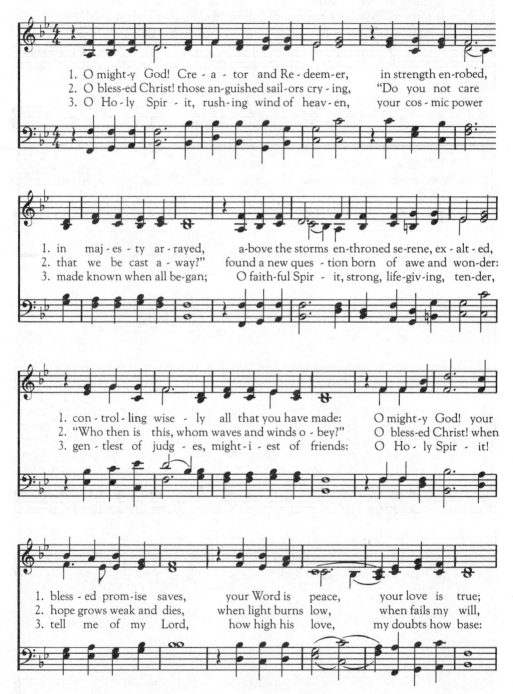

1. O might-y God! Cre - a - tor and Re - deem-er, in strength en-robed,
2. O bless-ed Christ! those an-guished sail-ors cry - ing, "Do you not care
3. O Ho - ly Spir - it, rush-ing wind of heav - en, your cos - mic power

1. in maj - es - ty ar - rayed, a-bove the storms en-throned se-rene, ex - alt - ed,
2. that we be cast a - way?" found a new ques - tion born of awe and won-der:
3. made known when all be-gan; O faith-ful Spir - it, strong, life-giv-ing, ten-der,

1. con - trol - ling wise - ly all that you have made: O might-y God! your
2. "Who then is this, whom waves and winds o - bey?" O bless-ed Christ! when
3. gen - tlest of judg - es, might-i - est of friends: O Ho - ly Spir - it!

1. bless - ed prom-ise saves, your Word is peace, your love is true;
2. hope grows weak and dies, when light burns low, when fails my will,
3. tell me of my Lord, how high his love, my doubts how base:

THE CHRISTIAN AS DISCIPLE

1. that love is might - ier than the rag - ing waves;
2. then let me hear your roy - al voice a - rise
3. show me the things of Christ, my King a - dored,

1. Lord, I be - lieve! I trust in you.
2. a - bove the tem - pest: "Peace! Be still!"
3. how small my fears how great his grace!

Ps. 93; Mk. 4:35ff, Mt. 8:23–27; Acts 2:2; Jn. 14:26ff

*If sung in parts, the basses and tenors
begin final line on the first beat of this measure.

Just as I Am, Without One Plea — 467

Charlotte Elliott, 1834
First Tune

SAFFRON WALDEN, 888.6

A. H. Brown, 1877

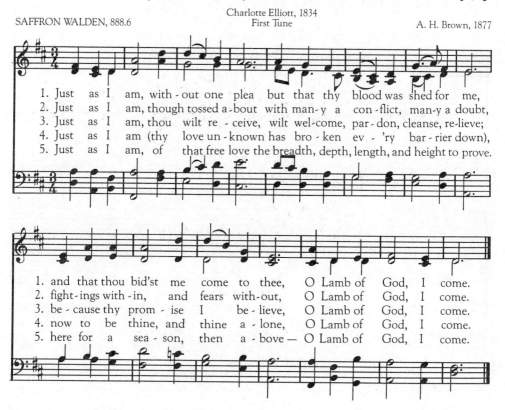

1. Just as I am, with - out one plea but that thy blood was shed for me,
2. Just as I am, though tossed a - bout with man - y a con - flict, man - y a doubt,
3. Just as I am, thou wilt re - ceive, wilt wel - come, par - don, cleanse, re - lieve;
4. Just as I am (thy love un - known has bro - ken ev - 'ry bar - rier down),
5. Just as I am, of that free love the breadth, depth, length, and height to prove.

1. and that thou bid'st me come to thee, O Lamb of God, I come.
2. fight - ings with - in, and fears with - out, O Lamb of God, I come.
3. be - cause thy prom - ise I be - lieve, O Lamb of God, I come.
4. now to be thine, and thine a - lone, O Lamb of God, I come.
5. here for a sea - son, then a - bove — O Lamb of God, I come.

Eph. 2:14

THE CHRISTIAN AS WITNESS

468 **Just as I Am, Without One Plea**

WOODWORTH, LM   Second Tune   W. B. Bradbury, 1849, 1860

1. Just as I am, with-out one plea but that thy blood was shed for me,
2. Just as I am, though tossed a-bout with man-y a con-flict, man-y a doubt,
3. Just as I am, thou wilt re-ceive, wilt wel-come, par-don, cleanse, re-lieve;
4. Just as I am (thy love un-known has bro-ken ev-'ry bar-rier down),
5. Just as I am, of that free love the breadth, depth, length, and height to prove,

1. and that thou bid'st me come to thee, O Lamb of God, I come, I come.
2. fight-ings with-in, and fears with-out, O Lamb of God, I come, I come.
3. be-cause thy prom-ise I be-lieve, O Lamb of God, I come, I come.
4. now to be thine, and thine a-lone, O Lamb of God, I come, I come.
5. here for a sea-son, then a-bove—O Lamb of God, I come, I come.

469 **Rejoice, Believer, in the Lord**

BRADFIELD, CM   John Newton, 1779   J. B. Calkin, 1872

1. Re-joice, be-liev-er, in the Lord, who makes your cause his own;
2. Though man-y foes be-set your road, and fee-ble is your arm,
3. Weak as you are, you shall not faint, or faint-ing, shall not die,
4. Though un-per-ceived by mor-tal sense, faith sees him al-ways near,
5. As sure-ly as he o-ver-came and tri-umphed once for you,

1. the hope that's built up-on his word shall ne'er be o-ver-thrown.
2. your life is hid with Christ in God be-yond the reach of harm.
3. Je-sus, the strength of ev-'ry saint, will aid you from on high.
4. a guide, a glo-ry, a de-fense; then what have you to fear?
5. so sure-ly you that love his name shall in him tri-umph too.

Alternative tunes: ST. STEPHEN, 473, ST. FULBERT, 474

THE CHRISTIAN AS WITNESS   *Phil. 4:4ff*

Lo! I Come with Joy

Charles Wesley, 1747

470

LLANGEITHO, 7.6.7.6.7.8.7.6

Anon. Welsh tune, 1839

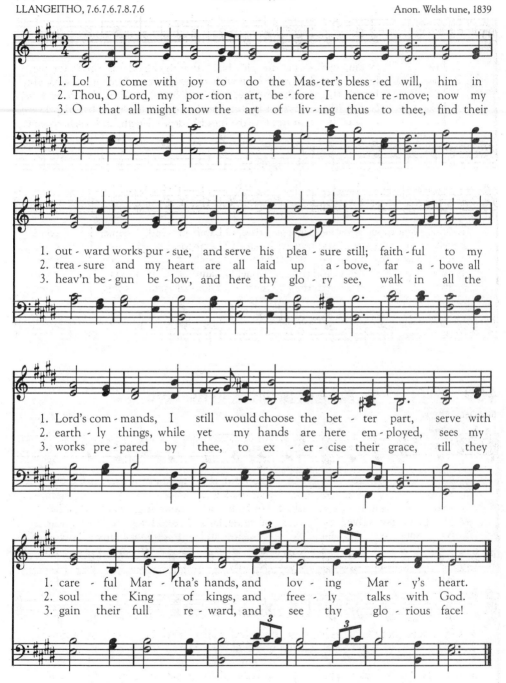

1. Lo! I come with joy to do the Mas-ter's bless-ed will, him in
2. Thou, O Lord, my por-tion art, be-fore I hence re-move; now my
3. O that all might know the art of liv-ing thus to thee, find their

1. out-ward works pur-sue, and serve his plea-sure still; faith-ful to my
2. trea-sure and my heart are all laid up a-bove, far a-bove all
3. heav'n be-gun be-low, and here thy glo-ry see, walk in all the

1. Lord's com-mands, I still would choose the bet-ter part, serve with
2. earth-ly things, while yet my hands are here em-ployed, sees my
3. works pre-pared by thee, to ex-er-cise their grace, till they

1. care-ful Mar-tha's hands, and lov-ing Mar-y's heart.
2. soul the King of kings, and free-ly talks with God.
3. gain their full re-ward, and see thy glo-rious face!

Ps. 40:7–8; Lk. 10:38–42

THE CHRISTIAN AS WITNESS

O Jesus, I Have Promised

J. E. Bode, 1868

WOLVERCOTE, 7.6.7.6 D

W. H. Ferguson, 1918

Unison

1. O Je-sus, I have prom - ised to serve thee to the end;
2. O let me feel thee near me! The world is ev - er near;
3. O let me hear thee speak - ing in ac - cents clear and still,
4. O Je-sus, thou hast prom - ised to all who fol -low thee

1. be thou for - ev - er near me, my Mas-ter and my Friend;
2. I see the sights that daz - zle, the tempt -ing sounds I hear;
3. a - bove the storms of pas - sion, the mur -murs of self - will!
4. that where thou art in glo - ry, there shall thy ser-vant be;

1. I shall not fear the bat - tle if thou art by my side,
2. my foes are ev - er near me, a - round me, and with - in;
3. O speak to re - as - sure me, to has -ten or con - trol!
4. and, Je - sus, I have prom -ised to serve thee to the end;

THE CHRISTIAN AS WITNESS

1. nor wan-der from the path - way if thou wilt be my Guide.
2. but, Je - sus, draw thou near - er, and shield my soul from sin.
3. O speak, and make me lis - ten, thou Guard-ian of my soul.
4. O give me grace to fol - low, my Mas - ter and my Friend!

Alternative version of this tune (SATB): 311; the two versions can be used together.

Jn. 12:26

Give Me, O Christ, the Strength That Is in Thee 472

KINGSTANDING, 10.10.10.10   Henry Child Carter, 1951   Erik Routley, 1940

Unison

1. Give me, O Christ, the strength that is in thee, that I may stand
2. Give me to see the foes that I must fight, pow'rs of the dark-
3. Give me to wear the ar-mor that can guard, o - ver my breast
4. Give me to wield the weap - on that is sure, tak - ing thro' pray'r

1. in ev - 'ry e - vil hour; faints my poor heart ex-cept to thee I flee,
2. ness throned where thou shouldst reign; read the di - rect-ings of thy wrath a - right,
3. thy blood-bought righ - teous - ness, faith for my shield, when fi-ery darts rain hard,
4. thy sword in - to my hand, word of thy wis-dom, peace-a-ble and pure,

1. rest - ing my weak - ness in thy per - fect pow'r.
2. lest, strik - ing flesh and blood, I strike in vain.
3. gird - ed with truth, and shod with zeal to bless.
4. so, Christ my Con - qu'ror, I shall con - qu'ror stand.

Eph. 6:10ff   THE CHRISTIAN AS WITNESS

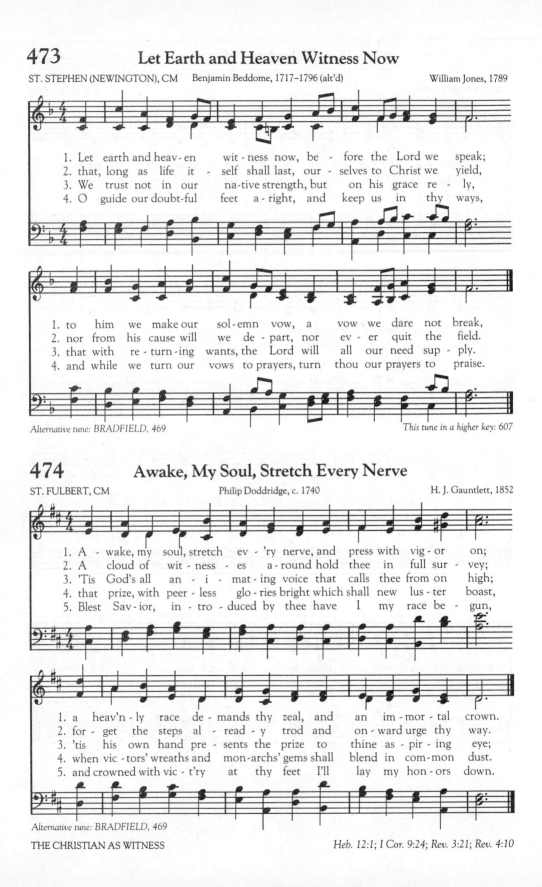

473   **Let Earth and Heaven Witness Now**

ST. STEPHEN (NEWINGTON), CM   Benjamin Beddome, 1717–1796 (alt'd)   William Jones, 1789

1. Let earth and heav-en wit-ness now, be-fore the Lord we speak;
2. that, long as life it-self shall last, our-selves to Christ we yield,
3. We trust not in our na-tive strength, but on his grace re-ly,
4. O guide our doubt-ful feet a-right, and keep us in thy ways,

1. to him we make our sol-emn vow, a vow we dare not break,
2. nor from his cause will we de-part, nor ev-er quit the field.
3. that with re-turn-ing wants, the Lord will all our need sup-ply.
4. and while we turn our vows to prayers, turn thou our prayers to praise.

Alternative tune: BRADFIELD, 469   *This tune in a higher key: 607*

474   **Awake, My Soul, Stretch Every Nerve**

ST. FULBERT, CM   Philip Doddridge, c. 1740   H. J. Gauntlett, 1852

1. A-wake, my soul, stretch ev-'ry nerve, and press with vig-or on;
2. A cloud of wit-ness-es a-round hold thee in full sur-vey;
3. 'Tis God's all an-i-mat-ing voice that calls thee from on high;
4. that prize, with peer-less glo-ries bright which shall new lus-ter boast,
5. Blest Sav-ior, in-tro-duced by thee have I my race be-gun,

1. a heav'n-ly race de-mands thy zeal, and an im-mor-tal crown.
2. for-get the steps al-read-y trod and on-ward urge thy way.
3. 'tis his own hand pre-sents the prize to thine as-pir-ing eye;
4. when vic-tors' wreaths and mon-archs' gems shall blend in com-mon dust.
5. and crowned with vic-t'ry at thy feet I'll lay my hon-ors down.

Alternative tune: BRADFIELD, 469

THE CHRISTIAN AS WITNESS   *Heb. 12:1; I Cor. 9:24; Rev. 3:21; Rev. 4:10*

Take My Life

Frances Ridley Havergal, 1874

HOLLINGSIDE, 77.77 D

J. B. Dykes, 1861

1. Take my life, and let it be con-se-crat-ed, Lord, to thee;
2. Take my voice, and let it sing al-ways, on-ly for my King;
3. Take my will, and make it thine; it shall be no long-er mine;

1. take my mo-ments and my days, let them flow in cease-less praise.
2. take my lips and let them be filled with mes-sag-es from thee.
3. take my heart, it is thine own; it shall be thy roy-al throne.

1. Take my hands, and let them move at the im-pulse of thy love;
2. Take my sil-ver and my gold, not a mite would I with-hold;
3. Take my love, my Lord, I pour at thy feet its trea-sure store;

1. take my feet, and let them be swift and beau-ti-ful for thee.
2. take my in-tel-lect and use ev-'ry power as thou shalt choose.
3. take my-self, and I will be ev-er, on-ly, all for thee.

I Sam. 3:9; Isa. 6:8; Lk. 21:2

THE CHRISTIAN AS WITNESS

476

Eternal Beam of Light Divine

Charles Wesley, 1739

J. F. Lampe, 1746

KENT, LM

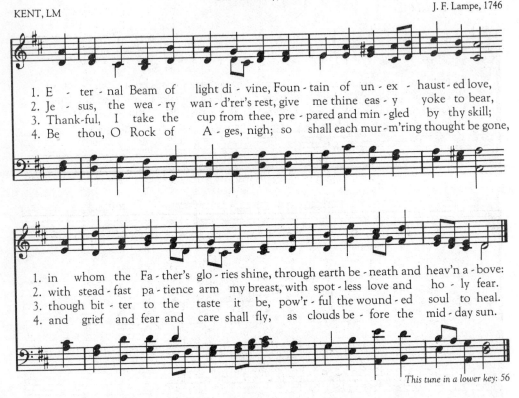

1. E - ter - nal Beam of light di - vine, Foun - tain of un - ex - haust - ed love,
2. Je - sus, the wea - ry wan - d'rer's rest, give me thine eas - y yoke to bear,
3. Thank-ful, I take the cup from thee, pre - pared and min - gled by thy skill;
4. Be thou, O Rock of A - ges, nigh; so shall each mur - m'ring thought be gone,

1. in whom the Fa - ther's glo - ries shine, through earth be - neath and heav'n a - bove:
2. with stead - fast pa - tience arm my breast, with spot - less love and ho - ly fear.
3. though bit - ter to the taste it be, pow'r - ful the wound - ed soul to heal.
4. and grief and fear and care shall fly, as clouds be - fore the mid - day sun.

This tune in a lower key: 56

5. Speak to my warring passions, "Peace";
   say to my wounded heart, "Be still!"
   Thy power my strength and fortress is,
   and all things serve thy sovereign will.

6. O death, where is thy sting? Where now
   thy boasted victory, O grave?
   Who shall contend with God? or who
   can hurt whom God delights to save?

THE CHRISTIAN AS WITNESS

Mt. 11:28; Lk. 22:42; I Cor. 15:55

I Have No Other Comfort

477

Alvin Grether, 1937; based on the Heidelberg Catechism, Question 1

ROCKPORT, 7.6.7.6 D

T. Tertius Noble, 1938

1. I have no oth-er com-fort which life and death en - dures
2. Thy blood is full a - tone-ment for all my sin and guilt;
3. What-ev-er things be - tide me must serve to save my soul;
4. And so thou mak'st me will - ing with all my heart and mind

1. than that I am my Sav - ior's whose death my life se - cures.
2. the cross is all my glo - ry; on thee my faith is built.
3. the Fa - ther watch - es o'er me to keep me safe and whole.
4. to live for thee, my Sav - ior, so lov - ing, true, and kind.

1. To thee with soul and bod - y, O Je - sus, I be - long;
2. And thou, my great de - liv - 'rer, art my pre - serv - er too;
3. Yes, by thy Ho - ly Spir - it I ful - ly am as - sured
4. To thee with soul and bod - y, O Je - sus, I be - long;

1. thou art my on - ly Mas - ter, and my Re-deem-er strong.
2. thou guid - est all my foot-steps, and lead-est me clear through.
3. that mine is life e - ter - nal ac - cord-ing to thy Word.
4. thou art my on - ly Mas - ter, and my Re-deem-er strong.

♮ *last stanza only*

Ps. 8:28

THE CHRISTIAN AS WITNESS

478 I Bind unto Myself Today

St. Patrick, c. 430; paraphrased by Cecil Frances Alexander, 1889

ST. PATRICK, LMD

Irish traditional melody; harmonized by Erik Routley

THE CHRISTIAN AS WITNESS

2. heav'n - ly way, his com - ing at the day of
3. shield to ward; the Word of God to give me
5. Spir - it, Word: praise to the God of my sal -

*   Fine

2. doom I bind un - to my - self to - day.
3. speech, his heav'n - ly host to be my guard. (st. 4 below)
5. va - tion, sal - va - tion is of Christ the Lord!

♮ last time only

DEIRDRE   Irish traditional melody; harmonized by C. V. Stanford, 1904

SATB

4. Christ be with me, Christ with - in me, Christ be - hind me, Christ be - fore me,
   Christ be - neath me, Christ a - bove me, Christ in qui - et, Christ in dan - ger.

After repeat D. C. al Fine

4. Christ be - side me, Christ to win me, Christ to com - fort and re - store me;
   Christ in hearts of all that love me, Christ in mouth of friend and strang - er.

THE CHRISTIAN AS WITNESS

479

Son of God, Eternal Savior

Somerset Corry Lowry, 1893 (alt'd)

BEECHER, 8.7.8.7 D

John Zundel, 1855

1. Son of God, e-ter-nal Sav-ior, source of life and truth and grace,
2. As thou, Lord, hast lived for oth-ers, so may we for oth-ers live;
3. Come, O Christ, and reign a-bove us, King of Love, and Prince of Peace;
4. Son of God, e-ter-nal Sav-ior, source of life and truth and grace,

1. wom-an's Son, whose birth a-mongst us hal-lows all our hu-man race:
2. free-ly have thy gifts been grant-ed, free-ly may thy ser-vants give.
3. hush the storm of strife and pas-sion, bid its cru-el dis-cords cease;
4. wom-an's Son, whose birth a-mongst us hal-lows all our hu-man race,

1. thou, our Head, who throned in glo-ry for thine own dost ev-er plead,
2. Thine the gold and thine the sil-ver, thine the wealth of land and sea,
3. by thy pa-tient years of toil-ing, by thy si-lent hours of pain,
4. thou who pray-edst, thou who will-est that thy peo-ple should be one,

1. fill us with thy love and pit-y, heal our wrongs, and help our need.
2. we but stew-ards of thy boun-ty held in sol-emn trust for thee.
3. quench our fe-ver'd thirst of plea-sure, shame our self-ish greed of gain.
4. grant, O grant our hope's fru-i-tion; here on earth thy will be done.

THE CHRISTIAN AS NEIGHBOR

Jn. 17:21

Awake, Awake to Love and Work

G. A. Studdert-Kennedy, 1921

Melody in *Kentucky Harmony* (1806);
harmonized by Charles Winfred Douglas, 1940

MORNING SONG, 8.6.8.6.8.6

1. A - wake, a - wake to love and work: the lark is in the sky,
2. Come, let thy voice be one with theirs, shout with their shout of praise,
3. to give, and give, and give a - gain what God hath giv - en thee,

1. the fields are wet with dia - mond dew, the worlds a - wake to cry
2. see how the gi - ant sun soars up, great lord of years and days!
3. to spend thy - self, nor count the cost, to serve right glo - rious - ly

1. their bless - ings on the Lord of life as he goes meek - ly by.
2. So let the love of Je - sus come and set thy soul a - blaze,
3. the God who gave all worlds that are, and all that are to be.

THE CHRISTIAN AS NEIGHBOR

Eternal God, Whose Power Upholds

H. H. Tweedy, 1929

HALIFAX, CMD

Adapted from a song by G. F. Handel, 1748;
arranged by Charles Winfred Douglas, 1941

1. E - ter - nal God, whose power up - holds both flower and flam - ing star,
2. O God of love, whose spir - it wakes in ev - 'ry hu - man breast,
3. O God of truth, whom sci - ence seeks and rev - 'rent souls a - dore,
4. O God of beau - ty, oft re - vealed in dreams of hu - man art,

1. to whom there is no here nor there, no time, no near nor far,
2. whom love, and love a - lone, can know, in whom all hearts find rest:
3. who light - est ev - 'ry ear - nest mind of ev - 'ry clime and shore:
4. in speech that flows to mel - o - dy, in ho - li - ness of heart:

1. no a - lien race, no for - eign shore, no child un - sought, un - known:
2. help us to spread thy gra - cious reign till greed and hate shall cease,
3. dis - pel the gloom of er - ror's night, of ig - no - rance and fear,
4. teach us to shun all ug - li - ness that blinds our eyes to thee,

1. O send us forth, thy proph - ets true, to make all lands thine own!
2. and kind - ness dwell in hu - man hearts, and all the earth find peace!
3. un - til true wis - dom from a - bove shall make life's path - way clear!
4. till all shall know the love - li - ness of lives made fair and free!

Alternative tune: FOREST GREEN, 9

THE CHRISTIAN AS NEIGHBOR

5. O God of righteousness and grace,
   seen in the Christ, thy Son,
  whose life and death reveal thy face,
   by whom thy will was done:
  inspire thy heralds of good news
   to live thy life divine,
  till Christ is formed in ev'ry heart,
   and ev'ry land is thine.

Where Cross the Crowded Ways of Life   482

Frank Mason North, 1903

GERMANY, LM

William Gardiner's *Sacred Melodies* (1815)

1. Where cross the crowd - ed ways of life, where sound the cries of race and clan, a - bove the noise of self - ish strife, we hear thy voice, O Son of Man.
2. In haunts of wretch - ed - ness and need, on shad - owed thresh - olds dark with fears, from paths where hide the lures of greed, we catch the vi - sion of thy tears.
3. The cup of wa - ter given for thee still holds the fresh - ness of thy grace; yet long these mul - ti - tudes to see the sweet com - pas - sion of thy face.
4. O Mas - ter, from the moun - tain - side, make haste to heal these hearts of pain; a - mong these rest - less throngs a - bide, O tread the cit - y's streets a - gain,
5. till all thy peo - ple know thy love, and fol - low where thy feet have trod; till glo - rious from thy heaven a - bove shall come the cit - y of our God.

Another version of this tune in a lower key: 295

THE CHRISTIAN AS NEIGHBOR

483 Almighty Father, Who for Us Thy Son Didst Give

George B. Caird, 1943

16th-century Dutch melody;
harmony mostly by John Wilson

WILHELMUS, 12 12.12 12

1. Al - might - y Fa - ther, who for us thy Son didst give,
2. We are thy stew - ards, thine our tal - ents, wis - dom, skill,
3. On just and un - just thou thy care dost free - ly shower;
4. Let not thy wor - ship blind us to the claims of love,

1. that all the na - tions through his pre - cious death might live,
2. our on - ly glo - ry that we may thy trust ful - fill,
3. make us, thy chil - dren, free from greed and lust for power,
4. but let thy man - na lead us to the feast a - bove,

1. in mer - cy guard us, lest by sloth and self - ish pride
2. that we thy plea - sure in our neigh - bors' good pur - sue,
3. lest hu - man jus - tice, yoked with our un - e - qual laws,
4. to seek the coun - try, which by faith we now pos - sess,

or

1. we cause to stum - ble those for whom the Sav - ior died.
2. if thou but work - est in us both to will and do.
3. op - press the need - y, and ne - glect the hum - ble cause.
4. where Christ, our Sav - ior, reigns in peace and righ - teous - ness.

THE CHRISTIAN AS NEIGHBOR

Mt. 12:14ff

Lord of Light, Whose Name Outshineth   484

Hywel Elfed Lewis, 1916

CHRIST CHURCH, ALEXANDRIA, 8.7.8.7 D   Richard Wayne Dirksen, 1973

1. Lord of light, whose name out-shin-eth all the stars and suns of space,
2. Grant that knowl-edge, still in-creas-ing, at thy feet may low-ly kneel;
3. By the prayers of faith-ful watch-ers, nev-er si - lent day or night,

1. deign to make us thy co-work-ers in the king-dom of thy grace;
2. with thy grace our tri-umphs hal-low, with thy char-i-ty our zeal;
3. by the cross of Je-sus, bring-ing peace to earth, and heal-ing light,

1. may our prayer ful-fill thy prom-ise in the gift of Christ thy Son;
2. lift the na-tions from the shad-ows to the glad-ness of thy sun;
3. by the love that pass-eth knowl-edge, mak-ing all thy chil-dren one,

Refrain

as in high-est heav-en, Fa-ther, so on earth thy will be done.

Mt. 6:10   THE CHRISTIAN AS NEIGHBOR

485 All Who Love and Serve Your City

Erik Routley, 1966
American folk hymn, *Southern Harmony* (1835);
arranged by Carlton R. Young, 1964

CHARLESTOWN, 8.7.8.7

Unison

1. All who love and serve your cit-y, all who bear its dai-ly stress,
2. In your day of loss and sor-row, in your day of help-less strife,
3. In your day of wealth and plen-ty, wast-ed work and wast-ed play,
4. For all days are days of judg-ment, and the Lord is wait-ing still,
5. Ris-en Lord, shall yet the cit-y be the cit-y of de-spair?

1. all who cry for peace and jus-tice, all who curse and all who bless.
2. hon-or, peace, and love re-treat-ing, seek the Lord, who is your life.
3. call to mind the word of Je-sus, "Work ye yet while it is day."
4. draw-ing near a world that spurns him, of-fering peace from Cal-vary's hill.
5. Come to-day, our Judge, our Glor-y; be its name, "the Lord is there!"

Jn. 9:4; Ezek. 48:35

486 Lord, Save Thy World

DISTRESS, LM

Albert F. Bayly, 1948
Melody in *Southern Harmony* (1835)

1. Lord, save thy world: in bit-ter need thy chil-dren lift their cry to thee;
2. Lord, save thy world: our souls are bound in i-ron chains of fear and pride;
3. Lord, save thy world: we strive in vain to save our-selves with-out thine aid;
4. Lord, save thy world: but thou hast sent the Sav-ior whom we sore-ly need;
5. Then save us now, by Je-sus' power, and use the lives thy love sets free

1. we wait thy lib-er-at-ing deed to sig-nal hope and set us free.
2. high walls of ig-no-rance a-round our fac-es from each oth-er hide.
3. what skill and sci-ence slow-ly gain is soon to e-vil ends be-trayed.
4. for us his tears and blood were spent, that from our bonds we might be freed.
5. to bring at last the glo-rious hour when all shall find thy lib-er-ty.

THE CHRISTIAN AS NEIGHBOR

Gen. 45:5; Gen. 50:20; Jn. 3:15ff

Lord Jesus, If I Love and Serve My Neighbor

Brian Wren, 1975

CITY OF GOD, 11.10.11.10

Daniel Moe, 1957

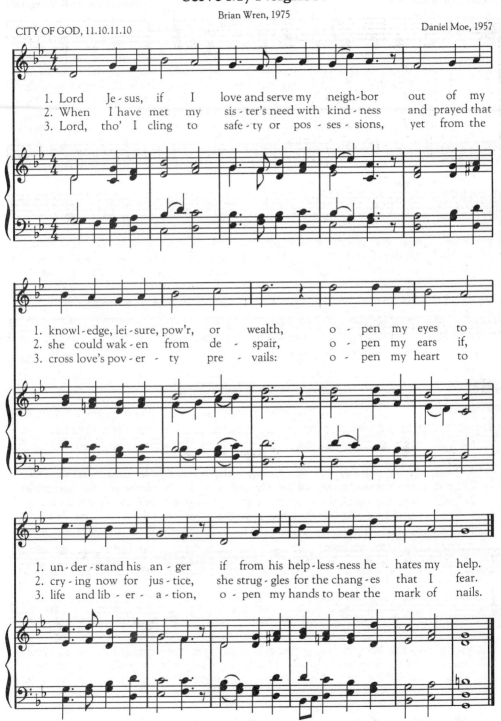

1. Lord Je-sus, if I love and serve my neigh-bor out of my
2. When I have met my sis-ter's need with kind-ness and prayed that
3. Lord, tho' I cling to safe-ty or pos-ses-sions, yet from the

1. knowl-edge, lei-sure, pow'r, or wealth, o-pen my eyes to
2. she could wak-en from de-spair, o-pen my ears if,
3. cross love's pov-er-ty pre-vails: o-pen my heart to

1. un-der-stand his an-ger if from his help-less-ness he hates my help.
2. cry-ing now for jus-tice, she strug-gles for the chang-es that I fear.
3. life and lib-er-a-tion, o-pen my hands to bear the mark of nails.

THE CHRISTIAN AS NEIGHBOR

488   Thou Judge, by Whom Each Empire Fell

Percy Dearmer, 1925

KIRKEN, 8.7.8.7.88.7

L. M. Lindeman, 1812–1887

1. Thou Judge, by whom each em-pire fell when pride of pow'r o'er-
2. Search, Lord, our spir-its in thy sight; in best and worst re-
3. Lo, fear-ing nought, we come to thee, though by our fault con-

1. came it, con-vict us now, if we re-bel, our na-tion
2. veal us; shed on our souls a blaze of light, and judge, that
3. found-ed; though self-ish, mean, and base we be, thy jus-tice

1. judge, and shame it: in each sharp cri-sis, Lord, ap-pear;
2. thou may'st heal us. The pres-ent be our judg-ment day,
3. is un-bound-ed, so large, it nought but love re-quires,

1. for-give, and show our du-ty clear — to serve thee by re-pen-tance.
2. when all our lack thou dost sur-vey; show us our-selves and save us.
3. and, judg-ing, par-dons and in-spires. De-liv-er us from e-vil!

Father Eternal, Ruler of Creation

489

Laurence Housman, 1919 (alt'd)

LANGHAM, 11.10.11.10.10

Geoffrey Shaw, 1921

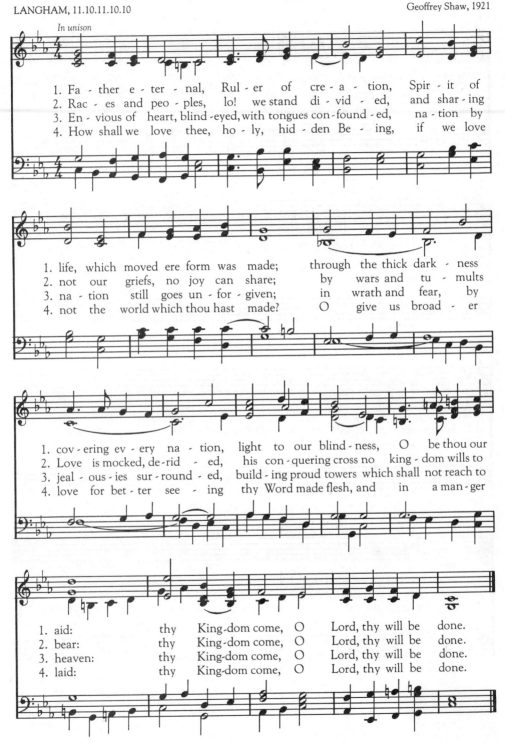

In unison

1. Fa - ther e - ter - nal, Rul - er of cre - a - tion, Spir - it of
2. Rac - es and peo - ples, lo! we stand di - vid - ed, and shar - ing
3. En - vious of heart, blind -eyed, with tongues con -found - ed, na - tion by
4. How shall we love thee, ho - ly, hid - den Be - ing, if we love

1. life, which moved ere form was made; through the thick dark - ness
2. not our griefs, no joy can share; by wars and tu - mults
3. na - tion still goes un - for - given; in wrath and fear, by
4. not the world which thou hast made? O give us broad - er

1. cov - ering ev - ery na - tion, light to our blind -ness, O be thou our
2. Love is mocked, de -rid - ed, his con -quering cross no king - dom wills to
3. jeal - ous -ies sur -round - ed, build - ing proud towers which shall not reach to
4. love for bet - ter see - ing thy Word made flesh, and in a man -ger

1. aid: thy King-dom come, O Lord, thy will be done.
2. bear: thy King-dom come, O Lord, thy will be done.
3. heaven: thy King-dom come, O Lord, thy will be done.
4. laid: thy King-dom come, O Lord, thy will be done.

Gen. 11:4; Jn. 1:14; Mt. 6:10

THE CHRISTIAN AS CITIZEN

490   O Christ, Our Savior, Who Must Reign

Francis Bland Tucker, 1971

NOEL, CMD

Arthur S. Sullivan, 1874

1. O Christ, our Sav - ior, who must reign till all the world is yours,
2. Your gos - pel to the na - tions take that you for all have died,
3. Go forth, O Christ, to vic - to - ry by God's de - sign most sure

1. let each one hear the joy - ful strain the heav - en - ly host out - pours.
2. for on - ly grat - i - tude can break our stub - born - ness and pride.
3. till all shall come in u - ni - ty, wise, pen - i - tent, ma - ture.

1. Your praise now makes your peo - ple one of many a name and birth;
2. Your grace a - lone can con - quer hate, can turn us to your ways,
3. Till root - ed, ground - ed in that love for us once sac - ri - ficed

1. the song in Beth - le - hem be - gun is hope of all the earth.
2. and of our thank - ful - ness cre - ate the fel - low - ship of praise.
3. your church at - tain the mea - sure of the full - ness of the Christ.

THE CHRISTIAN AS CITIZEN

Lk. 2:14; Eph. 4:13

O God of Love, O King of Peace 491

Henry Williams Baker, 1868

QUEBEC, LM

Henry Baker, 1854

1. O God of love, O King of peace, make wars through-out the world to cease;
2. Re - mem - ber, Lord, thy works of old, the won - ders that our fa - thers told;
3. Whom shall we trust but thee, O Lord? Where rest but on thy faith - ful word?
4. Where saints and an - gels dwell a - bove, all hearts are knit in ho - ly love;

1. the wrath of sin - ful flesh re - strain: give peace, O God, give peace a - gain!
2. re - mem - ber not our sin's dark stain: give peace, O God, give peace a - gain!
3. None ev - er called on thee in vain: give peace, O God, give peace a - gain!
4. O bind us in that heaven - ly chain: give peace, O God, give peace a - gain!

Let There Be Light, Lord God of Hosts! 492

ELTON, LM

William M. Vories, 1908

Lowell Mason, 1854

1. Let there be light, Lord God of hosts! Let there be wis - dom on the earth!
2. With - in our pas-sioned hearts in-still the calm that end - eth strain and strife;
3. Give us the peace of vi - sion clear to see in oth - ers' good our own,
4. Let woe and waste of war - fare cease, that use - ful la - bor yet may build

1. Let broad hu - man - i - ty have birth! Let there be deeds, in - stead of boasts!
2. make us thy min - is - ters of life; purge us from lusts that curse and kill!
3. to joy and suf - fer not a - lone: the love that cast - eth out all fear!
4. its homes with love and laugh - ter filled! God, give thy way - ward chil - dren peace!

Gen. 1:3

THE CHRISTIAN AS CITIZEN

493

God the Omnipotent!

St. 1-2, Henry F. Chorley, 1842; st. 3-4, John Ellerton,
1870 (alt'd)

RUSSIAN HYMN, 11.10.11.9

Alexis Lvov, 1833

1. God the Om - nip - o - tent! King, who or - dain - est thun - der thy
2. God the All - mer - ci - ful! earth hath for - sak - en thy ways all-
3. God the All - righ - teous One! we have de - fied thee; yet to e -
4. God the All - prov - i - dent! earth by thy chas - tening, yet shall to

1. clar - ion, the light - ning thy sword; show forth thy pit - y on
2. ho - ly, and slight - ed thy word; bid not thy wrath in its
3. ter - ni - ty stand - eth thy word; false - hood and wrong shall not
4. free - dom and truth be re - stored; through the thick dark - ness thy

1. high where thou reign - est: give to us peace in our time, O Lord.
2. ter - rors a - wak - en: give to us peace in our time, O Lord.
3. tar - ry be - side thee: give to us peace in our time, O Lord.
4. King - dom is has - tening: thou wilt give peace in thy time, O Lord.

THE CHRISTIAN AS CITIZEN

Hab. 1:13a

God of All Ages, Whose Almighty Hand

494

Daniel C. Roberts, 1876

NATIONAL HYMN, 10 10. 10 10

G. W. Warren, 1894

Trumpets, before each stanza
(Optional)

1. God of all a - ges, whose al - might - y
2. Thy love di - vine hath led us in the
3. From wars a - larms, from dead - ly pes - ti -
4. Re - fresh thy peo - ple on their toil - some

1. hand   leads forth in beau - ty   all the star - ry band
2. past;   in this free land   by thee our lot is cast;
3. lence,   be thy strong arm   our ev - er - sure de - fense;
4. way,   lead us from night   to nev - er - end - ing day;

1. of   shin - ing worlds   in   splen - dor through the   skies,
2. be   thou   our   Rul - er, Guard - ian, Guide, and   Stay;
3. thy   true   re - li - gion   in   our hearts in - crease,
4. fill   all   our   lives   with   love   and grace di - vine,

1. our   grate - ful songs   be - fore thy throne a - rise.
2. thy   word   our   law,   thy   paths   our   cho - sen   way.
3. thy   boun - teous good - ness   nour - ish   us   in   peace.
4. and   glo - ry, laud,   and   praise   be   ev - er   thine.

THE CHRISTIAN AS CITIZEN

495

It Is God Who Holds the Nations

Fred Pratt Green, 1976

VISION, 15 15 15.7

H. Walford Davies, 1915; arranged by John Wilson, 1977

1. It is God who holds the na-tions in the hol-low of his hand;
2. It is God whose pur-pose sum-mons us to use the pres-ent hour,
*3. When a thank-ful na-tion, look-ing back, u-nites to cel-e-brate
4. He re-minds us ev-ery sun-rise that the earth is ours on lease—

1. it is God whose light is shin-ing in the dark-ness of the land;
2. who re-calls us to our sens-es when a na-tion's life turns sour;
3. those who win our ad-mi-ra-tion by their ser-vice to the state,
4. for the sake of life to-mor-row may our love for it in-crease;

1. it is God who builds his Cit-y on the Rock and not on sand:
2. in the dis-ci-pline of free-dom we shall know his sav-ing power:
3. when self-giv-ing is a mea-sure of the great-ness of the great,
4. may all rac-es live to-geth-er, share its rich-es, be at peace:

1. may the liv - ing God be praised! _____
2. may the liv - ing God be praised! _____
3. may the liv - ing God be praised! _____
4. may the liv - ing God be praised! _____

Choir ad lib

1. may the liv - ing God be praised! God be praised!___
2. may the liv - ing God be praised! God be praised!___
3. may the liv - ing God be praised! God be praised!___
4. may the liv - ing God be praised! God be praised!___

Organ

st. 4

Isa. 40:12; Ps. 2

THE CHRISTIAN AS CITIZEN

God Bless Our Native Land

Gott segne Sachserland, st. 1–2 by S. A. Mahlmann, 1815;
tr. C. T. Brooks; st. 3, John S. Dwight, c. 1845

NATIONAL ANTHEM, 66.4.666.4

Anon. English melody, c. 1744;
harmonized by Gordon Jacob, 1953

1. God bless our na - tive land; firm may she ev - er stand
2. For her our prayer shall rise to God a - bove the skies;
3. Of man - y a race and birth from ut - most ends of earth,

1. through storm and night; when the wild tem - pests rave, rul - er of
2. on thee we wait; thou who art ev - er nigh, guard - ing with
3. God save us all! Bid strife and ha - tred cease, bid hope and

1. wind and wave, do thou our coun - try save by thy great might.
2. watch - ful eye, to thee a - loud we cry, "God save the state!"
3. joy in - crease, spread u - ni - ver - sal peace: God save us all!

THE CHRISTIAN AS CITIZEN

This Is My Song

St. 1–2, Lloyd Stone; st. 3, Georgia Harkness

FINLANDIA, 11.10.11.10.11.10

Jean Sibelius, 1899

1. This is my song, O God of all the na-tions, a song of peace for
2. My coun-try's skies are blu-er than the o-cean, and sun-light beams on
3. This is my prayer, O Lord of all earth's king-doms, thy king-dom come, on

1. lands a-far and mine; this is my home, the coun-try where my heart is;
2. clo-ver-leaf and pine; but oth-er lands have sun-light too, and clo-ver,
3. earth thy will be done; let Christ be lift-ed up till all shall serve him,

1. here are my hopes, my dreams, my ho-ly shrine: but oth-er hearts
2. and skies are ev-ery-where as blue as mine: O hear my song,
3. and hearts u-nit-ed learn to live as one: O hear my prayer,

1. in oth-er lands are beat-ing with hopes and dreams as true and high as mine.
2. thou God of all the na-tions, a song of peace for their land and for mine.
3. thou God of all the na-tions. My-self I give thee — let thy will be done.

This tune in a higher key: 154

THE CHRISTIAN AS CITIZEN

498 Christians, Lift Up Your Hearts

John E. Bowers, 1980

SALVE FESTA DIES, Irregular

R. Vaughan Williams, 1906

Descant (any stanza after first)

1. Chris-tians, lift up your hearts, and make this a day of re - joic - ing;

Refrain

1. Chris-tians, lift up your hearts, and make this a day of re - joic - ing;

1. God is our strength and song: glo - ry to his name! name!

1. God is our strength and song: glo - ry and praise to his name! name!

st. 1   *st. 7 Fine*

B

2. This is the house of the Lord, where seek - ers and find - ers are wel - come;
4. Here God's life - giv-ing word once more is pro - claimed to his peo - ple,
6. Sum-moned by Christ's com-mand, his peo - ple draw near to his ta - ble,

NOTE: *In performance the organ introduction should consist only of the measure marked st. 1. The choir should then sing the refrain and the congregation should repeat it after them. This applies only to the beginning of the hymn; thereafter, the refrain is sung by all after each stanza.*

GENERAL WORSHIP

2. en - ter its gates with your praise, fill all its courts with your song:
4. up - lift - ing those who are down, chal - leng - ing all with its truth.
6. glad - ly to greet their Lord, known in the break - ing of bread.

repeat refrain

C (this part may be sung by the choir alone)

3. All those bap - tized in - to Christ share the glo - ry of his res - ur -
5. Those who are bur - dened with sin find here the joy of for -
7. Strong and a - lert in his grace, God's peo - ple are one in their

3. rec - tion, dy - ing with him un-to sin, walk - ing in new - ness of life.
5. give - ness, lay - ing their sins be - fore Christ, par - don and peace their re - ward:
7. wor - ship; kept by his peace they de - part, rea - dy for serv - ing their Lord:

repeat refrain

repeat refrain

Ps. 118:14; Ps. 100:3; Rom. 6:4–5

GENERAL WORSHIP

499 Stand Up and Bless the Lord

CARLISLE, SM

James Montgomery, 1824

Charles Lockhart, 1769

1. Stand up and bless the Lord, ye peo-ple of his choice;
2. Though high a-bove all praise, a-bove all bless-ing high,
3. O for the liv-ing flame from his own al-tar brought,
4. God is our strength and song, and his sal-va-tion ours;
5. Stand up and bless the Lord; the Lord your God a-dore;

5. stand up and bless his glo-rious name, hence-forth for-ev-er-more.

1. stand up and bless the Lord your God with heart and soul and voice.
2. who would not fear his ho-ly name, and laud and mag-ni-fy?
3. to touch our lips, our minds in-spire, and wing to heav'n our thought!
4. then be his love in Christ pro-claimed with all our ran-somed powers.
5. stand up and bless his glo-rious name, hence-forth for-ev-er-more.

This tune in a lower key: 532

Neh. 9:5; Isa. 6:6

500 Gladly to God's Holy Temple

MICHAEL, 8.7.8.7.3.3.7

Erik Routley, 1981

Herbert Howells, 1930, 1977

1. Glad-ly to God's ho-ly tem-ple we in faith have found our way,
2. All a-long the pil-grims' path-way mer-cy's mon-u-ments we trace,
3. As for me and for my house-hold, we will love and serve the Lord,
*4. "Go, bap-tize the wait-ing na-tions: in God's name the peo-ples cheer;
5. Glo-ry to our kind Cre-a-tor, glo-ry to our liv-ing Lord!

GENERAL WORSHIP

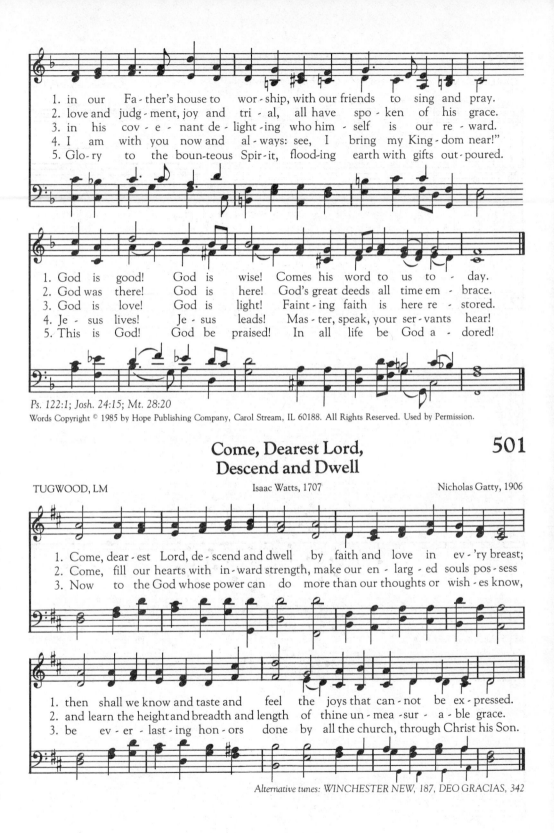

1. in our Fa-ther's house to wor-ship, with our friends to sing and pray.
2. love and judg-ment, joy and tri-al, all have spo-ken of his grace.
3. in his cov-e-nant de-light-ing who him-self is our re-ward.
4. I am with you now and al-ways: see, I bring my King-dom near!"
5. Glo-ry to the boun-teous Spir-it, flood-ing earth with gifts out-poured.

1. God is good! God is wise! Comes his word to us to-day.
2. God was there! God is here! God's great deeds all time em-brace.
3. God is love! God is light! Faint-ing faith is here re-stored.
4. Je-sus lives! Je-sus leads! Mas-ter, speak, your ser-vants hear!
5. This is God! God be praised! In all life be God a-dored!

Ps. 122:1; Josh. 24:15; Mt. 28:20

Come, Dearest Lord, Descend and Dwell

501

TUGWOOD, LM   Isaac Watts, 1707   Nicholas Gatty, 1906

1. Come, dear-est Lord, de-scend and dwell by faith and love in ev-'ry breast;
2. Come, fill our hearts with in-ward strength, make our en-larg-ed souls pos-sess
3. Now to the God whose power can do more than our thoughts or wish-es know,

1. then shall we know and taste and feel the joys that can-not be ex-pressed.
2. and learn the height and breadth and length of thine un-mea-sur-a-ble grace.
3. be ev-er-last-ing hon-ors done by all the church, through Christ his Son.

Alternative tunes: WINCHESTER NEW, 187, DEO GRACIAS, 342

Eph. 3:17—21

502

Open Now Thy Gates of Beauty

Thut mir auf die schöne Pforte, Benjamin Schmolck, 1732;
tr. Catherine Winkworth, 1863

UNSER HERRSCHER, 8.7.8.7.77

Joachim Neander, 1680

Descant, st. 5, by John Dykes Bower

5. Speak, O God, and I will hear thee; let thy will be done in-deed;

1. O - pen now thy gates of beau - ty; Zi - on, let me en - ter there,
2. Here, my God, I come be - fore thee, come thou al - so down to me;
3. Here thy praise is glad - ly chant - ed; here thy seed is du - ly sown;
4. Thou my faith in - crease and quick - en; let me keep thy gift di - vine;
5. Speak, O God, and I will hear thee; let thy will be done in - deed;

5. may I un - dis - turbed draw near thee, while thou dost thy peo - ple feed;

1. where my soul in joy - ful du - ty waits on him who an - swers prayer;
2. where we find thee and a - dore thee, there a heav'n on earth must be;
3. let my soul, where it is plant - ed, bring forth pre - cious sheaves a - lone,
4. how - so - e'er temp - ta - tions thick - en, may thy word still o'er me shine
5. may I un - dis - turbed draw near thee, while thou dost thy peo - ple feed;

5. here of life the foun - tain flows; here is balm for all our woes.

1. O how bless - ed is this place, filled with so - lace, light, and grace.
2. to my heart O en - ter thou, let it be thy tem - ple now.
3. so that all I hear may be fruit - ful un - to life in me.
4. as my guid - ing star through life, as my com - fort in all strife.
5. here of life the foun - tain flows; here is balm for all our woes.

GENERAL WORSHIP

Ps. 118:19

Lord God, Your Love Has Called Us Here 503

Brian Wren, 1973

ABINGDON, 8.8.8.8.88

Erik Routley, 1944

1. Lord God, your love has called us here as we, by love, for love were made.
2. We come with self-inflict-ed pains of bro-ken trust and cho-sen wrong,
3. Lord God, in Christ you call our name and then re-ceive us as your own
4. Then take the towel, and break the bread, and hum-ble us, and call us friends.
5. Lord God, in Christ you set us free, your life to live, your joy to share.

1. Your liv-ing like-ness still we bear, though marred, dis-hon-ored, dis-o-beyed.
2. half free, half bound by in-ner chains, by so-cial forc-es swept a-long,
3. not through some mer-it, right, or claim, but by your gra-cious love a-lone.
4. Suf-fer and serve till all are fed and show how grand-ly love in-tends
5. Give us your Spir-it's lib-er-ty to turn from guilt and dull de-spair

1. We come, with all our heart and mind, your call to hear, your love to find.
2. by pow'rs and sys-tems close con-fined, yet seek-ing hope for hu-man-kind.
3. We strain to glimpse your mer-cy seat and find you kneel-ing at our feet.
4. to work till all cre-a-tion sings, to fill all worlds, to crown all things.
5. and of-fer all that faith can do while love is mak-ing all things new.

Jn. 13:5; Jn. 15:14; Rom. 8:19; II Cor. 3:17

GENERAL WORSHIP

504   Only-Begotten Word of God Eternal

Christe sanctorum Dominator alme,
Latin, c. 9th century; tr. M. J. Blacker, 1906

ISTE CONFESSOR, 11.11.11.5 sapphic   Poitiers, *Antiphoner* (1746)

Unison

1. On - ly - be - got - ten   Word of God e - ter - nal,   Lord of cre - a - tion,
2. Here in our sick - ness   heal - ing grace a - bound - eth; light in our blind - ness,
3. Hal - lowed this dwell - ing where our Lord a - bid - eth;   this is none oth - er
4. Lord, we be - seech thee,   as we throng thy tem - ple,   by thy past bless - ings,
5. God in three per - sons,   Fa - ther ev - er - last - ing,   Son co - e - ter - nal,

1. mer - ci - ful and   might - y,   hear   now   thy   ser - vants
2. in   our toil re -   fresh - ment;   sin   is   for - giv - en,
3. than   the gate of   heav - en;   strang - ers   and   pil - grims
4. by   thy pres - ent   boun - ty,   smile   on   thy   chil - dren,
5. ev -   er bless - ed   Spir - it,   thine   be   the   glo - ry,

1. when their ea - ger   voic - es   rise   to thy pres   -   ence.
2. hope o'er fear pre -   vail - eth,   joy   o - ver sor   -   row.
3. seek - ing homes e -   ter - nal   pass through its por   -   tals.
4. and with ten - der   mer - cy   hear   our pe - ti   -   tions.
5. praise, and a - do -   ra - tion,   now   and for - ev   -   er.

GENERAL WORSHIP   *Ps. 118:19–20; II Chr. 6:21, 39*

Thy Mansion Is the Christian's Heart

William Cowper, 1779 (alt'd)

FESTUS, LM

Melody from the *Bristol Tune Book* (1863);
based on J. A. Freylinghausen, 1704

1. Thy man - sion is the Chris - tian's heart; let all but thoughts of thee de - part!
2. Prayer makes the dark - ened cloud with - draw; prayer climbs the lad - der Ja - cob saw,
3. Re - strain - ing prayer, we cease to fight; prayer keeps the Chris - tian's ar - mor bright;
4. When Mo - ses stood with arms spread wide, suc - cess was found on Is - rael's side;
5. O Lord, in - crease our faith and love, that we may all thy good - ness prove,

1. O Lord, thy dwell - ing place pre - pare; what peace shall reign when thou art there!
2. gives ex - er - cise to faith and love, brings ev - 'ry bless - ing from a - bove.
3. and Sa - tan trem - bles when he sees the weak - est saint up - on his knees.
4. but when through wea - ri - ness they failed, that mo - ment Am - a - lek pre - vailed.
5. and gain from thy ex - haust - less store the fruits of prayer for - ev - er - more.

Alternative tune: INVITATION, 243

Gen. 28:12; Ex. 17:11–12; Rom. 12:1

GENERAL WORSHIP

506 Not for Our Sins Alone

Henry Twells, 1889

REMISSION, 6.6.6.6.6.6

Leonard J. Blake, 1950

1. Not for our sins a - lone thy mer - cy, Lord, we sue;
2. The ho - liest hours we spend in prayer up - on our knees,
3. And all the gifts we bring, and all the vows we make,
4. And most, when we, thy flock, be - fore thine al - tar bend,
5. Bow down thine ear and hear! O - pen thine eyes and see.

1. let fall thy pity - ing glance on our de - vo - tions too,
2. the times when most we deem our songs of praise will please,
3. and all the acts of love we plan for thy dear sake,
4. and strange, be - wil - d'ring thoughts with those sweet mo - ments blend,
5. Our ver - y love is shame, and we must come to thee

1. what we have done for thee, and what we think to do.
2. thou search - er of all hearts, for - give - ness pour on these.
3. in - to thy par - d'ning thought, O God in mer - cy take.
4. by him whose death we plead, good Lord, thy help ex - tend.
5. to make it of thy grace what thou wouldst have it be.

Alternative tune: OLD 120th, 403

GENERAL WORSHIP

Lk. 15:25–30

What a Friend We Have in Jesus

507

Joseph Scriven, c. 1855

WHAT A FRIEND, 8.7.8.7 D

C. C. Converse, 1868

1. What   a friend we have in   Je - sus,   all   our sins and griefs to   bear!
2. Have   we tri - als and temp - ta - tions?   Is   there trou - ble an - y - where?
3. Are   we weak and heav - y   lad - en,   cum - bered with a load of   care?

1. What   a priv - i - lege to   car - ry   ev - ery - thing to God in   prayer!
2. We should nev - er   be dis - cour - aged: take   it   to the Lord in   prayer!
3. Pre - cious Sav - ior, still our   Ref - uge —   take   it   to the Lord in   prayer!

1. O   what peace we of - ten   for - feit,   O what need - less pain we   bear,
2. Can   we find a friend so   faith - ful,   who   will all our sor - rows share?
3. Do   thy friends de - spise, for - sake   thee?   take   it   to the Lord in   prayer!

1. all   be - cause we do not   car - ry   ev - ery - thing to God in   prayer!
2. Je - sus knows our ev - ery   weak - ness —   take   it   to the Lord in   prayer!
3. In   his arms he'll take and shield thee,   thou   wilt find a so - lace there.

Alternative tune: BLAENWERN, 115

GENERAL WORSHIP

508   When in Our Music God Is Glorified

Fred Pratt Green, 1971

ENGELBERG, 10 10 10.4

Charles Villiers Stanford, 1904

1. When in our mu-sic God is glo-ri-fied, and a-do-ra-tion leaves no room for pride, it is as though the whole cre-a-tion cried
2. How of-ten, mak-ing mu-sic, we have found a new di-men-sion in the world of sound, as wor-ship moved us to a more pro-found
3. So has the Church, in lit-ur-gy and song, in faith and love, through cen-tu-ries of wrong, borne wit-ness to the truth in ev-'ry tongue,
4. And did not Je-sus sing a psalm that night when ut-most e-vil strove a-gainst the Light? Then let us sing, for whom he won the fight,
5. Let ev-'ry in-stru-ment be tuned for praise! Let all re-joice who have a voice to raise! And may God give us faith to sing al-ways

st. 1,2,3,4   Al-le-lu-ia!

st. 5   Al-le-lu-ia!

This tune in a lower key: 345

Alternative tune: SINE NOMINE, 397

CHURCH MUSIC

Mk. 14:26

Almighty Father of All Things That Be

Ernest E. Dugmore, 1884, 1900

CHILTON FOLIAT, 10 10. 10 10

G. C. Martin, 1897

1. Al - might - y Fa - ther of all things that be, our
2. For well we know this wea - ry, soil - ed earth is
* 3. Thine still the change - ful beau - ty of the hills, the
4. Thou dost the strength to work - er's arm im - part; from

1. life, our work we con - se - crate to thee, whose heav'ns de - clare thy
2. yet thine own by right of its new birth, since that great cross up -
3. pur - ple val - leys flecked with sil - ver rills, the o - cean glis - t'ning
4. thee the skilled mu - si - cian's rea - soned art, the grace of po - et's

1. glo - ry from a - bove, whose earth be - low is wit - ness to thy love.
2. reared on Cal - va - ry re - deemed it from its fault and shame to thee.
3. 'neath the gold - en rays: they all are thine, and cease - less speak thy praise.
4. pen or paint - er's hand, to teach the love - li - ness of sea and land.

5. Then grant us, Lord, in all things thee to own,
to dwell within the shadow of thy throne,
to speak and work, to think and live and move
reflecting thine own nature, which is love;

6. that so, by Christ redeemed from sin and shame,
and hallowed by thy Spirit's cleansing flame,
ourselves, our work, and all our powers may be
a sacrifice acceptable to thee.

Ps. 19:1; Rom. 12:1

CHURCH MUSIC

510
When the Morning Stars Together

Albert F. Bayly, 1969

WEISSE FLAGGEN, 8.7.8.7 D

Cologne, 1741

1. When the morn-ing stars to-geth-er their Cre-a-tor's glo-ry sang,
2. When in syn-a-gogue and tem-ple voic-es raised the psalm-ists' songs,
3. Voice and in-stru-ment in un-ion through the a-ges spoke thy praise,
4. Lord, we bring our gift of mu-sic; touch our lips and fire our heart,

1. and the an-gel host all shout-ed till with joy the heav-ens rang,
2. of-fer-ing the a-do-ra-tion which a-lone to thee be-longs,
3. plain-song, tune-ful hymns, and an-thems told thy faith-ful gra-cious ways.
4. teach our minds and train our sens-es, fit us for this sa-cred art.

1. then thy wis-dom and thy great-ness their ex-ul-tant mu-sic told,
2. when the sing-ers and the cym-bals with the trum-pet made ac-cord,
3. Choir and or-ches-tra and or-gan each a sa-cred of-fring brought,
4. Then with skill and con-se-cra-tion we would serve thee, Lord, and give

1. all the beau-ty and the splen-dor which thy might-y works un-fold.
2. glo-ry filled the house of wor-ship, and all knew thy pres-ence, Lord.
3. while, in-spired by thine own Spir-it, po-et and com-pos-er wrought.
4. all our powers to glo-ri-fy thee, and in serv-ing ful-ly live.

CHURCH MUSIC

Job 38:7; II Chr. 5:13–14

O Day of Rest and Gladness

Christopher Wordsworth, 1862

CRÜGER, 7.6.7.6 D iambic

W. H. Monk, 1868; from J. Crüger, 1596–1662

1. O day of rest and glad - ness, O day of joy and light,
2. On thee at the cre - a - tion the light first had its birth,
3. New grac - es ev - er gain - ing from this our day of rest,

1. O balm of care and sad - ness, most beau - ti - ful, most bright!
2. on thee for our sal - va - tion Christ rose from depths of earth;
3. we reach the rest re - main - ing to spir - its of the blest.

1. On thee the high and low - ly be - fore th'e - ter - nal throne
2. on thee our Lord vic - to - rious, the Spir - it sent from heav'n,
3. To Ho - ly Ghost be prais - es, to Fa - ther and to Son;

1. sing "Ho - ly, ho - ly, ho - ly" to the great Three - in - One.
2. and thus on thee most glo - rious a tri - ple light was giv'n.
3. the Church her voice up - rais - es to thee, blest Three - in - One.

512

Come, Let Us with Our Lord Arise

Charles Wesley, 1763

COTSWOLD, 88.88.88

Alexander Brent Smith, c. 1925

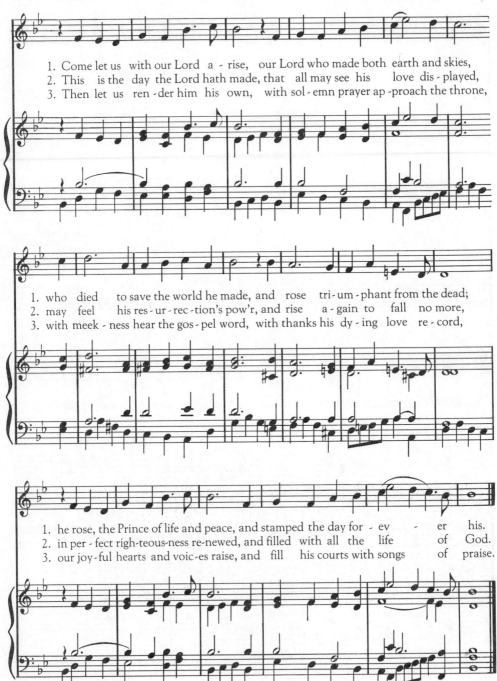

1. Come let us with our Lord a - rise, our Lord who made both earth and skies,
2. This is the day the Lord hath made, that all may see his love dis - played,
3. Then let us ren - der him his own, with sol - emn prayer ap - proach the throne,

1. who died to save the world he made, and rose tri - um - phant from the dead;
2. may feel his res - ur - rec - tion's pow'r, and rise a - gain to fall no more,
3. with meek - ness hear the gos - pel word, with thanks his dy - ing love re - cord,

1. he rose, the Prince of life and peace, and stamped the day for - ev - er his.
2. in per - fect righ - teous - ness re - newed, and filled with all the life of God.
3. our joy - ful hearts and voic - es raise, and fill his courts with songs of praise.

SPECIAL TIMES OF WORSHIP

Lord, as We Rise to Leave the Shell of Worship **513**

Fred Kaan, 1968

ARTISTS' PROCESSION, 11.11.11.5

Ronald L. Neal, 1978

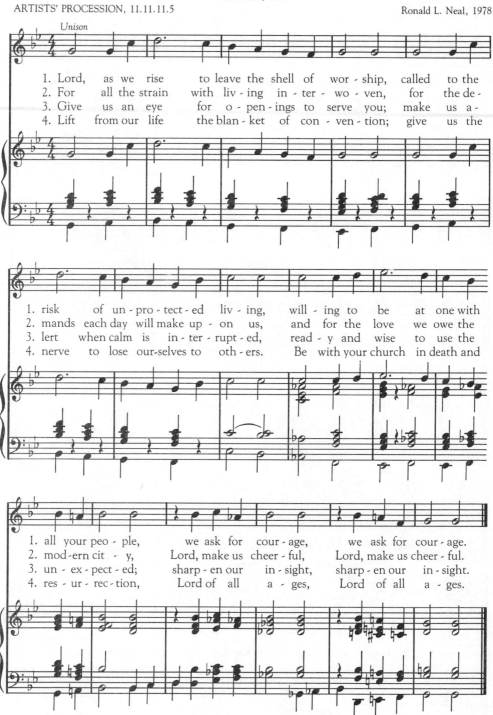

1. Lord, as we rise to leave the shell of wor-ship, called to the
2. For all the strain with liv-ing in-ter-wo-ven, for the de-
3. Give us an eye for o-pen-ings to serve you; make us a-
4. Lift from our life the blan-ket of con-ven-tion; give us the

1. risk of un-pro-tect-ed liv-ing, will-ing to be at one with
2. mands each day will make up-on us, and for the love we owe the
3. lert when calm is in-ter-rupt-ed, read-y and wise to use the
4. nerve to lose our-selves to oth-ers. Be with your church in death and

1. all your peo-ple, we ask for cour-age, we ask for cour-age.
2. mod-ern cit-y, Lord, make us cheer-ful, Lord, make us cheer-ful.
3. un-ex-pect-ed; sharp-en our in-sight, sharp-en our in-sight.
4. res-ur-rec-tion, Lord of all a-ges, Lord of all a-ges.

SPECIAL TIMES OF WORSHIP

514 The First Day of the Week

Fred Pratt Green, 1967

SANDYS, SM

English carol melody

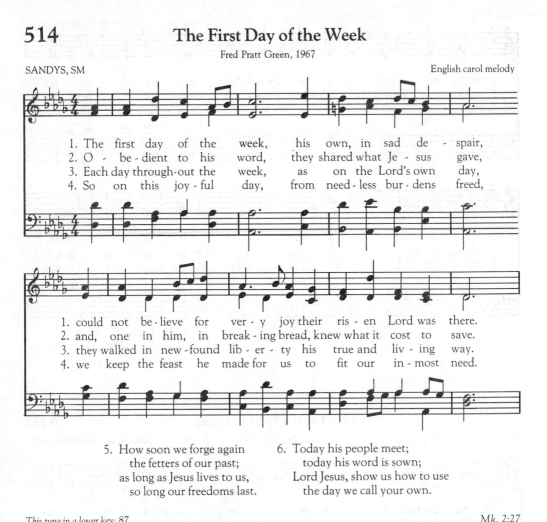

1. The first day of the week, his own, in sad de - spair,
2. O - be - dient to his word, they shared what Je - sus gave,
3. Each day through-out the week, as on the Lord's own day,
4. So on this joy - ful day, from need - less bur - dens freed,

1. could not be - lieve for ver - y joy their ris - en Lord was there.
2. and, one in him, in break - ing bread, knew what it cost to save.
3. they walked in new - found lib - er - ty his true and liv - ing way.
4. we keep the feast he made for us to fit our in - most need.

5. How soon we forge again
   the fetters of our past;
   as long as Jesus lives to us,
   so long our freedoms last.

6. Today his people meet;
   today his word is sown;
   Lord Jesus, show us how to use
   the day we call your own.

This tune in a lower key: 87

Mk. 2:27

515 Father, We Praise Thee, Now the Night Is Over

Nocte Surgentes, possibly by Pope Gregory I, d. 604; tr. Percy Dearmer, 1906

CHRISTE SANCTORUM, 11.11.11.5 sapphic

Later form of melody in *Paris Antiphoner* (1681)

1. Fa - ther, we praise thee, now the night is o - ver; ac - tive and
2. Mon - arch of all things, fit us for thy man - sions; ban - ish our
3. All - ho - ly Fa - ther, Son, and Ho - ly Spir - it, Trin - i - ty

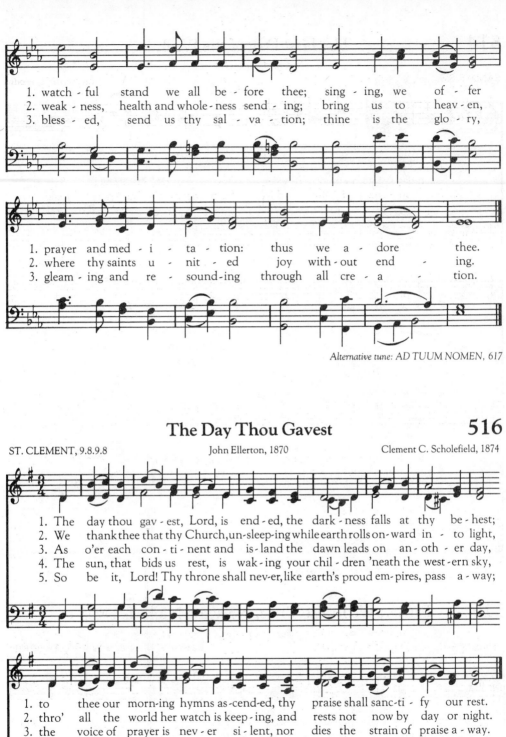

1. watch - ful stand we all be - fore thee; sing - ing, we of - fer
2. weak - ness, health and whole - ness send - ing; bring us to heav - en,
3. bless - ed, send us thy sal - va - tion; thine is the glo - ry,

1. prayer and med - i - ta - tion: thus we a - dore thee.
2. where thy saints u - nit - ed joy with - out end - ing.
3. gleam - ing and re - sound - ing through all cre - a - tion.

Alternative tune: AD TUUM NOMEN, 617

The Day Thou Gavest

516

ST. CLEMENT, 9.8.9.8   John Ellerton, 1870   Clement C. Scholefield, 1874

1. The day thou gav - est, Lord, is end - ed, the dark - ness falls at thy be - hest;
2. We thank thee that thy Church, un - sleep - ing while earth rolls on - ward in - to light,
3. As o'er each con - ti - nent and is - land the dawn leads on an - oth - er day,
4. The sun, that bids us rest, is wak - ing your chil - dren 'neath the west - ern sky,
5. So be it, Lord! Thy throne shall nev - er, like earth's proud em - pires, pass a - way;

1. to thee our morn - ing hymns as - cend - ed, thy praise shall sanc - ti - fy our rest.
2. thro' all the world her watch is keep - ing, and rests not now by day or night.
3. the voice of prayer is nev - er si - lent, nor dies the strain of praise a - way.
4. and hour by hour fresh lips are mak - ing thy won - drous do - ings heard on high.
5. thy king - dom stands and grows for - ev - er, till all thy crea - tures own thy sway.

517   Savior, Again to Thy Dear Name We Raise

John Ellerton, 1866

ELLERS, 10 10.10 10   E. J. Hopkins, 1869; harmonized by Sir Arthur Sullivan

1. Sav - ior, a - gain to thy dear name we raise with one ac -
*2. Grant us thy peace, Lord, through the com - ing night; turn thou for
3. Grant us thy peace through - out our earth - ly life; peace to thy
4. thy peace in life, the balm of ev - 'ry pain; thy peace in

1. cord our part - ing hymn of praise. Guard thou the lips from
2. us its dark - ness in - to light; from harm and dan - ger
3. church from er - ror and from strife; peace to our land, the
4. death, the hope to rise a - gain; then when thy voice shall

1. sin, the hearts from shame, that in this house have called up - on thy name.
2. keep thy chil - dren free, for dark and light are both a - like to thee.
3. fruit of truth and love; peace in each heart, thy Spir - it from a - bove;
4. bid our con - flict cease, call us, O Lord, to thine e - ter - nal peace.

NOTE: Omit st. 2 when the hymn is not sung in the evening.

518   Sun of My Soul, Thou Savior Dear

John Keble, 1827

HURSLEY, LM   Arranged (1861) from *Grosser Gott, wir loben dich*,
in *Katholischer Gesangbuch* (1774)

1. Sun of my soul, thou Sav - ior dear, it is not night if thou be near;
2. When the soft dews of kind - ly sleep my wea - ried eye - lids gent - ly steep,
3. A - bide with me from morn till eve, for with - out thee I can - not live;
4. Watch by the sick; en - rich the poor with bless - ings from thy bound - less store;
5. Come near and bless us when we wake, ere through the world our way we take,

1. O may no earth-born cloud a-rise to hide thee from thy ser-vant's eyes.
2. be my last thought, how sweet to rest for-ev-er on my Sav-ior's breast.
3. a-bide with me when night is nigh, for with-out thee I dare not die.
4. be ev-ery mourn-er's sleep to-night, like in-fants' slum-bers, pure and light.
5. till in the o-cean of thy love we lose our-selves in heav-en a-bove.

Surprised by Joy

519

Erik Routley, 1976

MELCOMBE (O SALUTARIS), LM

Samuel Webbe, 1782

1. Sur - prised by joy no song can tell, no thought can com - pass, here we stand
2. Be - yond an an - gel's mind is this, best gift, a - lone to mor - tals giv'n;
3. Faith, hope, and love here come a - live; God's ver - y be - ing is made known
4. For all this splen-dor, all this joy is ours be-cause a Fa - ther's care —
5. Your ban - ner o - ver us be love, your grace re - fresh our trav - 'ling days,

1. to cel - e - brate e - ter - nal Love, to reach for God's al - might - y hand.
2. the love of par - ent, lov - er, friend brings straight to earth the bliss of heaven.
3. when, giv - ing and for - giv - ing all, two are in - sep - a - ra - bly one.
4. large, gen - 'rous, pa - tient, strong as death—showed us in Christ what love can dare.
5. your power sus - tain, your beau - ty cheer; our words, our home, our lives be praise!

This tune in a higher key: 73

Alternative tune: HERONGATE, 71

MARRIAGE, FAMILY, FRIENDS

520

Crown with Love, Lord, This Glad Day

Ian Fraser, 1966

RATISBON, 7.7.7.7.77   Freylinghausen's *Gesangbuch* (1704); revised in Werner's *Gesangbuch* (1815)

1. Crown with love, Lord, this glad day, love to hum-ble and de-light,
2. Lord, give joy on this glad day, joy to face life's hurt and ill,
3. Crown with peace, Lord, this glad day, peace the world may not in-vent,

1. love which un-til death will stay, love to taste the depth and height
2. all that tests the wed-ded way, forg-ing un-ion deep or still,
3. nor mis-for-tune strip a-way: part-ners, in your will con-tent,

1. of that love which took our part, spend-thrift in its gen-'rous art.
2. joy like his who, for our gain, light-ly weighed the cross and pain.
3. know-ing love will nev-er cease from its source, who is our Peace.

MARRIAGE, FAMILY, FRIENDS   Jn. 14:27

Joyful, Joyful We Adore Thee

521

Henry Van Dyke, 1907

HYMN TO JOY, 8.7.8.7 D

Adapted by Elam Ives, 1846, and others, from a theme in the
Ninth Symphony of Ludwig van Beethoven, 1824

1. Joy - ful, joy - ful we a - dore thee, God of glo - ry, Lord of love;
2. All thy works with joy sur - round thee, earth and heaven re - flect thy rays,
3. Thou art giv - ing and for - giv - ing, ev - er bless - ing, ev - er blest.

1. hearts un - fold like flowers be - fore thee, o - pening to the sun a - bove.
2. stars and an - gels sing a - round thee, cen - ter of un - bro - ken praise.
3. Well - spring of the joy of liv - ing, o - cean depth of hap - py rest!

1. Melt the clouds of sin and sad - ness, drive the dark of doubt a - way;
2. Field and for - est, vale and moun - tain, flow - ery mead - ow, flash - ing sea,
3. Thou our Fa - ther, Christ our Broth - er, all who live in love are thine;

1. Giv - er of im - mor - tal glad - ness, fill us with the light of day.
2. chant - ing bird and flow - ing foun - tain, call us to re - joice in thee.
3. teach us how to love each oth - er, lift us to the joy di - vine.

Ps. 145:10a

MARRIAGE, FAMILY, FRIENDS

522

Our Father, by Whose Name †

F. Bland Tucker, 1938

RHOSYMEDRE, 6.6.6.6.888

John David Edwards, c. 1840

1. Our Fa - ther, by whose Name all fa - ther - hood is known,
2. O Christ, thy - self a child with - in an earth - ly home,
3. O Spir - it, who dost bind our hearts in u - ni - ty,

1. who dost in love pro - claim each fam - i - ly thine own,
2. with heart still un - de - filed, thou didst to man - hood come;
3. who teach - est us to find the love from self set free,

1. bless thou all par - ents, guard - ing well, with con - stant love
2. our chil - dren bless, in ev - 'ry place, that they may all
3. in all our hearts such love in - crease, that ev - 'ry home,

1. as sen - ti - nel, the homes in which thy peo - ple dwell.
2. be - hold thy face, and know - ing thee may grow in grace.
3. by this re - lease, may be the dwell - ing place of peace.

MARRIAGE, FAMILY, FRIENDS

Eph. 3:15

O Love That Casts Out Fear
523

Horatius Bonar, 1858

QUAM DILECTA, 6.6.6.6

Henry L. Jenner, 1861

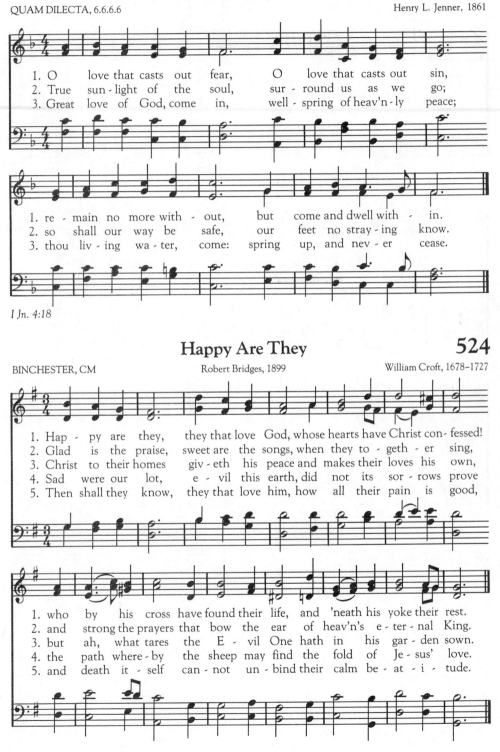

1. O love that casts out fear, O love that casts out sin,
2. True sunlight of the soul, surround us as we go;
3. Great love of God, come in, wellspring of heav'nly peace;

1. remain no more without, but come and dwell within.
2. so shall our way be safe, our feet no straying know.
3. thou living water, come: spring up, and never cease.

I Jn. 4:18

Happy Are They
524

BINCHESTER, CM

Robert Bridges, 1899

William Croft, 1678–1727

1. Happy are they, they that love God, whose hearts have Christ confessed!
2. Glad is the praise, sweet are the songs, when they together sing,
3. Christ to their homes giveth his peace and makes their loves his own,
4. Sad were our lot, evil this earth, did not its sorrows prove
5. Then shall they know, they that love him, how all their pain is good,

1. who by his cross have found their life, and 'neath his yoke their rest.
2. and strong the prayers that bow the ear of heav'n's eternal King.
3. but ah, what tares the Evil One hath in his garden sown.
4. the path whereby the sheep may find the fold of Jesus' love.
5. and death itself cannot unbind their calm beatitude.

MARRIAGE, FAMILY, FRIENDS

525   Eternal Father, Strong to Save

William Whiting, 1860

MELITA, 88.88.88

J. B. Dykes, 1861

1. E - ter - nal Fa - ther, strong to save, whose arm doth bind the rest - less wave,
2. O Sav - ior, whose al - might - y word the winds and waves sub - mis - sive heard,
3. O sa - cred Spir - it who didst brood up - on the cha - os dark and rude,
4. O Trin - i - ty of love and power, thy chil - dren shield in dan - ger's hour;

1. who bid'st the might - y o - cean deep its own ap - point - ed lim - its keep:
2. who walk - edst on the foam - ing deep and calm a - mid its rage didst sleep:
3. who bad'st its an - gry tu - mult cease, and gav - est light and life and peace:
4. from rock and tem - pest, fire and foe, pro - tect them where - so - e'er they go;

1. O hear us when we cry to thee for those in per - il on the sea.
2. O hear us when we cry to thee for those in per - il on the sea.
3. O hear us when we cry to thee for those in per - il on the sea.
4. and ev - er let there rise to thee glad hymns of praise from land and sea.

MARRIAGE, FAMILY, FRIENDS

Almighty Father, Strong to Save

526

Tune MELITA, opposite page

St. 1 and 4, William Whiting, 1860 (alt'd 1937);
st. 2 and 3, Robert Spencer, 1937

1. Almighty Father, strong to save,
whose arm hath bound the restless wave,
who bid'st the mighty ocean deep
its own appointed limits keep:
O hear us when we cry to thee
for those in peril on the sea.

2. O Christ, the Lord of hill and plain
o'er which our traffic runs amain
by mountain pass or valley low;
wherever, Lord, thy loved ones go,
protect them by thy guarding hand
from every peril on the land.

3. O Spirit, whom the Father sent
to spread abroad the firmament;
O Wind of heaven, by the might
save all who dare the eagle's flight,
and keep them by thy watchful care
from every peril in the air.

4. O Trinity of love and power,
thy children shield in danger's hour;
from rock and tempest, fire and foe,
protect them wheresoe'er they go;
thus evermore shall rise to thee
glad praise from air and land and sea.

We Praise You, Lord, for Jesus Christ

527

Judith O'Neill, 1975 (alt'd)

TALLIS' ORDINAL, CM

Thomas Tallis, c. 1557

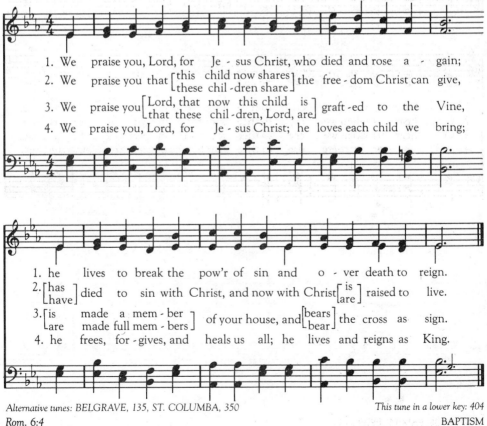

1. We praise you, Lord, for Je - sus Christ, who died and rose a - gain;
2. We praise you that [this child now shares / these chil -dren share] the free - dom Christ can give,
3. We praise you [Lord, that now this child is / that these chil -dren, Lord, are] graft -ed to the Vine,
4. We praise you, Lord, for Je - sus Christ; he loves each child we bring;

1. he lives to break the pow'r of sin and o - ver death to reign.
2. [has / have] died to sin with Christ, and now with Christ [is / are] raised to live.
3. [is / are] made a mem - ber / made full mem - bers] of your house, and [bears / bear] the cross as sign.
4. he frees, for - gives, and heals us all; he lives and reigns as King.

Alternative tunes: BELGRAVE, 135, ST. COLUMBA, 350

This tune in a lower key: 404

Rom. 6:4

BAPTISM

528 We Know That Christ Is Raised and Dies No More

John B. Geyer, 1964

ENGELBERG, 10.10.10 with Alleluia

Charles Villiers Stanford, 1904

1. We know that Christ is raised and dies no more; em-braced by
2. We share by wa - ter in his sav - ing death; this un - ion
3. The Fa - ther's splen - dor clothes the Son with life; the Spir - it's
4. A new cre - a - tion comes to life and grows as Christ's new

1. fu - tile death he broke its hold, and our de - spair he turned to
2. brings to be - ing one new cell, a liv - ing and or - gan - ic
3. fis - sion shakes the church of God; bap - tized, we live with God, the
4. Bod - y takes on flesh and blood; the u - ni - verse re - stored and

st. 1,2,3   *st. 4*

1. blaz - ing joy. Al - le - lu - ia!
2. part of Christ. Al - le - lu - ia!
3. Three - in - One: Al - le - lu - ia!
4. whole will sing, "Al - le - lu - ia!"

This tune in a lower key: 345

Alternative tune: SINE NOMINE, 397

BAPTISM

Rom. 6:4

Baptized into Your Name Most Holy

529

Ich bin getauft in deinem Namen, by J. J. Rambach, 1723;
tr. Catherine Winkworth, 1863; revised in *Lutheran Book of Worship* (1978)

MENTZER, 9.8.9.8.88   Melody in J. B. König's *Harmonischer Liederschatz* (1738)

1. Bap - tized in - to your name most ho - ly, O Fa - ther, Son, and
2. My lov - ing Fa - ther, you have made me to be your hon - ored
3. O faith - ful God, you nev - er fail me; your cov - 'nant sure - ly
4. All that I am and love most dear - ly, re - ceive it all, O

1. Ho - ly Ghost, I claim a place, though weak and low - ly, a -
2. child and heir; my faith - ful Sav - ior, here you make me the
3. will a - bide; let not e - ter - nal death as - sail me should
4. Lord, from me. Oh, let me make my vows sin - cere - ly, and

1. mong your seed, your cho - sen host. Bur - ied with Christ, and
2. fruit of all your sor - rows share; O Ho - ly Ghost, you
3. I trans - gress it on my side. Have mer - cy when I
4. help me your own child to be! Let noth - ing that I

1. dead to sin, I have your Spir - it now with - in.
2. com - fort me though threat - 'ning clouds a - round I see.
3. come de - filed; for - give, re - store, lift up your child.
4. am or own serve an - y will but yours a - lone.

St. 3–4 may be used on other occasions; alternative tune: NEUMARK, 151

Jn. 3:5   BAPTISM

530

Blessed Jesus, We Are Here

Liebster Jesu, by Benjamin Schmolck;
tr. Catherine Winkworth, 1863, and *Lutheran Book of Worship* (1978) (alt'd)

LIEBSTER JESU, 7.8.7.8.88

Later form of melody by J. R. Ahle, 1664

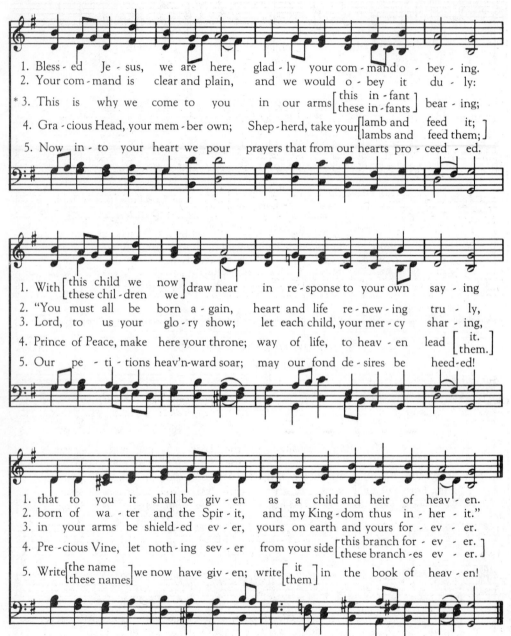

1. Bless-ed Je-sus, we are here, glad-ly your com-mand o - bey-ing.
2. Your com-mand is clear and plain, and we would o - bey it du - ly:
*3. This is why we come to you in our arms [this in-fant / these in-fants] bear-ing;
4. Gra-cious Head, your mem-ber own; Shep-herd, take your [lamb and feed it; / lambs and feed them;]
5. Now in-to your heart we pour prayers that from our hearts pro - ceed - ed.

1. With [this child we now / these chil-dren we] draw near in re-sponse to your own say - ing
2. "You must all be born a-gain, heart and life re-new-ing tru - ly,
3. Lord, to us your glo-ry show; let each child, your mer-cy shar - ing,
4. Prince of Peace, make here your throne; way of life, to heav - en lead [it. / them.]
5. Our pe - ti - tions heav'n-ward soar; may our fond de-sires be heed-ed!

1. that to you it shall be giv - en as a child and heir of heav'- en.
2. born of wa - ter and the Spir - it, and my King-dom thus in - her - it."
3. in your arms be shield-ed ev - er, yours on earth and yours for - ev - er.
4. Pre -cious Vine, let noth-ing sev - er from your side [this branch for - ev - er. / these branch -es ev - er.]
5. Write [the name / these names] we now have giv - en; write [it / them] in the book of heav - en!

BAPTISM

Rom. 6:4

Lord Jesus, Once a Child 531

Fred Pratt Green, 1971 (alt'd)

FRANCONIA, SM

W. H. Havergal, 1847; based on a chorale by J. B. König, 1738

1. Lord Je-sus, once a child, Sav-ior of young and old,
2. You drank the cup of life, its bit-ter-ness and bliss,
3. So help us, Lord, to trust, through this bap-tis-mal rite,

1. re-ceive [this lit-tle child of ours] [these lit-tle chil-dren now] in-to your flock and fold.
2. and loved us to the ut-ter-most for [such a child as this.] [chil-dren such as these.]
3. not in our own im-per-fect love, but in your sav-ing might.

This tune in a lower key: 236

Words Copyright © 1971 by Hope Publishing Company, Carol Stream, IL 60188. All Rights Reserved. Used by Permission.

The Son of God Proclaim 532

Basil E. Bridge, 1969

CARLISLE, SM

C. Lockhart, 1769

1. The Son of God pro-claim, the Lord of time and space;
2. He, God's cre-a-tive Word, the Church's Lord and Head,
*3. Be-hold his out-stretched hands; though all with-in his power.
4. The Lord of life and death with won-d'ring praise we sing;
5. We take this cup in hope; for he who glad-ly bore

1. the God who bade the light break forth now shines in Je-sus' face.
2. here bids us gath-er as his friends and share his wine and bread.
3. He took the towel and ba-sin then and serves us in this hour.
4. we break the bread at his com-mand and name him God and King.
5. the shame-ful cross is ris'n a-gain and reigns for-ev-er-more.

I Cor. 11:24-25   *This tune in a higher key: 499*   BAPTISM/LORD'S SUPPER

533

As the Disciples,
When Thy Son Had Left Them

Percy Dearmer, 1931

AD TUUM NOMEN, 11.11.11.5

Chartres Antiphoner (1784)

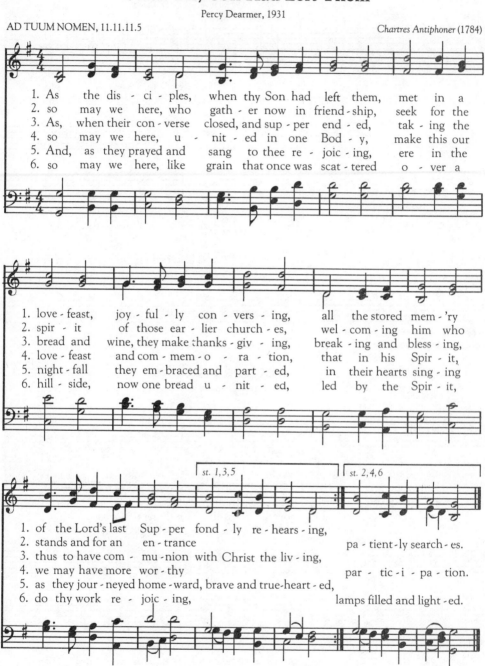

1. As the dis - ci - ples, when thy Son had left them, met in a
2. so may we here, who gath - er now in friend - ship, seek for the
3. As, when their con - verse closed, and sup - per end - ed, tak - ing the
4. so may we here, u - nit - ed in one Bod - y, make this our
5. And, as they prayed and sang to thee re - joic - ing, ere in the
6. so may we here, like grain that once was scat - tered o - ver a

1. love - feast, joy - ful - ly con - vers - ing, all the stored mem - 'ry
2. spir - it of those ear - lier church - es, wel - com - ing him who
3. bread and wine, they make thanks - giv - ing, break - ing and bless - ing,
4. love - feast and com - mem - o - ra - tion, that in his Spir - it,
5. night - fall they em - braced and part - ed, in their hearts sing - ing
6. hill - side, now one bread u - nit - ed, led by the Spir - it,

st. 1,3,5   *st. 2,4,6*

1. of the Lord's last Sup - per fond - ly re - hears - ing,
2. stands and for an en - trance   pa - tient - ly search - es.
3. thus to have com - mu - nion with Christ the liv - ing,
4. we may have more wor - thy   par - tic - i - pa - tion.
5. as they jour - neyed home - ward, brave and true - heart - ed,
6. do thy work re - joic - ing,   lamps filled and light - ed.

Alternative tune: CHRISTE SANCTORUM, 515

I Come with Joy to Meet My Lord

534

LAND OF REST, CM — Brian Wren, 1968 rev. — American folk melody

1. I come with joy to meet my Lord, for - giv - en, loved, and free,
2. I come with Chris - tians far and near to find, as all are fed,
3. As Christ breaks bread and bids us share, each proud di - vi - sion ends;
4. And thus with joy we meet our Lord; his pres - ence, al - ways near,
5. To - geth - er met, to - geth - er bound, we'll go our dif - f'rent ways,

1. in awe and won - der to re - call his life laid down for me.
2. the new com - mu - ni - ty of love in Christ's com - mu - nion bread.
3. the love that made us, makes us one, and strang - ers now are friends.
4. is in such friend - ship bet - ter known: we see and praise him here.
5. and as his peo - ple in the world we'll live and speak his praise.

Alternative tune: ST. AGNES, 359   *This tune in a higher key: 360*

Come, Be Our Hearts' Beloved Guest

535

Ach komm, du süsser Herzens-Gast, by Lueder Mencken, 1698;
tr. anon. in Moravian hymnals from 1784 (alt'd)

ACH GOTT UND HERR, 8.7.8.7 iambic — Arranged by J. S. Bach from a melody in *As hymnodus sacer* (1625)

1. Come, be our hearts' be - lov - ed guest, our joy be - yond all tell - ing,
2. O keep thy ban - quet, Lord, with us, with sin - ners poor and need - y,
3. We o - pen hearts and souls to thee, Lord Je - sus, to re - ceive thee;

1. for on - ly they on earth are blest with whom thou hast thy dwell - ing.
2. since gra - cious - ly thou call - est thus: "Come, all things now are read - y."
3. for thee we long most ar - dent - ly; O may we nev - er leave thee!

Lk. 14:17   *Alternative tune: MALABAR, 569*   LORD'S SUPPER

536

Deck Thyself, My Soul, with Gladness

Schmücke dich, by J. Franck, 1649; tr. Catherine Winkworth, 1863

SCHMUCKE DICH, 88.88 D trochaic

Melody by Johann Crüger, 1649

1. Deck thy-self, my soul, with glad-ness; leave the gloom-y haunts of sad-ness;
2. Sun who all my life dost bright-en, light who dost my soul en-light-en,
3. "Je-sus, Bread of life, I pray thee, let me glad-ly here o-bey thee;

1. come in-to the day-light's splen-dor, there with joy thy prais-es ren-der
2. joy the best a heart e'er know-eth, fount whence all my be-ing flow-eth:
3. nev-er to my hurt in-vit-ed, be thy love with love re-quit-ed;

1. un-to him whose grace un-bound-ed hath this won-drous ban-quet found-ed;
2. at thy feet I cry, "My Mak-er, let me be a fit par-tak-er
3. from this ban-quet let me mea-sure, Lord, how vast and deep its trea-sure;

1. high o'er all the heav'ns he reign-eth, yet to dwell with thee he deign-eth.
2. of this bless-ed food from heav-en for our good, thy glo-ry giv-en.
3. through the gifts thou here dost give me, as thy guest in heav'n re-ceive me."

LORD'S SUPPER

Lord, Enthroned in Heavenly Splendor

537

G. H. Bourne, 1874

ST. HELENA, 8.7.8.7.4.7

G. W. Martin, 1889

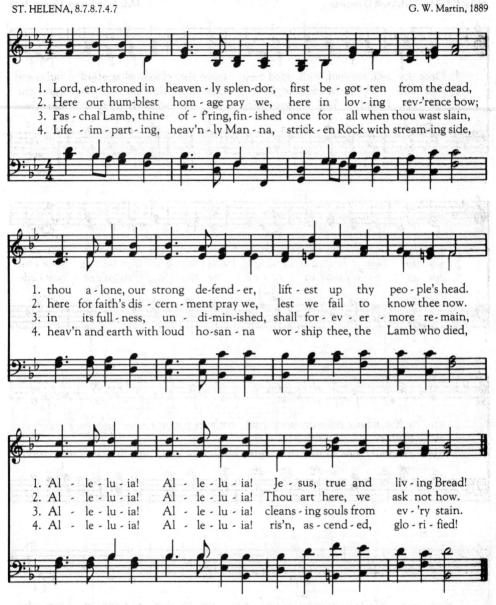

1. Lord, en-throned in heaven-ly splen-dor, first be-got-ten from the dead,
2. Here our hum-blest hom-age pay we, here in lov-ing rev-'rence bow;
3. Pas-chal Lamb, thine of-f'ring, fin-ished once for all when thou wast slain,
4. Life - im-part-ing, heav'n-ly Man-na, strick-en Rock with stream-ing side,

1. thou a-lone, our strong de-fend-er, lift-est up thy peo-ple's head.
2. here for faith's dis-cern-ment pray we, lest we fail to know thee now.
3. in its full-ness, un-di-min-ished, shall for-ev-er -more re-main,
4. heav'n and earth with loud ho-san-na wor-ship thee, the Lamb who died,

1. Al - le-lu-ia! Al - le-lu-ia! Je - sus, true and liv-ing Bread!
2. Al - le-lu-ia! Al - le-lu-ia! Thou art here, we ask not how.
3. Al - le-lu-ia! Al - le-lu-ia! cleans-ing souls from ev-'ry stain.
4. Al - le-lu-ia! Al - le-lu-ia! ris'n, as-cend-ed, glo-ri-fied!

Ex. 17:6; Num. 20:11; 1 Cor. 10:4

LORD'S SUPPER

538

Reap Me the Earth

Paul Inwood, 1972

WORLEBURY, 10.7.10.7.4.6.6.6 dactylic

John Ainslie, 1972

1. Reap me the earth as a har-vest to God, gath-er and bring it a
2. Go with your song and your mu-sic, with joy, go to the al-tar of
3. Glad-ness and pit-y and pas-sion and pain, all that is mor-tal in

1. gain, all that is his, to the Mak-er of all, lift it and
2. God, car-ry your of-fer-ings, fruits of the earth, work of your
3. life, lay all be-fore him, re-turn him his gift, God, to whom

Refrain

1. of-fer it high.
2. la-bor-ing hands. } Bring bread, bring wine, give glo-ry to the Lord.
3. all shall go home.

Whose is the earth but God's? Whose is the praise but his?

Ps. 24:1

Upon Thy Table, Lord, We Place

539

ELY, LM

M. F. C. Willson, 1884–1944 (alt'd)

Thomas Turton, 1844

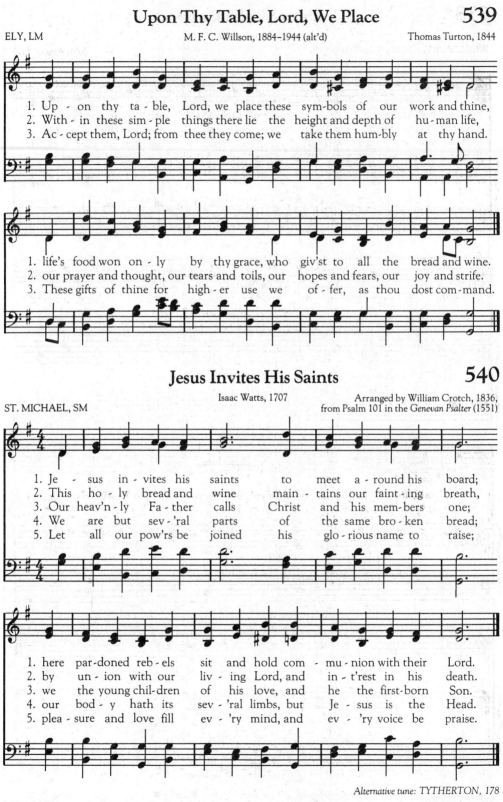

1. Up - on thy ta - ble, Lord, we place these sym-bols of our work and thine,
2. With - in these sim - ple things there lie the height and depth of hu - man life,
3. Ac - cept them, Lord; from thee they come; we take them hum-bly at thy hand.

1. life's food won on - ly by thy grace, who giv'st to all the bread and wine.
2. our prayer and thought, our tears and toils, our hopes and fears, our joy and strife.
3. These gifts of thine for high - er use we of - fer, as thou dost com - mand.

Jesus Invites His Saints

540

Isaac Watts, 1707

ST. MICHAEL, SM

Arranged by William Crotch, 1836,
from Psalm 101 in the *Genevan Psalter* (1551)

1. Je - sus in - vites his saints to meet a - round his board;
2. This ho - ly bread and wine main - tains our faint - ing breath,
3. Our heav'n - ly Fa - ther calls Christ and his mem-bers one;
4. We are but sev - 'ral parts of the same bro - ken bread;
5. Let all our pow'rs be joined his glo - rious name to raise;

1. here par-doned reb - els sit and hold com - mu - nion with their Lord.
2. by un - ion with our liv - ing Lord, and in - t'rest in his death.
3. we the young chil-dren of his love, and he the first-born Son.
4. our bod - y hath its sev - 'ral limbs, but Je - sus is the Head.
5. plea - sure and love fill ev - 'ry mind, and ev - 'ry voice be praise.

Alternative tune: TYTHERTON, 178

I Cor. 12:12

LORD'S SUPPER

541 **God, Your Glory We Have Seen in Your Son**

Dieu, nous avons vu ta gloire, by Didier Rimaud, 1957;
refrain tr. Ronald Johnson; stanzas tr. Brian Wren, 1964

DIEU NOUS AVONS VU TA GLOIRE, Irregular

Jean Langlais, 1957

God, your glory we have seen in your Son,

full of truth, full of heav'n-ly grace; in Christ make us live, his

love shine on our face, and the na-tions shall see in us the tri-umph

you have won.

1. In the fields of this world his good news he has
2. In his love, like a fire that con-sumes, he passed
3. He was bro-ken for us, God-for-sak-en his
4. He has tram-pled the grapes of new life on his
5. He has found-ed a king-dom that none shall de -

1. sown, and sends us out to reap till the har-vest is done.
2. by. The flame has touched our lips; let us shout, "Here am I!"
3. cry, and still the bread he breaks: to our-selves we must die.
4. cross. Now drink the cup and live; he has filled it for us.
5. stroy; the cor-ner-stone is laid; go to work, build with joy!

return to refrain

LORD'S SUPPER

Jn. 1:14; Isa. 6:6–8; Isa. 63:3

At Thy Command, Our Dearest Lord

542

Isaac Watts, 1707

TUGWOOD, LM

Nicholas Gatty, 1906

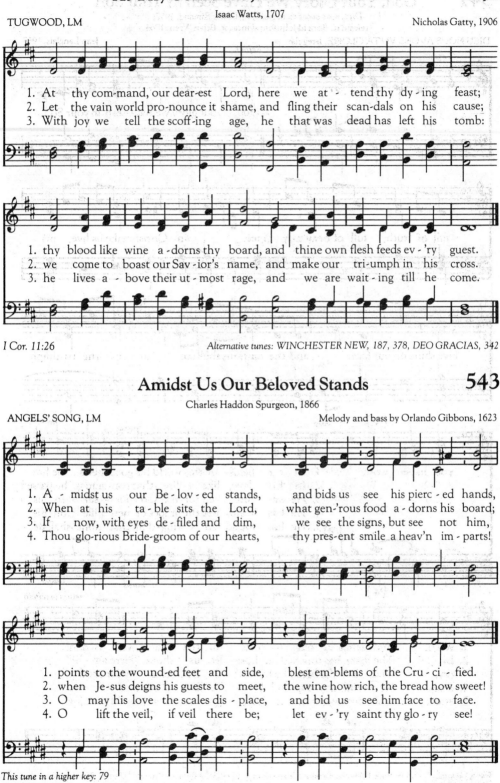

1. At thy com-mand, our dear-est Lord, here we at-tend thy dy-ing feast;
2. Let the vain world pro-nounce it shame, and fling their scan-dals on his cause;
3. With joy we tell the scoff-ing age, he that was dead has left his tomb:

1. thy blood like wine a-dorns thy board, and thine own flesh feeds ev-'ry guest.
2. we come to boast our Sav-ior's name, and make our tri-umph in his cross.
3. he lives a-bove their ut-most rage, and we are wait-ing till he come.

I Cor. 11:26

Alternative tunes: WINCHESTER NEW, 187, 378, DEO GRACIAS, 342

Amidst Us Our Beloved Stands

543

Charles Haddon Spurgeon, 1866

ANGELS' SONG, LM

Melody and bass by Orlando Gibbons, 1623

1. A-midst us our Be-lov-ed stands, and bids us see his pierc-ed hands,
2. When at his ta-ble sits the Lord, what gen-'rous food a-dorns his board;
3. If now, with eyes de-filed and dim, we see the signs, but see not him,
4. Thou glo-rious Bride-groom of our hearts, thy pres-ent smile a heav'n im-parts!

1. points to the wound-ed feet and side, blest em-blems of the Cru-ci-fied.
2. when Je-sus deigns his guests to meet, the wine how rich, the bread how sweet!
3. O may his love the scales dis-place, and bid us see him face to face.
4. O lift the veil, if veil there be; let ev-'ry saint thy glo-ry see!

This tune in a higher key: 79

Jn. 20:27

LORD'S SUPPER

544 **O Lord, Who Hast This Table Spread**

Edward A. Collier, 1889

ROCKINGHAM, LM

Adapted by Edward Miller, 1790, from an earlier tune (1780)

1. O   Lord, who hast this ta - ble spread, what roy-al fare thou dost pro - vide,
2. But   e'en this bread will be a stone, this cup of bless - ing mock our thirst,
3. O   come, then, Lord, and here pre-side: give thine own wel-come to each guest,
4. Then rich the por - tion thou wilt give; no more the hun-g'ring heart can need;

1. thy bro - ken bod - y   for our bread, the cup from thine own wounds sup-plied!
2. un - less thy gra-cious hand a - lone shall bless and give them as   at first.
3. nor let it   be to   love de - nied to lean con - fid - ing on thy breast.
4. thy - self the bread by which we live, thy pre-cious blood our   drink in - deed.

This tune in a lower key, with S. Webbe's harmonies: 292

5. Thus shall thy cross be lifted up
      till thou return, the King confessed,
   to call thine own with thee to sup
      within thy Father's Kingdom blest.

6. O Lord, on high now glorified,
      when wilt thou come to bring us home?
   Hear thou thy Spirit and thy Bride,
      and come, Lord Jesus, quickly come.

LORD'S SUPPER   *Lk. 14:15–24; Rev. 19:9–10; Rev. 22:17*

Anonymous

LET US BREAK BREAD, Irregular   American folk hymn

1. Let us break bread to-geth-er on our knees;

1. let us break bread to-geth-er on our knees. When I fall on my knees with my

Refrain

1. face to the ris-ing sun, O Lord, have mer-cy on me.

2. Let us drink wine together . . . .
3. Let us praise God together . . . .

NOTE: *(1) In places where Communion is not received kneeling, the lines may be sung: "Let us break bread together: praise the Lord!"*
(2) Improvisation of further verses following the pattern of those above is possible and appropriate; the refrain should remain unchanged.

LORD'S SUPPER

546   Lamb of God Unblemished

Hywel Elfed Lewis, 1916

WEM IN LEIDENSTAGEN, 6.5.6.5

F. Filitz, 1847

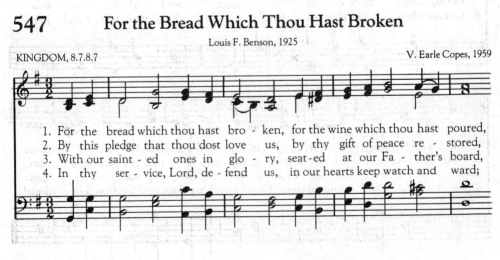

1. Lamb of God un-blem-ished, of-fered for our sin,
2. Love made thee our broth-er, love thine an-guish wrought;
3. By thy ho-ly pas-sion, and thine end-less love,
*4. By the cup of bless-ing and the bro-ken bread,

1. o'er our way-ward spir-its gra-cious tri-umph win.
2. love in thee was sov-'reign, love thy lost ones sought.
3. all that is un-like thee from our hearts re-move.
4. thy re-new-ing spir-it on us all be shed.

5. From each narrow purpose,
   from all barren strife,
   bring us to the fullness
   of the heavenly life.

*6. May each one partaking,
   Savior, be thy guest
   in the Father's kingdom,
   there forever bless'd.

NOTE: *If the starred verses are omitted, this hymn can be used otherwise than at Communion services.*

547   For the Bread Which Thou Hast Broken

Louis F. Benson, 1925

KINGDOM, 8.7.8.7

V. Earle Copes, 1959

1. For the bread which thou hast bro-ken, for the wine which thou hast poured,
2. By this pledge that thou dost love us, by thy gift of peace re-stored,
3. With our saint-ed ones in glo-ry, seat-ed at our Fa-ther's board,
4. In thy ser-vice, Lord, de-fend us, in our hearts keep watch and ward;

1. for the words which thou hast spo-ken, now we give thee thanks, O Lord.
2. by thy call to heav'n a - bove us, hal-low all our lives, O Lord.
3. may thy church that wait-eth for thee keep love's tie un-bro-ken, Lord.
4. in the world where thou dost send us, let thy king-dom come, O Lord.

Alternative tune: CROSS OF JESUS, 349

Father, We Greet Thee 548

J. G. Adderley, 1931

DONNE SECOURS (PSALM 12), 11.10.11.10   Melody in the *Genevan Psalter* (1551)

1. Fa - ther, we greet thee, God of love, whose glo - ry shines mir-rored
2. Fa - ther, we dare, by our great broth-er bid - den, take up the
*3. Here we pre - sent our - selves, our souls and bod - ies, strength-ened with
4. Friends at his ta - ble, priests a - round his al - tar, sol - diers of

1. in the face of Je - sus Christ, who by his per - fect
2. cross and hum-bly fol - low him; send out thy light and
3. bread, the food of ev - 'ry land, read - y to love and
4. Christ, dis - ci - ples of thy Son, Fa - ther, we stand, pre -

1. life of love and la - bor, and in his per-fect death was sac - ri - ficed.
2. truth that they may lead us; show us the way a - mid the dark-ness dim.
3. work, but yet con - fess-ing lone - ly we can-not, by his grace we can.
4. pared to do thy bid-ding; come, God's own king-dom, and God's will be done!

LORD'S SUPPER

549   Here, O My Lord, I See Thee Face to Face

Horatius Bonar, 1858

LANGRAN, 10.10.10.10

James Langran, 1861

1. Here, O my Lord, I see thee face to face; here would I touch and handle things unseen, here grasp with firmer hand th'eternal grace, and all my weariness upon thee lay.

2. Here would I feast upon the bread of God, here drink with thee the royal wine of heav'n; here would I lay aside each earthly load, here taste afresh the calm of sin forgiv'n.

3. This is the hour of banquet and of song; this is the heav'nly table spread for me; here let me feast, and feasting still prolong this hallowed hour of fellowship with thee.

* 4. Too soon we rise: the symbols disappear; the feast, though not the love, is past and gone; the bread and wine remove, but thou art here, nearer than ever, still my Shield and Sun.

*5. I have no help but thine; nor do I need
    another arm save thine to lean upon;
  it is enough, my Lord, enough indeed;
    my strength is in thy might, thy might alone.

*6. Feast after feast thus comes and passes by,
    yet, passing, points to that glad feast above,
  giving sweet foretaste of the festal joy,
    the Lamb's great bridal feast of bliss and love.

NOTE: *The last three stanzas may be separated and sung after the Communion.*

LORD'S SUPPER

Rev. 19:9

Come, Risen Lord, and Deign to Be Our Guest 550

G. W. Briggs, 1931

SURSUM CORDA, 10.10.10.10   Alfred Morton Smith, 1940

1. Come, ris-en Lord, and deign to be our Guest; nay, let us be thy
2. We meet, as in that up-per room they met; thou at the ta-ble,
3. One bod-y we, one bod-y who par-take, one Church u-nit-ed
4. One with each oth-er, Lord, for one in thee, who art our Sav-ior

1. guests; the feast is thine; thy-self at thine own board made man-i-
2. bless-ing, yet dost stand: "This is my bod-y": so thou giv-est
3. in com-mu-nion blest; one name we bear, one bread of life we
4. and our liv-ing Head; then o-pen thou our eyes, that we may

1. fest in this, our sac-ra-ment of bread and wine.
2. yet: faith still re-ceives the cup as from thy hand.
3. break, with all thy saints on earth and saints at rest.
4. see: be known to us in break-ing of the bread.

Lk. 22:12ff; I Cor. 11:24; I Cor. 12:27; Lk. 24:35   LORD'S SUPPER

551

Stanza 1: Bread of the World, in Mercy Broken

Reginald Heber, 1783–1826

Stanza 2 and 3: Father, We Thank Thee Who Hast Planted

Francis Bland Tucker, 1941; based on the *Didache* (c. 200)

RENDEZ A DIEU, 9.8.9.8 D

Strasbourg Psalter (1545); revised in Genevan Psalter (1551)

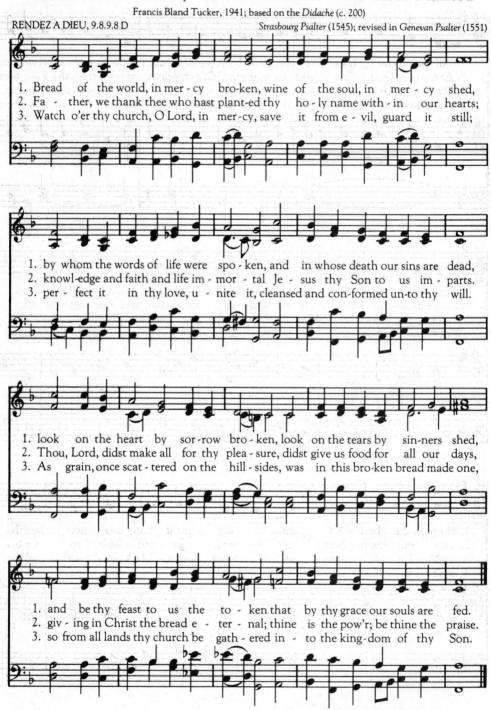

1. Bread of the world, in mer-cy bro-ken, wine of the soul, in mer-cy shed,
2. Fa-ther, we thank thee who hast plant-ed thy ho-ly name with-in our hearts;
3. Watch o'er thy church, O Lord, in mer-cy, save it from e-vil, guard it still;

1. by whom the words of life were spo-ken, and in whose death our sins are dead,
2. knowl-edge and faith and life im-mor-tal Je-sus thy Son to us im-parts.
3. per-fect it in thy love, u-nite it, cleansed and con-formed un-to thy will.

1. look on the heart by sor-row bro-ken, look on the tears by sin-ners shed,
2. Thou, Lord, didst make all for thy plea-sure, didst give us food for all our days,
3. As grain, once scat-tered on the hill-sides, was in this bro-ken bread made one,

1. and be thy feast to us the to-ken that by thy grace our souls are fed.
2. giv-ing in Christ the bread e-ter-nal; thine is the pow'r; be thine the praise.
3. so from all lands thy church be gath-ered in-to the king-dom of thy Son.

This tune in a higher key with a different harmony: 119

LORD'S SUPPER

All Speech Far Transcending

Paraphrase of John Calvin, 1509–1564, by Ford Lewis Battles, 1970

ADORO TE DEVOTE, 6.5.6.5 D

Processional (Paris, 1697)

1. All speech far tran - scend-ing and be-yond all thought, won-der-ful ex - chang-ing
2. Son of God now with us, make us God's chil-dren; com-ing from the Fa - ther,
3. Word of God now call-ing us to pu - ri - ty, of this sup-per make us
4. Au - thor of all jus - tice, turn our un-just ways; heal-er of all sick - ness,

1. pov - er - ty for wealth: to our hope-less weak-ness give your might - y power;
2. raise us now to him. Dy-ing with us hu - man, give us God-like life;
3. wor-thy to par - take; flood us with thanks - giv - ing for your sac-ri - fice,
4. cure our dread dis-ease. In this meal de - clar - ing your death till you come,

1. through the bod - y's eat - ing grant our souls new health.
2. knit our mem - bers to you, fas - ten limb to limb.
3. once for all time of - fered hum - bly for our sake.
4. make us all your house - hold liv - ing in your peace.

I Cor. 11:26

LORD'S SUPPER

553

Come, Bread of Life

Daniel and Melody Meeter, 1981

GENEVA 32, 11 11.10 10 D

Pseaulmes Cinquante (L. Bourgeois), 1547; revision of 1551

1. Come, Bread of life, come down to us from heav-en, as man-na
2. Come, liv-ing Wa-ter, come to us from heav-en, re-fresh-ment

1. to your hun-gry chil-dren giv-en. O come and feed us
2. for your thirst-y chil-dren giv-en. Come, make a riv-er

1. in the wil-der-ness, and with un-end-ing life your chil-dren
2. in the wil-der-ness, a well to sat-is-fy our thirst-i-

1. bless. The ho-ly bread be-fore us is the to-ken by which you
2. ness. The ho-ly wine be-fore us is the to-ken; thus we o-

1. give your pre-cious bod-y bro-ken; who-ev-er eats this
2. bey the word our Lord has spo-ken, who bids us drink, and,

1. bread, O Lord, we know, will nev-er die, and nev-er hun-gry go.
2. deep-ly drink-ing, know that liv-ing wa-ters shall for-ev-er flow.

LORD'S SUPPER

Jn. 6:32, 35

Glory, Love, and Praise, and Honor

Charles Wesley, 1746

BENIFOLD, 8.33.6 D

Francis Westbrook, 1969

1. Glo - ry, love, and praise, and hon - or for our food now be-stowed
2. Thank-ful for our ev - ery bless-ing, let us sing Christ the Spring
3. He dis - pels our sin and sad-ness, life im-parts, cheers our hearts,

1. ren - der we the Do - nor. Boun-teous God, we now con - fess thee;
2. nev - er, nev - er ceas - ing. Source of all our gifts and grac - es,
3. fills with food and glad - ness. Who him - self for all hath giv - en,

1. God, who thus bless-est us, meet it is to bless thee.
2. Christ we own; Christ a - lone calls for all our prais - es.
3. us he feeds, us he leads to a feast in heav - en.

LORD'S SUPPER

555 And Now, O Father, Mindful of the Love

William Bright, 1873

SONG 1, 10.10.10.10.10 10

Melody and bass by Orlando Gibbons, 1623

1. And now, O Father, mindful of the love that bought us, once for all, on Calvary's tree, and having with us him that pleads above, we here present, we here spread forth to thee, that only offering perfect in thine eyes, the one true, pure, immortal sacrifice.

2. Look, Father, look on his anointed face, and only look on us as found in him; look not on our misusings of thy grace, our prayer so languid, and our faith so dim; for lo! between our sins and their reward, we set the passion of thy Son, our Lord.

3. And so we come; O draw us to thy feet, most patient Savior who canst love us still! And by this food, so aweful and so sweet, deliver us from every touch of ill; in thine own service make us glad and free, and grant us nevermore to part with thee.

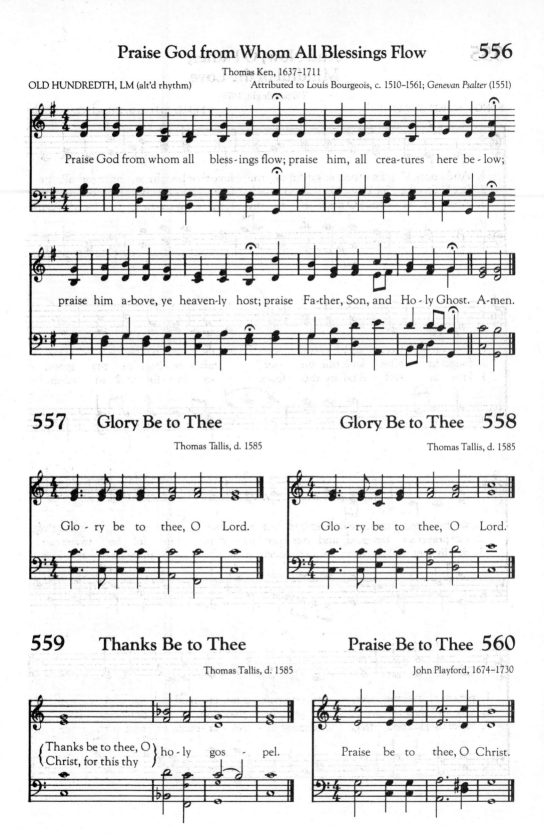

Praise God from Whom All Blessings Flow 556

Thomas Ken, 1637–1711

OLD HUNDREDTH, LM (alt'd rhythm) Attributed to Louis Bourgeois, c. 1510–1561; *Genevan Psalter* (1551)

Praise God from whom all bless-ings flow; praise him, all crea-tures here be-low;

praise him a-bove, ye heaven-ly host; praise Fa-ther, Son, and Ho-ly Ghost. A-men.

557 Glory Be to Thee Glory Be to Thee 558

Thomas Tallis, d. 1585 Thomas Tallis, d. 1585

Glo-ry be to thee, O Lord. Glo-ry be to thee, O Lord.

559 Thanks Be to Thee Praise Be to Thee 560

Thomas Tallis, d. 1585 John Playford, 1674–1730

{ Thanks be to thee, O } ho-ly gos - pel. Praise be to thee, O Christ.
{ Christ, for this thy }

LORD'S SUPPER

561   **Glory Be to the Father**

SETTING I

Henry W. Greatorex, 1813–1858

Glo - ry be to the Fa - ther, and to the Son, and to the
Ho - ly Ghost; as it was in the be - gin - ning, is now, and ev - er
shall be, world with - out end. A - men. A - men.

562   **Glory Be to the Father**

SETTING II

Charles Meineke, 1782–1850

Glo - ry be to the Fa - ther and to the Son and to the
Ho - ly Ghost; as it was in the be - gin - ning, is
now, and ev - er shall be, world with - out end. A - men, A - men.

LORD'S SUPPER

Glory Be to the Father

SETTING III

EHR 'SEI DEM VATER, Tone V

Adapted by Regina H. Fryxell, 1958

Glo - ry be to the Fa - ther, and to the Son,

and to the Ho - ly Ghost: as it was in the be - gin - ning,

is now, and ev - er shall be, world with-out end. A - men.

LORD'S SUPPER

Communion Service I

John Merbecke, 1549

KYRIE

Lord, have mer - cy up - on us; Christ, have mer - cy up - on us; Lord, have mer - cy up - on us.

SANCTUS

Ho - ly, ho - ly, ho - ly, Lord God of hosts;

Heav'n and earth are full of thy glo - ry: Glo - ry be to thee,

BENEDICTUS

O Lord, most high. Bless - ed is he that com - eth

in the name of the Lord. Ho - san - na in the high - est.

LORD'S SUPPER

MISSA PAROCHIALIS

George Oldroyd, 1927

KYRIE

Lord have mer - cy, mer - cy; Christ have mer - cy, mer - cy; Lord have mer - cy, mer - cy.

SANCTUS

Ho - ly, ho - ly, ho - ly, Lord God of hosts, Heav - en and earth are full of

thy glo - ry, Glo - ry be to thee, O Lord most high.

BENEDICTUS

Bless - ed, bless - ed, bless - ed is he, that com - eth in the name of the

Lord, Ho - san - na, ho - san - na, ho - san - na, in the high - est.

(Organ)

KYRIE

Healey Willan, 1928

Lord, have mer - cy up - on us, Christ, have mer - cy up -

on us. Lord, have mer - cy up - on us.

SANCTUS

Ho - ly, ho - ly, ho - ly, Lord God of hosts,

Heav-en and earth are full . . . of thy glo - ry: Glo - ry be to

thee, O Lord most high. A - men.

LORD'S SUPPER

An Upper Room

Fred Pratt Green, b. 1903

FOLKSONG, 9.8.9.8

English traditional melody; harmonized by John Wilson, b. 1905

1. An up-per room did our Lord pre-pare for those he
2. A last-ing gift Je-sus gave his own: to share his
3. And af-ter sup-per he washed their feet, for ser-vice,
4. No end there is! We de-part in peace. He loves be-

1. loved un-til the end, and his dis-ci-ples still gath-er
2. bread, his lov-ing cup. What-ev-er bur-dens may bow us
3. too, is sac-ra-ment. In him our joy shall be made com-
4. yond our ut-ter-most: in ev-ery room in our Fa-ther's

1. there, to cel-e-brate their ris-en friend.
2. down, he by his cross shall lift us up.
3. plete, sent out to serve, as he was sent.
4. house, he will be there, as Lord and host.

Strengthen for Service, Lord, the Hands

Liturgy of Malabar, 4th century, in Syriac;
tr. C. W. Humphries and Percy Dearmer, 1906

MALABAR, 8.7.8.7 iambic

David McK. Williams, 1941

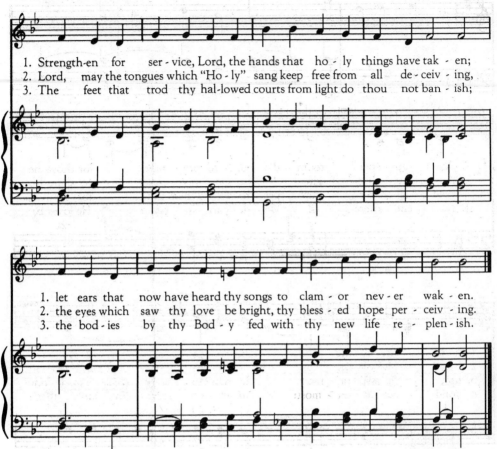

1. Strength-en for ser - vice, Lord, the hands that ho - ly things have tak - en;
2. Lord, may the tongues which "Ho - ly" sang keep free from all de - ceiv - ing,
3. The feet that trod thy hal-lowed courts from light do thou not ban - ish;

1. let ears that now have heard thy songs to clam - or nev - er wak - en.
2. the eyes which saw thy love be bright, thy bless - ed hope per - ceiv - ing.
3. the bod - ies by thy Bod - y fed with thy new life re - plen - ish.

Alternative tune: ACH GOTT UND HERR, 535

LORD'S SUPPER

570

Thee Will I Love,
My God and King

Robert Bridges, 1899

GENEVA 138, 8.9.8.9 D

Melody in *Genevan Psalter* (1551)

1. Thee will I love, my God and King; thee will I sing, my strength and tow-er;
2. Set in my heart thy love I find; my wan-d'ring mind to thee thou lead-est;
3. O more and more thy love ex-tend, my life be-friend with heav'n-ly plea-sure,

1. for-ev-er-more thee will I trust, O God most just of truth and pow-er,
2. my trem-bling hope, my strong de-sire with heav'n-ly fire thou kind-ly feed-est.
3. that I may win thy Par-a-dise, thy pearl of price, thy count-less trea-sure.

1. who all things hast in or-der placed, yea, for thy plea-sure hast cre-at-ed;
2. Lo, all things fair thy path pre-pare; thy beau-ty to my spir-it call-eth.
3. Since but in thee I can go free from earth-ly care and vain op-pres-sion,

1. and on thy throne, un-seen, un-known, reign-est a-lone in glo-ry seat-ed.
2. thine to re-main, in joy or pain, and count it gain what-e'er be-fall-eth.
3. this prayer I make for Je-sus' sake, that thou me take in thy pos-ses-sion.

Come, Let Us Join Our Cheerful Songs

571

RICHMOND, CM   Isaac Watts, 1707   T. Haweis, 1734–1820

1. Come, let us join our cheer-ful songs with an-gels round the throne;
2. "Wor-thy the Lamb that died," they cry, "to be ex-alt-ed thus!"
3. Je-sus is wor-thy to re-ceive hon-or and pow'r di-vine;
4. Let all cre-a-tion join in one to bless the sa-cred name

1. ten thou-sand thou-sand are their tongues, but all their joys are one.
2. "Wor-thy the Lamb," our lips re-ply, "for he was slain for us."
3. and bless-ings more than we can give be, Lord, for-ev-er thine.
4. of him who sits up-on the throne, and to a-dore the Lamb.

Rev. 5:11–14   *Alternative tune: BRISTOL, 251*   *This tune in a higher key: 362*

Let Saints on Earth in Concert Sing

572

Variant from Charles Wesley, 1759

DUNDEE, CM   *Scottish Psalter (1615); harmony from Ravenscroft's Psalms (1621)*

1. Let saints on earth in con-cert sing with those whose work is done,
2. One fam-i-ly, we dwell in him, one church a-bove, be-neath,
3. One ar-my of the liv-ing God, to his com-mand we bow;
4. E'en now to their e-ter-nal home there pass some spir-its blest,
5. Je-sus, be thou our con-stant guide; then, when the word is giv'n,

1. for all the ser-vants of the King in earth and heav'n are one.
2. though now di-vid-ed by the stream, the nar-row stream of death.
3. part of his host hath crossed the flood, and part is cross-ing now.
4. while oth-ers to the mar-gin come, wait-ing their call to rest.
5. bid Jor-dan's nar-row stream di-vide, and bring us safe to heav'n.

This tune in the older rhythm: 45   This tune in a lower key: 131
Alternative tune: LONDON NEW, 36

CLOUD OF WITNESSES

573 Sing Alleluia Forth in Loyal Praise

MARTINS, 10 10.7   *Alleluia perenne*, Latin, before 800; tr. composite   Percy C. Buck, 1913

Descant, st. 5 and 8, Erik Routley

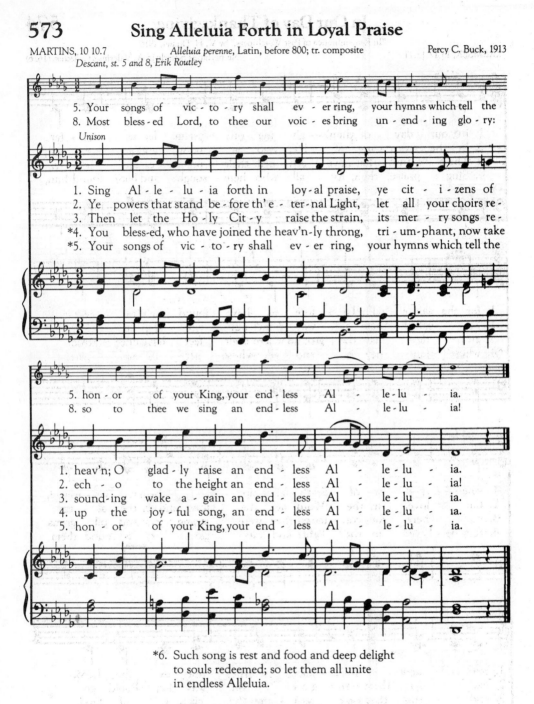

5. Your songs of vic - to - ry shall ev - er ring, your hymns which tell the
8. Most bless - ed Lord, to thee our voic - es bring un - end - ing glo - ry:

Unison

1. Sing Al - le - lu - ia forth in loy - al praise, ye cit - i - zens of
2. Ye powers that stand be - fore th' e - ter - nal Light, let all your choirs re -
3. Then let the Ho - ly Cit - y raise the strain, its mer - ry songs re -
*4. You bless-ed, who have joined the heav'n-ly throng, tri - um-phant, now take
*5. Your songs of vic - to - ry shall ev - er ring, your hymns which tell the

5. hon - or of your King, your end - less Al - le - lu - ia.
8. so to thee we sing an end - less Al - le - lu - ia!

1. heav'n; O glad - ly raise an end - less Al - le - lu - ia.
2. ech - o to the height an end - less Al - le - lu - ia!
3. sound-ing wake a - gain an end - less Al - le - lu - ia.
4. up the joy - ful song, an end - less Al - le - lu - ia.
5. hon - or of your King, your end - less Al - le - lu - ia.

*6. Such song is rest and food and deep delight
to souls redeemed; so let them all unite
in endless Alleluia.

7. And here on earth God's blessed name we praise,
whose grace adorns and brightens all our days,
with endless Alleluia.

8. Most blessed Lord, to thee our voices bring
unending glory: so to thee we sing
an endless Alleluia!

CLOUD OF WITNESSES

In Our Day of Thanksgiving

574

"In Remembrance of Past Worshipers," by W. H. Draper, 1916

KREMSER, 13.12.13.11

Netherlands melody in A. Valerius's *Collection* (1626)

1. In our day of thanks- giv- ing one psalm let us of- fer
2. In the morn- ing of life, and at noon, and at e- ven,
3. These stones that have ech- oed their prais- es are ho- ly,
4. Sing praise, then, for all who here sought and here found him,

1. for the saints who be- fore us have found their re- ward;
2. he called them a- way from our wor- ship be- low;
3. and dear is the ground where their feet have once trod;
4. whose jour- ney is end- ed, whose per- ils are past;

1. when the shad- ow of death fell up- on them we sor- rowed,
2. but love, in the Word, at the font, and on the al- tar
3. yet here they con- fessed they were strang- ers and pil- grims,
4. they be- lieved in the light; and its glo- ry is round them

1. but now we re- joice that they rest in the Lord.
2. had girt them with grace for the way they should go.
3. and still they were seek- ing the cit- y of God.
4. where the clouds of earth's sor- rows are lift- ed at last.

This tune in a higher key: 62

Heb. 11:13

CLOUD OF WITNESSES

575   Come, We That Love the Lord

St. 1 and 5, Isaac Watts, 1707; st. 2–4, William Hammond, 1745
First Tune

VINEYARD HAVEN, SM with refrain   Richard Wayne Dirksen, 1974

1. Come, we that love the Lord, and let our joys be known; join
2. Sing till we feel our hearts as-cend-ing with our tongues, sing
3. Ye pil-grims on the road to Zi-on's cit-y, sing; re-
4. There shall each rap-tured tongue his end-less praise pro-claim, and
5. Then let our songs a-bound, and let our tears be dry; we're

1. in a song with sweet ac-cord, and thus sur-round the throne.
2. till the love of sin de-parts, and grace in-spires our songs:
3. joice ye in the Lamb of God, in Christ th' e-ter-nal King:
4. sing in sweet-er notes the song of Mo-ses and the Lamb:
5. march-ing through Im-man-uel's ground to fair-er worlds on high!

Refrain

Ho - san - na! Ho - san - na! Re - joice, give thanks, and sing!

Tune © MCMLXXIV Harold Flammer, Inc.   *Rev. 15:2–8*

576   Come, We That Love the Lord

ST. THOMAS, SM   Second Tune   Aaron Williams, *Psalmody* (1770)

1. Come, we that love the Lord, and let our joys be known;
2. Sing till we feel our hearts as-cend-ing with our tongues,
3. Ye pil-grims on the road to Zi-on's cit-y, sing;
4. There shall each rap-tured tongue his end-less praise pro-claim,
5. Then let our songs a-bound, and let our tears be dry;

CLOUD OF WITNESSES

1. join in a song with sweet ac - cord, and thus sur - round the throne.
2. sing till the love of sin de - parts, and grace in - spires our songs.
3. re - joice ye in the Lamb of God, in Christ th' e - ter - nal King.
4. and sing in sweet - er notes the song of Mo - ses and the Lamb.
5. we're march-ing through Im-man-uel's ground to fair - er worlds on high!

This tune in a lower key: 409   *Alternative tune: SONG 20, 177*

None Lacks a Friend Who Hath Thy Love   577

Richard Baxter, 1663

WHITEHALL (PSALM VIII), LM   Henry Lawes, 1637

1. None lacks a friend who hath thy love, and may con - verse and walk with thee,
2. In the com - mu - nion of God's saints is wis-dom, safe - ty, and de - light;
3. As for my friends, they are not lost; the sev -'ral ves - sels of thy fleet,
4. Still we are cen - tered all in thee, mem-bers, though dis - tant, of one Head;

1. and with the saints, here and a - bove, with whom for - ev - er I must be.
2. and when my heart de - clines and faints, it's lift - ed by their warmth and light.
3. though part-ed now, by tem-pests toss'd, shall safe - ly in the ha - ven meet.
4. in the same fam - i - ly we be, by the same faith and Spir - it led.

5. Before thy throne we daily meet
   as joint petitioners to thee;
   in spirit we each other greet,
   and shall again each other see.

6. The heavenly hosts, world without end,
   shall be my company above;
   and thou, my best and surest friend,
   who shall divide me from thy love?

CLOUD OF WITNESSES

578

Ye Holy Angels Bright

J. H. Gurney, 1838; based on Richard Baxter, 1672

DARWALL, 6.6.6.6.4.44.4

John Darwall, 1770

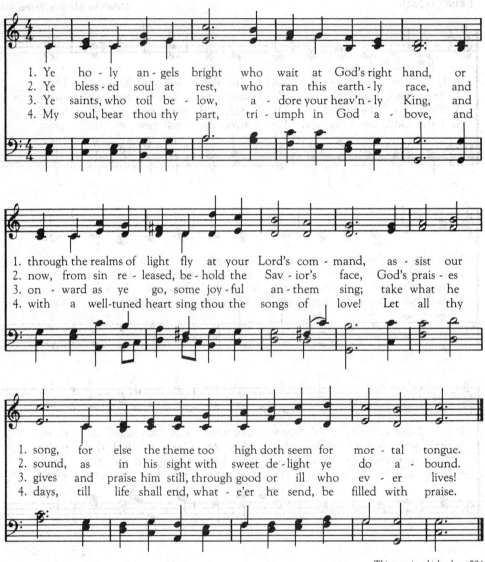

1. Ye ho - ly an - gels bright who wait at God's right hand, or
2. Ye bless - ed soul at rest, who ran this earth - ly race, and
3. Ye saints, who toil be - low, a - dore your heav'n - ly King, and
4. My soul, bear thou thy part, tri - umph in God a - bove, and

1. through the realms of light fly at your Lord's com - mand, as - sist our
2. now, from sin re - leased, be - hold the Sav - ior's face, God's prais - es
3. on - ward as ye go, some joy - ful an - them sing; take what he
4. with a well-tuned heart sing thou the songs of love! Let all thy

1. song, for else the theme too high doth seem for mor - tal tongue.
2. sound, as in his sight with sweet de - light ye do a - bound.
3. gives and praise him still, through good or ill who ev - er lives!
4. days, till life shall end, what - e'er he send, be filled with praise.

This tune in a higher key: 596

CLOUD OF WITNESSES

Jerusalem the Golden

Hora Novissima, by Bernard of Cluny, 12th century;
tr. J. M. Neale, 1861

579

EWING, 7.6.7.6 D

Melody by Alexander Ewing, 1861

1. Je - ru - sa - lem the gold - en, with milk and hon - ey blest,
2. They stand, those halls of Zi - on, con - ju - bi - lant with song,
3. There is the throne of Da - vid, and there, from sin re - leased,
4. There God, our King and Por - tion, the full - ness of his grace

1. be - neath thy con - tem - pla - tion sink heart and voice op - press'd;
2. and bright with man - y an an - gel, and man - y a mar - tyr throng;
3. the song of them that tri - umph, the shout of them that feast,
4. shall we be - hold for - ev - er and wor - ship face to face.

1. I know not, Oh, I know not what joys a - wait us there,
2. the cross is all their splen - dor, the Cru - ci - fied their praise;
3. and they who with their Lead - er have con-quered in the fight,
4. Then all the halls of Zi - on for aye shall be com - plete,

1. what ra - dian - cy of glo - ry, what bliss be - yond com - pare.
2. his laud and ben - e - dic - tion his ran-somed peo - ple raise.
3. for - ev - er and for - ev - er are clad in robes of white.
4. and in the land of beau - ty all things of beau - ty meet.

HEAVENLY COMPANY

580 Ten Thousand Times Ten Thousand

Henry Alford, 1867

KOMM SEELE, 7.6.8.6 D

Melody by J. W. Franck, c. 1681

1. Ten thou-sand times ten thou-sand in spar-kling rai-ment bright,
2. What rush of Al - le - lu - ias fills all the earth and sky!
3. O then, what rap-tured greet-ings on Ca-naan's hap-py shore,
4. Bring near thy great sal - va - tion, thou Lamb for sin-ners slain;

1. the ar - mies of the ran-somed saints throng up the steeps of light;
2. What ring-ing of a thou-sand harps be - speaks the tri - umph nigh!
3. what knit-ting sev-ered friend-ships up, where part - ings are no more!
4. fill up the roll of thine e - lect, then take thy power and reign;

1. "'Tis fin-ished, all is fin-ished!"—their fight with death and sin;
2. O day for which cre - a - tion and all its tribes were made!
3. Then eyes with joy shall spar - kle that brimmed with tears of late,
4. ap - pear, De - sire of Na - tions, thine ex - iles long for home;

1. fling o - pen wide the gold - en gates, and let the vic - tors in!
2. O joy, for all its for - mer woes a thou-sand-fold re - paid!
3. or - phans no long-er fa - ther-less, nor wid - ows des - o - late.
4. show in the heav'n thy prom - ised sign; thou Prince and Sav - ior, come!

HEAVENLY COMPANY

Far Off I See the Goal

581

Robert R. Roberts, 1925

MOAB, 6.5.6.5.666.5

John Roberts (Ieuan Gwyllt), 1870

1. Far off I see the goal — O Sav-ior, guide me;
2. When-e'er thy way seems strange, go thou be-fore me,
3. Should earth-ly plea-sures wane, and joy for-sake me,
4. There, with the ran-somed throng who praise for-ev - er

1. I feel my strength is small — be thou be-side me;
2. and, lest my heart should change, O Lord, watch o'er me;
3. and lone-ly hours of pain at length o'er-take me,
4. the love that made them strong to serve for-ev - er,

1. with vi-sion ev-er clear, with love that con-quers fear,
2. but, should my faith prove frail, and I through blind-ness fail,
3. my hand in thine hold fast till sor-row be o'er - past,
4. I too would seek thy face, thy fin-ished work re - trace,

1. and grace to per-se - vere, O Lord, pro-vide me.
2. O let thy grace pre - vail, and still re-store me.
3. and gen-tle death at last for heaven a-wake me.
4. and mag-ni - fy thy grace, re - deemed for-ev - er.

HEAVENLY COMPANY

582

Here from All Nations

C. M. Idle, 1974

O QUANTA QUALIA, 11.10.11.10 dactylic

Later form (1861) of melody in *Paris Antiphoner* (1681)

1. Here from all na-tions, all tongues, and all peo-ples, count-less the crowd, but their
2. These have come out of the hard-est op-pres-sion; now they may stand in the
3. Gone is their thirst, and no more shall they hun-ger: God is their shel-ter, his
4. He will go with them to clear liv-ing wa-ter flow-ing from springs which his

1. voic-es are one. Vast is the sight and ma-jes-tic their
2. pres-ence of God, serv-ing their Lord day and night in his
3. pow'r at their side; sun will not pain them, no burn-ing shall
4. mer-cy sup-plies. Gone is their grief, and their tri-als are

1. sing-ing: "God has the vic-t'ry, he reigns from the throne!"
2. tem-ple, ran-somed and cleansed by the Lamb's pre-cious blood.
3. tor-ture: Je-sus the Lamb is their Shep-herd and Guide.
4. o-ver; God wipes a-way ev-'ry tear from their eyes.

This tune in a higher key: 602

5. Blessing and glory and wisdom and power
   be to the Savior again and again.
   Might and thanksgiving and honor forever,
   be to our God, Alleluia! Amen!

HEAVENLY COMPANY

Rev. 7:13ff

O What Their Joy
and Their Glory Must Be

and Their Glory Must Be

O quanta qualia, by Peter Abelard, 12th century;
tr. J. M. Neale, 1851

Tune O QUANTA QUALIA, opposite page

1. O what their joy and their glory must be,
   those endless sabbaths the blessed ones see!
   Crown for the valiant, to weary ones rest,
   God shall be all, and in all ever blest.

2. Truly Jerusalem name we that shore:
   "Vision of peace" that brings joy evermore!
   Wish and fulfilment can severed be ne'er,
   nor the thing prayed for come short of the prayer.

3. We, where no trouble distraction can bring,
   safely the anthems of Zion shall sing,
   while for thy grace, Lord, their voices of praise
   thy blessed people shall evermore raise.

4. Now, in the meanwhile, with hearts raised on high,
   we for that country must yearn and must sigh,
   seeking Jerusalem, dear native land,
   through our long exile on Babylon's strand.

5. Low before him with our praises we fall,
   of whom, and in whom, and through whom are all:
   of whom, the Father, and through whom, the Son,
   in whom, the Spirit, with these ever One.

This tune in a higher key: 602

584

Lord, It Is in Thy Tender Care

from Richard Baxter, 1681

WIGTON, CM

Scottish Psalter (1635)

1. Lord, it is in thy ten-der care wheth-er I die or live;
2. If life be long, I will be glad that I may long o-bey;
3. Christ leads me thro' no dark-er rooms than he went thro' be-fore;
4. Come, Lord, when grace hath made me meet thy bless-ed face to see:
5. My knowl-edge of that life is small, the eye of faith is dim,

1. to love and serve thee is my share, and this thy grace must give.
2. if short, yet why should I be sad to soar to end-less day?
3. all who in-to God's king-dom come must en-ter by this door.
4. for if thy work on earth be sweet, what will thy glo-ry be?
5. but 'tis e-nough that Christ knows all, and I shall be with him.

This tune in a higher key: 255

Phil. 1:21

585

Children of the Heavenly Father

Tryggare kan ingen vara, by Caroline V. Sandell Berg, c. 1850;
tr. Ernst W. Olson, 1925

CHILDREN OF THE HEAVENLY FATHER, 88.88 trochaic

Swedish folk melody

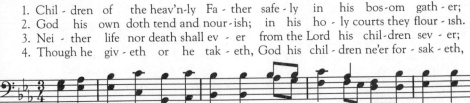

1. Chil-dren of the heav'n-ly Fa-ther safe-ly in his bos-om gath-er;
2. God his own doth tend and nour-ish; in his ho-ly courts they flour-ish.
3. Nei-ther life nor death shall ev-er from the Lord his chil-dren sev-er;
4. Though he giv-eth or he tak-eth, God his chil-dren ne'er for-sak-eth,

HEAVENLY COMPANY

Rev. 7:16; Rom. 8:38–39

Jesus, Still Lead On

586

Jesu, geh' voran, by Nicolaus von Zinzendorf, 1700–1761;
tr. Jane Borthwick, 1858 (alt'd)

SEELENBRÄUTIGAM, 55.88.55

Adam Drese, 1668

1. nes-tling bird or star in heav-en such a ref-uge ne'er was giv-en.
2. From all e-vil things he spares them; in his might-y arms he bears them.
3. un-to them his grace he show-eth, and their sor-rows all he know-eth.
4. his the lov-ing pur-pose sole-ly to pre-serve them pure and ho-ly.

1. Je - sus, still lead on till our rest be won,
2. If the way be drear, if the foe be near,
3. When we seek re - lief from a long - felt grief,
4. Je - sus, still lead on till our rest be won;

1. and al-though the way be cheer - less, we will fol - low,
2. let no faith - less fears o'er-take us, let not faith and
3. when temp-ta - tions come al-lur - ing, make us pa - tient
4. heav'n-ly Lead - er, still di - rect us, still sup-port, con-

1. calm and fear - less; guide us by your hand to our prom-ised land.
2. hope for-sake us; safe - ly past the foe to our home we go.
3. and en-dur - ing; show us that bright shore where we weep no more.
4. sole, pro-tect us, till we safe - ly stand in our prom-ised land.

This tune in a higher key: 384

HEAVENLY COMPANY

587   The Sands of Time Are Sinking

Anne Ross Cousin, 1857; based on sayings of Samuel Rutherford, 1600–1661

LLANGLOFFAN, 7.6.7.6.7.6.7.5

David Evans, 1865

1. The sands of time are sink - ing; the dawn of heav-en breaks;
2. The King there in his beau - ty with - out a veil is seen;
3. With mer - cy and with judg - ment my web of time he wove,

1. the sum-mer morn I've sighed for, the fair, sweet morn, a - wakes.
2. it were a well-spent jour - ney though sev'n deaths lay be - tween!
3. and aye the dews of sor - row were lus-tered by his love;

1. Dark, dark hath been the mid - night, but day-spring is at hand,
2. The Lamb, with his fair ar - my, doth on Mount Zi - on stand,
3. I'll bless the hand that guid - ed; I'll bless the heart that planned;

Refrain

and glo - ry, glo - ry dwell - eth in Im-man-uel's land.

This tune in a higher key: 80   *Alternative tunes: KING'S LYNN, 395, LANCASHIRE, 423*

HEAVENLY COMPANY   *Isa. 33:17*

No Saint on Earth

588

J. W. Schulte-Nordholt; tr. Norman J. Kansfield, 1982

NIEMAND VAN ONS, 10 10.10 10.10 10

Jaap Geraedts

1. No saint on earth lives life to self a-lone or dies a-lone, for we with
2. For to this end our Lord by death was slain, that to new life he might a-

1. Christ are one. So if we live, for him our life we live, and
2. rise a-gain. Through sor-row on to tri-umph Christ has led, and

1. if we die, to Christ our dy-ing give. In liv-ing and in dy-ing,
2. reigns o'er all: the liv-ing and the dead. In liv-ing and in dy-ing,

1. this con-fess: We are the Lord's, safe in his faith-ful-ness.
2. him we bless. We are the Lord's, safe in his faith-ful-ness.

Rom. 14:7–9

HEAVENLY COMPANY

589

For Those We Love Within the Veil

William Charter Piggott, 1931

RIPPONDEN, 8.8.8.4

Norman Cocker, 1951

1. For those we love with-in the veil, who once were com-rades
2. Free from the fret of mor-tal years, and know-ing now thy
3. O full - er, sweet - er is that life, and larg - er, am - pler
4. nor know to what high pur-pose thou dost yet em - ploy their
5. And life for them is life in - deed, the splen-did goal of

1. of our way, we thank thee, Lord, for they have won to cloud - less day.
2. per - fect will, with quick-ened sense and height-ened joy they serve thee still.
3. is the air: eye can - not see nor heart con-ceive the glo - ry there;
4. rip - ened powers, nor how at thy be - hest they touch this life of ours.
5. earth's strait race; and where no shad - ows in - ter-vene they see thy face.

Alternative tune: MEYER, 379; original key, E

I Cor. 2:9

590

Go, Happy Soul

George Ratcliffe Woodward, 1910 (alt'd)

COMMANDMENTS, 9.8.9.8

Melody in the *Genevan Psalter* (1551);
bass by C. Goudimel, 1565

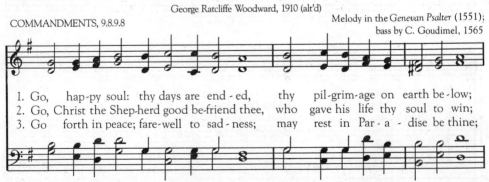

1. Go, hap-py soul: thy days are end - ed, thy pil-grim-age on earth be-low;
2. Go, Christ the Shep-herd good be-friend thee, who gave his life thy soul to win;
3. Go forth in peace; fare-well to sad - ness; may rest in Par - a - dise be thine;

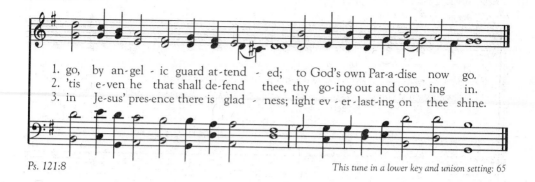

1. go,   by an-gel - ic guard at-tend - ed;   to God's own Par-a-dise   now   go.
2. 'tis   e-ven he that shall de-fend   thee, thy go-ing out and com - ing   in.
3. in   Je-sus' pres-ence there is glad - ness; light ev-er-last-ing on   thee shine.

Ps. 121:8

This tune in a lower key and unison setting: 65

How Blest Are They Who Trust in Christ   591

Fred Pratt Green, 1972

TALLIS' CANON, LM

Thomas Tallis, 1557

In unison or in canon. Slowly

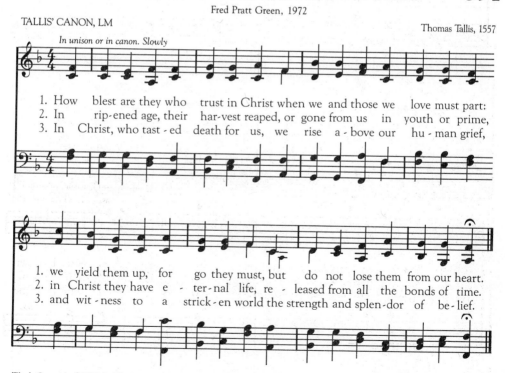

1. How   blest are they who   trust in Christ when we and those we   love must part:
2. In   rip-ened age, their har-vest reaped, or gone from us in   youth or prime,
3. In   Christ, who tast-ed death for us, we   rise a-bove our   hu-man grief,

1. we   yield them up, for   go they must, but   do not lose them from our heart.
2. in Christ they have e - ter-nal life, re - leased from all   the bonds of time.
3. and wit-ness to   a   strick-en world the strength and splen-dor of be-lief.

This tune in a higher key: 77

HEAVENLY COMPANY

592

O Lord of Life, Where'er They Be

Frederick Lucian Hosmer, 1888

GELOBT SEI GOTT, 888 with Alleluias

Melody by M. Vulpius, 1609

1. O Lord of life, wher-e'er they be, safe in thine own e-ter-ni-ty, our dead are liv-ing un-to thee. Al-le-lu-ia! Al-le-lu-ia! Al-le-lu-ia!
2. All souls are thine, and here or there they rest with-in thy shel-t'ring care; one prov-i-dence a-like they share. Al-le-lu-ia! Al-le-lu-ia! Al-le-lu-ia!
3. Thy word is true, thy ways are just; a-bove the re-quiem, "Dust to dust," shall rise our psalm of grate-ful trust. Al-le-lu-ia! Al-le-lu-ia! Al-le-lu-ia!
4. O hap-py they in God who rest, no more by fear and doubt op-pressed; liv-ing or dy-ing, they are blest. Al-le-lu-ia! Al-le-lu-ia! Al-le-lu-ia!

This tune in a higher key: 326

HEAVENLY COMPANY

Job. 34:15

All Hail the Power of Jesus' Name

St. 1–4, Edward Perronet, 1779, 1780; st. 5, John Rippon, c. 1795
First Tune

CORONATION, CM extended

Oliver Holden, 1793

1. All hail the power of Je-sus' name, let an-gels pros-trate fall;
*2. Crown him, ye morn-ing stars of light, who fixed this float-ing ball;
*3. Ye seed of Is-rael's cho-sen race, ye ran-somed of the fall,
4. Let ev-'ry tongue and ev-'ry tribe on this ter-res-trial ball

1. bring forth the roy-al di-a-dem, and crown him Lord of all!
2. now hail the Strength of Is-rael's might, and crown him Lord of all!
3. hail him who saves you by his grace, and crown him Lord of all!
4. to him all maj-es-ty as-cribe, and crown him Lord of all!

1. Bring forth the roy-al di-a-dem, and crown him Lord of all.
2. Now hail the Strength of Is-rael's might, and crown him Lord of all.
3. Hail him who saves you by his grace, and crown him Lord of all.
4. To him all maj-es-ty as-cribe, and crown him Lord of all.

5. Oh that with yonder sacred throng
   we at his feet may fall!
   We'll join the everlasting song,
   and crown him Lord of all!
   We'll join the everlasting song,
   and crown him Lord of all.

Rev. 5:12–13

ENTHRONED ETERNALLY

594　All Hail the Power of Jesus' Name

Second Tune

MILES LANE, CM extended

William Shrubsole, 1779

1. All hail the power of Je - sus' name, let an - gels pros - trate fall;
*2. Crown him, ye morn - ing stars of light, who fixed this float - ing ball;
3. Ye seed of Is - rael's cho - sen race, ye ran - somed of the fall,
4. Let ev - 'ry tribe and ev - 'ry tongue on this ter - res - trial ball

1. bring forth the roy - al di - a - dem, and crown him,
2. now hail the Strength of Is - rael's might, and crown him,
3. hail him who saves you by his grace, and crown him,
4. to him all maj - es - ty as - cribe, and crown him,

1. crown him, crown him, crown him Lord of all.
2. crown him, crown him, crown him Lord of all.
3. crown him, crown him, crown him Lord of all.
4. crown him, crown him, crown him Lord of all.

5. Oh that with yonder sacred throng
we at his feet may fall!
We'll join the everlasting song,
and crown him, crown him,
crown him, crown him Lord of all.

ENTHRONED ETERNALLY

The God of Abr'am Praise

Thomas Olivers, 1770

Thomas Olivers and Meyer Lyon, 1770;
based on a Jewish melody

LEONI, 6.6.8.4 D

1. The God of A-bram praise, who reigns en-throned a-bove;
2. He by him-self hath sworn, I on his oath de-pend;
3. The God who reigns on high the great arch-an-gels sing,
4. The whole tri-um-phant host give thanks to God on high,

1. An - cient of ev - er - last - ing days, and God of love:
2. I shall on ea - gles' wings up-borne, to heav'n as - cend;
3. and "Ho - ly, Ho - ly, Ho - ly!" cry, "Al - might - y King!
4. "Hail, Fa-ther, Son, and Ho - ly Ghost!" they ev - er cry:

1. the Lord, the great I AM, by earth and heav'n con - fess'd:
2. I shall be-hold his face, I shall his power a - dore,
3. who wast and art the same, and ev - er-more shalt be;
4. Hail! A-br'am's God and mine (I join the heav'n-ly lays),

1. I bow and bless the sa - cred name, for - ev - er bless'd.
2. and sing the won - ders of his grace for - ev - er - more.
3. the Lord, our Fa - ther! great I AM, we wor - ship thee."
4. all might and maj - es - ty be thine and end - less praise!

Alternative tune: SEVENTH TUNE, 271

Ex. 3:6; Gen. 12:1; Gen. 22:16–17; Rev. 4:8; Rev. 5:13

ENTHRONED ETERNALLY

596
Rejoice, the Lord Is King

DARWALL, 6.6.6.6.88

Charles Wesley, 1746
First Tune

John Darwall, 1770

1. Re - joice, the Lord is King: your Lord and King a - dore!
2. Je - sus the Sav - ior reigns, the Lord of truth and love;
3. His king-dom can - not fail; he rules o'er earth and heav'n;

1. Re - joice, give thanks, and sing, and tri-umph ev - er - more.
2. when he had purged our stains he took his seat a - bove.
3. the keys of death and hell are to our Je - sus giv'n.

Refrain

Lift up your heart, lift up your voice: re-joice, a-gain I say, re - joice!

This tune in a lower key: 578

Heb. 1:3; Rev. 1:18

597
Rejoice, the Lord Is King

GOPSAL 6.6.6.6.88

Second Tune

Voices in unison

G. F. Handel, c. 1747; realized from original
figured bass by John Wilson, 1964, 1968

1. Re - joice, the Lord is King: your Lord and King a - dore!
2. Je - sus the Sav - ior reigns, the Lord of truth and love;
3. His king-dom can - not fail; he rules o'er earth and heav'n;

Organ introduction

ENTHRONED ETERNALLY

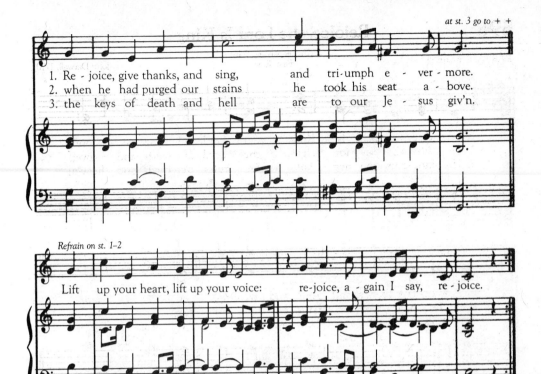

at st. 3 go to + +

1. Re - joice, give thanks, and sing, and tri-umph e - ver - more.
2. when he had purged our stains he took his seat a - bove.
3. the keys of death and hell are to our Je - sus giv'n.

Refrain on st. 1–2

Lift up your heart, lift up your voice: re-joice, a - gain I say, re - joice.

+ + Refrain on st. 3

Lift up your heart, lift up your voice: re-joice, a - gain I say, re -

joice. *Organ postlude after st. 3*

Heb. 1:3; Rev. 1:18

ENTHRONED ETERNALLY

598

Ye Servants of God

Charles Wesley, 1744

LYONS, 10 10.11 11

William Gardiner, 1815

1. Ye ser-vants of God, your Mas-ter pro-claim,
2. God rul-eth on high, al-might-y to save;
3. "Sal-va-tion to God who sits on the throne!"
4. Then let us a-dore and give him his right,

1. and pub-lish a-broad his won-der-ful name;
2. and still he is nigh, his pres-ence we have;
3. let all cry a-loud and hon-or the Son;
4. all glo-ry and power, all wis-dom and might,

1. the name all-vic-to-rious of Je-sus ex-tol;
2. the great con-gre-ga-tion his tri-umph shall sing,
3. the prais-es of Je-sus the an-gels pro-claim,
4. all hon-or and bless-ing with an-gels a-bove,

1. his king-dom is glo-rious and rules o-ver all.
2. as-crib-ing sal-va-tion to Je-sus our King.
3. fall down on their fac-es and wor-ship the Lamb.
4. and thanks nev-er ceas-ing, and in-fi-nite love.

Alternative tunes: HANOVER, 2, LAUDATE DOMINUM, 143

ENTHRONED ETERNALLY

Rev. 5:12

Look, Ye Saints, the Sight Is Glorious

Thomas Kelly, 1809

WESTMINSTER ABBEY, 8.7.8.7.4.7

From an anthem by Henry Purcell, 1658–1695

1. Look, ye saints, the sight is glo - rious, see the Man of
2. Crown the Sav - ior, an - gels, crown him, rich the tri - umphs
3. Sin - ners in de - ri - sion crowned him, mock - ing thus the
4. Hark, those bursts of ac - cla - ma - tion, hark, those loud tri -

1. Sor - rows now, from the fight re - turned vic - to - rious,
2. Je - sus brings; in the seat of pow'r en - throne him
3. Sav - ior's claim, saints and an - gels throng a - round him,
4. um - phant chords, Je - sus takes the high - est sta - tion,

1. ev - 'ry knee to him shall bow. Crown him! Crown him!
2. while the vault of heav - en rings. Crown him! Crown him!
3. own his ti - tle, praise his name. Crown him! Crown him!
4. oh, what joy the sight af - fords. Crown him! Crown him!

1. Crown him! Crown him! Crowns be - come the Vic - tor's brow.
2. Crown him! Crown him! Crown the Sav - ior King of kings.
3. Crown him! Crown him! Spread a - broad the Vic - tor's fame.
4. Crown him! Crown him! King of kings and Lord of lords!

A lower setting of this tune, with inner parts slightly simplified: 392

Alternative tune: REGENT SQUARE, 229

Isa. 63:1; Phil. 2:11; Mt. 27:29

ENTHRONED ETERNALLY

600 Crown Him with Many Crowns

Matthew Bridges, 1851

DIADEMATA, SMD

G. J. Elvey, 1868

1. Crown him with man-y crowns, the Lamb up-on his throne;
2. Crown him the Lord of love; be-hold his hands and side,
3. Crown him the Lord of peace; whose power a scep-ter sways
4. Crown him the Lord of years, the Po-ten-tate of time;

1. hark! how the heaven-ly an-them drowns all mu-sic but its own:
2. rich wounds, yet vis-i-ble a-bove, in beau-ty glo-ri-fied:
3. from pole to pole, that wars may cease, ab-sorbed in prayer and praise:
4. cre-a-tor of the roll-ing spheres, in-ef-fa-bly sub-lime:

1. a-wake, my soul, and sing of him who died for thee,
2. no an-gel in the sky can ful-ly bear that sight,
3. his reign shall know no end; and round his pierc-ed feet
4. all hail, Re-deem-er, hail! for thou hast died for me:

1. and hail him as thy match-less King through all e-ter-ni-ty.
2. but down-ward bends his burn-ing eye at mys-ter-ies so bright.
3. fair flowers of Par-a-dise ex-tend their fra-grance ev-er sweet.
4. thy praise shall nev-er, nev-er fail through-out e-ter-ni-ty.

ENTHRONED ETERNALLY

Rev. 19:12

Hark, the Song of Jubilee

James Montgomery, 1818 (alt'd)

ST. GEORGE'S WINDSOR, 7.7.7.7 D

G. J. Elvey, 1858

1. Hark, the song of ju-bi-lee loud as might-y thun-ders roar,
2. Al - le - lu - ia! hark, the sound from the depths un - to the skies,
3. He shall reign from pole to pole with il - lim - it - a - ble sway;

1. or the full-ness of the sea when it breaks up - on the shore:
2. wakes a-bove, be - neath, a - round all cre - a-tion's har - mo-nies;
3. he shall reign when, like a scroll, yon - der heav'ns have passed a - way;

1. Al - le - lu - ia! for the Lord God om - nip - o - tent shall reign!
2. see the Vic-tor's ban-ner furled; sheathed his sword, he speaks—"'Tis done!"—
3. then the end: be - neath his rod his last en - e - my shall fall;

1. Al - le - lu - ia! let the word sound from cit - y, hill, and plain.
2. and the king-doms of this world are the king-dom of his Son.
3. Al - le - lu - ia! Christ in God, God in Christ, is all in all.

This tune in a lower key: 18

Rev. 19:6

ENTHRONED ETERNALLY

602   Blessing and Honor and Glory and Power

Horatius Bonar, 1858

O QUANTA QUALIA, 10 10.10 10   Later form of melody in *Paris Antiphoner* (1681)

1. Bless - ing and hon - or and glo - ry and pow'r, wis - dom and
2. In - to the heav'n of the heav'ns hath he gone, sit - teth he
3. Sound - eth the heav'n of the heav'ns with his name, ring - eth the
4. Ev - er as - cend - eth the song and the joy; ev - er de -

1. rich - es and strength ev - er - more give ye to him who our
2. now in the joy of the throne, wear - eth he now of the
3. earth with his glo - ry and fame, o - cean and moun-tain, stream,
4. scend - eth the love from on high; sing we the song of the

1. bat - tle hath won, whose are the king-dom, the crown, and the throne.
2. king - dom the crown, sing - eth he now the new song with his own.
3. for - est, and flow'r ech - o his prais-es and tell of his pow'r.
4. Lamb that was slain, dy - ing in weak-ness and ris - ing to reign.

Alternative (later) version of this measure

This tune in a lower key: 582

ENTHRONED ETERNALLY   *Rev. 5:13*

You, Living Christ, Our Eyes Behold

603

Edmund R. Morgan, 1950, 1973 (alt'd)

PALACE GREEN, 8.7.8.7.88.7

Michael Fleming, 1958

1. You, liv-ing Christ, our eyes be-hold a - mid your church ap-
2. Your glo-rious feet have sought and found your own in ev-'ry
3. O ris - en Christ, to - day a - live, a - mid your church a-

1. pear - ing, all girt a - bout your breast with gold, and bright ap-
2. na - tion; with ev - er - last-ing voice you sound the call of
3. bid - ing, who still your blood and bod - y give, new life and

1. par - el wear - ing; your coun-te-nance is burn-ing bright, a sun re-
2. our sal - va - tion; you search us still with eyes of flame; you know and
3. strength pro-vid - ing, we join the heav'n-ly com-pa - ny to sing your

1. splen - dent in its might: Lord Christ, we see your glo - ry.
2. call us all by name: Lord Christ, we see your glo - ry.
3. praise tri - um-phant - ly, for we have seen your glo - ry.

Rev. 1;13–14; Jn. 1:14

ENTHRONED ETERNALLY

604

Ah! Think Not the Lord Delayeth

Percy Dearmer, 1931

AUCTOR OMNIUM BONORUM, 88.7 D

J. Lohner, 1691; adapted by J. S. Bach; harmony simplified

1. Ah! think not the Lord de - lay - eth; "I am with you,"
2. For e'en now the reign of heav - en spreads through-out the
3. Not for us to find the rea - sons, or to know the

1. still he say - eth; "do you not yet un - der-stand?"
2. world like leav - en, un - ob - served and ver - y near;
3. times and sea - sons, comes the Lord when strikes the hour;

1. Look not back, the past re - gret - ting; on the dawn your
2. like the seed when no one know - eth, like the shel - t'ring
3. ours to bear the faith - ful wit - ness which can shape the

1. hearts be set - ting; rise and hear the Lord's com - mand.
2. tree that grow - eth, comes the life e - ter - nal here.
3. world to fit - ness; thine, O God, to give the pow'r.

COMING IN GLORY

Lk. 12:45

Lo! He Comes

Charles Wesley, 1758

HELMSLEY, 8.7.8.7.4.7

18th-century English melody

1. Lo! he comes with clouds de-scend-ing, once for fa-vored
2. To his love and sav-ing Pas-sion all our hap-pi-
3. Yea, A-men! let all a-dore thee, high on thine e-

1. sin-ners slain; thou-sand thou-sand saints at-tend-ing
2. ness we owe, par-don, ho-li-ness, sal-va-tion,
3. ter-nal throne: Sav-ior, take the pow'r and glo-ry,

A   B

1. swell the tri-umph of his train. Al-le-lu-ia! Al-le-
2. heav'n a-bove and heav'n be-low. Grace and glo-ry, grace and
3. claim the king-dom for thine own. Al-le-lu-ia! Al-le-

All

1. lu-ia! Al-le-lu-ia! God ap-pears, on earth to reign.
2. glo-ry, grace and glo-ry from that o-pen foun-tain flow.
3. lu-ia! Al-le-lu-ia! Thou shalt reign, and thou a-lone!

NOTE: At "A" and "B" the phrases may be given to different groups of voices.

Mt. 24:30

COMING IN GLORY

606

"Sleepers, Wake!"

Wachet Auf, by Philipp Nicolai, 1598; tr. Carl P. Daw, Jr. (b. 1944), and others

WACHET AUF, 89.8.89.8.66.4.88

P. Nicolai, 1598; arranged by J. S. Bach (Cantata 140)

1. "Sleep-ers, wake!" A voice as-tounds us; the shout of ram-part
2. Zi-on hears the night-watch sing - ing; her heart with joy-ful
3. Lamb of God, the heavens a-dore you; let saints and an-gels

1. guards sur-rounds us: "A - wake, Je-ru-sa-lem, a-rise!"
2. hope is spring - ing, she wakes and hur-ries through the night.
3. sing be-fore you, as harps and cym-bals swell the sound.

1. Mid-night's peace their cry has bro - ken, their ur-gent sum-mons
2. Forth he comes, the Bride-groom glo - rious in strength of grace, in
3. Twelve great pearls, the cit-y's por - tals: through them we stream to

1. clear-ly spo - ken: "The time has come, O maid-ens wise!
2. truth vic-to - rious: her star is risen, her light grows bright.
3. join th' im-mor - tals as we with joy your throne sur-round.

COMING IN GLORY

1. Rise up, and give us light; the Bride-groom is in sight. Al-le-lu-ia!
2. Now come, most wor-thy Lord, God's Son, In-car-nate Word, Al-le-lu-ia!
3. No eye has known the sight, no ear heard such de-light: Al-le-lu-ia!

1. Your lamps pre-pare and has-ten there, that you the wed-ding feast may share."
2. We fol-low all in-to the hall to join the wed-ding fes-ti-val.
3. There-fore we sing to greet our King; for-ev-er let our prais-es ring.

Eph. 5:14; Mt. 25:1–13

The King Shall Come When Morning Dawns   607

Anon. Greek hymn; tr. James Brownlie, 1908

ST. STEPHEN, CM

William Jones, 1789

1. The King shall come when morn-ing dawns, and light tri-um-phant breaks;
2. Not as of old a lit-tle child to bear, and fight, and die,
3. O bright-er than the ris-ing morn when he, vic-to-rious, rose,
4. O bright-er than that glo-rious morn shall this fair morn-ing be,
5. The King shall come when morn-ing dawns, and light and beau-ty brings:

1. when beau-ty gilds the east-ern hills, and life to joy a-wakes.
2. but crowned with glo-ry like the sun that lights the morn-ing sky.
3. and left the lone-some place of death, de-spite the rage of foes —
4. when Christ, our King, in beau-ty comes, and we his face shall see!
5. hail, Christ the Lord! Thy peo-ple pray, "Come quick-ly, King of kings."

This tune in a lower key: 473   Alternative tune: BRADFIELD, 469

Lk. 21:28

COMING IN GLORY

608

Lord Christ, When First You Came

Walter Russell Bowie, 1928 (alt'd)

NEWNHAM, 8.7.8.7.88.7

Herbert Howells, 1964

1. Lord Christ, when first you came to earth up - on a cross they
*2. O won - drous love, which found no room in life, where sin de -
3. New ad - vent of the love of Christ, shall we a - gain re -
4. O wound - ed hands of Je - sus build in us your new cre -

1. bound you, and mocked your sav - ing king - ship then by thorns with
2. nied you, and, doomed to death, must bring to doom the power which
3. fuse you, till in the night of hate and war we per - ish
4. a - tion; our pride is dust, our vaunt is stilled, we wait your

1. which they crowned you; and still our wrongs may weave you now new
2. cru - ci - fied you, till not a stone was left on stone, and
3. as we lose you? From old un - faith our souls re - lease to
4. rev - e - la - tion. O Love that tri - umphs o - ver loss, we

1. thorns to pierce that stead - y brow, and robe of sor - row 'round you.
2. all a na - tion's pride o'er-thrown, went down to dust be - side you.
3. seek the king - dom of your peace by which a - lone we choose you.
4. bring our hearts be - fore your cross to fin - ish your sal - va - tion.

*Eb minor is the original key.

COMING IN GLORY

Mk. 13:2

We Believe in One True God

609

St. 1, 2, 4, Tobias Clausnitzer, 1668; tr. Catherine Winkworth, 1863;
st. 3, 5, 6, Howard G. Hageman, 1982

RATISBON, 7.7.7.7.77

Arranged from J. G. Werner's *Choralbuch* (1815)

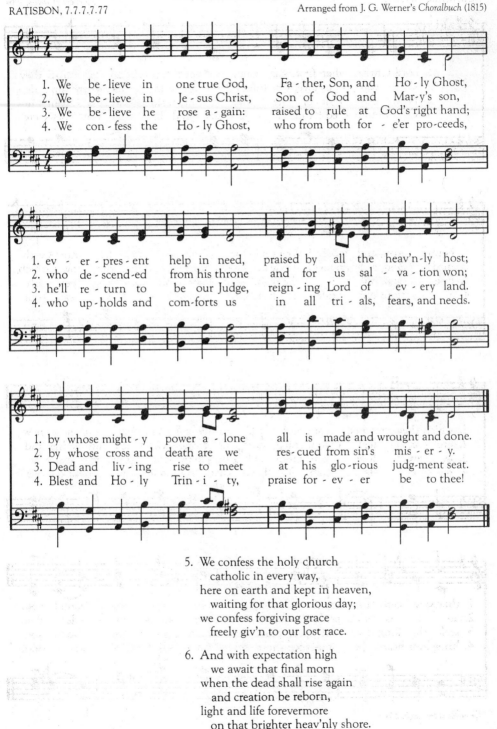

5. We confess the holy church
   catholic in every way,
   here on earth and kept in heaven,
   waiting for that glorious day;
   we confess forgiving grace
   freely giv'n to our lost race.

6. And with expectation high
   we await that final morn
   when the dead shall rise again
   and creation be reborn,
   light and life forevermore
   on that brighter heav'nly shore.

FULLNESS OF GOD

610

Our Song of Hope

SONG OF HOPE, Irregular   Eugene P. Heideman, 1974   Roger J. Rietberg, 1975, 1983

OUR SONG

We sing to our Lord a new song; we sing in our world a sure hope: our God loves his world, he called it in-to be-ing, he re-news it through Je-sus Christ, he gov-erns it by his Spir-it. God is the world's true hope.

OUR PRAYER

Come, Lord Je-sus: we are o-pen to your Spir-it. We a-wait your full pres-ence. Our world finds rest in you a-lone.

FULLNESS OF GOD

Holy, Holy, Holy! Lord God Almighty!   611

Richard Heber, 1783–1826

NICAEA, 11.12.12.10

J. B. Dykes, 1861

Descant, st. 4, by David McK. Williams

4. Ho - ly, ho - ly, ho - ly! Ho - ly,

1. Ho - ly, ho - ly, ho - ly! Lord God Al - might - y! Ear - ly in the
2. Ho - ly, ho - ly, ho - ly! All the saints a - dore thee, cast - ing down their
3. Ho - ly, ho - ly, ho - ly! Though the darkness hide thee, though the eye of
4. Ho - ly, ho - ly, ho - ly! Lord God Al - might - y! All thy works shall

4. ho - ly, ho - ly! Ho - ly, ho - ly,

1. morn - ing our song shall rise to thee; ho - ly, ho - ly, ho - ly!
2. gold - en crowns a - round the glass - y sea; cher - u - bim and ser - a - phim
3. sin - ful - ness thy glo - ry may not see; on - ly thou art ho - ly;
4. praise thy name, in earth and sky and sea; ho - ly, ho - ly, ho - ly!

4. ho - ly! God in three per - sons, bless - ed Trin - i - ty.

1. mer - ci - ful and might - y! God in three per - sons, bless - ed Trin - i - ty!
2. fall - ing down be - fore thee, who wert, and art, and ev - er - more shalt be.
3. there is none be - side thee, per - fect in power, in love, and pu - ri - ty.
4. mer - ci - ful and might - y! God in three per - sons, bless - ed Trin - i - ty!

Isa. 6:1–3; Rev. 4:8; 15:4   FULLNESS OF GOD

612 Bright the Vision That Delighted

Richard Mant, 1837

LAUS DEO, 8.7.8.7

Richard Redhead, 1853

Descant, st. 3 and 6, by S. H. Nicholson

"Lord, thy glo - ry fills the heav - en, earth is with its full - ness stored;

1. Bright the vi - sion that de - light - ed once the sight of Ju - dah's seer,
2. Round the Lord in glo - ry seat - ed cher - u - bim and ser - a - phim
3. "Lord, thy glo - ry fills the heav - en, earth is with its full - ness stored;
4. Heav'n is still with glo - ry ring - ing, earth takes up the an - gels' cry,

un - to thee be glo - ry giv - en, Ho - ly, ho - ly, ho - ly Lord."

1. sweet the count - less tongues u - nit - ed to en - trance the proph - et's ear.
2. filled his tem - ple and re - peat - ed each to each th' al - ter - nate hymn:
3. un - to thee be glo - ry giv - en, Ho - ly, ho - ly, ho - ly Lord!"
4. "Ho - ly, ho - ly, ho - ly," sing - ing, "Lord of hosts, the Lord most high."

5. With his seraph train before him,
with his holy church below,
thus conspire we to adore him,
bid we thus our anthem flow:

6. "Lord, thy glory fills the heaven,
earth is with its fullness stored;
unto thee be glory given,
Holy, holy, holy Lord."

FULLNESS OF GOD

Isa. 6:1–3

God Is in His Temple

613

W. T. Matson, 1887, based on *Gott ist gegenwärtig;*
Gerhardt Tersteegen, 1697–1767

TYSK, 6.686.686.6.6.

Hymnal–1940, from a chorale sung at Stockholm, 1718

1. God is in his tem - ple, the al - might - y Fa - ther;
2. Christ comes to his tem - ple: we, his word re - ceiv - ing,
3. Come and claim thy tem - ple, gra - cious Ho - ly Spir - it;

1. round his foot - stool let us gath - er;
2. are made hap - py in be - liev - ing;
3. in our hearts thy home in - her - it;

1. him with a - do - ra - tion serve, the Lord most ho - ly,
2. lo! from sin de - liv - ered he hath turned our sad - ness,
3. make in us thy dwell - ing, thy high work ful - fill - ing,

1. who hath mer - cy on the low - ly; let us raise hymns of praise
2. our deep gloom, to joy and glad - ness; let us raise hymns of praise,
3. in - to ours thy will in - still - ing, till we raise hymns of praise

1. for his great sal - va - tion: God is in his tem - ple.
2. for our bonds are sev - ered: Christ comes to his tem - ple.
3. be - yond mor - tal tell - ing, in th' e - ter - nal tem - ple.

Hab. 2:20

FULLNESS OF GOD

614

Praise Ye the Lord,
Ye Servants of the Lord

From a passage (Greek) in the *Apostolic Constitutions*, 3rd century;
tr. G. R. Woodward, 1910 (alt'd)

OLD 124th, 10.10 10 10.10

Genevan Psalter (1551); harmony from W. Parsons, 1563

1. Praise ye the Lord, ye ser-vants of the Lord;
2. Fa - ther of Christ — of him whose work was done

1. praise ye his name, his lord - ly hon - or sing:
2. when by his death he took our sins a - way —

1. thee we a - dore, to thee glad hom-age bring;
2. to thee be - long - eth wor - ship day by day;

1. thee we ac - knowl - edge, God to be a - dored
2. yea, ho - ly Fa - ther, ev - er - last - ing Son,

1. for thy great glo - ry, sov-'reign Lord and King.
2. and Ho - ly Spir - it, praise be thine for aye.

FULLNESS OF GOD

Lord, Keep Us Steadfast in Your Word

615

Erhalt'uns, Herr, by Martin Luther, 1533;
tr. Catherine Winkworth, 1863, and *Lutheran Book of Worship* (1978)

ERHALT'UNS, HERR, LM

Klug, *Geistliche Lieder* (1543)

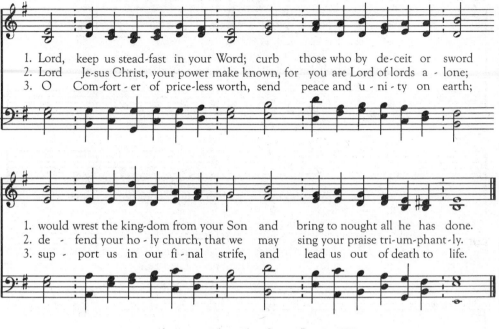

1. Lord, keep us stead-fast in your Word; curb those who by de-ceit or sword
2. Lord Je-sus Christ, your power make known, for you are Lord of lords a - lone;
3. O Com-fort - er of price-less worth, send peace and u - ni - ty on earth;

1. would wrest the king-dom from your Son and bring to nought all he has done.
2. de - fend your ho - ly church, that we may sing your praise tri-um-phant-ly.
3. sup - port us in our fi - nal strife, and lead us out of death to life.

Alternative translation, from Cantate Domino *(1972)*

1. Father, with all your Gospel's power,
   protect us in temptation's hour,
   when in his pride the Evil One
   seeks your Anointed to dethrone.

2. Our King of glory, Jesus Christ,
   power in obedience manifest,
   defend your church in dangerous days,
   and liberate us for your praise.

3. Spirit, by Christ's atonement given
   to bring together earth and heaven,
   in us, between us, silence strife
   and lead us out of death to life.

616   O God, We Praise Thee, and Confess

Te Deum Laudamus, 5th century;
versified in the *Supplement to the New Version* (1703)

LADYWELL, CMD

W. H. Ferguson, c. 1911; harmony slightly simplified

1. O God, we praise thee, and con - fess that thou the on - ly Lord
2. O ho - ly, ho - ly, ho - ly Lord, whom heav'n - ly hosts o - bey,
3. The ho - ly church through-out the world, O Lord, con - fess - es thee,
4. O Christ, of glo - ry thou art King, who from on high didst come

1. and ev - er - last - ing Fa - ther art, by all the earth a - dored.
2. the world is with the glo - ry filled of thy ma - jes - tic ray.
3. that thou e - ter - nal Fa - ther art of bound-less maj - es - ty.
4. to save us all, and didst not then dis - dain the vir - gin's womb.

1. To thee all an - gels cry a - loud; to thee the pow'rs on high,
2. Th' a - pos - tles' glo - rious com - pa - ny and proph-ets crowned with light,
3. Thine hon-ored, true, and on - ly Son, and Ho - ly Ghost, the spring
4. And, hav - ing o - ver - come the sting of death, thou o - pen'st wide

1. both cher - u - bim and ser - a - phim con - tin-ual - ly do cry.
2. with all the mar - tyrs' no - ble host thy con-stant praise re - cite.
3. of end - less joy, the Lord of life: blest Trin - i - ty we sing.
4. the gates of heav'n to all who firm in thy be - lief a - bide.

Alternative tune: ST. MATTHEW, 92

FULLNESS OF GOD

Father Most Holy, Merciful, and Loving   617

O Pater sancte, c. 10th century; tr. A. E. Alston, 1904

AD TUUM NOMEN, 11.11.11.5 sapphic   Melody from *Chartres Antiphoner* (1784)

1. Fa - ther most ho - ly, mer - ci - ful, and lov - ing, Je - sus, Re -
2. three in a won - drous u - ni - ty un - bro - ken, one per - fect
3. all thy cre - a - tion serv - eth its cre - a - tor; thee ev - 'ry
4. Lord God al - might - y, un - to thee be glo - ry, One in three

1. deem - er, ev - er to be wor - shiped, life - giv - ing Spir - it,
2. God - head, love that nev - er fail - eth, light of the an - gels,
3. crea - ture prais - eth with - out ceas - ing; we, too, would sing the
4. Per - sons, o - ver all ex - alt - ed; thine, as is meet, be

1. Com - fort - er most gra - cious, God ev - er - last - ing;
2. suc - cor of the need - y, hope of all liv - ing;
3. psalms of true de - vo - tion; hear, we be - seech thee.
4. hon - or, praise, and bless - ing, now and for - ev - er.

Alternative tune: CHRISTE SANCTORUM, 515

FULLNESS OF GOD

618
Come, Thou Almighty King

Anon. English, c. 1757

ITALIAN HYMN, 66.4.666.4

Felice de Giardini, 1769

1. Come, thou al-might-y King, help us thy name to sing,
2. Come, thou in-car-nate Word, gird on thy might-y sword,
3. Come, Ho-ly Com-fort-er, thy sa-cred wit-ness bear
4. To the great One in Three e-ter-nal prais-es be

1. help us to praise: Fa-ther all glo-ri-ous, o'er all vic-
2. our prayer at-tend; come and thy peo-ple bless, and give thy
3. in this glad hour: thou who al-might-y art, now rule in
4. hence ev-er-more; his sov-'reign maj-es-ty may we in

1. to-ri-ous, come and reign o-ver us, An-cient of Days.
2. word suc-cess; Spir-it of ho-li-ness, on us de-scend.
3. ev-'ry heart, and ne'er from us de-part, Spir-it of power.
4. glo-ry see and to e-ter-ni-ty love and a-dore.

FULLNESS OF GOD

Dan. 7:9

Holy God, We Praise Your Name

Grosser Gott, wir loben dich, attributed to I. Franz, 1770;
st. 1–4 tr. *Lutheran Book of Worship* (1978);
st. 5 tr. R. Birch Hoyle, 1923 (alt'd)

619

GROSSER GOTT, 7.8.7.8.77
Descant, st. 5

Melody in *Katholisches Gesangbuch* (1774)

5. Glo - ry through e - ter - ni - ty: Spir - it, Son, and bless - ed Fa - ther,

1. Ho - ly God, we praise your name; Lord of all, we bow be-fore you.
2. Hark, the glad ce - les - tial hymn an - gel choirs a - bove are rais-ing:
3. Lo, the a - pos - tol - ic train join your sa - cred name to hal-low;
4. Ho - ly Fa - ther, ho - ly Son, Ho - ly Spir - it, Three we name you,
5. Glo - ry through e - ter - ni - ty: Spir - it, Son, and bless - ed Fa - ther,

5. God of gra - cious ten - der-ness, at your feet we sin - ners gath-er.

1. All on earth your scep-ter claim; all in heav'n a - bove a-dore you.
2. cher - u - bim and ser - a - phim, in un - ceas - ing cho - rus prais-ing,
3. proph - ets swell the glad re-frain, and the white-robed mar - tyrs fol-low;
4. though in es - sence on - ly One; un - di - vid - ed God, we claim you,
5. God of gra - cious ten - der-ness, at your feet we sin - ners gath-er.

5. All your great and won-drous love we shall through the a - ges prove.

1. In - fi - nite your vast do-main; ev - er - last - ing is your reign.
2. fill the heav'ns with sweet ac-cord— "Ho - ly, ho - ly, ho - ly, Lord!"
3. and from morn to set of sun through the church the song goes on.
4. and, a - dor - ing, bend the knee while we own the mys - ter - y.
5. All your great and won-drous love we shall through the a - ges prove.

Rev. 4:8

FULLNESS OF GOD

620 All Glory Be to God on High

Allein Gott in der Hoh' sei Ehr, by N. Decius, 1522;
tr. F. Bland Tucker, 1977

ALLEIN GOTT IN DER HOH' SEI EHR, 8.7.8.7.88.7   Melody in *Geistliche Lieder* (Leipzig, 1539)

1. All glo-ry be to God on high, and peace on earth from
2. O Lamb of God, Lord Je-sus Christ, whom God the Fa-ther
3. You on-ly are the Ho-ly One, who came for our sal-

1. heav-en, and God's good-will un-fail-ing-ly to
2. gave us, who for the world was sac-ri-ficed up-
3. va-tion, and on-ly you are God's true Son, the

1. hu-man-kind be giv-en. We bless, we wor-ship you, we raise for
2. on the cross to save us; and, as you sit at God's right hand, and
3. first-born of cre-a-tion. You on-ly, Christ, as Lord we own and,

1. your great glo-ry thanks and praise, O God, Al-might-y Fa-ther.
2. we for judg-ment there must stand, have mer-cy, Lord, up-on us.
3. with the Spir-it, you a-lone share in the Fa-ther's glo-ry.

Ancient of Days

William C. Doane, 1886, 1892

EASTWOOD, 11.10.11.10

Eric Shave, 1951

1. An - cient of Days, who sit-test throned in glo - ry, to thee all
2. O Ho - ly Fa - ther, who hast led thy chil-dren in all the
3. O Ho - ly Je - sus, Prince of Peace and Sav - ior, to thee we
4. O Ho - ly Ghost, the Lord and the Life - giv - er, thine is the

1. knees are bent, all voic - es pray; thy love has blessed the wide world's
2. a - ges, with the fire and cloud, through seas dry-shod, through wea-ry
3. owe the peace that still pre - vails, still - ing the rude wills of our
4. quick-ening power that gives in - crease; from thee have flowed, as from a

1. won - drous sto - ry, with light and life since E - den's dawn - ing day.
2. wastes be - wil-d'ring: to thee in rev-'rent love our hearts are bowed.
3. wild be - hav - ior, and calm-ing pas-sion's fierce and storm-y gales.
4. pleas - ant riv - er, our plen - ty, wealth, pros-per-i - ty, and peace.

5. O Triune God, with heart and voice adoring,
      praise we the goodness that doth crown our days;
   pray we that thou wilt hear us, still imploring
      thy love and favor, kept to us always.

Ex. 13:20–14:28; Dan. 7:9

FULLNESS OF GOD

622   Come, You People, Rise and Sing

C. A. Alington, 1872–1955

BOUNDLESS MERCY, 7.6.7.6 D trochaic

Union Harmony (1830)

1. Come, you peo-ple, rise and sing praise to God who made you,
2. Praise we God the Fa-ther's name for our world's cre-a-tion,
3. Praise we God the on-ly Son who in mer-cy sought us;
4. Ho-ly Spir-it, grant, we pray, that we come to know him

1. and to heav'n's e-ter-nal King bring the prayers he bade you;
2. and his sav-ing health pro-claim un-to ev-'ry na-tion;
3. born to save a world un-done, out of death he brought us;
4. more and more, and ev-'ry day in our lives we show him,

1. bring your praise for mer-cies past, all his love con-fess-ing,
2. till, his name by all con-fess'd, ev-'ry heart en-throne him,
3. here, a-while he showed his love, suf-fered un-com-plain-ing;
4. that with hearts by you made brave, strong, and wise, and ten-der,

1. and in life, while life shall last, ask your Fa-ther's bless-ing.
2. and from far-thest east to west, all his chil-dren own him.
3. now he pleads for us a-bove, ris'n, as-cend-ed, reign-ing.
4. we, with all the pow'rs we have, ser-vice meet may ren-der.

5. Father, Son, and Holy Ghost, help us to adore you,
   till with all the angel host low we fall before you,
   till throughout our earthly days, guided, loved, forgiven,
   we can blend our song of praise with the song of heaven.

FULLNESS OF GOD

O Gladsome Light

623

Greek hymn, 3rd century; tr. Robert Bridges, 1899

NUNC DIMITTIS, 66.7.66.7

Genevan Psalter (1551): version of melody in *First Book of Psalms* (Lyon, 1547);
edited by L. Bourgeois; harmonized by C. Goudimel, 1565

1. O glad-some light, O grace of God the Fa-ther's face, th' e-
2. Now, ere day fad - eth quite, we see the eve- ning light, our
3. To thee of right be - longs all praise of ho - ly songs, O

1. ter - nal splen-dor wear - ing; ce - les-tial, ho - ly, blest, our
2. wont-ed hymn out - pour - ing; Fa - ther of might un - known, thee,
3. Son of God, Life - giv - er; thee, there-fore, O Most High, the

1. Sav - ior Je - sus Christ, joy - ful in thine ap - pear - ing.
2. his in - car - nate Son, and Ho - ly Spirit a - dor - ing.
3. world doth glo - ri - fy, and shall ex - alt for - ev - er.

624 We Give Immortal Praise

Isaac Watts, 1707

CROFT'S 136th, 6.6.6.6.88

Melody and bass by William Croft, 1708

1. We give im-mor-tal praise to God the Fa-ther's love, for all our com-forts here, and bet-ter hopes a-bove; he sent his own e-ter-nal Son to die for sins that we had done.
2. To God the Son be-longs im-mor-tal glo-ry too, who bought us with his blood from ev-er-last-ing woe; and now he lives, and now he reigns, and sees the fruit of all his pains.
3. To God the Spir-it's name im-mor-tal wor-ship give, whose new cre-at-ing power makes the dead sin-ner live; his work com-pletes the grand de-sign and wills the world with joy di-vine.
4. Al-might-y God, to thee be end-less hon-or done, the un-di-vid-ed Three and the mys-te-rious One; where rea-son fails with all her powers, there faith prevails, and love a-dores.

GUIDES TO WORSHIP

ORDER OF WORSHIP

The service of worship ordinarily begins with the Votum, Sentences, and Salutation. Or it may begin with the Hymn, especially if it is a processional, followed by the Votum, Sentences, and Salutation. The portions printed in bold type are intended to be read by the congregation.

THE APPROACH TO GOD

VOTUM

Our help is in the name of the Lord, who made heaven and earth. **Amen.**

Psalm 124:8

SENTENCES

The following, or other appropriate portions of Scripture, may be used.

O come, let us worship and bow down, let us kneel before the Lord, our Maker! For he is our God, and we are the people of his pasture, and the sheep of his hand.   *Psalm 95:6-7*

and/or

Psalm 33:1-5	*Psalm 100*	*Zechariah 8:7-8*
Psalm 43:3-4	*Exodus 15:2*	*John 4:24*
Psalm 96:1-3	*Isaiah 55:1, 6-7*	

SALUTATION

Grace to you and peace from God our Father and the Lord Jesus Christ. **Amen.**

or

Galatians 1:3-5	*II Peter 1:2*	*Jude 2*
I Timothy 1:2	*II John 3*	*Revelation 1:4-5*
Titus 1:4		

HYMN

PRAYER OF CONFESSION

The minister may introduce the prayer with the following or another suitable call to confession.

Let us confess our sins to almighty God. Let us pray.

All shall join in one of the following prayers or another appropriate confession.

Have mercy upon us, O God, according to your steadfast love; according to your abundant mercies, blot out our transgressions. Wash us thoroughly from our iniquity, and cleanse us from our sin. For we know our transgressions, and our sin is ever before us. Create in us a clean heart, O God, and put a new and right spirit within us. Cast us not away from your presence, and take not your Holy Spirit from us. Restore to us the joy of your salvation, and uphold us with a willing spirit. Through Jesus Christ our Lord. Amen.   *Adapted from Psalm 51*

or

Most holy and merciful Father, we acknowledge and confess before you our sinful nature, prone to evil and slow to do good; and all our shortcomings and offenses. You alone know how often we have sinned: in wandering from your ways, in wasting your gifts, in forgetting your love. But, O Lord, have mercy on us, who are ashamed and sorry for all wherein we have displeased you. Teach us to hate our errors; cleanse us from our secret faults; and forgive our sins; for the sake of your dear Son. And, O most holy and loving God, help us to live in your light and walk in your ways, according to the commandments of Jesus Christ, our Savior. Amen.

A brief period for silent prayers may be allowed. The following or another suitable response may then be said or sung: (see hymns 564-567):

Lord, have mercy upon us.
Christ, have mercy upon us.
Lord, have mercy upon us.

ASSURANCE OF PARDON

One of the following scriptural assurances or one drawn from other portions of Scripture may be used to convey an assurance of God's promise freely to pardon all who come to him in repentance and faith.

The LORD is merciful and gracious, slow to anger and abounding in steadfast love. He does not deal with us according to our sins, nor requite us according to our iniquities. For as the heavens are high above the earth, so great is his steadfast love toward those who fear him; as far as the east is from the west, so far does he remove our transgressions from us.   *Psalm 103:8, 10-12*

or

With everlasting love I will have compassion on you, says the LORD your Redeemer. I, I am he who blots out your transgressions for my own sake, and I will not remember your sins. Return to me, for I have redeemed you.
Isaiah 54:8; 43:25; 44:22

or

Can a woman forget her sucking child, that she have no compassion on the child of her womb? As a mother comforts her child, so will I comfort you, says the LORD.   *Isaiah 49:15; 66:13*

or

For God so loved the world that he gave his only Son, that whoever believes in him should not perish, but have eternal life. For God sent the Son into the world, not to condemn the world, but that the world might be saved through him.   *John 3:16-17*

or

Psalm 130:3-4, 7	*Isaiah 44:21-22*	*John 8:34-36*
Psalm 145:18-19	*Luke 1:68, 77-78*	*Colossians 1:11-14*

At the conclusion of the scriptural assurance, the minister shall add:

Believe this Gospel and go forth to live in peace. **Amen.**

THE LAW OF GOD

The Law may be read or sung, or the service may proceed to the reading of the Summary. To sing a metrical version of the law use hymn 65.

God spoke all these words, saying, I am the LORD your God who brought you out of the land of Egypt, out of the house of bondage.

You shall have no other gods before me.

You shall not make yourself a graven image, or any likeness of anything that is in the heaven above, or that is in the earth beneath, or that is in the water under the earth; you shall not bow down to them or serve them; for I the LORD your God am a jealous God, visiting the iniquity of the fathers upon the children to the third and fourth generation of those who hate me, but showing steadfast love to thousands of those who love me and keep my commandments.

You shall not take the name of the LORD your God in vain; for the LORD will not hold him guiltless who takes his name in vain.

Remember the sabbath day, to keep it holy. Six days you shall labor, and do all your work; but the seventh day is the sabbath to the LORD your God; in it you shall not do any work, you, or your son, or your daughter, your manservant, or your maidservant, or your cattle, or the sojourner who is within your gates; for in six days the LORD made heaven and earth, the sea, and all that is in them, and rested the seventh day; therefore the LORD blessed the sabbath day and hallowed it.

Honor your father and your mother, that your days may be long in the land which the LORD your God gives you.

You shall not kill.

You shall not commit adultery.

You shall not steal.

You shall not bear false witness against your neighbor.

You shall not covet your neighbor's house; you shall not covet your neighbor's wife, or his manservant, or his maidservant, or his ox, or his ass, or anything that is your neighbor's.   *Exodus 20:1-17*

and/or

Hear what our Lord Jesus Christ says:

You shall love the Lord your God with all your heart, and with all your soul, and with all your mind. This is the great and first commandment. And a second is like it, you shall love your neighbor as yourself. On these two commandments depend all the law and the prophets.   *Matthew 22:37-40*

or as it is recorded in Mark 12:29-31.

PSALTER AND GLORIA PATRI

A selection from the Psalms and the Gloria Patri or another appropriate hymn may be used to express gratitude to God.

THE WORD OF GOD
IN PROCLAMATION AND SACRAMENT

PRAYER FOR ILLUMINATION

This prayer or another petition may be offered.

Guide us, O Lord, by your Word and Holy Spirit, that in your light we may see light, in your truth find freedom, and in your will discover peace; through Jesus Christ our Lord. **Amen.**

HYMN

A hymn setting forth the theme of the Scripture reading(s) or praising God for the revelation in his Word may be sung here, between the lessons, or before the sermon.

LESSONS

There will ordinarily be two or three lessons, one from the Old Testament, one from the portion of the New Testament other than the Gospels, and one from the Gospels. The lessons may be announced as follows:

The Word of the Lord from _____

After the reading of the lesson there may be the response.

This is the Word of the Lord.

Thanks be to God.

The Gospel may be announced as follows:

The Gospel of our Lord Jesus Christ according to _____

The following may be used as a response to the Gospel.

This is the Gospel of the Lord.

Praise to you, O Christ.

SERMON

The minister shall deliver a sermon proclaiming the Scripture of the day.

PRAYER FOR BLESSING

Almighty God, grant that the words we have heard this day may, through your grace, be so grafted within our hearts that they may bring forth in us the fruits of the Spirit, to the honor and praise of your name; through Jesus Christ our Lord. **Amen.**

The minister shall move to the table.

When worship includes only the grace of the WORD IN PROCLAMATION, then the Creed, Offering, Doxology, Prayers of Thanksgiving and Intercession, Hymn, and Benediction may be understood as the congregation's RESPONSE TO GOD.

CONFESSION OF FAITH

The minister shall call the people to join in an affirmation of the Christian faith.

Let us confess our Christian faith using the Nicene [*or* Apostles' (see p. 566)] Creed:

When all have risen, the minister shall say:

Let us say what we believe.

I. THE NICENE CREED

We believe in one God,
   the Father, the Almighty,
   maker of heaven and earth,
   of all that is, seen and unseen.

We believe in one Lord, Jesus Christ,
   the only Son of God,
   eternally begotten of the Father,
   God from God, Light from Light,
   true God from true God,
   begotten, not made,
   of one being with the Father.
   Through him all things were made.
   For us and for our salvation
      he came down from heaven:
   by the power of the Holy Spirit
      he became incarnate from the virgin Mary,
      and was made man.
   For our sake he was crucified under Pontius Pilate;
      he suffered death and was buried.
      On the third day he rose again
         in accordance with the Scriptures;
      he ascended into heaven
         and is seated at the right hand of the Father.
   He will come again in glory to judge the living and the dead,
      and his kingdom will have no end.

We believe in the Holy Spirit, the Lord, the giver of life,
   who proceeds from the Father and the Son.
   With the Father and the Son he is worshiped and glorified.
   He has spoken through the Prophets.
   We believe in one holy catholic and apostolic Church.
   We acknowledge one baptism for the forgiveness of sins.
   We look for the resurrection of the dead,
      and the life of the world to come. Amen.

or

II. THE NICENE CREED

We believe in one God,
   the Father almighty,
   maker of heaven and earth,
   and of all things visible and invisible;

And in one Lord Jesus Christ,
   the only-begotten Son of God,
   begotten of his Father before all worlds,
   God of God, Light of Light,
   very God of very God,
   begotten, not made,
   being of one substance with the Father;
   by whom all things were made;
   who for us and for our salvation
      came down from heaven,
   and was incarnate by the Holy Ghost of the Virgin Mary,
      and was made man;
   and was crucified also for us under Pontius Pilate;
   he suffered and was buried;
   and the third day he rose again according to the Scriptures,
   and ascended into heaven,
   and sitteth on the right hand of the Father;
   and he shall come again, with glory,
      to judge both the quick and the dead;
   whose kingdom shall have no end.

And we believe in the Holy Ghost, the Lord and giver of life,
   who proceedeth from the Father and the Son;
   who with the Father and the Son together is worshiped
      and glorified;
   who spake by the Prophets.
   and we believe one holy catholic and apostolic Church;
   we acknowledge one baptism for the remission of sins;
   and we look for the resurrection of the dead,
      and the life of the world to come. Amen.

or

I. THE APOSTLES' CREED

I believe in God, the Father almighty,
    creator of heaven and earth.

I believe in Jesus Christ, his only Son, our Lord.
    He was conceived by the power of the Holy Spirit
        and born of the Virgin Mary.
    He suffered under Pontius Pilate,
        was crucified, died, and was buried.
    He descended to the dead.
    On the third day he rose again.
    He ascended into heaven,
        and is seated at the right hand of the Father.
    He will come again to judge the living and the dead.

I believe in the Holy Spirit,
    the holy catholic Church,
    the communion of saints,
    the forgiveness of sins,
    the resurrection of the body,
    and the life everlasting. Amen.

or

II. THE APOSTLES' CREED

I believe in God, the Father almighty,
    maker of heaven and earth;

And in Jesus Christ, his only Son, our Lord;
    who was conceived by the Holy Ghost,
    born of the Virgin Mary,
    suffered under Pontius Pilate,
    was crucified, dead, and buried.
    He descended into hell.
    The third day he rose again from the dead.
    He ascended into heaven,
    and sitteth on the right hand of God the Father almighty.
    From thence he shall come to judge the quick and the dead.

I believe in the Holy Ghost,
    the holy catholic Church,
    the communion of saints,
    the forgiveness of sins,
    the resurrection of the body,
    and the life everlasting. Amen.

    N.B. A metrical version of the creed may be sung using hymn 609.

PEACE

The minister may introduce the Peace with these, or other appropriate words of Scripture:

Let the peace of Christ rule in your hearts since as members of one body you were called to peace.   *Colossians 3:15*

The peace of Christ be with you.

And also with you.

The congregation may then exchange the Peace using the same greeting and response or through other appropriate words and actions.

OFFERING

An offering shall be received to provide for a ministry within the congregation, to gather resources for the ministries of others, and to provide the elements for the celebration of the Lord's Supper.

DOXOLOGY

This hymn, or another ascription of praise, may be used as the offerings are brought forward.

MEANING OF THE SACRAMENT

Beloved in the Lord Jesus Christ, the holy Supper which we are about to celebrate is a feast of remembrance, of communion, and of hope.

We come in remembrance that our Lord Jesus Christ was sent of the Father into the world to assume our flesh and blood and to fulfil for us all obedience to the divine law, even to the bitter and shameful death of the cross. By his death, resurrection, and ascension he established a new and eternal covenant of grace and reconciliation that we might be accepted of God and never be forsaken by him.

We come to have communion with this same Christ who has promised to be with us always, even to the end of the world. In the breaking of the bread he makes himself known to us as the true heavenly Bread that strengthens us unto life eternal. In the cup of blessing he comes to us as the Vine in whom we must abide if we are to bear fruit.

We come in hope, believing that this bread and this cup are a pledge and foretaste of the feast of love of which we shall partake when his kingdom has fully come, when with unveiled face we shall behold him, made like unto him in his glory.

Since by his death, resurrection, and ascension Christ has obtained for us the life-giving Spirit who unites us all in one body, so are we to receive this Supper in true love, mindful of the communion of saints.

INVITATION

The minister, in the name of Christ, shall extend an invitation to all communicants present to participate in the Sacrament. The following, or a similar invitation, may be said.

All those who have confessed their faith in Christ and are members of a Christian church are welcome at the Lord's Table. Come, for all things are now ready.

COMMUNION PRAYER

The Lord be with you.

And also with you.

Lift up your hearts!

We lift them up to the Lord.

Let us give thanks to the Lord our God.

For it is holy and right to do so!

Holy and right it is, and our joyful duty to give thanks to you at all times and in all places, O Lord our Creator, almighty and everlasting God! You created heaven with all its hosts and the earth with all its plenty. You have given us life and being, and preserve us by your providence. But you have shown us the fullness of your love in sending into the world your Son, Jesus Christ, the eternal Word, made flesh for us and for our salvation. For the precious gift of this mighty Savior who has reconciled us to you we praise and bless you, O God. With your whole Church on earth and with all the company of heaven we worship and adore your glorious name.

Here all shall say or sing (where sung see hymns 564-567):

Holy, holy, holy, Lord God of hosts! Heaven and earth are full of your glory. Hosanna in the highest!

Blessed is he that comes in the name of the Lord. Hosanna in the highest!

A short period of silence

Most righteous God, we remember in this Supper the perfect sacrifice offered once on the cross by our Lord Jesus Christ for the sin of the whole world.

In the joy of his resurrection and in expectation of his coming again, we offer ourselves to you as holy and living sacrifices. Send your Holy Spirit upon us, we pray, that the bread which we break and the cup which we bless may be to us the communion of the body and blood of Christ. Grant that, being joined together in him, we may attain to the unity of the faith and grow up in all things into Christ our Lord.

And as this grain has been gathered from many fields into one loaf, and these grapes from many hills into one cup, grant, O Lord, that your whole Church may soon be gathered from the ends of the earth into your kingdom. Even so, come, Lord Jesus!

COMMUNION

The minister shall declare the Words of Institution:

The Lord Jesus, the same night he was betrayed, took bread; and when he had given thanks, he broke it and gave it to them, saying, "Take, eat; this is my body which is broken for you: do this in remembrance of me."

The minister shall break the bread.

After the same manner also, he took the cup when they had supped, saying, "This cup is the new testament in my blood: this do, as often as you drink it, in remembrance of me."

The minister shall lift the cup.

In partaking of the bread it shall be said:

The bread which we break is the communion of the body of Christ.

In partaking of the cup it shall be said:

The cup of blessing which we bless is the communion of the blood of Christ.

THE RESPONSE TO GOD

THANKSGIVING AFTER COMMUNION

Brothers and sisters, since the Lord has now fed us at his Table, let us praise God's holy name with heartfelt thanksgiving!

Bless the LORD, O my soul;

and all that is within me, bless his holy name!

Bless the LORD, O my soul,

and forget not all his benefits,

who forgives all your iniquity,

who heals all your diseases,

who redeems your life from the Pit,

who crowns you with steadfast love and mercy.

The LORD is merciful and gracious,

slow to anger and abounding in steadfast love.

He does not deal with us according to our sins,

nor requite us according to our iniquities.

For as the heavens are high above the earth,

so great is his steadfast love toward those who fear him;

as far as the east is from the west,

so far does he remove our transgressions from us.

As a father pities his children,

so the LORD pities those who fear him.

Who did not spare his own Son, but gave him up for us all, and will also give us all things with him.

Therefore shall my mouth and heart show forth the praise of the Lord, from this time forth forevermore. Amen.   *From Psalm 103 with additions*

N.B. This thanksgiving can be sung using hymn 121, 122, or 144.

INTERCESSION

The following prayers may be used. Intercessions may be selected from other sources or may be in the minister's own words. The intercessions shall conclude with the Lord's Prayer.

Let us pray.

We praise and thank you, O Lord, that you have fed us at your Table. Grateful for your gifts and mindful of the communion of your saints, we offer to you our prayers for all people.

God of compassion, we remember before you the poor and the afflicted, the sick and the dying, prisoners and all who are lonely, the victims of war, injustice, and inhumanity, and all others who suffer from whatever their sufferings may be called.

Silence

O Lord of Providence, who holds the destiny of the nations in your hand, we pray for our country. Inspire the hearts and minds of our leaders that they, together with all our nation, may first seek your kingdom and righteousness so that order, liberty, and peace may dwell with your people.

Silence

O God the Creator, we pray for all nations and peoples. Take away the mistrust and lack of understanding that divide your creatures; increase in us the recognition that we are all your children.

Silence

O Savior God, look upon your Church in its struggle upon the earth. Have mercy on its weakness, bring to an end its unhappy divisions, and scatter its fears. Look also upon the ministry of your Church. Increase its courage, strengthen its faith, and inspire its witness to all people, even to the ends of the earth.

Silence

Author of grace and God of love, send your Holy Spirit's blessing to your children here present. Keep our hearts and thoughts in Jesus Christ, your Son, our only Savior

who has taught us to pray:	*or*	who has taught us when we pray to say:

Our Father in heaven,	**Our Father, who art in heaven,**
hallowed be your name,	**hallowed be thy name,**
your kingdom come,	**thy kingdom come,**
your will be done,	**thy will be done,**
on earth as in heaven.	**on earth as it is in heaven.**
Give us today our daily bread.	**Give us this day our daily bread.**
Forgive us our sins	**And forgive us our debts,**
as we forgive those	**as we forgive our debtors.**
who sin against us.	**And lead us not into temptation,**
Save us from the time of trial,	**but deliver us from evil.**
and deliver us from evil.	**For thine is the kingdom,**
For the kingdom, the power,	**and the power, and the glory,**
and the glory are yours,	**for ever. Amen.**
now and for ever. Amen.	

N.B.: *The Lord's Prayer may be sung using hymn 262.*

HYMN   *A hymn or psalm of thanksgiving may be sung.*

BENEDICTION   *Facing the congregation, the minister shall give the blessing:*

The grace of the Lord Jesus Christ and the love of God and the fellowship of the Holy Spirit be with you all. **Amen!**   *II Corinthians 13:14*

or

Numbers 6:24-26	Luke 2:29-32	II Thessalonians 3:16
Psalm 67:1-2	Romans 15:5-6	Hebrews 13:20-21

PSALMS FOR LITURGICAL READING

PSALM 1

Blessed are they
    who do not follow the advice
        of the wicked,
    nor loiter in the way of sinners,
    nor seat themselves in company
        with the scoffers.
Their delight is in the law of the LORD,
    and on his law they meditate
        day and night.

They are like trees planted by water-brooks,
    that bear fruit in season,
    with leaves that never wither.
In everything they do, they prosper.

It is not thus with the wicked!
    They are like chaff blown away
        by the wind;
    the wicked cannot withstand the Judgment,
    nor will sinners be within the company
        of the just.
For the LORD knows the way of the just,
    but the way of the wicked will perish.

PSALM 8

O LORD, our Lord,
    how glorious is your name
        in all creation!

Your majesty is praised above the heavens;
    it is sung below by babes
        and little children.

You have founded a stronghold
    against your foes,
    to silence your enemies and avengers.

When I look up to your sky,
    the work of your fingers,
    the moon and the stars
        that you set in their courses,

what are human beings
    that you should be mindful of them,
    or their offspring
        that you should care for them?

Yet you made them in the image of yourself,
    and crowned them with glory and honor.

You gave them rule over your handiwork,
    and put all things
        under their dominion:

all sheep and cattle,
    and also the wild animals;

birds of the air, fish of the sea,
    and whatever makes its path
        through the waters.

O LORD, our Lord,
    how glorious is your name
        in all creation!

PSALM 19

I

The heavens declare the glory of God;
    the vault of the sky
        shows his handiwork.

Day after day tells it out,
    and night after night makes it known.

There are no words, no language,
    nor voices that are heard.

Yet their sound has gone out to all lands,
    and their words to the end of the world.

In the heavens he pitched a tent for the sun,
    who comes out from his canopy
        as a bridegroom,
    and rejoices as a champion in a race.

He rises from one edge of the heavens,
    and makes his circuit to the other:
    and nothing is hidden from his heat.

II

The law of the LORD is perfect,
    and renews life.

The decrees of the LORD are trustworthy,
    and make the simple wise.

The statutes of the LORD are just,
    and give new joy to the heart.

The commands of the LORD are clear,
    and enlighten the eyes.

The fear of the LORD is holy,
    and endures for ever.

The judgments of the LORD are true,
    every one of them is righteous.

They are more desirable than gold,
    more than the purest gold.

Sweeter are they than honey,
    than honey from the comb.

By your law your servant is taught;
    and in keeping it there is great reward.

Who can discern one's faults? —
    for those of which I am not aware,
    forgive me.

Keep your servant away from the insolent,
    lest they get the better of me.

Then shall I be blameless,
    and innocent of grievous offense.

Let the words of my mouth,
and the thoughts of my heart,
    find favor in your sight,
    O LORD, my rock and my redeemer.

PSALM 22 (verses 1-11, 19, 22-31)

I

My God, my God, why have you forsaken me?
    Why are you so far from helping me,
    and from the cry of my distress?

My God, I cry to you in the daytime,
    but you do not answer;
    and in the night also,
        but I find no rest.

Yet you are the Holy One,
    enthroned above the praises of Israel.

The generations that preceded us
    put their trust in you;
    they trusted you,
    and you delivered them.

When they cried to you, you set them free;
    they trusted you
    and were not put to shame.

As for me, I am a worm and barely human,
    scorned by everyone
    and despised by the people.

All who see me deride me
    and make sport of me,
    curling their lips
    and tossing their heads:
    "He trusted in the LORD;
    let him save him!
    Let him rescue him
    if he delights in him!"

Yet you drew me out of the womb,
    and made me safe on my mother's breast.

I have been cast on your care
    since my birth;
    from my mother's womb you have been
    my God.

Do not be far from me,
    for trouble is at hand;
    be near, for there is no one to help.

Be not far off from me, LORD;
    you are my strength, hasten to help me.
    O God, answer me!

II

I shall proclaim your Name
　　to the congregation;
**in the midst of the assembly
　　I shall praise you.**

My praise shall be of you
　　in the great assembly;
**I will pay my vows among those
　　who revere you:**

Praise the LORD, you who fear him!
　　Give him glory, you offspring of Jacob!
　　Stand in awe of him,
　　　　you children of Israel!
**He does not despise the poor
　　in their need,
　　nor does he hide his face from them;
　　but when they cry out, he hears them.**

The poor will eat and be satisfied;
　　those who seek the LORD will praise him.
Long may they live!

Let all the ends of the earth remember
　　and turn to the LORD.

Let all the families of the nations
　　do homage before him.

For the kingdom is the LORD's,
　　and he rules over the nations.

Before him all who sleep in the earth
　　bow down,
　　and all who go down to the dust.

Our posterity will serve him,
　　**and tell of the LORD
　　　　to coming generations.**

They shall proclaim to a people yet unborn
　　the deeds that he has done.

PSALM 23

The LORD is my shepherd;
　　there is nothing I lack.

He gives me rest in green pastures,
　　and leads me by quiet waters.

He revives my spirit
　　and guides me in right paths,
　　for his name's sake.

Though I walk through valleys of darkness,
　　I fear no evil.

You are always beside me
　　with your club and staff
　　to protect me.

You spread out a banquet before me
　　in sight of my foes.

You anoint my head with perfume;
　　my cup overflows.

Surely your goodness and mercy follow me
　　all my life long;

And I will dwell in the house of the LORD,
　　now and for ever.

PSALM 24

I

The whole earth is the LORD's,
  the world and all who live in it.

He has founded it upon the seas,
  and set it firm above the deep waters.

"Who can ascend the LORD's mountain?
Who can stand in his holy place?"
  **"Only one who has clean hands
    and a pure heart,
  who is not given to deceit
    nor sworn to lies.**

Only such a person shall receive
    the LORD's blessing,
and just reward from the God
    of our salvation."
  **Such are the people who seek him,
  who seek the God of Jacob face to face.**

II

Lift up your heads, O gates!
  Open wide, you everlasting doors!

Let the King of glory come in.
  Who is the King of glory?

The LORD of power and might,
the LORD, mighty in battle.
  Lift up your heads, O gates!

Open wide, you everlasting doors!
  Let the King of glory come in.

Who is the King of glory?
  **The LORD of power and might,
  he is the King of glory.**

PSALM 25 (verses 1-11, 18-22)

To you, LORD, I lift up my heart:
  my God, I trust in you,
    let me not be put to shame;
  nor let my foes exult over me.

Let none who hope in you be put to shame;
  **let them be shamed who are treacherous
    without cause.**

Make me know your ways, LORD,
  and teach me your paths.

Lead me in your truth and teach me;
  **for you are the God of my salvation,
  in whom I put my trust
    all the day long.**

Remember, LORD, your mercy and love,
  for they are from everlasting.
  Remember not the sins of my youth
    or my offenses;
  **according to your love remember me
  for the sake of your goodness, LORD.**

The LORD is good and upright;
  therefore he teaches sinners his way.

He guides the humble in what is right,
  and teaches the humble his way.

All the paths of the LORD are love
    and faithfulness,
  **for those who keep his covenant
    and his commands.**

For the sake of your Name, LORD,
  forgive my sin, for it is great.

Look upon my affliction and misery,
  and forgive me all my sin.

Look at my enemies, how many they are,
  how violent their hatred is for me.

Protect my life and rescue me;
  **let me not be ashamed,
    for in you I have my hope.**

Let my protection be integrity
    and uprightness;
  **for in you I have placed my hope.
  O God, redeem Israel
  out of all their troubles.**

PSALM 27

I

The LORD is my light and my salvation;
  whom shall I fear?
The LORD is the strength of my life;
  of whom shall I be afraid?

When evil-doers press hard upon me,
  to destroy me,
it is they, my foes and adversaries,
  who stumble and fall.

Though an army encamp against me,
  my heart will not fear;
though they raise up war against me,
  yet my trust is in him.

One thing I ask of the LORD;
  one thing I seek:
That I may dwell in the house of the LORD
  all the days of my life,
to behold the beauty of the LORD,
  to consult in his temple.

For he will shelter me under his tent,
  in the day of trouble.
He will hide me secretly in his dwelling,
  and set me high on a rock.

Now is my head lifted up—
  above my foes round about.

Therefore, I shall offer sacrifices
    in his tent
  with shouts of joy;
I will sing and make melody—
  melody to the LORD.

II

Hear my voice, LORD, when I cry;
  have mercy and answer me.

You have said to my heart, "Seek my face!"
  Your face, LORD, do I seek.

Do not hide your face from me,
  nor turn me away in anger.

You have been my help;
    do not cast me off or forsake me,
  God of my salvation!
Though my father and mother have
    forsaken me,
  the LORD will uphold me.

Teach me your way, O LORD;
  guide me on a level path
  because of my enemies.

Deliver me not into the will of my foes;
  false witnesses have risen against me,
  such as those who breathe violence.

I do believe that I shall see
  the goodness of the LORD
  in the land of the living.

Put your hope in the LORD.
  Be strong and take courage.
  Put your hope in the LORD.

PSALM 31 (verses 1-5, 14-16, 19-20, 24)

In you, O LORD, I take refuge;
   let me never be put to shame.

In your righteousness deliver me;
   bend your ear to me
     and hasten to save me.

You are the rock of my refuge,
   a strong fortress where I am safe.

You are my crag and my stronghold;
   for your name's sake
     lead me and guide me.

Get me out of the net they have hidden
   for me,
   for you are my tower of strength.

Into your hand I commend my life, O LORD.
   You will redeem me, O God of truth.

As for me, I have trusted in you, O LORD,
   and have said, "You are my God!"

My times are in your hand;
   deliver me from my foes and persecutors.

Let your face shine upon your servant,
   and save me in your loving-kindness.

How great is your goodness, O LORD,
   laid in store for those who fear you.

Which you do in the sight of all,
   for those who put their trust in you.

In the covert of your presence you hide them
   from the slanders of others.

Be strong; let your hearts have courage,
   all you who hope in the LORD.

PSALM 34

I

I will bless the LORD at all times;
   his praise shall be ever in my mouth.

In the LORD I will make my boast;
   let the humble hear and rejoice.

Magnify the LORD with me;
   let us together exalt his name.

I sought the LORD and he answered me,
   and delivered me from all my fears.

Look to him, and you will be radiant;
   and your faces will not be ashamed.

This poor one called and the LORD heard,
   and I was saved from all my troubles.

The LORD's angel encamps
     about those who fear him,
   and he will deliver them.

Taste and see that the LORD is good;
   happy are they who trust in him.

Fear the LORD, you saints of his;
   for those who fear him lack nothing.

The lions suffer want and hunger;
   those who seek the LORD lack nothing
     that is good.

II

Come, children, and listen to me;
   and I will teach you to fear the LORD.

Who is there that loves life;
   who desires a long life
     to enjoy prosperity?

Keep your tongue from speaking evil,
   and your lips from telling lies.

Turn from evil and do what is good;
   seek peace and pursue it.

The LORD's eyes are open to the righteous,
   and his ears open to their prayer.

The LORD's face is against evil-doers,
   to cut off their remembrance
     from the earth.

When the righteous call,
     the LORD hears them,
   and rescues them
     from all their troubles.

The LORD is near the broken in heart,
and saves those who are crushed
in spirit.

The righteous have many troubles,
but the LORD rescues them out of all.

He will keep all of their bones safe;
not one of them will be broken.

Evil will bring death to the wicked;
those who hate the righteous
will be punished.

The LORD will redeem the life
of his servants;
none who trust in him will be condemned.

PSALM 36 (verses 5-10)

Your loving-kindness, O LORD,
reaches to the heavens,
and your faithfulness to the clouds.

Your righteousness is strong
as the mountains,
and your judgments vast as the deeps.

You, LORD, save human being and beast;
how priceless is your love, O God.

We take refuge under the shadow
of your wings;
we feast on the rich abundance
of your house.

We drink from the river of your pleasures,
for with you is the fountain of life
and in your light we see light.

Continue your goodness
to those who know you,
and your justice
to those true of heart.

PSALM 42 (verses 1-5, 8-11)

As a deer pants for the water-brooks,
so longs my soul for you, O God.

My soul thirsts for God, for the living God;
how long before I come
and behold his face?

My tears have been my food day and night,
while they say to me all day long,
where now is your God?

As I pour out my soul, I remember
how I went with the throngs,
and led them into the house of God,

with shouts of praise and thanksgiving,
among the crowds keeping festival.

Why are you downcast, my soul?
Why so distraught within me?

Put your trust in God;
I shall again praise him,
my help and my God.

By day and by night his song is with me,
a prayer to the God of my life.

I will say to God, my rock:
Why have you forgotten me?
Why do I mourn
because my foes oppress me?

My bones break as my enemies mock me,
while they say to me all day long,
where now is your God?

Why are you downcast, my soul?
Why so distraught within me?

Put your trust in God;
I shall again praise him,
my help and my God.

PSALM 46

God is our refuge and strength,
  an ever ready help in time of trouble.

We shall not fear if the earth is shaken,
  if the mountains fall into the deeps
    of the sea;

Even if the waters rage and foam,
  and the mountains quake
    in the surging tide,

the mighty LORD is with us;
  the God of Jacob is our fortress.

There are river-streams that make glad
  the city of God,
  the holy dwelling place
    of the most high.

God is in her midst; she cannot be shaken.
  God will help her
    at the breaking of dawn.

Nations are in tumult
  and kingdoms are tottering;
  God speaks and the earth melts away.

The mighty LORD is with us;
  the God of Jacob is our fortress.

Come, see the works of the LORD,
  the awesome deeds he has done
    in the earth.

He puts an end to wars in all the world;
  he breaks the bow
    and shatters the spear,
  and burns up the chariots with fire.

Be still and know that I am God;
  I am exalted among the nations,
  I am exalted in the earth.

the mighty LORD is with us;
  the God of Jacob is our fortress.

PSALM 51 (verses 1-15)

Have mercy on me, O God,
  in your loving-kindness;
  in your compassion
    blot out my offenses.

Wash me thoroughly from my iniquity,
  and cleanse me from my sin.

I know full well my misdeeds,
  and my sin is ever before me.

Against you, against you only,
  have I sinned,
  and done what is evil in your sight.

You are just in your sentence,
  and righteous in your judgment.

I was conceived in iniquity,
  and a sinner from my mother's womb.

Yet you look for truth in my inmost being,
  and teach me wisdom in my heart.

Purify me that I may be clean;
  wash me, make me whiter than snow.

Let me hear joy and gladness,
  that the bones you have broken
    may rejoice.

Hide your face from my sins,
  and wipe out all my iniquity.

Create in me a pure heart, O God,
  and renew a right spirit within me.

Cast me not away from your presence,
  and take not your Holy Spirit from me.

Restore to me the joy of your salvation,
  and uphold me in a free will
    of obedience,

that I may teach transgressors your ways,
  and turn sinners back to you.

Deliver me from death, O God my savior,
  that my tongue may sing
    of your justice.

O Lord, open my lips,
  and my mouth shall proclaim your praise.

PSALM 67

God be gracious to us and bless us;
    may the light of your face
        shine upon us,

that your ways may be known on the earth,
    your salvation among all nations.

Let the peoples praise you, O God.
    Let all the peoples praise you.

Let the nations exult in you,
    and shout with joy;

for with justice you judge the peoples,
    and rule the nations of the earth.

Let the peoples praise you, O God.
    Let all the peoples praise you.

The earth has yielded its increase;
    God, our own God, has blessed us.

May God continue to give us his blessing,
    until all the ends of the earth
        worship him.

Let the peoples praise you, O God.
    Let all the peoples praise you.

PSALM 84

How lovely is your dwelling place,
O LORD of might!
    My soul longs and faints
    for the courts of the LORD.
    My whole being rejoices
    in the living God.

The sparrow finds a home,
the swallow a nest,
    where she may lay her young,
        near your altars,
    O LORD of might,
        my King and my God.

Blest are they who dwell in your house,
ever singing your praise!
    Blest are they who have in you
        their strength;
    in whose hearts are the highways
        to Zion!

They go through a barren valley,
and find it a place with springs;
    for the early rains
    have filled it with pools.

They go from height to height;
    for the God of gods
    will be seen in Zion.

LORD God of might, hear my prayer;
    give ear to me, God of Jacob.

Look with favor on our King, O God;
    behold the face of your anointed.

One day in your courts is better
    than a thousand elsewhere.

I would rather stand at the door
        of God's house
    than dwell in the tents of the wicked.

For the LORD God is a sun and shield;
    the LORD bestows grace and glory.

No good thing does the LORD withhold
    from those who live uprightly.

O LORD of might,
    blest is everyone
    who trusts in you!

PSALM 89 (verses 5-16)

Let the heavens praise your wonders, O LORD,
  and your faithfulness in the council
    of the gods.

Who in the skies can be compared
  to the LORD?
  Who is like the LORD among the gods?

God is to be feared in the council
  of the gods,
  great and terrible
    to all those around him.

Who is like you, LORD, God of might?
  Your power and faithfulness, O LORD,
  surround you.

You rule over the raging of the sea;
  when its waves ride high,
  you subdue them.

You crushed to death Rahab, the monster
  of the deep;
  with your mighty arm
  you scattered your foes.

The heavens are yours, and the earth also;
  the world and all that is in it
  you have founded.

You created the limits of the north
  and the south;
  Mounts Tabor and Hermon rejoice
  in your Name.

Your arm is mighty, your hand is strong;
  your right hand is lifted high.

Righteousness and justice
  are the foundation of your throne;
  love and faithfulness
  go ever before you.

Blest are the people
  who know the festal shout;
  they walk, O LORD,
  in the light of your presence.

They rejoice all day long in your Name,
  and exult in your righteousness.

PSALM 90 (verses 1-12, 16-17)

Lord, you have been our home and refuge
  from generation to generation.

Before the mountains were brought forth,
  or the earth and the world were formed,
  from ages to ages you are God.

You are able to turn us back to dust,
  and can say,
    "Return, O children of earth."

A thousand years in your sight
are but a yesterday that is gone.
  As a watch in the night
  or a fleeting dream,
  they are like grass
    that flourishes and fades.

In the morning it sprouts up and is green;
  in the evening it dries up and withers.

Are we to be consumed by your anger,
  or perish from your displeasure?

You have laid bare our iniquities
  before you,
  our secret sins in the light
  of your face.

All our days pass away in your anger;
  our years come to an end like a sigh.

The number of our years is perhaps seventy,
  or even eighty if we are strong.

Yet their span is but toil and trouble;
  they go swiftly and fly away.

Who understands the power of your anger;
  who fears aright your indignation?

So teach us to take account of our days,
  that we may give our hearts to wisdom.

Show your wonders to your servants,
  and your glorious splendor
  to their children.

May the favor of the Lord God be upon us:
  prosper, O prosper the work of our hands.

PSALM 91

Whoever dwells under the shelter
　　of the Most High,
　　and abides in the shade
　　　of the Almighty,

shall say of the LORD,
　　"My refuge, my fortress,
　　my God in whom is my trust."

For he rescues you from the hunter's snare,
　　and from deadly pestilence.

He covers you with his pinions,
　　and under his wings you find refuge;
　　his faithfulness is a shield and buckler.

You will not be afraid of terror
　　in the night,
　　nor of arrows that fly in the day—

neither the pestilence that stalks
　　in the darkness,
　　nor a sudden sickness that strikes
　　　at noontime.

A thousand may fall at your side,
ten thousand at your right hand;
　　but you will be unharmed.

Your eyes have only to look
　　to see the reward of the wicked.

Because you have made the LORD your refuge,
　　and made the Most High your home,

no evil will happen to you,
　　nor calamity come near your dwelling.

He will give charge over you to his angels,
　　to guard you in all your ways.

In their hands they will hold you
　　lest you stub your foot on a stone.

You will tread on poisonous serpents;
　　you will trample young lions
　　　and dragons.

Because you hold fast to me in love,
　　I will save you.

Because you know my Name,
　　I will protect you.

When you call upon me,
　　I will answer you.

In trouble I will be with you;
　　I will rescue and honor you.

With long life I will satisfy you,
　　and show you my salvation.

PSALM 95 (verses 1-7)

Come, let us sing to the LORD;
　　let us shout for joy
　　　to the Rock of our salvation.

Let us come before his presence
　　with thanksgiving,
　　and raise a loud shout to him
　　　in psalms.

For the LORD is a great God,
　　and a great King above all gods.

In his hand are the deep places
　　of the earth,
　　and the high peaks of the mountains
　　　are his also.

The sea is his, for he made it;
　　and his hands formed the dry land.

Come, let us bow down and give homage,
and kneel before the LORD our Maker.
　　For he is our God;
　　and we are his people,
　　and sheep of his pasture.

Today will you listen to his voice?

PSALM 96

Sing to the LORD a new song;
   sing to the LORD, all the earth.

Sing to the LORD, bless his Name;
   proclaim his salvation from day to day.

Tell out his glory among the nations,
   and his marvelous works to all peoples.

The LORD is great and worthy to be praised;
   he is awesome above all gods.

The gods of the peoples
   are nothing but idols;
   but the LORD made the heavens.

Glory and majesty surround him;
   power and splendor adorn his sanctuary.

Give to the LORD, you families of peoples;
   give to the LORD glory and power.

Give to the LORD the honor due his Name;
   bring offerings
     and come into his courts.

Worship the LORD in the beauty of holiness;
   let the whole earth dance before him.

Declare among the nations:
   "The LORD is King!
   He has established the world
     firm and immovable."

Let the heavens rejoice
   and the earth be glad;
   let the sea resound,
     and everything in it.

Let the fields be joyful
   and everything in them,
   and the trees of the wood shout for joy,

before the LORD when he comes,
   when he comes to judge the earth.

He will judge the world with justice,
   and the peoples with his truth.

PSALM 98

Sing to the LORD a new song,
   for he has wrought a marvelous thing.

With his right hand and holy arm,
   he himself has brought salvation.

The LORD has made known his salvation;
   his righteousness is open to the nations.

He has remembered his love to Jacob,
   his faithfulness to the house of Israel.

All the ends of the earth have seen
   the salvation of our God.

Lift a jubilant shout to the LORD, O earth;
   rejoice and ring out his praises.

Sing psalms to the LORD with the harp;
   with the harp and the melody of songs.

With trumpets and the sound of the horn,
   shout with joy before the King,
     the LORD.

Let the sea resound and everything in it;
   the world and all who dwell therein.

Let the rivers clap their hands,
   and the hills sing together for joy.

Before the LORD who comes to judge the earth.
   He will judge the earth with justice,
   and the peoples with equity.

PSALM 100

Shout for joy to the LORD, all the earth;
   serve the LORD with gladness,
   come before him with singing.

Know that the LORD—he is God;
   he made us, we belong to him,
   we are his people,
     the sheep of his pasture.

Enter his gates with thanksgiving;
   go into his courts with praise,
   give him thanks, bless his Name.

For the LORD is good;
   his merciful love is for ever,
   his faithfulness from age to age.

PSALM 103

Bless the LORD, O my soul;
>with all my being, bless his holy Name!

Bless the LORD, O my soul,
>and forget not all his benefits.

He forgives all your sins,
>and heals all your diseases.

He redeems your life from the grave,
>and crowns you with mercy
>>and loving-kindness.

He fills all your years with good,
>and renews your youth like an eagle's.

The LORD gives righteous judgments,
>and justice for all who are oppressed.

He made known his ways to Moses,
>and his deeds to the children of Israel.

The LORD is merciful and compassionate,
>slow to anger and rich in enduring love.

He will not always scold us,
>nor will he remain angry for ever.

He has not treated or punished us,
>as our sins and misdeeds deserve.

As high as the heavens are above the earth,
>so great is his mercy
>>to those who revere him.

As far as the east is from the west,
>so far has he removed our sins from us.

As a father has compassion for his children,
>so the LORD has compassion
>>for those who revere him.

For he knows of what we are made;
>he remembers that we are but dust.

As for us, our days are like the grass,
>and like a wild flower in blossom.

When the wind blows over it, it is gone,
>and the place of it is known no more.

The love of the LORD for those who revere him
>endures for ever and ever.

His righteousness extends
>to their descendants,
>who keep his covenant
>>and obey his commandments.

The LORD has fixed his throne in heaven,
>and his kingdom rules over all.

Bless the LORD, you angels of his,
>his mighty ones who do his bidding,
>and obey the voice of his word.

Bless the LORD, you heavenly armies,
>his servants who do his will.

Bless the LORD, all his works,
>in all places of his dominion.
>Bless the LORD, O my soul!

PSALM 104 (verses 1-15, 24-35)

I

Bless the LORD, O my soul!
>O LORD, my God,
>>how supreme is your greatness;
>you are clothed with majesty and glory.

You robe yourself with a mantle of light,
>and stretch out the heavens
>>like a curtain.

You lay the beams of your dwelling
>>on the waters,
>and make the clouds your chariot,
>to ride on the wings of the wind.

You make the winds your messengers;
>and flames of fire are your servants.

You make springs
>>that stream into the valleys,
>and run among the hills.

They give water for all the beasts
>>of the field;
>in them the wild asses
>>quench their thirst.

Beside them the birds of the air
>>make their nests,
>and sing among the branches.

From your dwelling you water the mountains;
>the earth is filled with the fruit
>>of your works.

You make the grass grow for the cattle,
>and plants for the use of people.

That we may bring forth food from the earth:
>wine to gladden our hearts;

Oil to make our faces attractive
>and bread to make us strong.

II

How manifold are your works, O LORD!
  In wisdom you have made them all;
  the earth is full of your creatures.

And there is the sea, vast and wide,
  with its swarms of living things
    without number,
  creatures both great and small.

They move there like ships;
  and there is Leviathan
  whom you made to play with.

All of them look to you
  to give them their food in due season.

When you give it to them, they gather it;
  when you open your hand,
  they are filled with good.

When you hide your face, they are troubled;
  when you take away their breath,
  they die and return to the dust.

When you send forth your Spirit,
  they are created,
  and you renew the face of the earth.

The glory of the LORD is everlasting;
  the Lord rejoices in his works.

If he looks at the earth, it trembles;
  if he touches the mountains,
  they smoke.

I will sing to the LORD as long as I live;
  I will praise my God
  as long as I breathe.

May my meditation please him;
  I will rejoice in the LORD.

Let sinners vanish from the earth,
  and let the wicked be no more.

Bless the LORD, O my soul!
  Hallelujah!

PSALM 107

I

Hallelujah!
Give thanks to the LORD, for he is good;
  his merciful love endures for ever.

So let the redeemed of the LORD proclaim,
  those whom he rescued
  from the enemy's hand,

those whom he gathered out of the lands,
  from east and west,
  from north and south.

Some wandered through desert wastes,
  finding no way to a settled city.

They became hungry and thirsty;
  their spirit was almost spent.

Then they cried to the LORD
    in their trouble,
  and he delivered them
  from their distress.

He set their course on a straight way,
  to a city where they might dwell.

Let them give thanks to the LORD
    for his mercy,
  and the wonders that he did for them.

For he satisfies those who are thirsty,
  and fills the hungry with good fare.

II

Some lived in darkness and gloom,
  bound in misery with iron fetters.

For they rebelled against the words of God,
  and spurned the counsel
  of the Most High.

He humbled their spirit with hard labor;
  when they fell, there was none to help.

Then they cried to the LORD
    in their trouble,
  and he delivered them
  from their distress.

He brought them out of darkness and gloom,
  and broke asunder their bonds.

Let them give thanks to the LORD
    for his mercy,
  and the wonders that he did for them.

For he shatters the gates of bronze,
  and breaks the bars of iron in two.

III

Some were sick because of sinful ways;
  their iniquities made them miserable.

They loathed any kind of food,
  and were very near to death's door.

Then they cried to the LORD
    in their trouble,
  and he delivered them
    from their distress.

He sent forth his word and healed them,
  and rescued them from the grave.

Let them give thanks to the LORD
    for his mercy,
  and the wonders that he did for them.

Let them offer sacrifices of thanksgiving,
  and declare his works
    with joyful acclaim.

IV

Some went down to the sea in ships,
  to ply their trade in deep waters.

They saw the works of the LORD
  and his wonders in the deep.

With his voice he sent a gale
  that tossed high above them the waves,

lifted to the sky, then down in the deep;
  their spirit was dismayed and troubled.

They reeled and staggered like drunkards,
  and were at their wit's end.

Then they cried to the LORD
    in their trouble,
  and he delivered them
    from their distress.

He stilled the storm to a whisper,
  until the waves of the sea were quiet.

He brought them, glad at the calm,
  to the harbor where they were bound.

Let them give thanks to the LORD
    for his mercy,
  and the wonders that he did for them.

Let them extol him in the assembly
    of the people,
  and praise him in the council
    of the elders.

V

The LORD changed rivers to a desert,
  and water-springs to an arid land,

a fertile ground into a salt marsh,
  because the people who dwelt there
    were wicked.

Again, he turned deserts to pools of water,
  and arid ground to flowing springs,

where he gave the hungry a home,
  to build a city to dwell in.

They sowed fields and planted vineyards,
  that yielded a fruitful harvest.

He blessed them, so that they multiplied;
  nor did he let their herds decrease.

When they were diminished and humbled
  by oppression, adversity, and sorrow,

he poured his contempt on their rulers,
  and made them wander
    in trackless wastes.

Yet he raised the needy from affliction,
  and increased their families
    like a flock.

The righteous shall see this and rejoice,
  and the mouth of the wicked
    will be shut.

Whoever is wise will give heed,
  and consider the loving-kindness
    of the LORD.

PSALM 112

Hallelujah!
Blessed are they who fear the LORD,
　and have great delight
　　in his commandments.

Their offspring will be powerful
　in the land,
　and their children who are upright
　　will be blest.

In their house are wealth and riches;
　their righteousness stands firm
　　for ever.

Light shines in darkness for the upright,
　for they are merciful and kind.

It is good for them to be generous
　in lending,
　and to manage their affairs
　　with justice.

Never will the righteous be perturbed;
　and they will always be remembered.

They will not fear any news that is evil;
　their heart is fixed,
　　for they trust in the LORD.

Without any fear their heart is confident;
　they will see the downfall
　　of their enemies.

With open hand they give to the poor;
　their righteousness stands firm
　　for ever;
　they will hold up their head
　　with honor.

The wicked see it and are filled with anger;
　they grind their teeth, then fade away,
　for their hopes have come to nothing.

PSALM 113

Hallelujah!
Praise the LORD, you servants of his;
　praise the Name of the LORD.

Blessed be the Name of the LORD,
　now and for evermore.

From the rising of the sun to its setting,
　let the Name of the LORD be praised.

The LORD is high above all nations,
　and his glory is above the heavens.

Who is like the LORD our God,
　seated enthroned on high?

Yet he humbles himself to behold
　the heavens and the earth.

He takes up the weak from the dust,
　and lifts the poor
　　out of the trash-heap,

to seat them in the company of princes,
　with the princes of his people.

He gives the childless woman a home,
　as a happy mother of children.

PSALM 118

I

Give thanks to the LORD, for he is good;
  his steadfast love endures for ever.

Let the household of Israel now say:
  "His steadfast love endures for ever."

Let the household of Aaron now say:
  "His steadfast love endures for ever."

Let all who revere the LORD now say:
  "His steadfast love endures for ever."

I called out to the LORD in my plight;
  he answered me and came to my rescue.

The LORD is on my side, I shall not fear;
  what can any person do to me?

The LORD is on my side, he is my helper;
  I shall see my victory over my enemies.

It is better to take refuge in the LORD
  than to put trust in any person.

It is better to take refuge in the LORD
  than to put any trust in princes.

All the heathen peoples surround me;
  in the Name of the LORD
    I shall repel them.

They surround me,
    they surround me on every side;
  in the Name of the LORD
    I shall repel them.

They surround me like bees,
    like fire in brushwood;
  in the Name of the LORD
    I shall repel them.

I was very hard pressed and almost fell;
  but the LORD came to my rescue.

The LORD is my strength and my song;
  he has become my salvation.

Hear the shouts of joy and victory
  in the tents of the righteous:
  the right hand of the LORD,
  the right hand of the LORD is victorious!

I shall not die but live,
  to declare the deeds of the LORD.

He has given me a sore punishment,
  but he has not handed me over to death.

II

Open to me the gates of victory,
  that I may enter
    and give thanks to the LORD.

"This is the gate of the LORD;
  the righteous may enter it."

I thank you because you answered me;
  and you have become my salvation.

"The stone that the builders rejected
  has become the chief cornerstone."

This is the LORD's doing;
  it is marvelous in our sight.

"This is the day in which the LORD has acted;
  let us rejoice and be glad in it!"

Hosanna! Hosanna!
  Save us, LORD, and prosper us, we pray.

"Blessed is he who comes in the Name
    of the LORD;
  we bless you from the house of the LORD."

The LORD is God; his light shines upon us;
  form the procession with branches
    up to the altar.

"You are my God and I will praise you!
  You are my God and I will exalt you!"

Give thanks to the LORD, for he is good;
  his loving-kindness endures for ever.

PSALM 121

I will lift my eyes to the hills:
"**Whence comes my help?**"

My help comes from the LORD,
the maker of heaven and earth.

He will not let your foot slip;
your keeper will not sleep.

He who keeps watch over Israel
never slumbers nor sleeps.

The LORD watches over you as a shade,
over you and beside you,

so that the sun shall not hurt you in the day,
nor the moon in the night.

The LORD will defend you from all evil,
and keep you in safety.

The LORD watches over your going out
and coming in,
now and for evermore.

PSALM 122

I rejoiced when they said to me,
"Let us go to the house of the LORD."
**Now at last we are standing
within your gates, O Jerusalem.**

Jerusalem is built as a city
bound firmly together in unity.
**There the tribes go up,
the tribes of the LORD—**

as he decreed for Israel—
to praise the Name of the LORD.
**There are the seats of justice,
the thrones of the house of David.**

Pray for the peace of Jerusalem:
"Prosperity to those who love you!
**Peace within your ramparts!
Safety behind your towers!**"

For love of my family and friends
I say, "Peace be with you!"
**For love of the house
of the LORD our God,
I will seek to do you good.**

PSALM 130

Out of the depths have I called to you, LORD.
Lord, hear my voice,
**O let your ear be attentive
to the voice of my plea.**

LORD, if you take account of our sins,
who then can stand?
**But with you there is forgiveness,
that you may be worshipped.**

I wait, I wait for the LORD;
in his word is my hope.
**I wait for the LORD
more than the watchers
who look for the dawn.**

O Israel, look for the LORD's mercy and love,
for his bounteous redemption.
**For he will set Israel free
from all their sins.**

PSALM 138

With my whole heart I will thank you, O LORD;
before the gods I will sing your praise.

I will bow down and worship
at your holy temple,
**and praise your Name
for your faithfulness and love.**

Your Name and your word are exalted
above all things;
**yet when I called, you answered
and strengthened me.**

All the kings of the earth will praise you,
O LORD,
**when they have heard the words
of your mouth.**

They will sing of the ways of the LORD,
how great is the glory of the LORD.

For though the LORD is high,
he has regard for the lowly;
**as for the proud,
he considers them from afar.**

Though I walk in the midst of trouble,
you save me;
**against the fury of my foes,
you stretch out your hand.**

With your right hand you deliver me;
the LORD will fulfill his purpose for me.

Your steadfast love, O LORD, endures for ever;
do not forsake the work of your hands.

PSALM 139

O LORD, you have searched me;
  and you know me thoroughly.

You know whether I sit down or stand up;
  you can discern my thoughts from afar.

You watch where I walk and lie down,
  and are familiar with all my ways.

There is not a word on my lips,
  but you, LORD, know it already.

You surround me behind and before;
  your hand is ever laid upon me.

Such knowledge is too wonderful for me,
  so high that I cannot reach it.

Where shall I escape from your Spirit?
  Where can I flee from your presence?

If I climb up to heaven, you are there;
  **you are there
    if my bed be in the underworld.**

If I take wing to the dawning sun,
  or dwell at the limits of the sea,

even there will your hand lead me,
  and your right hand will hold on to me.

If I say, "Surely the darkness will hide me,
  and the night will cover me round about,"

yet darkness is not dark to you,
  **for the night is as bright as the day;
  darkness and light to you are both alike.**

You have created my inmost being,
  and formed me in my mother's womb.

I praise you in awe for making me;
  **your work is wondrous,
    and I know it well.**

My body was not hidden from you
  when moulded secretly in the depths.

In your book you wrote of me unformed,
  and of my deeds that should come to pass.

How unsearchable are your thoughts, O God!
  How without limit is the sum of them!

To count them would be more
    than the grains of sand;
  were I to finish, you would still be there.

Search me, O God, and know my heart;
  test me and know my thoughts.

Watch lest I walk in any evil way,
  and lead me in the way everlasting.

PSALM 145

I will exalt you, O God my King,
  and bless your Name for ever and ever.

Day after day will I bless you,
  and praise your Name for ever and ever.

Great is the LORD
    and worthy of great praise;
  there is no limit to his greatness.

Age to age praises your works,
  and proclaims your mighty deeds.

They ponder the splendor and glory
    of your majesty,
  and all your marvelous wonders.

They will relate your awesome acts,
  and recount your greatness.

They will call to remembrance
    your great goodness,
  and sing out with joy your righteousness.

The LORD is gracious and merciful,
  slow to anger and steadfast in love.

The LORD is good to everyone;
  **his compassion reaches all
    whom he has made.**

All your creation praises you, O LORD;
  all your faithful people bless you.

They proclaim the glory of your kingdom,
  and tell of all your power;

That everyone may know of your might,
  **and the glorious splendor
    of your kingdom.**

Your kingdom is an everlasting one
  that endures throughout all ages.

The LORD is faithful in all his words,
  and gracious in all his deeds.

The LORD upholds all who have fallen,
  and raises up those who are bowed down.

The eyes of all creatures look to you,
  **and you give them their food
    in due time.**

You open your hand wide,
  **and satisfy the want
    of all living things.**

The LORD is just in all his ways,
  and gracious in all his deeds.

The LORD is near to all who call to him,
to all who call to him sincerely.

He fulfills the desires
of those who revere him;
he hears their cry and saves them.

The LORD preserves all those who love him;
but those who are wicked he destroys.

My mouth will speak the praise of the LORD;
**let every creature bless his holy Name
for ever.**

PSALM 146

Hallelujah!
Praise the LORD, O my soul!

I will praise the LORD all my days;
I will sing to my God while I live.

Put not your trust in princes,
nor in people in whom is no help.

When they breathe their last,
they return to the earth;
their plans perish on that very day.

Happy are they whose help is the God
of Jacob,
whose hope is in the LORD their God,

who made the heaven and the earth,
the sea, and all that is in them.

He keeps his promise for ever;
he renders justice to the oppressed.

He gives bread to the hungry;
the LORD sets the prisoners free.

The LORD opens the eyes of the blind;
**the LORD lifts up
those who are bowed low.**

The LORD cares for the strangers,
and supports the widow and orphan.

The LORD loves the righteous;
but he thwarts the way of the wicked.

The LORD shall reign for ever;
**your God, O Zion, for all generations.
Hallelujah!**

PSALM 147

Hallelujah!
How good to make melody to our God;
how pleasant to honor him with praise!

The LORD rebuilds Jerusalem,
and gathers the exiles of Israel.

He heals the brokenhearted,
and binds up all their wounds.

He numbers all the stars,
and calls each one by its name.

Our LORD is great and mighty;
his wisdom is without measure.

The LORD lifts up the lowly,
**but casts the wicked to the ground.
Hallelujah!**

Sing to the LORD and give him thanks;
make melody to our God with the harp!

He veils the heavens with clouds,
and provides rain for the earth.

He clothes the hillsides with grass,
and with green plants for our needs,

with fodder for the cattle,
and food for the calling ravens.

The strength of a horse or a human
is not what pleases the LORD;

But his delight is in those who revere him,
**and who hope in his gracious love.
Hallelujah!**

Praise the LORD, O Jerusalem!
O Zion, praise your God!

He makes strong the bars of your gates,
and blesses your children within you.

He establishes peace in your borders,
and satisfies you with the finest wheat.

He sends out his command to the earth,
and his word runs very swiftly.

He showers the snow, white as wool,
and scatters the hoar-frost like ashes.

He sprinkles the ice like bread-crumbs,
and the cold becomes unbearable;

then he utters his word, the ice thaws;
his wind blows and the waters flow.

To Jacob he makes known his word,
his statutes and judgments to Israel.

He has not done this for any other nation,
**nor revealed to them his decrees.
Hallelujah!**

PSALM 148

Hallelujah!
Praise the LORD from the heavens;
praise him in the heights.

Praise him, all you angels;
praise him, all his host.

Praise him, sun and moon;
praise him, all you stars of light.

Praise him, highest heavens,
and you waters above the heavens.

Let them all praise the Name of the LORD,
for at his command they were created;

He made them fast for ever and ever,
with a law they shall never breach.

Praise the LORD from the earth:
sea-monsters and all deeps;

fire and hail, snow and fog,
storm-wind, obeying his word;

mountains and all hills,
fruit-trees and all cedars;

wild animals and all cattle,
reptiles and winged birds;

kings of the earth and all peoples,
princes and all rulers of the world;

young men and maidens,
elders and children together.

Let them all praise the Name of the LORD,
**for his Name alone is exalted;
his majesty is above earth and heaven.**

He raised up strength for his people;
**he is the praise
of all his faithful ones,
Israel's children,
a people near to him.
Hallelujah!**

PSALM 150

Hallelujah!
Praise God in his holy place.
Praise him in the heaven of his power.

Praise him for his mighty deeds.
Praise him for his excelling greatness.

Praise him with blast of the horn.
Praise him with harp and lyre.

Praise him with drum and dance.
Praise him with strings and pipe.

Praise him with resounding cymbals.
Praise him with clashing cymbals.

Let everything with breath
**Praise the LORD.
Hallelujah!**

TOPICAL INDEX

HYMNS WITH DESCANTS

INDEX OF SCRIPTURAL ALLUSIONS

INDEX OF AUTHORS, TRANSLATORS, AND SOURCES OF HYMNS

Knapp, Shepherd (1873–1946), 432
Knox, Ronald A. (1888–1957), 174

Landsberg, Max (1845–1928), 6
Lewis, H. Elfed (1860–1953), 435, 484, 546
Littledale, Richard F. (1833–1890), 444
Liturgy of Malabar (4th century), 569
Liturgy of St. James (4th century), 188
Livingston, John Henry (1746–1825), 40
Lowry, Robert S. (1826–1899), 443
Lowry, Somerset C. (1855–1932), 479
Luther, Martin (1483–1546), 134, 179, 189, 207, 324, 377, 615
Lutheran Book of Worship (1978), 13, 69, 158, 283, 322, 367, 387, 389, 420, 529, 530, 615, 619
Lynch, Thomas T. (1818–1871), 253, 271
Lyte, Henry F. (1793–1847), 108, 142, 144, 440

McBean, Lachlan (1853–1931), 215
Macdonald, George (1824–1905), 377
Macdonald, Mary (1789–1872), 215
MacGregor, Duncan (1854–1923), 337
Magdeburg, Joachim (c. 1525–1583), 152
Mahlmann, S.A. (1771–1826), 496
Mann, Newton (1836–1926), 6
Mant, Richard (1776–1848), 612
March, Daniel (1816–1909), 431
Massie, Richard (1800–1887), 134, 324
Matheson, George (1842–1906), 442
Matson, William T. (1833–1899), 613
Medley, Samuel (1738–1799), 296, 321
Meeter, Daniel James (b. 1953), 65, 112, 553
Meeter, Melody (b. 1954), 553
Mencken, Lueder (1658–1726), 535
Micklem, Nathaniel (1888–1976), 305
Micklem, T. Caryl (b. 1925), 16, 426, 462
Milman, Henry H. (1791–1868), 280, 281
Milton, John (1608–1674), 136, 165
Mitre Hymn Book (1836), 236
Miwa, Genzō (20th century), 211
Mohr, Joseph (1792–1848), 216
Moment, John J. (1785–1959), 39
Monsell, John S.B. (1811–1875), 19
Montgomery, James (1771–1854), 95, 105, 115, 229, 232, 247, 261, 262, 375, 378, 499, 601
Montgomery-Campbell, Jane (1817–1878), 17
Moravian hymnals (1784), 535
Morgan, Edmund R. (1888–1979), 603
Morison, John (1750–1798), 37, 167
Moss, John (b. 1925), 211
Mote, Edward (1797–1874), 459, 460
Moultrie, Gerard (1829–1885), 188
Murrayfield Psalms, The (1954), 92, 94, 106, 125, 127, 128

Nazianzen, Gregory (c. 329–389), 439
Neale, John M. (1818–1866), 190, 218, 246, 256, 279, 286, 287, 289, 290, 308, 314, 315, 316, 317, 318, 332, 342, 343, 372, 392, 579, 583

Neander, Joachim (1650–1680), 145, 156, 157
Nelson, Earl (19th century), 269
Neumark, Georg (1621–1681), 151
Newbolt, Michael Robert (1874–1956), 415
Newton, John (1725–1807), 364, 393, 456, 469
Nicolai, Philipp (1556–1608), 367, 606
Noel, Caroline (1817–1877), 336
North, Frank Mason (1850–1935), 482

Oakeley, Frederick (1802–1880), 195
Olearius, Johann (1611–1684), 169
Olivers, Thomas (1725–1799), 595
Olson, Ernest W. (1870–1958), 585
O'Neill, Judith (b. 1930), 527
Oudaen, Joachim (17th century), 329
Oxenham, John (1852–1941), 410

Palgrave, Francis T. (1824–1897), 403
Palmer, Ray (1808–1887), 273, 278, 446
Park, J. Edgar (1879–1956), 250
Patrick, Saint (372–466), 478
Peacey, John R. (1896–1971), 373
Perronet, Edward (c. 1726–1792), 593, 594
Piae Cantiones (1582), 212, 226
Pierpoint, Folliott S. (1835–1917), 5
Pierpont, John (1785–1866), 272
Piggott, W. Charter (1872–1943), 589
Pitt-Watson, Ian (b. 1923), 138
Polish Carol, 221
Post, Marie J. (b. 1919), 103
Poston, Elizabeth (b. 1905), 220
Pott, Francis (1832–1909), 319
Prudentius, Aurelius Clemens (348–413), 190, 191
Psalter, The (1912), 81, 83, 88, 96, 97, 100, 102, 104, 107, 113, 114, 118, 125, 131, 132, 141

Quinn, James (b. 1919), 406, 413

Rambach, J.J. (1693–1735), 529
Reed, Edith M.G. (1885–1933), 221
Rees, Timothy (1874–1939), 34, 42, 381
Reynolds, W.M. (1822–1876), 189
Rimaud, Didier (b. 1919), 541
Rinckart, Martin (1586–1649), 61
Rippon, John (1751–1836), 593, 594
Ritsema, Herbert (b. 1929), 32
Robbins, Howard C. (1876–1952), 376
Roberts, Daniel C. (1841–1907), 494
Roberts, Robert R. (1865–1945), 581
Robinson, Robert (1735–1790), 348, 449
Rodigast, Samuel (1649–1708), 153
Romanis, William (1824–1899), 264
Routley, Erik (1917–1982), 82, 101, 119, 307, 466, 485, 500, 519
Russell, Arthur T. (1806–1874), 330
Rutherford, Samuel (c. 1600–1661), 587

Saward, Michael (b. 1932), 133
Schlegel, Katharina von (b. 1697), 154

Schmolck, Benjamin (1672–1737), 502, 530
Schulte-Nordholt, J.W. (b. 1920), 588
Schütz, Johann J. (1640–1690), 146
Scott, Lesbia (b. 1898), 401
Scott, Robert B.Y. (b. 1899), 178, 344
Scottish Paraphrases (1781), 37, 45, 166, 167, 170, 339, 340, 341
Scottish Psalter: (1565), 120; (1650), 89, 90, 93, 106, 116
Scriven, Joseph (1819–1886), 507
Sedulius, Coelius (5th century), 192
Shairp, John C. (1819–1885), 160
Shurtleff, Ernest W. (1862–1917), 423
Smith, Elizabeth L. (1817–1898), 366
Smith, Walter C. (1824–1908), 7
Snow, Ann B. (20th century), 163
Spencer, Robert N. (1877–1961), 526
Spurgeon, Charles H. (1834–1892), 543
Sternhold, Thomas (d. 1549), 86, 91
Stevenson, Isabella (20th century), 370
Stocking, Jay T. (1870–1936), 238
Stone, Lloyd (b. 1912), 497
Stone, Samuel J. (1839–1900), 394
Strasbourg Psalter (1553), 366
Studdert-Kennedy, Geoffrey A. (1883–1932), 480
Supplement to the New Version (1703), 616
Symphonia Serenum Selectarum (1695), 319
Synesius of Cyrene (375–430), 248
Sywulka, Anna Marie (b. 1939), 72

Tate, Nahum (1652–1715), 199, 200
Tate, Nahum (1652–1715), and Nicholas Brady (1659–1726), 98
Taylor, Jeremy (1613–1667), 269
Taylor, Sarah E. (1883–1954), 389
Tersteegen, Gerhardt (1697–1769), 452, 613
Theodulph of Orleans (c. 760–c. 821), 279
Theoktistus (9th century), 308
Thomas à Kempis (1380–1471), 342, 343
Thomson, Mary A. (1834–1923), 421
Threlfall, Jeannette (1821–1880), 282
Tindall, Adrienne (b. 1935), 85
Tisserand, Jean (d. 1494), 318
Toplady, Augustus M. (1740–1778), 177, 447
Toth, William (1905–1963), 49
Troeger, Thomas F. (b. 1945), 25
Tucker, F. Bland (1895–1984), 241, 288, 345, 350, 490, 522, 551, 620

Tuttiett, Lawrence (1825–1897), 78
Tweedy, Henry H. (1868–1953), 481
Twells, Henry (1823–1900), 252, 506

Van Dyke, Henry (1852–1933), 521
Vanstone, W.H. (b. 1923), 351
Vogel, Heinrich (20th century), 395
Vories, William M. (1880–1964), 492

Wardlaw, Ralph (1779–1853), 455
Warner, Anna B. (1820–1915), 457
Watts, Isaac (1674–1748), 1, 10, 53, 87, 91, 99, 110, 121, 122, 126, 127, 128, 129, 130, 135, 139, 140, 175, 198, 233, 243, 244, 283, 292, 293, 294, 295, 347, 369, 400, 411, 412, 501, 540, 542, 571, 575, 576, 624
Webb, Benjamin (1819–1885), 332, 342, 343
Weisse, Michael (1484–1531), 323
Weissel, Georg (1590–1635), 185
Wesley, Charles (1707–1788), 46, 47, 51, 52, 79, 183, 196, 240, 245, 325, 331, 362, 363, 385, 405, 438, 450, 451, 463, 464, 470, 476, 512, 554, 572, 596, 597, 598, 605
Wesley, John (1703–1791), 140, 148, 149, 150, 452, 454
Whitehouse, W.A. (b. 1915), 395
Whiting, William (1825–1878), 525, 526
Whittier, John Greenleaf (1807–1892), 254, 358
Wilbur, Richard (b. 1920), 205
Wile, Frances W. (1878–1939), 9
Williams, Peter (1722–1796), 50
Williams, William (1717–1791), 50
Willson, M.F.C. (1884–1944), 539
Winkworth, Catherine (1827–1878), 61, 69, 145, 151, 153, 169, 185, 202, 368, 420, 448, 502, 529, 530, 536, 609, 615
Winslow, Jack (1882–1974), 68
Wolcott, Samuel (1813–1886), 422
Woodward, George R. (1848–1934), 328, 590, 614
Wordsworth, Christopher (1807–1885), 231, 334, 511
Wortman, Denis (1835–1922), 429
Wren, Brian A. (b. 1936), 22, 257, 275, 380, 419, 487, 503, 534, 541

Zinzendorf, Nicolaus L. von (1700–1761), 586

INDEX OF COMPOSERS, ARRANGERS, AND SOURCES OF TUNES

HARMONIZATIONS AND ARRANGEMENTS
BY ERIK ROUTLEY

These harmonizations were prepared by Erik Routley for this book.

ALPHABETICAL INDEX OF TUNES

When a tune appears in this book in more than one key, the key for each hymn number is indicated in parentheses after the number. Where a tune has been suggested as an alternate, this has been indicated by an "X" followed by the number of the hymn. Certain names in foreign languages are given also in English form: these are starred.

METRICAL INDEX OF TUNES

ST. CATHERINE, 454
STELLA, 452
SURREY, 47
VATER UNSER, 35
VENI IMMANUEL, 184
WOODBURY, 46

8.8.8.8.88 with refrain
SAGINA, 451

88.88.88
COTSWOLD, 512
GOTTLOB, 114
MELITA, 525, 526
ST. PETERSBURG, 113

888.888
OLD 113th, 140

89.8.89.8.66.4.88
WACHET AUF, 606

8.9.8.9 D
GENEVA 138, 570

9.8.8.8.88
SOUTH CERNEY, 85

9.8.9.8
COMMANDMENTS, 65, 590
FOLKSONG, 568
ST. CLEMENT, 516

9.8.9.8 D
RENDEZ A DIEU, 119, 551

9.8.9.8 D amphibrachic
CRUGYBAR, 391

9.8.9.8.88
MENTZER, 529
NEUMARK, 151

9.10.9.10.10 10
DIR, DIR, JEHOVA, 420

9 10.99 with refrain
ASSURANCE, 453

9.10.10.9
LONSDALE, 22

10 4.66.66.10 4
AUGUSTINE, 11

10.4.10.4.10 10
ALBERTA, 58
SANDON, 59

10.7.10.7.4.6.6.6 dactylic
WORLEBURY, 538

10.8.10.8
SRI LAMPANG, 82

10 10 with refrain
CRUCIFER, 415

10 10.7
MARTINS, 573

10 10.9 10 dactylic (irregular)
SLANE, 67

10 10 10 with alleluias
SINE NOMINE, 397

10 10 10.4
ENGELBERG, 345, 508, 528

10.10.10.6
PEACE, 162

10.10.10.10
LANGRAN, 549
LONGWOOD, 60
MORECAMBE, 445
SURSUM CORDA, 138, 550
WOODLANDS, 171, 182

10 10.10 10
CHILTON FOLIAT, 509
ELLERS, 517
EVENTIDE, 440
JULIUS, 430
KINGSTANDING, 472
MAGDA, 373
NATIONAL HYMN, 494
O QUANTA QUALIA, 602
SHELDONIAN, 269
SURSUM CORDA, 434
TOULON, 366, 429

10.10 10 10.10
OLD 124th, 614

10.10.10.10.10 10
FINLANDIA, 154
SONG 1, 402, 555

10 10.10 10.10 10
NIEMAND VAN ONS, 588
STOCKPORT, 197

10 10.11 11
LYONS, 598
OLD 104th, 398

10 11.11 11 dactylic
SLANE, 68

11.10.10.11
GENEVA 87, 112

11.10.11.9
RUSSIAN HYMN, 493

11.10.11.10
CHARTERHOUSE, 389
CITY OF GOD, 487
DONNE SECOURS, 414, 548
EASTWOOD, 621
FOREST HILL, 250
INTERCESSOR, 55
VICAR, 31
WELWYN, 432
WESLEY, 180

11.10.11.10 dactylic
ECOLOGY, 23
MORNING STAR, 230
O QUANTA QUALIA, 582, 583

11.10.11.10 with refrain
PILGRIMS, 174
TIDINGS, 421

11.10.11.10 D dactylic
FAITHFULNESS, 155

11.10.11.10.10
LANGHAM, 489

11.10.11.10.10.8.10.8
O STORE GUD, 466

11.10.11.10.11.10
FINLANDIA, 497

11 11.10 10 D
GENEVA 32, 553

11.11.11.5
AD TUUM NOMEN, 533, 617
DIVA SERVATRIX, 307
ARTISTS' PROCESSION, 513

11.11.11.5 sapphic
CHRISTE SANCTORUM, 515
ISTE CONFESSOR, 504

11 11.11.5
HERZLIEBSTER JESU, 285

11.11.11.11 dactylic
O QUANTA QUALIA, 39

11 11.11 11
AWAY IN A MANGER, 214
MONTGOMERY, 355
MUELLER, 213
ST. BASIL, 344

11 11.11 11 anapaestic
FOUNDATION, 172
ST. DENIO, 7

11.12.12.10
NICAEA, 611

12.11.12.11
KREMSER, 62, 63

12 12.12 12
WILHELMUS, 32, 483

13.12.13.11
KREMSER, 574

14 14.4 7.8
LOBE DEN HERREN, 145

15 15 15.7
VISION, 495

Irregular
BALM IN GILEAD, 465
DIEU NOUS AVONS VU TA GLOIRE, 541
GRAND ISLE, 401
LAUDATE PUERI, 123
LET US BREAK BREAD, 545
NU ZIJT WELLECOME, 220
PURPOSE, 425
RESONET IN LAUDIBUS, 354
SALVE FESTA DIES, 371, 498
SILENT NIGHT, 216
SONG OF HOPE, 610
STILLE NACHT, 216

Irregular with refrain
GOD REST YOU MERRY, 209
GO TELL IT ON THE MOUNTAIN, 224
THE FIRST NOWELL, 223

INDEX OF FIRST LINES

PERMISSIONS

The committee and the publisher express their sincere gratitude and appreciation to those individuals and publishers who kindly granted permission for use of their copyrighted materials. Every effort has been made to trace the ownership of all copyrighted material, although in some instances exact ownership is obscure. If for this reason any omissions have been made, it is hoped that these will be brought to our attention so that proper acknowledgment may be made in future printings of the book.

2 Descant by John Wilson, used by permission of Oxford University Press
4 Trans. W. H. Draper, copyright © 1926 by J. Curwen & Sons, Ltd., used by permission of G. Schirmer, Inc., U.S. agents; music harmonized by Ralph Vaughan Williams (1872–1958) from the *English Hymnal*, used by permission of Oxford University Press
5 Descant by S. Nicholson, used by permission of The Royal School of Church Music
9 Words by Frances W. Wile (1912), used by permission of Dorothy M. W. Bean; music coll. adpt. and arr. by Ralph Vaughan Williams (1872–1958) from the *English Hymnal*, used by permission of Oxford University Press
11 Words by Erik Routley (1964), copyright © 1976 by Hinshaw Music, Inc. and used by permission 4-19-84
13 Text copyright 1978 *Lutheran Book of Worship*, used by permission of Augsburg Publishing House
14, 15 Music harmonized by David Hugh Jones from *The Hymnbook*, copyright MCMLV by John Ribble, renewed 1983, used by permission of Westminster Press
16 Words and music by Caryl Micklem (1975), used by permission
20 Words by Albert F. Bayly (1901–1984), used by permission of Oxford University Press
21 Words by Frederick Pratt Green, copyright © 1970 by Hope Publishing Co. and used by permission; music by Francis Jackson (1969), copyright © 1969 by Francis Jackson and used by permission
22 Words by Brian Wren, copyright © 1975 by Hope Publishing Co. and used by permission; music by Erik Routley, copyright © 1985 by Hope Publishing Co. and used by permission
23 Words by Frederick Pratt Green, copyright © 1973 by The Hymn Society of America and used by permission; music by Austin C. Lovelace, copyright 1974 by Augsburg Publishing House and used by permission
24 Words by Ian Fraser (1964), copyright © 1969 by Stainer & Bell, Ltd., used by permission of Galaxy Music Corp., sole U.S. agent; music by Richard Proulx (1977), copyright © 1980 by G.I.A. Publications, Inc.
25 Words by Thomas H. Troeger (1985), used by permission of Oxford Univ. Press; music by Carol Doran (1985), used by permission of Oxford Univ. Press
26 Words by G. W. Briggs (1875–1959), used by permission of Oxford University Press
27 Words by Elizabeth J. Cosnett, used by permission; music by Melville Cook (1968), used by permission
29 Words by Catherine Cameron, copyright © 1967 by Hope Publishing Co. and used by permission

by permission of Augsburg Publishing House

163 Words by Ann B. Snow (1959) from *Songs and Hymns for Primary Children*, copyright © 1963 by W. L. Jenkins, used by permission of Westminster Press

171 Words by Paul Inwood (1972), used by permission of Mayhew McCrimmon, Ltd.; music by Walter Greatorex (1877–1949), used by permission of Oxford University Press

173 Descant by Eric H. Thiman, used by permission of the United Reformed Church

176 Words by Albert F. Bayly (1901–1984), used by permission of Oxford University Press; music by Erik Routley, copyright © 1969 by Hope Publishing Co. and used by permission

178 Words by Robert B. Y. Scott (1958), used by permission

181 Words by G. W. Briggs (1875–1959), used by permission of Oxford University Press; music by Deborah Holden (1980), used by permission

182 Words by Timothy Dudley-Smith, copyright © 1962 by Hope Publishing Co. and used by permission; music by Walter Greatorex (1877–1949), used by permission of Oxford University Press

183 Descant by John Wilson, used by permission of Oxford University Press

188 Music arr. Ralph Vaughan Williams (1872–1958) from the *English Hymnal*, used by permission of Oxford University Press

190 Music arr. C. W. Douglas (1916), used by permission of The Church Hymnal Corp.

193 Music coll. adpt. and arr. by Ralph Vaughan Williams (1872–1958) from the *English Hymnal*, used by permission of Oxford University Press

199 Descant by Alan Gray from *A Book of Descants* by Alan Gray (1923), published by Cambridge University Press and used by permission

201 Music by H. J. Gauntlett (1858), harmonized by A. H. Mann (1919), reproduced by permission of Novello & Co., Ltd.

203 Words by Frederick Pratt Green, copyright © 1978 by Hope Publishing Co. and used by permission; music arr. John Wilson, used by permission of Oxford University Press

205 Words by Richard Wilbur (1961) from *Advice to Prophet and Other Poems*, copyright © 1961 by Richard Wilbur, reprinted by permission of Harcourt Brace Jovanovich, Inc.

208 Trans. G. B. Caird (1951), used by permission; music music harmonized by Ralph Vaughan Williams (1872–1958) from the *English Hymnal*, used by permission of Oxford University Press.

210 Words by Joseph Simpson Cook, copyright © 1956, 1958 by Gordon V. Thompson, Ltd., International Copyright secured, and used by permission of Carl Fischer, Inc., agents on behalf of Alta Lind Cook and Gordon V. Thompson, Ltd.

211 Trans. John Moss (1957), used by permission of John A. Moss and the United Church of Christ in Japan; music by Chûgorô Torii (1941), used by permission of the United Church of Christ in Japan

212 Trans. Jane M. Joseph (1894–1929); music arr. Gustav Holst (1925), copyright © 1924 by J. Curwen & Sons, Ltd., used by permission of G. Schirmer, Inc., U.S. agents

218 Music harmonized by John Stainer (1871) from *The Hymnbook*, used by permission of Westminster Press

220 Words by Elizabeth Poston from *The Penguin Book of Christmas Carols*, ed. Elizabeth Poston, reprinted by permission of Penguin Books Ltd.; music harmonized by Adriaan Engels from the *Liedboek voor de Kerken*, used by permission

221 Words paraphrased by Edith M. G. Reed, copyright © 1925, used by permission of Bell & Hyman Ltd.; music harmonized by David Hugh Jones from *The Hymnbook*, copyright MCMLV by John Ribble, renewed 1983, used by permission of Westminster Press

224 Words and music from *American Negro Songs* by J. W. Work, used by permission

226 Trans. Percy Dearmer (1928) from *The Oxford Book of Carols*, used by permission of Oxford University Press; music arr. Geoffrey Shaw (1928) from *Enlarged Songs of Praise*, used by permission of Oxford University Press

227 Music harmonized by G. R. Woodward (1910), used by permission of A. R. Mowbray & Co., Ltd.

232 Music copyright renewal © 1968 assigned to Abingdon Press and used by permission

235 Words by Timothy Dudley-Smith, copyright © 1969 by Hope Publishing Co. and used by permission

237 Music by Erik Routley, copyright © 1985 by Hope Publishing Co. and used by permission

238 Music by Lee Hastings Bristol, Jr. (1951), copyrighted and used by permission

239 Words by G. W. Briggs (1875–1959), used by permission of Oxford University Press

241 Words by F. Bland Tucker (1977), used by permission of The Church Hymnal Corp.

242 Trans. Maurice F. Bell (1862–1947) from the *English Hymnal*, used by permission of Oxford University Press

245 Music by Erik Routley, copyright © 1985 by Hope Publishing Co. and used by permission

249 Words by G. W. Briggs (1875–1959), used by permission of Oxford University Press; music by Kenneth Finlay (1936) from *Congregational Praise*, © Independent Press

250 Music by Walford Davies (1869–1941) from *A Students' Hymnal*, used by permission of Oxford Univ. Press

253 Music by Annabeth McClelland Gay (1958), copyright © 1958 by the Pilgrim Press and used by permission

257 Words by Brian Wren; music by Peter Cutts, copyright © 1977 by Hope Publishing Co. and used by permission

258 Music coll. adpt. and arr. by Ralph Vaughan Williams (1872–1958) from the *English Hymnal*, used by permission of Oxford University Press

263 Words by Norman Elliott (1951), used by permission of the United Reformed Church

265 Mean parts by John Wilson, used by permission of Oxford University Press

269 Music by Cyril V. Taylor, copyright © 1962 by Hope Publishing Co. and used by permission

270 Music by David McKay Williams (1941), used by permission of The Church Hymnal Corp.

273 Music adpt. by John Wilson, used by permission of Oxford University Press

275 Words by Brian Wren, copyright © 1968 by Hope Publishing Co.; music by John Wilson, copyright © 1981 by Hope Publishing Co. and used by permission

277 Music by Ralph Vaughan Williams, copyright © 1971 by Stainer & Bell, Ltd., used by permission of Galaxy Music Corp., sole U.S. agent

280 Music by Graham George (1938), used by permission of Belwin Mills Publishing Corp.

283 Text and setting copyright 1978 *Lutheran Book of Worship*, used by permission of Augsburg Pub. House

284 Music by John Ireland (1918), used by permission of the Executors of N. K. Kirby (Dec'd)

286 Music by Percy Buck (1871–1947), used by permission of Oxford University Press

289 Music arr. Ralph Vaughan Williams (1872–1958) from the English Hymnal, used by permission of Oxford University Press

301 Words by H. E. Hardy (c. 1930), used by permission of A. R. Mowbray & Co., Ltd.; music by Erik Routley, copyright © 1985 by Hope Publishing Co. and used by permission

303, 304 Words by Frederick Pratt Green, copyright © 1973 by Hope Publishing Co. and used by permission; First Tune ed. John Wilson, used by permission of Oxford University Press

305 Words amended by Nathaniel Micklem, used by permission

307 Paraphrased by Erik Routley (1974), copyright © 1976 by Hinshaw Music, Inc. and used by permission; music arr. Erik Routley, copyright © 1976 by Hinshaw Music, Inc. and used by permission 4-19-84

309 Words by G. G. Gillett (1873–1948) from the English Hymnal, used by permission of Oxford Univ. Press

311 Second Tune by William H. Ferguson (1874–1950), used by permission of Oxford University Press

325 Music harmonized by Ralph Vaughan Williams (1872–1958) from the English Hymnal, used by permission of Oxford University Press

326 Words by C. A. Alington (1925), used by permission of Hymns Ancient & Modern, UK

327 Trans. R. Birch Hoyle (1923), used by permission of World Student Christian Federation

328 Words by G. R. Woodward (1894), used by permission of A. R. Mowbray & Co., Ltd.

329 Trans. Frederick Pratt Green, copyright © 1982 by Hope Publishing Co. and used by permission

332 Music harmonized by Erik Routley (1976), harmonization copyright © 1976 by Hinshaw Music, Inc. and used by permission 4-19-84

334 Music copyright by Dilys Evans and Eluned Grump, used by permission

336 Music by Ralph Vaughan Williams (1872–1958) from Enlarged Songs of Praise, used by permission of Oxford University Press

344 Words by Robert B. Y. Scott (1938), © The Hymn Book, 1971, used by permission; music by Healey Willan, © Executors of H. Willan's Estate and used by permission

345 Words by F. Bland Tucker (1940), used by permission of The Church Hymnal Corp.

350 Words by F. Bland Tucker (1940), used by permission of The Church Hymnal Corp.; music harmonized by Walford Davies (1869–1941) from A Students' Hymnal, used by permission of Oxford University Press

352 Words by Percy Dearmer (1867–1936), after J. M. Neale; music harmonized by Ralph Vaughan Williams (1872–1958), both from the English Hymnal, used by permission of Oxford University Press

353 Music from The Hymnbook, copyright 1954 by John Ribble, renewed 1982, used by permission of Westminster Press

356 Music coll. Lucy Broadwood, arr. Ralph Vaughan Williams (1872–1958) from the English Hymnal, used by permission of Oxford University Press

360 Music American folk hymn, arr. Erik Routley (1976), harmonization copyright © 1976 by Hinshaw Music, Inc.

371 Words copyright © 1980 by John E. Bowers and used by permission; music by Ralph Vaughan Williams

(1872–1958) from the English Hymnal, and used by permission of Oxford University Press

372 Trans. R. E. Roberts (1879–1953) from the English Hymnal, and used by permission of Oxford Univ. Press

373 Words by John R. Peacey (1969), used by permission of M. E. Peacy; music by Ralph Vaughan Williams (1872–1958) from Enlarged Songs of Praise, and used by permission of Oxford University Press

374 Words by T. C. Hunter-Clare (1950), and by permission of Arthur C. F. Davies, Executor of the Estate of T. C. Hunter-Clare

379 Words by Frederick Pratt Green, copyright © 1979 by Hope Publishing Co. and used by permission

380 Words by Brian Wren; music by John Wilson, copyright © 1979 by Hope Publishing Co. and used by permission

381 Words by Timothy Rees (1922) from The Mirfield Mission Hymn Book, used by permission of A. R. Mowbray & Co., Ltd.

382 Words by Margaret Clarkson (1982), © 1976 Inter-Varsity Christian Fellowship and used by permission

383 Words by Michael Hewlett (1916–) from English Praise, used by permission of Oxford University Press; music by Christopher Dearnley (1930–) from English Praise, used by permission of Oxford University Press

384 Words by T. C. Hunter-Clare, used by permission of Arthur C. F. Davies, Executor of the Estate of T. C. Hunter-Clare

385 Music by Melville Cook (1968), used by permission

386 Words by Martin Franzmann (1969), adpt. from Worship Supplement, copyright © 1969 Concordia Publishing House and used by permission; music by Alfred Fedak (1980) and used by permission

388 Words by George B. Caird (1945), used by permission

389 Words by Sarah E. Taylor, copyright © 1952 by Hope Publishing Co. and used by permission; renewal 1980 by The Hymn Society of America; music by David Evans (1874–1948) from the Revised Church Hymnary 1927, used by permission of Oxford University Press

390 Words by R. T. Brooks, copyright 1954, renewal 1982 by Hope Publishing Co.; music by Erik Routley, copyright © 1985 by Hope Publishing Co. and used by permission

391 Words by Granton Douglas Hay, © 1977, from Australian Hymn Book, and used by permission; music based on the harmony by David Evans (1874–1948) from the Revised Church Hymnary 1927, used by permission of Oxford University Press

393 Music by Cyril V. Taylor, copyright © 1942, renewal 1970 by Hope Publishing Co. and used by permission

395 Music coll. adpt. and arr. by Ralph Vaughan Williams (1872–1958) from the English Hymnal, used by permission of Oxford University Press

396 Words by G. K. A. Bell (1883–1958) from Enlarged Songs of Praise, used by permission of Oxford Univ. Press

397 Music by Ralph Vaughan Williams (1872–1958) from the English Hymnal, used by permission of Oxford University Press

398 Words by Frederick Pratt Green, copyright © 1973, 1980 by Hope Publishing Co. and used by permission

401 Words by Lesbia Scott (1929), reprinted by permission of Morehouse-Barlow Co., Inc.

406 Words copyright © 1969, James Quinn, S.J., printed by permission of Geoffrey Chapman, a division of Cassell, Ltd.; music by Gregory Murray (1940), used by permission of The Grail, England

411 First Tune by Paul Manz (1973), used by permission

413 Words copyright © James Quinn, S.J., by permission

of Geoffrey Chapman, a division of Cassell, Ltd.

414 Words by Georgia Harkness, copyright 1954, renewal 1982 by The Hymn Society of America and used by permission

415 Words by G. W. Kitchin, rev. 1916 by M. G. Newbolt, by permission of Hymns Ancient & Modern, UK

416 Words by H. E. Fosdick (1930; alt'd), used by permission

418 Words copyright © 1974 by Ruth Duck, used by permission

419 Words by Brian Wren, copyright © 1975 by Hope Publishing Co.; music by John Wilson, copyright © 1980 by Hope Publishing Co. and used by permission

422 Music by Eric H. Thiman (1951), used by permission of the United Reformed Church

424 Words by C. A. Alington (1950), used by permission of Hymns Ancient & Modern, UK; music by Cyril V. Taylor, copyright © 1942, renewal 1970 by Hope Publishing Co. and used by permission

425 Music by Martin Shaw (1875–1958) from Enlarged Songs of Praise, used by permission of Oxford Univ. Press

426 Words by Caryl Micklem (1977), used by permission

430 Words by Albert F. Bayly (1901–1984), used by permission of Oxford University Press; music by Martin Shaw (1935), used by permission of The Royal School of Church Music

433 Words by Frederick Pratt Green, copyright © 1982 by Hope Publishing Co. and used by permission

435 Words by Hywel Elfed Lewis (1883), used by permission of the United Reformed Church

444 Music by Ralph Vaughan Williams (1872–1958) from the English Hymnal, used by permission of Oxford University Press

460 Words by Edward Mote (c. 1834) with additions by Norman Kansfield (1982), used by permission

462 Words and music by Caryl Micklem (1975), used by permission

465 Music harmonized by Betty Pulkingham, arr. copyright © 1974 Celebration Services International, Ltd. and used by permission

466 Words by Erik Routley (1982), used by permission

471 Music by William H. Ferguson (1874–1950), used by permission of Oxford University Press

472 Words by Henry Child Carter (1951), used by permission of the United Reformed Church; music by Erik Routley (1940), copyright © 1976 by Hinshaw Music, Inc. and used by permission 4-19-84

477 Music copyright renewal © 1968 assigned to Abingdon Press and used by permission

478 Music harmonized by Erik Routley (1976), copyright © 1976 by Hinshaw Music, Inc. and used by permission 4-19-84

480 Words by G. A. Studdert-Kennedy (1921), used by permission of Hodder & Stoughton, Ltd.; music harmonized by Charles Winfred Douglas (1940), used by permission of The Church Hymnal Corp.

481 Music arr. Charles Winfred Douglas (1941), used by permission of The Church Hymnal Corp.

483 Words by George B. Caird (1943), used by permission; music harmonized mostly by John Wilson, used by permission of Oxford University Press

484 Words by Hywel Elfed Lewis (1916), used by permission of the United Reformed Church; music by Richard Dirksen, copyright © 1977 by Hope Publishing Co. and used by permission

485 Words by Erik Routley (1966), copyright © 1969 by Galliard Ltd., used by permission of Galaxy Music Corp., sole U.S. agent; music American folk hymn,

arr. Carlton R. Young (1964), harmonization copyright © 1965 by Abingdon Press and used by permission

486 Words by Albert F. Bayly (1901–1984), used by permission of Oxford University Press

487 Words by Brian Wren, copyright © 1983 by Hope Publishing Co. and used by permission; music by Daniel Moe (1957), tune and setting copyright Augsburg Publishing House and used by permission

488 Words by Percy Dearmer (1867–1936) from Enlarged Songs of Praise, used by permission of Oxford Univ. Press

489 Words by Laurence Housman (1865–1959), used by permission of Oxford University Press; music by Geoffrey Shaw (1921), © League of Nations Union and used by permission

490 Words by F. Bland Tucker (1971), copyright © 1971 by Walton Music Corp. and used by permission

492 Words by William M. Vories (1908), used by permission of Heldref Publications

495 Words by Frederick Pratt Green, copyright © 1976 by Hope Publishing Co. and used by permission; music by H. Walford Davies (1865–1941), arr. John Wilson, used by permission of Oxford University Press

496 Music harmonized by Gordon Jacob (1953), reproduced by permission of Novello & Co., Ltd.

497 Words by Lloyd Stone (st. 1 and 2) and Georgia Harkness (st. 3), used by permission of the Lorenz Corp.; music by Jean Sibelius (1899), used by permission of Breithopf & Härtel, Wiesbaden

498 Words copyright © 1980 by John E. Bowers and used by permission; music by Ralph Vaughan Williams (1872–1958) from the English Hymnal, used by permission of Oxford University Press

500 Words by Erik Routley (1981), copyright © 1985 by Hope Publishing Co. and used by permission; music by Herbert Howells (1930, 1977), reproduced by permission of Novello & Co., Ltd.

502 Descant by John D. Bower, used by permission of Hymns Ancient & Modern, UK

503 Words by Brian Wren; music by Erik Routley, copyright © 1977 by Hope Publishing Co. and used by permission

506 Music by Leonard J. Blake (1950), used by permission of Hymns Ancient & Modern, UK

508 Words by Frederick Pratt Green, copyright © 1972 by Hope Publishing Co. and used by permission

510 Words by Albert F. Bayly (1901–1984), used by permission of Oxford University Press

513 Words by Fred Kaan (1968), copyright © 1968 by Hope Publishing Co. and used by permission; ARTISTS' PROCESSION by Ronald L. Neal, Jr. (1978), used by permission

514 Words by Fred Pratt Green, copyright © 1969 by Hope Publishing Co. and used by permission

515 Words by Percy Dearmer (1867–1936) from the English Hymnal, used by permission of Oxford Univ. Press

519 Words by Erik Routley, copyright © 1985 by Hope Publishing Co. and used by permission

520 Words by Ian Fraser (1966), copyright © 1969 by Galliard, Ltd., used by permission of Galaxy Music Corp., sole U.S. agent

521 Words by Henry Van Dyke (1907), used by permission of Charles Scribner & Sons

522 Words by F. Bland Tucker (1938), used by permission of The Church Hymnal Corp.

526 Words by W. Whiting (st. 1 and 4) and R. Spencer (st. 2 and 3), used by permission of The Church Hymnal Corp.

527 Words by Judith O'Neill (1975), used by permission